# A PEOPLE
# THAT SHALL
# DWELL ALONE

# A PEOPLE THAT SHALL DWELL ALONE

## Judaism as a Group Evolutionary Strategy

### Kevin MacDonald

Human Evolution, Behavior, and Intelligence
*Seymour W. Itzkoff, Series Editor*

Westport, Connecticut
London

**Library of Congress Cataloging-in-Publication Data**

MacDonald, Kevin.
    A people that shall dwell alone  :  Judaism as a group evolutionary
strategy / Kevin MacDonald.
        p.    cm.—(Human evolution, behavior, and intelligence,
ISSN 1063–2158)
    Includes bibliographical references and index.
    ISBN 0–275–94869–2 (alk. paper)
    1. Jews—Social conditions.   2. Jews—Identity.   3. Jews—
Segregation.   4. Collectivism.   5. Judaism—History—Philosophy.
6. Antisemitism.   I. Title.   II. Series.
DS140.M28   1994
296′.01′57—dc20        94–16446

British Library Cataloguing in Publication Data is available.

Library of Congress Catalog Card Number: 94–16446
ISBN: 0–275–94869–2
ISSN: 1063–2158

First published in 1994

Praeger Publishers, 88 Post Road West, Westport, CT  06881
An imprint of Greenwood Publishing Group, Inc.

Printed in the United States of America

The paper used in this book complies with the
Permanent Paper Standard issued by the National
Information Standards Organization (Z39.48–1984).

10  9  8  7

# CONTENTS

# PREFACE

This project attempts to develop an understanding of Judaism based on modern social and biological sciences. It is, broadly speaking, a successor to the late-19th-century effort to develop a *Wissenschaft des Judentums*—a scientific understanding of Judaism. The fundamental paradigm derives from evolutionary biology, but there will also be a major role for the theory and data derived from several areas of psychology, including especially the social psychology of group behavior.

In the present volume, the basic focus will be the attempt to adduce evidence relevant to the question of whether Judaism can reasonably be viewed as a group evolutionary strategy. The basic proposal is that Judaism can be interpreted as a set of ideological structures and behaviors that have resulted in the following features: (1) the segregation of the Jewish gene pool from surrounding gentile societies as a result of active efforts to prevent the influx of gentile-derived genes; (2) resource and reproductive competition between Jews and gentiles; (3) high levels of within-group cooperation and altruism among Jews; and (4) eugenic efforts directed at producing high intelligence, high-investment parenting, and commitment to group, rather than individual, goals.

I believe that there is no sense in which this book may be considered anti-Semitic. This book and its companion volume are intended to stand or fall on their merits as scientific works. This implies an attempt on my part at developing a scientifically valid account of Judaism. Nevertheless, one cannot read very far in Jewish history without being aware that historical data do not exist in a theoretically pristine state in which they lend themselves to only one interpretation. While by no means always the case, the historiography of Jewish history has to an extraordinary degree been characterized by apologia and a clear sense of personal involvement by both Jews and gentiles, and this has been the case from the very earliest periods in classical antiquity. There is therefore considerable controversy about key issues in the history of Judaism which are of great importance to an evolutionary perspective. Jewish history, more so than any other area I am familiar with, has been to a considerable extent a social construction performed by highly interested parties intent on vindicating very basic moral and philosophical beliefs about the nature of Judaism, Christianity, and gentile society generally.

Indeed, I would suggest that the very fact that the history of Judaism represents such a minefield for an evolutionary theorist (or any theorist) attempting to understand Judaism is itself an important fact about this endeavor that is highly compatible with an evolutionary perspective on Judaism: Theories of Judaism often reflect the interests of their proponents. These issues are discussed extensively in the companion volume, *Separation and Its Discontents: Toward an Evolutionary Theory of Anti-Semitism* (MacDonald 1995). The only point here is to say that, like any other scientific account, this one is open to rational, logical debate.

In addition, there are enormous difficulties in attempting to present the empirical data that would be relevant to an evolutionary theory. Much of the historical record is quite scanty and difficult to interpret even for those with the most dispassionate intentions. This is, of course, typical of historical research generally and is especially true when one is attempting to understand events that occurred over two millennia ago. These difficulties are compounded by the fact that at present there is simply no overlap between scholars who are working in the area of applying evolutionary models to human behavior and professional historians in the field of Jewish history. Nevertheless, the proposal here is that it is possible to provide an account of Judaism that fits quite well with the idea that Judaism is an evolutionary group strategy and to do so by relying on a substantial body of scholarly research in the field of Jewish history, the vast majority of which has been written by Jews themselves.

This project has obviously been quite wide-ranging, and I have profited a great deal from the comments of a number of scholars in the areas of evolutionary biology and psychology, including C. Davison Ankney, Hiram Caton, David Dowell, Martin Fiebert, William Gardner, John Hartung, Peter LaFreniére, John Pearce, J. Philippe Rushton, and David Sloan Wilson. Regrettably, there are others who have made helpful comments but have asked that their names not appear here. I would also like to give special thanks to Seymour Itzkoff, the editor of this series, for his helpful comments on earlier versions of the manuscript.

# OVERVIEW

The organization of this volume is as follows: Chapter 1 develops the basic theoretical perspective of the book, including especially the idea of a group evolutionary strategy. Evolutionary group strategies are proposed to be theoretically unconstrained on a variety of dimensions, and the remaining chapters flesh out the specific characteristics of Judaism as a group evolutionary strategy. Chapter 2 discusses the evidence from modern studies on genetic differences between Jewish and gentile populations. This material is relevant to the hypothesis that Judaism represents a group strategy that is fairly (but not completely) closed to penetration from gentile gene pools. The data indicate that Jews have remained genetically distinct from the groups they have lived among despite having lived among them for centuries. In addition, Jewish populations in very diverse areas have significantly more genetic commonality than is the case between Jews and the gentile populations they have lived among for centuries.

Chapter 3 discusses some preliminary issues that are important for the general theory that Judaism can be viewed as a group evolutionary strategy. This chapter has three purposes. Evolutionary anthropologists have found that stratified societies tend to be characterized by polygyny by wealthy males. The society depicted in the writings of the *Tanakh* (i.e., the Old Testament) conforms quite well to this expectation. There is indeed ample evidence for reproductive competition and for intensive polygyny by wealthy males. Evolutionary anthropology also emphasizes the importance of endogamy and kinship for understanding human societies. The second purpose of this chapter is to show that there is a pronounced tendency toward idealizing endogamy and condemning exogamy apparent in these writings. Close kinship relationships and consanguineous marriage are also very important themes in these writings, and are especially important for understanding the activities of the patriarchs. Finally, and perhaps most important to the present undertaking, it is shown that much of the ideology of Judaism as an evolutionary strategy for maintaining genetic and cultural segregation in a diaspora context is apparent in the writings of the Priestly stratum of the Tanakh. There is scholarly agreement that this material was written by Israelite priests during the period of the Babylonian exile. It is proposed therefore that Judaism as an evolutionary strategy dates from this period.

Chapter 4 discusses the manner in which Jewish religious ideology and practice have facilitated the genetic and cultural separation of Jews and gentiles, and is thus relevant to the hypothesis that Judaism is a self-chosen, genetically fairly closed evolutionary strategy. Of the hundreds of human groups in the ancient world, only Judaism avoided the powerful tendencies toward cultural and genetic assimilation. Judaism as a group strategy depends on the development of social controls reinforcing group identity and preventing high levels of genetic admixture from surrounding groups. This genetic separation has been maintained by a variety of cultural practices: religious practices and beliefs, language and mannerisms, physical appearance, customs, occupations, and physically separated areas of residence which were administered by Jews according to Jewish civil and criminal law. All of these practices date from very early stages of the diaspora. This chapter surveys these ideologies and behaviors with a particular emphasis on their role in severely limiting the numbers of gentile converts to Judaism and preventing intermarriage between Jews and gentiles.

Chapter 5 reviews evidence of resource and reproductive competition between Jews and gentiles, as well as evidence supporting the proposition that anti-Semitism has been strongest among gentiles most in competition with Jews. The evidence indicates that Jews were commonly utilized as an intermediary group between ruling elites (and especially alien elites) and the native population. In these situations, the elite gentile group actively encouraged Jewish economic interests to the detriment of other sectors of the native population. After summarizing data on this type of relationship in widely dispersed parts of the world, separate sections are devoted to resource competition between Jews and gentles in Spain prior to the Inquisition, in early modern Poland, and in Europe and the United States following Jewish Emancipation.

Chapter 6 discusses data indicating the importance of kin-based cooperation and altruism within Judaism, its role in resource competition with gentiles, and its importance in maintaining cohesion within the Jewish community. Data are presented indicating that Jewish economic activities have often been characterized by a high degree of nepotism and within-group charity which are central to conceptualizing Judaism as an evolutionary strategy. Group interests, rather than individual interests, have been of primary importance throughout Jewish history.

Further, it is shown that within-group charity and altruism have been facilitated by strong social controls within traditional Jewish communities, which enforced a high level of within-group altruism. Traditional Jewish communities were also characterized by strong social controls against Jews who cooperated with gentiles against Jewish interests or who patronized gentile businesses or aided gentiles in economic activities. Finally, data are discussed indicating that there were limits on within-group altruism among Jews. Although altruism toward poor Jews was an important aspect of Judaism, there was also discrimination against poorer Jews, especially in times of economic and demographic crises. There was also discrimination between different Jewish groups as recipients of altruistic behavior as a function of genetic distance.

Chapter 7 discusses hypotheses related to the issue of whether Judaism constitutes an ecologically specialized evolutionary strategy. The following five propositions are of interest: (1) Judaism can be characterized in ecological terms as a high-investment reproductive strategy that facilitates resource competition by Jews with the gentile host society; (2) success in mastering the vast and complex Jewish religious writings was strongly associated with prestige within the Jewish community and was ultimately linked rather directly to control of resources and reproductive success; (3) Jewish religious and social practices fostered the development of the high-investment patterns of childrearing necessary for successful resource competition and a role in society above that of primary producer; (4) Judaism has been characterized by assortative mating and by cultural and natural selection for intelligence and other traits related to obtaining resources within stratified human societies; data are reviewed indicating that Jewish populations have a higher average intelligence than their gentile counterparts, as well as a number of other demographic markers indicating that Jews as a group engage in high-investment parenting; (5) Jewish groups have been characterized by a set of practices aimed at socializing individuals into identifying strongly with the group.

Finally, Chapter 8 discusses the origins of Judaism as a group evolutionary strategy. As indicated above, part of the argument in Chapter 1 is that evolutionary group strategies need not be viewed as determined by ecological contingencies or evolutionary theory. Group strategies are viewed as experiments in living that can be developed and maintained by purely cultural processes. Chapter 8 modifies this perspective by suggesting that the development of Judaism as an evolutionary strategy was facilitated by a combination of three historically contingent factors: (1) a strong predisposition to ethnocentrism characteristic of Middle Eastern cultures generally; it is argued that this predisposition is genetically influenced, but that the tendency toward ethnocentrism has been exacerbated as a result of selective effects resulting from Jewish cultural practices; (2) unique historical experiences (including especially the sojourn in Egypt) that showed that a diaspora strategy could be successful; and (3) the unique early organization of the Israelite tribes, which resulted in a powerful class of priests and Levites whose status depended on their genealogy and whose own individual interests were intimately bound up with the fate of the entire group. These individuals benefited most from the group strategy which ultimately evolved into historical Judaism.

While clearly of great interest in its own right, the present endeavor should be viewed as a necessary prologue to developing an evolutionary theory of anti-Semitism. This book's companion volume, *Separation and Its Discontents: Toward an Evolutionary Theory of Anti-Semitism* (MacDonald 1995; hereafter referred to as *SAID*), will extend this paradigm to develop a theory of anti-Semitism based on an evolutionary interpretation of social identity theory and the psychology of individualism/collectivism. *SAID* reviews historical data on Jewish-gentile interaction in a wide range of historical societies, including an emphasis on gentile anti-Semitic strategies as well as Jewish strategies for combatting anti-Semitism.

It is my hope that these two volumes together not only will result in a greater scientific understanding of the extraordinary phenomenon of Judaism and its effects on gentile societies, but also will indicate the mechanisms that would end the extraordinary levels of intrasocietal violence and hostility that have been directed at the Jews over their history. However, this aspect of the project must be deferred to *SAID*. The purpose of the present volume is to give a scientific account of Judaism as a group evolutionary strategy.

# A PEOPLE THAT SHALL DWELL ALONE

# 1

# INTRODUCTION AND THEORY

Beginning with the pioneering work of Richard Alexander (1979), approaches based on evolutionary biology have been applied to an increasingly wide range of human societies, including hunter-gatherer societies (e.g., Chagnon 1983; Hill & Kaplan 1988), tribal societies (e.g., Barkow 1991; Irons 1979) and stratified societies (e.g., Dickemann 1979; Betzig 1986; Kroll & Bachrach 1990; MacDonald 1990; Weisfeld 1990). The research thus far indicates that evolutionary biology provides a powerful paradigm for understanding human behavior and suggests that this body of theory will eventually provide a paradigm that encompasses all of the social and behavioral sciences. The purpose of this essay is to extend the evolutionary paradigm to the study of possible group strategies occurring within human societies.

This book is likely to be highly controversial and troubling to many, since it depicts Judaism as a fundamentally self-interested group strategy, which has often been in competition with at least some sections of gentile society. Bear in mind, however, that evolutionary theory is not a "feel good" theory. The theory of Judaism presented here implies that Judaism must be understood as exhibiting universal human tendencies for self-interest, ethnocentrism, and competition for resources and reproductive success. But an evolutionary theory must also suppose that these tendencies are in no way exclusive to Judaism. Indeed, the theory of anti-Semitism proposed in a companion volume, *Separation and Its Discontents: Toward an Evolutionary Theory of Anti-Semitism* (MacDonald 1995; hereafter referred to as *SAID*), essentially states that gentiles also are self-interested, are ethnocentric, and engage in competition for resources and reproductive success.

The evolutionist is regarded in many circles as a nasty and unwelcome interpreter of ethnicity and ethnic conflict. But the evolutionist is also keenly aware of the ways in which our ideologies can rationalize our self-serving behavior. And, in a very real sense, we cannot afford to continue to hide our heads in the sand while ethnic conflict continues to escalate. A basic thesis of these volumes is that ethnic conflict can be greatly illuminated by evolutionary theory. But evolutionary and psychological theory also provides some strong suggestions regarding the mechanisms for ameliorating this conflict. Only by understanding the past can we attempt to change the future in an intelligent manner.

# THE IDEA OF A GROUP EVOLUTIONARY STRATEGY

The question of whether Judaism is properly conceptualized as a group evolutionary strategy is of great theoretical interest. Mainstream Darwinism from its origins has emphasized natural selection at the level of the individual or the gene, not the group. This powerful tendency has continued in most recent formulations of sociobiology, beginning with the seminal work of G. C. Williams (1966) and culminating in E. O. Wilson's (1975) synthesis.

Within this tradition, applications of evolutionary theory to human behavior have tended to conceptualize individuals as free agents whose self-interested behavior has been shaped by evolutionary forces acting on psychological mechanisms. Human social relationships are viewed as permeated by conflicts of interest, but research has tended to focus on the individual actor confronting an infinitely fractionated social space. Within that social space, individual strategy is viewed as depending crucially on biological relatedness to other individuals (the result of kin selection theory [Hamilton 1964]), as well as on several other individual difference variables, such as sex, age, and resource control.

Within this individualist perspective, the group is nothing more than a concatenation of self-interested individuals. Cooperation among individuals is understood as depending on perceived benefits to each individual. For example, Alexander (1979, 1987) emphasizes that humans tend to cooperate or even behave "altruistically" in the face of external threats--a point that is of some importance in developing an evolutionary understanding of Jewish history (see below and Chapter 6). Thus, Alexander's theory of socially imposed monogamy proposes that wealthy males give up their ability to have many wives or concubines in order to elicit the cooperation of lower-ranking males. The result is an egalitarian mating system, since each male would then have access to the same number of females independent of such characteristics as wealth and social status. Alexander proposes that such an egalitarian group would have a great deal of internal cohesion because lower-status males would have a stake in the system and would therefore cooperate more with the elite. Such a group would therefore have an advantage over other groups in which lower-ranking males perceive themselves to be exploited by higher-ranking males.

Note that in this analysis of behavior within the group each individual male is viewed as continually assessing his self-interest. If external conditions become less threatening, so that there is no need for the wealthy males to elicit the cooperation of lower-ranking males, the wealthy males would be expected to revert to a strategy in which they maximize their accumulation of concubines and wives. Correspondingly, lower-status males would be expected to continually assess the benefits versus the costs of continued group cooperation versus defection.

The idea of group strategies presents a quite different paradigm for human behavior. From a group strategy perspective, human societies are seen as ecosystems in which different human groups are analogous to species occupying a common ecosystem and engaging in competition and/or reciprocity with each other. Thus, in the natural world, an ecosystem may comprise producer species as well as several levels of predator species and parasitic (and hyperparasitic) species. Species may also enter into mutually advantageous roles *vis-à-vis* each other--what ecologists term *mutualism*. Each species may be viewed as having an evolutionary strategy by which it adapts to a particular ecosystem.

The analogy with humans would be that stratified human societies offer the possibility of complex intrasocietal ecological strategies. D. S. Wilson (1989; see also Wilson & Sober 1994) has developed the theory of group-structured populations in which groups of individuals (coalitions) separate themselves off from the other members of the species. These groups can then be proposed to vary in their level of within-group altruism, ranging from extremely altruistic to completely individualistic. Because of their very high level of cooperation and even self-sacrifice, individuals within altruistic groups may then have higher biological fitness on average (i.e., leave more offspring) than individuals in individualistic groups. The result is that there is natural selection between groups.

A main purpose of the following section is to develop the theoretical basis for the claim that humans, perhaps uniquely among animals, are able to create and maintain groups that impose high levels of altruism on their members. Moreover, it is argued that the fundamental mechanisms rely ultimately on human abilities to monitor and enforce group goals, to prevent defection, and to create ideological structures that rationalize group aims both to group members and to outsiders.

These uniquely human abilities to create and enforce group strategies essentially remove all theoretical strictures regarding human social organization. For humans, the limits of human social organization are defined only by the limits of the human imagination. We shall see, however, that such a proposition most certainly does not imply that evolutionary thinking is therefore irrelevant to thinking about human social organization. It may indeed be the case that there are no interesting theoretical limits on the types of strategies that humans can invent, but whether or not these strategies are evolutionarily successful is a question that inevitably remains. And, in the present case, a primary burden of this book will be to show that Judaism as a group evolutionary strategy has often been a highly successful strategy for acquiring resources and achieving reproductive success within gentile host societies.

# THEORETICAL BASICS: THE PLACE OF SOCIAL CONTROLS, IDEOLOGY, AND PLASTICITY IN EVOLUTIONARY THEORY

## Evolution and Social Controls

Crucial to the discussion of Judaism in traditional societies will be evidence that social controls acting within the Jewish community have had an important role in maintaining the strategy. This in turn raises the general issue of the role of social controls in an evolutionary theory of human societies.[1]

Social controls can range from subtle effects of group pressure on modes of dressing to laws or social practices that result in large penalties to violators. Stratified societies are characterized by the possibility of very stringent controls on human behavior, and Betzig (1986) presents many examples in which high levels of centralized political control (i.e., despotism) are associated with control over the persons and behavior of others. In the case of Judaism, there were often powerful community controls that minutely prescribed behavior in a wide range of settings, including modes of dressing, religious observance, business practices, and the type and extent of contact with gentiles.

Social controls that regulate behavior need not be viewed as determined by ecological contingencies or by evolutionary theory. For example, social controls supporting a socialist economic system may be viewed as being in the interests of many individual members of human society (presumably the lower social classes). On the other hand, social controls supporting a *laissez faire* capitalist society may also be viewed as being in the interests of other members of the society (presumably including successful capitalists). That the imposition of social controls will result in these types of economic or political systems is always a possibility, and there is thus no evolutionary reason to suppose that one or the other will necessarily characterize a given society. Conflict of interest over the distribution of economic resources is predicted by evolutionary theory, but whether socialism, *laissez faire* capitalism, or some intermediate form results from this conflict is underdetermined by evolutionary theory.

Within the present theoretical perspective, therefore, social controls are viewed as the outcome of internal political processes whose nature is underdetermined by evolutionary/ecological theory. Corresponding to this indeterminacy, these social controls may be quite insensitive to the genotypic or phenotypic characteristics of the individuals to whom they apply and cannot be analyzed reductionistically (i.e., as a genetic characteristic of individuals): Thus, whether or not one supports the idea of welfare payments to the poor, there may be strong penalties on avoiding taxes. Similarly, it will be seen in Chapter 6 that individual Jews could be prevented by the Jewish authorities from avoiding taxes that helped support the Jewish poor or from overbidding for economic franchises in competition with other Jews. Group interests could therefore be maintained, even if individual interests suffered.

## Evolution and Ideology

Besides social controls, another theoretically important feature of the present treatment is the proposal that the religious ideology of Judaism is essentially a blueprint for a group evolutionary strategy (see Chapter 3). The point here is that although ideology often rationalizes evolutionary goals, it is underdetermined by evolutionary theory. Ideologies, like group strategies generally, may be viewed as "hopeful monsters" whose adaptiveness is an empirical matter.

The present essay describes Judaism as an evolutionary ideology and provides some indication of how this ideology has succeeded or failed in practice. Ideologies imply that factors internal to the individual, such as an individual's personal beliefs, norms, and attitudes, often motivate and rationalize behavior. An evolutionary analysis of ideology proposes that individuals tend to believe what is in their self-interest (e.g., E. O. Wilson 1978), and there is certainly good evidence for this phenomenon in the psychological literature (e.g., Krebs, Denton, & Higgins 1988). However, like social controls, ideologies can be relatively insensitive to individual self-interest and are underdetermined by biological theory (see also Boyd & Richerson 1985).

The main reasons for supposing that ideologies in general are underdetermined by evolutionary theory are that (1) ideologies often characterize an entire society (or, in this case, the subculture of Judaism), and (2) ideologies are often intimately intertwined with various social controls. In the case of Judaism, and as described in Chapters 3-6, these social controls act within the Jewish community to enforce the stated ideological goals of maintaining internal cohesion, preventing marriage with gentiles, enforcing altruistic behavior toward other Jews, and excluding those who fail to conform to group goals. To the extent that an ideology characterizes an entire group, it becomes insensitive to individual self-interest, and to the extent that it is reinforced by social controls, it is possible that individuals who do not benefit from adopting the ideology will be socialized to do so. This is especially important because the thesis here is that Judaism is an altruistic group strategy in which the interests of individuals are subservient to the interests of the group (see especially Chapter 6).

As in the case of social controls and also because ideologies are so often intricately bound up with social controls, it is not possible to predict which ideology will prevail within a particular group. For example, ideologies may be egalitarian or anti-egalitarian. They may promote the deregulation of human behavior, or they may foster strong social controls on behavior. Like social controls, personal ideologies are strongly influenced by complex, group-level political processes and are thus not analyzable in a reductionistic manner as solely the property of an individual.

Theoretically, the ideologies and internal social controls that form the basis of group strategies are thus seen as underdetermined. Although group strategies are influenced by evolved human psychological mechanisms (see below), group strategies are in an important sense *unnecessary*. As the great Jewish historian Salo Baron notes, "It is clear, therefore, that to answer our question concerning the survival of the Jews as a separate entity in the Diaspora we must turn to the Jews themselves. The decision was one which they were free to make" (Baron 1952a, 118). At certain times and places, individual humans have developed and participated in group strategies, and others living in the same areas have not.

Ideologies can underlie altruistic group strategies, such as that of ancient Sparta (described below; see MacDonald 1988a, 301-304), or they may underlie individualistic systems, such as traditional English liberal political theory, which has recently been triumphant in the West. In some cases, ideologies may be quite successful in presenting a blueprint of a successful group strategy, or the ideology may result in a system that is a complete failure. Thus, Alexander (1979) describes a religious sect that forbade sexual relations of any kind between its members. Not surprisingly, the sect was short-lived. Moreover, while the group strategy of the ancient Spartans was successful for a significant period, it was ultimately a failure.

The perspective adopted here is thus non-deterministic. Within this framework, historical analysis focuses on the origin and maintenance of Judaism as an evolutionary ideology and as characterized by a particular set of internal social controls on the behavior of Jews, but with no implication that Judaism is in some sense ecologically or genetically determined or that it is necessarily adaptive for Jews at any stage of their history. Because of the indeterminacy of social controls and ideology, these contextual variables can be influenced by such historical events as the outcome of military engagements, which are themselves theoretically underdetermined (e.g., the successful conquest of Canaan after the Exodus--surely a necessary condition for the development of Judaism) or the outcome of particular historical events such as the Egyptian sojourn, recounted in Genesis and Exodus.

Within this framework, it is quite possible that successful experience in following a particular strategy will influence whether that strategy is continued in the future or is instead altered in some basic manner. Thus, for example, if living as a minority among the Egyptians during the original sojourn recounted in Genesis and Exodus had resulted in a large increase in wealth and population, a similar diaspora strategy might be viewed as viable in the future--a point that we shall return to in Chapter 8 when I attempt to develop an evolutionary perspective on the origins of Judaism as a group evolutionary strategy. The success of such a diaspora strategy could not have been foreseen with certainty, and its success may well not have been known beforehand by its participants, but, given the early indications of success, it would be rational to continue the strategy.

An evolutionary group strategy thus may be conceived, at least partly (see below), as an "experiment in living," rather than as the determinate outcome of natural selection acting on human populations or the result of ecological contingencies acting on universal human genetic propensities. Supporting these experiments in living are ideological structures that explain and rationalize the group strategy, including the social controls utilized by the strategy.

Social controls in the service of achieving internal discipline (such as, for example, preventing exploitation by cheaters or non-cooperators) are theoretically important for the development of a successful altruistic group evolutionary strategy (D. S. Wilson 1989; see below). But there is no reason why an experiment in living must include such controls. One could perfectly well imagine a group strategy in which there were no provisions at all to exclude cheaters and exploiters. Such a strategy would presumably fail in the long run, just as Alexander's (1979) celibate religious sect failed. But that is not the point. Experiments are experiments: Some are successful and well designed, and others are not. The evidence reviewed in later chapters suggests that Judaism has survived as a group evolutionary strategy (albeit with several important changes) at least since the Babylonian captivity. If this is so, there is the implication that it has been a well-designed evolutionary strategy.

From the present perspective, humans (and probably only humans) are viewed as having sophisticated cognitive abilities that enable them to develop strategies in pursuit of evolutionary ends (MacDonald 1991; Itzkoff 1993). Within this perspective, the evolved goals of humans have been genetically influenced by our evolutionary past, but there are no constraints at all on how humans attempt to achieve these goals. As Itzkoff (1993) notes, the evolved motivational goals of humans can be achieved through uniquely human cortical/symbolic systems, with the result that behavior is only indirectly linked with reproductive success.

This is an extremely important aspect of the present conceptualization. As an example that illustrates the general principle, many evolutionary psychologists propose that human males have evolved traits that result in their attempting to copulate with nubile females, so that, for example, the prospect of mating with such a female would be accompanied by positive affective responses (including pleasurable sexual arousal).

Such a goal may be evolutionarily programmed, but the means by which individual males achieve such an evolved goal may vary widely and may well not be under any genetic control whatever. Thus, a male with the affective goal of copulating with females may pursue a wide range of strategies, involving, perhaps, resource accumulation and exchange, seduction accompanied by deception, courting and falling in love, military engagements in which women are seized, or even rape--all of which would result in the ability to mate with females. None of these strategies for obtaining this evolutionary goal need be genetically determined. Any could be invented by the human mind utilizing its extremely sophisticated domain-general cognitive abilities (MacDonald 1991).

These strategies therefore need not be the result of natural selection, but may be a completely invented or "made up" product of the human mind. Some such strategies may fail miserably, but there is no question that humans can attempt a wide range of solutions for achieving evolutionary goals. The conclusion must be that we cannot develop a deterministic theory of a creature whose behavior can be significantly manipulated by "voluntary symbolic meanings" (Itzkoff 1993, 292).

Whether these strategies are successful is therefore a purely empirical question, but there is no theoretical reason to suppose that a strategy needs to be ultimately adaptive in order to persist for long periods of time. Nevertheless, as will be seen, the data presented in subsequent chapters indicate that Judaism has been quite successful in an evolutionary sense over fairly long stretches of historical time, although it has been subject to rather extreme swings of fortune, chiefly as the result of anti-Semitic actions. As is the case with any group strategy in which the strategizing group resides within a wider human society, the ecological limits of success are importantly determined by the actions of the other members of the society.

In summary, Judaism is here considered fundamentally as a cultural invention that is underdetermined by evolutionary/ecological theory and whose adaptiveness is an empirical question. However, it does not follow that there are no biological predispositions at all for developing the type of group evolutionary strategy represented by Judaism. In Chapter 8, I suggest that the ancient Israelites were genetically predisposed to be high on a cluster of psychological traits centering around group allegiance, cultural separatism, ethnocentrism, concern with endogamy, and a collectivist, authoritarian social structure. Evidence cited there indicates that these tendencies are very strong among widely dispersed Jewish groups in traditional societies and that they appear to be more common among other Near Eastern peoples compared to prototypical Western societies. Further, it is suggested that Judaism itself resulted in a "feed-forward" selection process in which Jewish groups become increasingly composed of individuals who are genetically and phenotypically predisposed to these traits.

Thus, while the theory presented in Chapter 8 falls well short of being a deterministic theory, an important component of the theory is that being relatively high on certain psychological systems has constituted a powerful predisposition for the development of Judaism as a group evolutionary strategy.

## Evolution and Plasticity

Because of the "made up," unnecessary character of human group evolutionary strategies, these strategies actually assume an important role for human plasticity. Humans possess a great deal of behavioral plasticity and flexibility and are able to manipulate their own environments in order to produce adaptive (and sometimes maladaptive) outcomes (MacDonald 1988a, 1988b, 1989, 1991). A major misconception of many critics of evolutionary approaches is their supposition that evolutionary accounts necessarily imply a high degree of genetic determination of human phenotypes. However, there is overwhelming evidence that in fact human behavior is significantly (but not infinitely) plastic. For example, behavior genetic research on intelligence and personality indicates that although genetic variation is indeed an important source of individual variation among humans, environmental variation is also important.

This finding that environmental variation affects human development implies an important role for human plasticity--the idea that the observed level of a trait can be altered depending upon which environment is experienced (from the set of all normally experienced and even abnormal, extreme environments). Behavior genetic studies attempt to sample a representative range of environments normally encountered in a given society (not the effects of extreme environments), and within these studies environmental variation typically accounts for approximately half of the variation for personality traits (see Digman [1990]; Plomin & Daniels [1987] for summaries). There is also considerable evidence for environmental influences on intelligence, although genetic variation is also important (e.g., Plomin & Daniels 1987; Scarr & Weinberg 1983).

Human plasticity, which also includes mechanisms such as various forms of learning, provides a mechanism such that humans can adapt to environmental uncertainty and lack of recurring structure within a finite range. The point here is that societies and subcultures are able to take advantage of this plasticity and manipulate their own environments in order to produce adaptive phenotypes. In the case of Judaism, it will be argued in Chapter 7 that both eugenic practices (taking advantage of human genetic variation) and manipulation of environments (taking advantage of human plasticity) have been enshrined in religious ideology and intensively practiced. By manipulating environments in this manner, Judaism has been able to develop a highly specialized group strategy, which has often been highly adaptive in resource competition within stratified human societies.

# CONCEPTUALIZING HUMAN GROUP STRATEGIES

The general topic of group strategies among humans is central to the present endeavor. Since this topic is yet fairly unexplored territory, it is of interest to make some general statements regarding human group strategies and to attempt to briefly describe some prominent examples.

*1. A group is defined as a discrete set of individuals that is identifiably separate from other individuals (who themselves may or may not be members of groups).* As Rabbie (1991, 238) notes, there is no agreement on the definition of a social group among social psychologists. The present definition is a very minimal requirement, stating only that the groups must be well defined and distinct from other individuals or groups. Thus broadly defined, the concept would apply to football teams or members of modern corporations where membership is quite fluid and permeable. Political entities would also be groups in this sense. In the present case, evidence will be provided in Chapter 4 that Judaism has been characterized throughout its history by segregation from gentile societies and that there was very little permeability between Jewish and gentile groups, at least in traditional societies.

*2. Separation between groups can be actively maintained or maintained as the result of coercion. Groups actively maintaining separation between themselves and other groups are defined as engaging in group evolutionary strategies.* It is of some practical importance to distinguish group partitions that are voluntary and self-imposed from those that are involuntary and imposed by others. Genetic and cultural segregation and a particular pattern of relationships may be imposed on one group by some other group(s) in the society. Thus, if slavery and genetic segregation of one ethnic group is imposed by another ethnic group, it is reasonable to view the behavior of the latter as a group evolutionary strategy because it is actively maintaining genetic and cultural segregation from the other group. Such a situation would hardly qualify as a strategy on the part of the enslaved group, but may well be a strategy by the enslaving group.

In the present case, the evidence provided in Chapters 3 and 4 indicates that Judaism has actively maintained genetic and cultural segregation and thus qualifies as a group evolutionary strategy. There are many other historical examples where group partitions have been actively imposed on another group. For example, the ancient Spartans enslaved another ethnic group (the Helots) (Hooker 1980). The point here is that this arrangement would qualify as a group evolutionary strategy for the Spartans because the genetic segregation is actively maintained by the strategizing group, but it would not qualify as an evolutionary strategy for the enslaved Helots, since there is good evidence that the Helots attempted to end their enslavement. Similarly, the *Nethinim* lived among the ancient Israelites as a genetically and culturally segregated lower caste, perhaps deriving from the peoples originally displaced after the Exodus (see discussion in Chapter 3). The *Nethinim* were never incorporated within the Jewish people.

*3. Strategizing groups can range from complete genetic segregation from the surrounding population to complete panmixia (i.e., random mating).* Strategizing groups maintain a group identity separate from the population as a whole, but there is no theoretical necessity that the group be genetically segregated from the rest of the population. Thus, Wilson, Pollock, and Dugatkin (1992) note that one theoretically attractive possibility for the evolution of altruism in some life forms is that altruism could evolve in populations of "alternating viscosity." In these populations, altruism within a group of close relatives early in the life cycle (the viscous phase) allows the group to have more offspring. However, individuals from these altruistic groups must then disperse and mate randomly with individuals from the rest of the gene pool (the non-viscous phase). Since population regulation is postulated to occur only during the non-viscous phase, the altruistic groups are protected from invasion by selfish individuals. But this is accomplished despite the fact that genetic segregation is not maintained in the non-viscous phase.

At a theoretical level, therefore, a group strategy does not require a genetic barrier between the strategizing group and the rest of the population. Group evolutionary strategies may be viewed as ranging from completely genetically closed (at the extreme end of which there is no possibility of genetic penetration by surrounding populations) to genetically open (at the extreme end of which there is completely random mating [termed *panmixia*]). In the case of Sparta, membership in the group of Spartan citizens was entirely hereditary, and there is no indication of any interbreeding between the Spartans and the Helots (see MacDonald 1988a, 301ff). In the case of Judaism, evidence will be provided in Chapter 2 that in fact there have been significant genetic barriers between Jews and gentiles, and in Chapters 3 and 4, it will be shown that these barriers were actively maintained by a variety of cultural barriers erected by Jews against significant gentile penetration of the Jewish gene pool. The evidence provided there indicates that through the vast majority of its history Judaism has been near the completely genetically closed end of this continuum.

However, while it is clear that panmixia between Jews and gentiles has never occurred, there has been some gentile penetration of the Jewish gene pool. In the present volume, therefore, it is hypothesized that historical Judaism has been a fairly genetically closed group evolutionary strategy in which genetic differences between Jews and gentiles have been actively maintained by Jews. Moreover, the data summarized in Chapters 3 and 4 indicate that extremely powerful cultural barriers have been erected by Jews in order to prevent assimilation into gentile societies.[2,3]

*4. Altruism within strategizing groups may be facilitated by kinship relationships within the group.* Beginning with Hamilton's (1964) seminal essay on kin selection theory, evolutionary models have shown that relatives have a lower threshold of altruism than non-relatives (D. S. Wilson 1991; Wilson &

Sober 1994). From an evolutionary perspective, it is expected that the cohesiveness of the group and altruism within the group are facilitated by the existence of significant genetic commonality within the segregating group and a corresponding genetic gradient between the segregating group and the rest of the society. Further, if there were a genetic gradient separating the segregating group from the surrounding society, the temptation for individuals of the segregating group to defect from the group strategy is lower.

In Chapter 2, it will be shown that Judaism has been characterized by the existence of a genetic gradient separating Jews from gentiles and that indeed there is significant genetic commonality among Jewish groups widely separated in time and space. From the standpoint of evolutionary theory, the thesis of this essay is that Judaism may be viewed as consisting of a large kinship group whose members are widely separated in space, but whose behavior is nevertheless strongly influenced by their kinship ties (see especially Chapter 6). Moreover, since many diaspora Jewish communities were founded by only a very few families and since immigration to these communities by other Jews was often discouraged, biological relatedness within Jewish communities was often quite high (Fraikor 1977). The fundamental kinship nature of Judaism and its role in facilitating within-group altruism will thus figure prominently in the present treatment. Similarly, the very high levels of altruism characteristic of Spartan society (see below) may well have been facilitated by the close kinship ties of the group.[4]

*5. Powerful group controls on individual behavior are often an important mechanism for promoting altruism and ensuring conformity to group interests in strategizing human groups.* Although high levels of kinship within strategizing human groups are expected to lower the threshold for altruism, kinship by itself is not expected to be sufficient to result in high levels of altruism. The entire edifice of modern evolutionary theory implies that self-sacrificing behavior is highly problematic. Models of group selection face the difficulty that the forces of population regulation inevitably lead to the evolution of selfishness within groups (Wilson, Pollock, & Dugatkin 1992). This problem is especially acute in large groups where the ties of genetic relatedness become quite weak and are thus unable to support high levels of self-sacrifice. As a result, in the absence of coercion, individuals are expected to quickly defect from group strategies in which individual interests are not being maximized.

Boyd and Richerson (1992) have shown that punishment allows for the natural selection of altruism (or anything else). In the case of human groups, punishment that effectively promotes altruism and inhibits non-conformity to group goals can be effectively carried out as the result of culturally invented social controls on the behavior of group members. Thus, while it may well be that group-level evolution is relatively uncommon among animals due to their limited abilities to prevent cheating, human groups are able to regulate themselves via social controls so that theoretical possibilities regarding invasion by selfish types from surrounding human groups or from within can be eliminated or substantially reduced (Wilson & Sober 1994).

Facilitating altruism by punishing non-altruists can be viewed as a special case of the general principal that social controls can act to promote group interests that are in opposition to individual self-interest. Group strategies must typically defend themselves against "cheaters" who benefit from group membership, but fail to conform to group goals. Human societies are able to institute a wide range of social controls that effectively channel individual behavior, punish potential cheaters and defectors, and coerce individuals to be altruistic.

In the case of Judaism, the central authority of the *kehilla* system of self-government in the diaspora provided a powerful mechanism for excluding Jews (often termed "informers") who failed to conform to group goals by, for example, collaborating with gentiles against the interests of the Jewish community or who engaged in behavior such as dishonest business practices with gentiles that was likely to lead to anti-Semitism. Moreover, as indicated in Chapters 4 and 6, there were strong community sanctions on individuals (and their families) who violated group norms against intermarriage with gentiles, socialized with gentiles, patronized businesses owned by gentiles, or attempted to bid against other Jews who owned franchises obtained from gentiles.

Another example of a group evolutionary strategy based on high levels of within-group altruism supported by community controls is provided by the ancient Spartans (see MacDonald 1988a, 301-304); 1990). The Spartans originated as a group of biologically related Dorian tribes. As proposed here also with respect to Judaism, these kinship ties within the Spartan community presumably lowered the threshold for altruism, but ultimately it was the highly centralized political authority of the state that produced a strong sense of group goals and self-sacrifice among the Spartan citizens. As Hammond (1986) notes, the Dorian state formed "a remarkably compact and almost indestructible community . . . it generated an intense patriotism and dynamic energy" (p. 101). The Spartans were known for their self-sacrifice and willingness to give their lives for the state. "[T]he Spartan, from his childhood on, has learnt to give his life for his country, without any hesitation. Not only the state, the laws, the leaders, and the comrades expect this of him, even his own mother finds it natural that her son should be either victorious or dead" (Tigerstedt 1974, 20).[5]

*6. Altruistic group strategies often develop controls that effectively limit the extent of within-group altruism.* Altruistic group strategies run the risk that an altruistic strategy could be invaded by freeloaders who would take advantage of the altruism of some group members. This indeed is the fundamental difficulty that makes the evolution of altruistic groups in the natural world so problematic. Strictly speaking, there is no theoretical requirement that altruistic group strategies adopt limits on altruism, but evolutionary theory suggests that without such limits the strategy is likely to fail. In the case of Judaism, the evidence presented in Chapter 6 indicates that there were indeed limits on Jewish altruism, including various sorts of discrimination against poorer Jews by setting quotas on marriage and minimum dowries and by directing Jewish charity preferentially toward more closely related Jews.[6]

7. *The minimization of conflicts of interest within the group is expected to facilitate the willingness of individuals to cooperate and engage in altruism.* As indicated in the above discussion of Alexander's (1979) theory of socially imposed monogamy, egalitarian institutions are expected to facilitate cooperation and altruism within the group. This point can perhaps best be seen by considering the expected consequences of despotism on cooperation and self-sacrifice by lower-status males. Research in evolutionary anthropology has indicated that the vast majority of stratified human societies have been characterized by despotism and intensive polygyny by wealthy males (e.g., Betzig 1986; Dickemann 1979; MacDonald 1983). In a despotic situation, lower-status males are more likely to perceive themselves as exploited by upper-status males and as benefiting little from cooperation or altruism. Self-sacrifice and voluntary cooperation in such a situation are expected to be minimal because the benefits of such behavior are more likely to accrue to the despot while the costs are borne by the lower-status males. At the extreme, if the lower-status male is a slave, cooperation and self-sacrifice can only occur as the result of coercion. The expected association between egalitarianism and altruism can be seen by again considering ancient Sparta. We have already noted the high level of altruism among the Spartans, but there is also evidence for a pervasive egalitarianism among the Spartan citizens, including sexual egalitarianism (Hammond 1986, 104; Jones 1967, 37).

Egalitarianism may well facilitate altruism and cooperation within strategizing groups by minimizing social conflict, but there is no reason to suppose that egalitarianism is the only mechanism available to a strategizing group that would have this effect. The important point is to minimize conflicts of interest within the group, and although egalitarianism accomplishes this result, other mechanisms are possible.

In the case of Judaism, the material reviewed in Chapters 5-7 indicates that there were indeed powerful forces that tended to minimize conflict of interest within the Jewish community, including economic cooperation and patronage and high levels of charity. Nevertheless, the data do not indicate that Judaism has typically been characterized by a high degree of social and political egalitarianism. Rather, the historical record suggests that Judaism for much of its history has been characterized by the development of a highly competent elite who acted in the interests of the entire group and whose wealth came ultimately not from exploiting other Jews, but as a result of economic transactions with the gentile community.

In Chapter 7, evidence is provided that Jewish education and eugenic practices were directed at producing such an elite and that access to elite status was meritocratic. Thus, although Jewish groups have been far from egalitarian, the allegiance of lower-status Jews may well have been fostered because they benefited both directly and indirectly from the economic activities of the elite and because they could hope that they or their children could attain elite status through merit. Conflict of interest within the community was minimized.

8. *Altruism and internal cohesion within a strategizing group are expected to be maximized in situations of external threat.* The importance of group conflict in producing powerful cohesion within groups combined with hostility toward outgroups is apparent in the writings of several 19th- and early-20th-century anthropologists, such as Spencer, Tylor, and Sumner (see van der Dennen 1987). Among evolutionary theorists, Alexander (1979, 1987) has emphasized the importance of external threat in creating high levels of cohesion, cooperation, and self-sacrifice. In situations of external threat, individual self-interest increasingly coincides with the survival interest of the group, and since Jews have typically lived as a minority group in the midst of an often hostile gentile society, this mechanism for producing altruism and within-group solidarity may well be of considerable importance. Although statements linking altruistic behavior with external threat are difficult to verify, several historians of Judaism have concluded that external threat has indeed been an important mechanism for social cohesion and altruism among Jews (see Chapter 6). The external threats represented by the other Greek city-states and the Persian Empire may well also have been a strong influence on the extraordinary levels of social cohesion and altruism exhibited by the Spartans.

9. *In addition to mechanisms of social control that involve monitoring and enforcing compliance with group goals and excluding cheaters, group strategies may also rely on psychological mechanisms that predispose humans toward adopting group strategies.* The theoretical analysis of groups presented here has emphasized the importance of social controls that monitor and enforce group goals and exclude cheaters. Nevertheless, it has also been suggested that group strategies may be facilitated by specific evolved psychological mechanisms promoting group allegiance, cultural separatism, ethnocentrism, concern with endogamy, and a collectivist, authoritarian social structure. Such mechanisms will be a vital concern here. Individuals high on these traits may be more prone to develop highly cohesive, exclusionist group strategies, and, once constituted, there may be self-selection processes that ensure that individuals who are high on these traits are less likely to defect from the group strategy and individuals who are low on these traits are likely to be forcibly excluded from the group. These issues are discussed in Chapters 7 and 8.

10. *Because of the problematic nature of altruistic behavior, altruistic group strategies will tend to have highly elaborated mechanisms of group socialization.* Besides the psychological mechanisms mentioned in the previous section, another very important psychological aspect of Judaism as a group evolutionary strategy appears to involve intense socialization toward group identification and within-group altruism. There is good reason to suppose that, in the absence of social controls, natural selection alone could not have produced altruistic human groups. Psychological mechanisms are thus likely to be biased

toward self-interest, and, as a result, it is not surprising to find that altruistic group evolutionary strategies among humans are characterized by intensive socialization pressures focused on the inculcation of altruism and acceptance of group, rather than individual, goals. A major theme of Chapter 7 will be that Judaism, at least in traditional societies, has been characterized by community-controlled education in which children are socialized to accept group goals, such as cultural separatism and within-group altruism, and to reject important elements of gentile culture.

Other altruistic group strategies have also placed an important emphasis on socialization for group goals. Among the Anabaptist groups (including the Hutterites mentioned above), there is an important emphasis on being able to have complete control over children's education and to avoid education in secular schools (see Hostetler 1992). An important feature of ancient Sparta was that the state assumed the entire responsibility for childrearing after the early years. Children were viewed as the property of the state and were taken away from the home and educated "according to a rigorous discipline of quasi-military type" (Hooker 1980, 137). Complete obedience to authority and total allegiance to group goals were emphasized, including the acceptance of making the ultimate sacrifice for the good of the group.

*11. While competition between groups is a common consequence of group strategies, between-group competition is not a necessary consequence of the development of group strategies.* The thesis of Chapter 5 of this volume is that Jews as a cohesive, genetically and culturally segregated group have often engaged in intense resource and reproductive competition with the host society. However, such between-group competition is not necessary to the general concept of an evolutionary group strategy.

Certain fundamentalist religious groups, such as the Amish, may well be examples of non-competitive group strategies. These strategies essentially advertise to the surrounding society that they are not going to engage in resource competition with the larger society. Thus, the Amish have continued to utilize the technology of the 18th century in their agricultural practices, minimizing competitive relationships with the host society. One might tentatively term these strategies "benign group strategies," since, although as a defenseless minority they appear to rely on the host society's good will for their very existence, there is no attempt to compete with the host society. Indeed, by adopting outmoded agricultural practices and avoiding modern secular education there is the virtual assurance that they will not outcompete the host society. It is as if they say to the host society: "We want to go our separate way; we promise not to compete with you and will only engage in economic reciprocity and never attempt to economically exploit you." Hasidic Jews may function in this manner in contemporary societies and their non-competitive status would ameliorate anti-Semitism directed against them (see *SAID*, ch. 2).

*12. Strategizing groups span the range from ecological specialists to ecological generalists.* A further dimension that is relevant to the conceptualization of group strategies is whether there is a consistent set of relationships between the strategizing group and other groups such that in ecological terms the strategizing group may be viewed as an ecological specialist. In the case of the Spartans, there was a consistent relationship between themselves and their Helot slaves. Moreover, Sparta was completely specialized as a military state to the point that its citizens produced no art or literature. Every male adult was a citizen-soldier in the service of the state. Clearly, the Spartan group strategy was highly specialized, and training in this highly specialized military role began early in life. This intensive socialization for military prowess (as well as for self-sacrifice and a group orientation) was extremely rigorous, and the results were spectacularly successful: Despite their small size, the Spartans achieved the status of a world power and remained undefeated in military engagements on land for at least two centuries until the attrition caused by the constant warfare eventually resulted in Sparta's decline.

The specialization of the Spartans undoubtedly was an element in their success as a group, but there is no theoretical reason to suppose that group strategizers must necessarily specialize in a distinct role *vis-à-vis* other groups. It was suggested above (see note 3) that upper-caste Indian Brahmins may be viewed as following a genetically fairly open group evolutionary strategy. This caste clearly had a highly specific caste relationship to other groups in Indian society, but there is no reason to suppose that they developed a highly specialized set of behaviors analogous to the military specialization of the Spartans.

Moreover, it is quite conceivable that a strategizing group would be entirely opportunistic in its relationships with other groups within a society—adopting one strategy under one set of circumstances and a quite different strategy under another. Nevertheless, although an opportunistic strategy is conceivable, it is unlikely to be as successful as specialization for abilities that are always advantageous in economically advanced human societies. As in a natural ecosystem, it verges on theoretical impossibility for one species to develop the role of predator, parasite, and primary producer.

Similarly, in the extremely competitive human environment, a high level of specialization appears to be advantageous. Specialization allows for the development of cultural practices directed at becoming extremely competent at a particular type of role. If this role is commonly available within human societies or is useful in intersocietal competition, then the strategizing group will be able to be highly competitive because the group can specialize in traits suited to that role.

The strategizing group can engage in intragroup eugenic practices for traits conducive to the successful pursuit of the ecological role. (The Spartans practiced infanticide against any weak or sickly children. Significantly, the decision was made not by the parents, but by the central authorities—another indication of the privileged position of group interests over individual interests.) In addition, the strategizing group can develop environments that are ideally suited for the development of the desired traits. (In the case of Sparta, there was a prolonged and intensive education in military skills, as well as a strong emphasis on socializing affective bonding among the male citizens.)

In the case of Judaism, it will be argued that there has been a considerable degree of specialization such that Jews have in general attempted to fulfill and have quite often succeeded in fulfilling a particular type of economic and social role within human societies. The evidence reviewed in Chapter 7 indicates that Judaism has emphasized eugenic practices as well as cultural practices and ideological structures that foster a specific set of phenotypic traits (especially intelligence, high-investment parenting, and allegiance to the group) that are advantageous in stratified human societies. By specializing in these traits, Jews have been able to compete successfully with gentile members of many societies for positions in which literacy and intelligence are important (see Chapter 5). Moreover, because Jews have possessed these traits and because Jews have maintained genetic and cultural segregation from the societies they have resided in, Jews have often been utilized by alien ruling elites as an administrative class governing native subjects (see Chapter 5). Thus, the thesis of this volume is that Jews have attempted to develop and have often succeeded in developing a specialized role within human societies.

Moreover, another result of this specialization is that Jews in the diaspora have almost never been engaged in what ecologists term *primary production* (i.e., in the human case, working as a laborer in agriculture). Rather, the data reviewed in this volume (see especially Chapter 5) indicate that Jews have become specialized for occupational niches at the upper levels of the human energy pyramid. And in ecological terms, this implies that Jews as a group, like other high-status groups in traditional human societies, serve as consumers of energy produced by lower-status gentile members of society laboring in the area of primary production.

# CONCLUSION: THE FIVE INDEPENDENT DIMENSIONS OF HUMAN GROUP EVOLUTIONARY STRATEGIES

These twelve statements are related to five theoretically significant independent dimensions relevant to conceptualizing human group structure in evolutionary terms: (1) a dimension ranging from complete voluntarism, in which the strategizing group voluntarily adopts its strategy, at one extreme to complete coercion, in which the group is forced to adopt significant aspects of its strategy, at the other; (2) a dimension ranging from complete genetic closure, in which the group is closed to penetration from other individuals or groups, at one extreme to complete genetic openness (panmixia), at the other; (3) a dimension ranging from high levels of within-group altruism and submergence of individual interest to group interests at one extreme to complete within-group selfishness at the other; (4) a dimension ranging from high between-group resource and reproductive competition at one extreme to very little between-group resource and reproductive competition at the other; and (5) a dimension ranging from high levels of ecological specialization at one extreme to ecological generalization at the other. It is proposed that human group evolutionary strategies vary along all of these dimensions independently.

Because of the lack of theoretical strictures on human group evolutionary strategies, the structure of this volume will reflect the need to provide empirical evidence regarding the status of Judaism on these five dimensions. Although qualifications to these propositions will be necessary at various points in the argument, the burden of this essay will be to show that historical Judaism can be reasonably conceptualized as follows: (1) Judaism is a self-imposed, non-coerced evolutionary strategy, although at times anti-Semitic actions have had effects that dovetailed with Judaism as an evolutionary strategy; (2) Judaism is a fairly closed group strategy in which much effort has been devoted to resisting genetic assimilation with surrounding populations, and, moreover, this effort has been substantially successful; (3) Jews have typically engaged in resource and reproductive competition with gentile societies, often successfully; (4) there is a significant (but limited) degree of within-group altruism, traditionally enforced by powerful social controls and always enshrined in religious ideology; and (5) there is a significant degree of role specialization, specifically specialization for a role in society above the level of primary producer characterized by cultural and eugenic practices centered around intelligence, the personality trait of conscientiousness, high-investment parenting, and group allegiance.

At a fundamental level, a closed group evolutionary strategy for behavior within a larger human society, as proposed here for Judaism, may be viewed as pseudospeciation: Creation of a closed group evolutionary strategy results in a gene pool that becomes significantly segregated from the gene pool of the surrounding society. Within the strategizing group, there is increasing specialization so that the group is able to become extremely adept at occupying a specific type of niche that is commonly available in human societies. If the strategizing group then undergoes a diaspora and therefore lives among a wide range of human societies, members of the strategizing group, like conspecifics in the natural world, will have greater genetic ties with the dispersed members of their ingroup than with the other members of the society in which they live. Moreover, the within-group genetic commonality predisposes strategizing group members to relatively high levels of within-group altruism and cooperation, while the genetic barrier between the strategizing group and the surrounding society facilitates instrumental behavior directed toward the surrounding society. Moreover, the strategizing group is able to protect itself against freeloading individuals by instituting powerful social controls and belief systems so that a significant level of altruism is maintained within the strategizing group and cheaters who compromise group interests are punished.

Evidence supporting the thesis that Judaism is an ecologically specific strategy can reasonably be found by looking at Jewish religious ideology and practice as well as by examining marriage practices that might suggest inbreeding for specific traits. Contemporary data on distributions of phenotypic traits, such as intelligence and parental investment, among Jews is also confirmatory evidence for cultural selection for particular specialized traits. Moreover, the theory of a specific strategy is supported if there is evidence that Jews have tended to hold particular types of occupations in a wide range of societies and that the individuals holding these occupations have been relatively fertile compared to others within the Jewish community. If these patterns are a reasonably expectable outcome of Jewish religious ideology and practice and if they recur in a wide range of historical societies, then it is reasonable to suppose that this pattern of relationships is not the result of coercion, but represents an evolutionary strategy.

One difficulty in establishing that Judaism is an evolutionary strategy is that one must deal with immense stretches of historical time—at least the time span from the Babylonian captivity (587 B.C.) to the present. There is thus likely to be considerable historical variation in the extent to which these hypotheses are correct, and there is certainly variation in the amount and trustworthiness of available historical data.

Nevertheless, much of this difficulty can be obviated by the availability of contemporary genetic data on populations that have been separated for many centuries. Thus, even if we do not know the extent of conversions and intermarriage in many historical eras or the extent to which Judaism officially or unofficially encouraged genetic admixture at particular times, the finding of significant genetic segregation in contemporary populations would indicate that endogamy (non-panmixia) within the Jewish community was a significant force throughout Jewish history and thereby would support the hypothesis that Judaism has been a predominantly closed group evolutionary strategy.

It should be noted that there has in fact been a great deal of similarity among Jewish communities scattered around the world in traditional societies. For example, Katz (1961b, 9) states that "Jewish history to some extent repeats itself, not only in the temporal dimension, but primarily in the spatial dimensions. The history of Jewish communities, though they still possess their own unique ingredients, read like variations of the same theme." To a great extent, "the widely scattered sections of the Jewish people represent a uniform social entity" (p. 11; see also Ritterband 1981, 3).

This powerful commonality over historical time can also be seen at the ideological level. Neusner (1987, 165) finds that although there have been several "Judaic systems" throughout history, they are "of a type":

All of the continuator-Judaisms claimed to stand in a linear and incremental relationship to the original. They made constant reference to the established and authoritative canon. They affirmed the importance of meticulous obedience to the law. Each one in its way proposed to strengthen or purify or otherwise confirm the dual Torah of Sinai. . . . One system after another took shape and made its own distinctive statement, but every one of them affirmed the definitive symbolic system and structure of the original.

Thus, although it will be necessary to consider some very interesting and important variations among historical Jewish communities, it will be apparent that there is also an overwhelming social and ideological unity to historical Judaism. To anticipate the conclusion, the evidence reviewed in the following chapters indicates that for all practical purposes Judaism may be viewed as a unitary group evolutionary strategy.

# NOTES

1. The discussion in this and the following section follows MacDonald (1983, 1988a, 1988b, 1989, 1990).

2. However, the data discussed in *SAID* (ch. 10) indicate that the relaxation of these cultural barriers in recent times has led to fairly high rates of genetic admixture, although the ultimate status within the Jewish community of these genetically mixed individuals remains doubtful, and some Jewish groups continue to completely resist genetic assimilation. These data strongly suggest that the perpetuation of a group evolutionary strategy in which there is a genetic gradient between the segregating group and the host society is extremely difficult and must be actively maintained.

3. An example of a fairly open group evolutionary strategy is provided by the caste system of India, as described by E. O. Wilson (1975, 555). In India, wealthy, powerful males were able to mate with many lower-status concubines (Betzig 1986; Dickemann 1979). As a result, even though the upper-caste males had a high level of reproductive success, there were only slight variations in gene frequencies and morphological traits between the castes. Presumably, in the case of India, there was a relative homogenization of the genetic composition of the population because of female hypergamy: The genetic composition of the entire population came to resemble the composition of the reproductively successful upper-class males. Nevertheless, since there were indeed some differences in gene frequencies resulting ultimately from rigid social barriers between the castes, upper-caste status in India may be viewed as a group evolutionary strategy that approaches panmixia, but that closes access to positions of highest breeding potential to genetic penetration from lower castes. Alterations in gene frequency thus occurred in a top-down manner, as wealthy, powerful Brahmin males were able to have a disproportionate effect on population gene frequencies.

Zenner (1991, 79) notes that overseas Hindus living in diaspora conditions have tended to strongly resist genetic assimilation with the surrounding society. Such behavior contrasts with that of the overseas Chinese: Zenner (1991, 78ff) shows that, despite considerable ethnocentrism, overseas Chinese living in diaspora conditions were quite tolerant of intermarriage and actively participated in local religions. Such behavior would be expected in the long run to lead to complete assimilation.

4. There is no general expectation that human group strategies will be characterized by high levels of within-group altruism based on kinship ties. In the case of the Indian caste system described in note 3, there is no reason to suppose that upper-caste status is in any way based on within-group altruism. Based on Dickemann (1979), upper-caste males controlled high levels of resources and political power, and there was a high level of intermarriage among the elite. Such marriages among the elite functioned quite differently than concubinage relationships with lower-status females, since the offspring of such marriages were assured of inheritance rights. However, there is no reason to suppose that these upper-caste males behaved in an altruistic, self-sacrificing manner toward each other (although there was presumably a great deal of caste solidarity among them). And, obviously, there is no reason whatever to suppose that the use of lower-status females as concubines of the wealthy represented altruism on the part of lower-status males. Coercion is a far more likely explanation for this state of affairs.

5. Sexual relationships in Sparta also indicate a high level of within-group altruism. Lacey (1968) notes a Spartan ideology opposed to sexual jealousy and the persistent and unequivocal evidence for wife-sharing among them. Community social controls that facilitate within-group altruism have occurred in other human groups. Writing of pre-industrial England, Laslett (1983; see also Quaife 1979) notes that solvent households took in paupers as servants, perhaps as official village welfare policy, and he also notes the commonness of transfer payments from the households of the more prosperous to those of the less prosperous during the 17th and 18th centuries. The Hutterites, as described by D. S. Wilson (1989; see also Wilson & Sober 1994), appear to represent a highly self-sacrificing group strategy, which simply excludes those not willing to submerge their own interests to those of the group.

6. Although there were community controls favoring altruism in 17th-century England, altruism was far from complete. Although starvation was not common, Quaife (1979, 22) finds that individuals who had been forced to accept apprentices and servants sometimes responded by treating them very badly. Moreover, Quaife finds that the authorities strongly discouraged illegitimate offspring because these individuals would have to be supported by the poor rate. Wrightson (1980) and Amussen (1988) also note the very harsh treatment of bastard bearers in mid-17th-century England, with repeat offenders committed to a year in prison.

# 2

# GENETIC SEGREGATION OF JEWS AND GENTILES

[T]he Israelite marries only another Israelite. . . . Foreign elements do not intermingle with them. (Medieval Islamic author al-Jahiz, reprinted in Stillman 1979, 170)

I live not far from the city of Worms, to which I am bound by the tradition of my forefathers, and from time to time I go there. . . . I go over to the Jewish cemetery consisting of crooked, cracked, shapeless, random stones. . . . The dust is there, no matter how thinly scattered. There lies the corporeality of man. . . . I have stood in the dust, and through it with the Patriarchs. (Martin Buber [1933]; quoted in Margalit 1993, 69)

## THE SEGREGATION OF THE JEWISH GENE POOL

The present thesis that Judaism is an evolutionary strategy does not rely on the proposition that Jews represent a distinct race. The minimal requirement for the present theory of Judaism as a fairly closed group strategy is that there be genetic gradients between well-defined groups of Jews and gentiles within particular societies that are maintained by cultural practices. It is the genetic gradient and the coincident competition between significantly different gene pools that are of interest to the evolutionist. Clearly, such a proposal is compatible with some genetic admixture from the surrounding populations. However, an evolutionary perspective must also consider the hypothesis that widely dispersed Jewish populations have significantly more genetic commonality than local Jewish populations have with their gentile co-habitants, since this hypothesis is relevant to developing an evolutionary theory of the patterns of altruism and cooperation among widely scattered Jewish populations.

It should be noted at the outset that there are good reasons to suppose that there will be some differentiation of the Jewish gene pool among the different Jewish groups of the diaspora. These groups were separated, in many cases for two millennia or more, so that, even in the absence of genetic admixture with surrounding populations, one would expect that genetic drift as well as natural selection resulting, for example, from differences in climate or parasites, would begin to differentiate these populations genetically. Regarding genetic drift, the high frequencies of recessive disorders among Jewish populations and the fact that recessive disorders tend to be unique to particular communities strongly suggest that Jewish populations have been susceptible to founder effects and genetic drift (Chase & McKusick 1972; Fraikor 1977; Mourant, Kopec, & Domaniewska-Sobczak 1978). The general picture is that Jewish communities often originated with a very few families who married within the group, typically with high levels of inbreeding (see Chapters 4 and 8).

There is also evidence that selection within the diaspora environment has been important in differentiating Jewish populations. Thus, Motulsky (1977b, 425) proposes that, given the clear evidence for the genetic distinctiveness of the Ashkenazi gene pool, the resemblance in physical characteristics and the ABO blood group between the Ashkenazim and the gentile European population is due to convergent selection (see also below). Lenz (1931, 667-668) suggests that the phenotypic resemblance of Jews to the local gentile population may arise from natural and sexual selection for individuals who resembled the local population, just as different species of butterflies may come to resemble each other. It is thus theoretically possible that a fairly small set of genes promoting phenotypic similarity could be amplified via natural selection within Jewish populations without precluding a large overall genetic distance between Jewish and gentile gene pools.

Selective processes within far-flung Jewish communities might also lead to genetic divergence between them. For example, in Chapter 7, data are discussed indicating a great deal of assortative mating for traits related to intelligence, high-investment parenting, and group cohesion within Jewish communities. Although eugenic selection for a common phenotype may result in selection for the same genes, this certainly need not be the case, since different Jewish populations may accrue different genetic mutations related to intelligence as well as different genes resulting from low levels of genetic admixture with local gentile populations. Supporting this possibility, Eldridge (1970; see also Eldridge & Koerber 1977) suggests that a gene causing primary torsion dystonia, which occurs at high levels among Ashkenazi Jews, may have a heterozygote advantage because of beneficial effects on intelligence. Further supporting the importance of selective processes, eight of the 11 genetic diseases found predominantly among Ashkenazi Jews involve the central nervous system, and three are closely related in their biochemical effects (see Goodman 1979, 463).[1]

Thus, there is no expectation that the various populations of diaspora Judaism will remain genetically uniform. Moreover, the possibilities of natural selection and drift suggest that the most important confirmatory data for the present evolutionary hypothesis are positive indications of genetic commonality between separated Jewish groups combined with differences from co-habitant populations. Thus, if in fact gene frequency data for some loci fail to support the genetic segregation hypothesis, such findings are less important than the findings that many other genetic systems and morphological traits do fit the hypothesis (e.g., Kobyliansky et al. 1982).

Despite these caveats, there is overwhelming evidence for the proposition that the Jewish gene pool has been significantly segregated from the gene pools of the populations that Jews have lived among for centuries, while at the same time there is significant genetic commonality between Jewish groups that have been separated for centuries.[2] Mille and Kobyliansky (1985), using dermatoglyphic data, have found that Eastern European Jews are far more similar to North African and Middle Eastern Jews than to non-Jewish Eastern Europeans. Indeed, they are more similar to Caucasians from the Caucasus Mountains or middle Asia than to Caucasians from Eastern Europe. Similarly, Sachs and Bat-Miriam (1957) have found striking similarities among Jews from nine countries in Central Europe, North Africa, and the Middle East in various indices of fingerprint patterns, a phenotype that is largely under genetic control. These similarities are accompanied by striking differences between Jews and non-Jews in all of these countries and North America, while at the same time Jews are much more similar to non-Jewish groups from the Eastern Mediterranean region (e.g., Egyptian Copts and Israeli Arabs) than they are to non-Jewish groups from other parts of the world. "Even Jews living in Europe and North America therefore show clear evidence of what one may call their original Eastern Mediterranean gene pool," despite "being widely dispersed for centuries in different parts of the world" (p. 125).

Sofaer, Smith, and Kaye (1986) have found greater similarity in dental morphology among three widely scattered, long-separated Jewish groups from Eastern Europe, Morocco, and Kurdish Iraq than among five non-Jewish groups living relatively near them. Moreover, a 3,000-year-old Jewish skeletal group is more similar to these three Jewish groups than to all but one non-Jewish group studied. (The Druse, a sect derived from the Arabs in the 11th century, clustered with the Jewish groups.) In another study using cluster analysis on 25 morphological characteristics, Kobyliansky and Livshits (1985) have found that Jewish groups from the USSR are six times more distant from the Russian group than the Russians are from the German group. In addition, Jews are completely separate from 24 ethnic groups living in Russia, Poland, and Germany. Moreover, this divergence in morphology is highly correlated with divergence in biochemical characteristics based on the data of Kobyliansky and his colleagues (1982).

Several studies of genetic distance between Jews and non-Jews have been performed using blood group data. Karlin, Kenett, and Bonné-Tamir (1979; see also Bonné-Tamir, Ashbel & Kenett 1977), using 14 polymorphic loci, have found no significant differences among Jews from Libya, Iraq, Germany, Poland, and Russia. However, all of these Jewish populations are significantly separated from Arabs, Germans, and Armenians. The distance between Jewish and non-Jewish populations living in the same area is three to five times greater than the distances between several Ashkenazi groups. Bonné-Tamir and his colleagues (1977, 75) conclude "not much admixture has taken place between Ashkenazi Jews and their Gentile neighbors during the last 700 years or so."

Similarly, Kobyliansky and his colleagues (1982) have calculated genetic distance on the basis of 13 blood polymorphisms from six Jewish groups originating in Eastern Europe, Central Europe, Southern Europe, the Middle East, North Africa, and Yemen and have compared them with those of non-Jews from the same areas. Small differences were found among the Jewish populations in the direction of the frequencies of the non-Jewish population of the same area. Cluster analysis revealed that all of the Jewish populations (except the Yemenite population) clustered together with the non-Jewish Middle Eastern population, while Eastern, Central and Southern European non-Jews formed a second cluster, and the North African non-Jews formed a third cluster. Jews who remained in the Middle East retained greater similarity to the ancestral Jewish population than did the migrants.

Mourant, Kopec, and Domaniewska-Sobczak (1978) conclude their very broad survey of blood group data of Jewish groups from Asia, Europe, and Africa by commenting that "[i]t may be said that, in general, blood-group data . . . support the relative homogeneity of the main historical Jewish communities and their distinctness from one another" (p. 57). They find that neither the Ashkenazim nor the Sephardim closely resembled the populations they had resided among for centuries, and although there were a number of differences between these groups, overall the differences were so small that they conclude that Jews represent essentially a single population.

Similarly, Carmelli and Cavalli-Sforza (1979), using a discriminant analysis based on three loci, have found that, with the exception of Jewish isolates, the centroids of all Jewish groups, including the Ashkenazi and the Sephardic Jews, are nearer the non-Jewish Middle Eastern centroid than the Southern or Central European centroids. Roychoudhury (1974), in a study based on results from nine loci, has found Ashkenazi Jews and North African Jews to be more closely related to each other than to non-Jewish Europeans and North Africans, respectively. Finally, Szeinberg (1977) characterizes data on fingerprint patterns and polymorphic blood proteins as indicating general similarities among Ashkenazi Jews, non-Ashkenazi Jews, and non-Jewish Mediterranean peoples, but as indicating differences between these groups and Western, Central, and Eastern European populations.

Kobyliansky and his colleagues (1982) have also found evidence that some of the divergence of Jewish gene frequencies is due to selection in the diaspora environment, since in the case of Yemenite Jews, while there are major differences in frequency for several loci, at others the Jewish groups are relatively similar to the local populations. This suggests that selection has occurred at some loci in the direction of a greater similarity to the local population, but significant admixture is counterindicated because major differences between Jews and non-Jews remain on other loci. Other investigators have found a similar pattern. Thus, Bonné-Tamir, Ashbel, and Kenett (1977) have found little difference between Jews and non-Jews in the ABO system, while, for example, the Rh system shows a major difference, and Szeinberg (1977) has found that the PGM blood group system among Ashkenazi Jews is quite similar to that found in European populations. Thus, while some natural selection in the direction of European populations may have occurred among the Ashkenazim, there is little evidence for admixture, a conclusion also reached by Cavalli-Sforza and Carmelli (1977).

I conclude that these studies of genetic distance point to the common genetic origins of all of the Jewish populations of the world (e.g., Kobyliansky et al. 1982). They also indicate that, although there is some genetic admixture with surrounding populations as well as some natural selection toward the frequencies of local populations, all Jewish populations have a significant degree of segregation from native populations and a significant degree of commonality with other Jewish groups derived from widely separated parts of the world. Finally, the data support the proposal that, with the exception of non-Jewish Middle Eastern populations, all Jewish groups are more closely related to each other than to any non-Jewish group.

# GENTILE REPRESENTATION IN THE JEWISH GENE POOL

We have seen that Jewish populations tend to resemble local populations to some extent genetically. Although these findings could be due to selection in the diaspora environment, they are also compatible with the possibility of some gene flow between populations. Indeed, it would be rather remarkable if there was no gene flow at all into the Jewish gene pool from gentile populations living in close proximity over several centuries. The data reviewed in Chapter 4 indicate that in fact there have been low levels of gentile proselytism to Judaism over the centuries, and Patai and Patai (1989) suggest that the rape of Jewish women by gentiles as well as the illicit affairs of Jewish women with gentile men may also have influenced the representation of gentile genes in the Jewish gene pool.

It is possible that even this relatively small genetic admixture from surrounding populations could be adaptive for a strategizing group because the group would benefit from new genetic combinations. For example, genes related to intellectual abilities occurring in gentile populations could enter the Jewish gene pool even with very low levels of intermixing. These genes could then be propagated within the Jewish community via Jewish eugenic practices (for which there is substantial evidence; see Chapter 7) and other sources of natural selection because they enhance the competitive abilities of those bearing the genes, while gentile-derived genes, which conferred no such advantage, would be allowed to drift or could actually be selected against. The overall result would be that only a relatively few gentile genes would enter the Jewish population so that the basic genetic rationale of Judaism as a fairly closed evolutionary strategy would not be significantly compromised. Moreover, even though some gentile-derived genes were being selected for their effects on resource-obtaining abilities within the Jewish community, the gentile-derived genes may also have pleiotropic effects that would result in greater phenotypic similarity between Jews and gentiles.

Evidence in favor of this hypothesis would be that Jewish proselytism, while highly limited and restricted (see Chapter 4), has been far more successful among wealthy, intelligent, and talented individuals and that this pattern was actively encouraged by the Jewish community. Accounts of proselytes (see, e.g., Patai & Patai 1989) indicate that proselytism was more common among talented and wealthy people. For example, Patai and Patai (1989, 83), in describing proselytes in Germany, note that "[o]nce again history records only the conversions of those few proselytes in Germany who were exceptional among the many converts to Judaism because they were of high status in Gentile society prior to their conversion, or because they achieved renown after they had become Jewish."

The finding that converts are disproportionately intelligent and successful may be the result of biased reporting, as suggested by Patai and Patai (1989), but there is no actual evidence that this is the case. The actual historical record therefore is highly consistent with the hypothesis that converts have been disproportionately wealthy, talented individuals, but there may indeed be some underreporting of the poor and obscure.

However, besides actual data on the conversions of the poor and obscure, there are excellent reasons for supposing that in fact Jewish proselytes would tend disproportionately to be intelligent and successful. There is overwhelming evidence for the existence of an extremely strong emphasis on the establishment of an elite characterized by high intelligence and resource control within the Jewish communities of the diaspora throughout Jewish history (see Chapters 6 and 7). Given this strong bias, it is highly unlikely that poor and obscure gentiles would be interested in joining the Jewish community where they would be at considerable reproductive disadvantage. Nor is it likely that historical Jewish communities would have welcomed such individuals. There is no question that poor and uneducated gentiles would be relegated to a very low social status as proselytes in the Jewish community and every reason to suppose that such individuals would not have been welcomed by the Jewish community. Consistent with this proposal, of the eight gentile proselytes found by Simon (1986, 279-280) in the period from A.D. 135 to the end of the fourth century, seven were scholars.

Moreover, as might be expected, given the strong emphasis on elitism within the Jewish community, there is evidence that Jewish apostates tended disproportionately to be poor and obscure Jews, at least into the 19th century: Lea (1906-07, I:111, 139) notes that prior to the forced conversions of 1391 in Spain, the converts to Christianity had been mostly of humble status, and prior to the expulsion of 1492, only the lowest classes of the remaining Jews converted to Christianity.[3] Similarly, Weinryb (1972, 94) notes that, although voluntary conversions of Jews to Christianity in traditional Poland were small in number, they mostly involved poor and obscure Jews. Moreover, Kaplan (1983, 275) shows that poor Jewish girls who could not afford an adequate dowry were forced to marry gentiles as a last resort. Pullan (1983, 294ff) finds 12 cases of Jewish apostasy in 16th-century Venice, of whom 9 were poor Jews attempting to better their economic conditions. All three of the wealthy individuals apostatized in order to marry or have sexual intercourse with gentile females and/or obtain property, and in at least two of the cases, the conversions themselves appear to have been insincere. This trend for apostates to be disproportionately of humble status was altered beginning with the trend toward emancipation, but the reverse trend did not occur even then. During this period, Jewish apostates included many individuals hoping to advance their career options, but, as Katz (1986, 54) points out, the apostates did not differ economically or in terms of education or social success from those who remained Jews.

If in fact poor and obscure Jews were disproportionately abandoning Judaism, there is no reason whatever to suppose that poor and obscure gentiles were even proportionately represented as proselytes to Judaism. Similarly, recent surveys in the United States indicate that more highly educated Jews and those with higher socioeconomic status are more likely to marry endogamously (Ellman 1987), again suggesting a greater identification with Judaism among elite individuals. These findings are highly compatible with the idea that the few proselytes in traditional societies who did convert to Judaism were in fact disproportionately drawn from among the talented, educated, and wealthy.

Besides low levels of proselytism on the part of disproportionately wealthy and intelligent gentiles, another reason for some gentile penetration into the Jewish gene pool could be that gentile genetic admixture may have resulted from behavior that was adaptive to individual Jews, but that actually conflicted with Judaism as a group evolutionary strategy. From an evolutionary perspective, it is not in the least surprising that there are conflicts between group and individual interests and, in the case of Judaism, that individual Jews may attempt to contravene the group strategy and engage in behavior that is forbidden by the community.[4]

For example, a Jewish male without an heir by a Jewish woman may further his genetic interests by fathering children by gentile women (e.g., slaves and concubines among the Sephardim in pre-expulsion Spain or among the Jews living in Muslim areas) and then scheming to get these children recognized as legitimate heirs. Or it may well be in the interests of the children themselves to become legitimate heirs and members of the Jewish community. There is historical evidence for such behavior. Patai and Patai (1989) show that some concubine owners attempted to have their children by these women become their heirs. They suggest that the significant admixture of African genes among the Mzab Jews occurred because the male offspring of Jews and their slave girls may have had sexual relations with the master's wife.

Similarly, it may have been in the interests of individual Jewish women to bear children who were illicitly conceived by gentile men with attractive phenotypic or genetic traits. Such women could expect that their offspring would also have these traits—an aspect of female choice originally proposed by Darwin as an evolutionary mechanism (see discussion in MacDonald 1991). It is interesting in this regard that in the Ottoman Jewish community male vigilance of female behavior increased to truly obsessive proportions during a period of economic decline and intense persecution (Shaw 1991, 137ff). One might speculate that during periods of economic decline and intense persecution there would be greater concern for defection of females from the group strategy and a greater attraction to gentile males. Community control over female behavior during this period was truly remarkable. For example, women were expected to be extremely deferential toward men, and they were not allowed to leave their homes to shop for food if they had a servant. If they did not have a servant, they were forced to conduct their purchases in the doorway of the shop so that they could be seen from the street.

It may also have been in the interests of a woman to rear a child sired by a gentile rapist. A Jewish woman would be behaving quite adaptively if she clandestinely rears the child of a gentile rapist, rather than accepting one of the alternatives: having no children at all or having herself and her child shunned by the community and rejected by her husband. Such a woman is certainly deviating from the ideal of a closed group evolutionary strategy, but her behavior may be individually adaptive.

Patai and Patai (1989) indicate that both illicit affairs and rape occurred among Jewish populations. Rape was probably fairly common in some eras, especially in Eastern Europe during pogroms or war, such as the Cossack uprisings of the 17th century. Graetz (1898, III: 40-41) recounts an incident in Roman times when German soldiers fathered children by Jewish prisoners of war.

These individually adaptive behaviors must be viewed as events that, if they occurred sufficiently often, would have completely destroyed the genetic gradients separating Jewish and gentile populations. Clearly, however, the level of influx was not sufficient to destroy the essential unity of the Jewish gene pool. Also, it is important to note that this genetic influx was illicit in the sense that it was not socially approved by the Jewish authorities themselves and, as indicated in Chapter 4, there were active attempts to lower the social status of individuals with doubtful or alien parentage. Patai and Patai (1988, 128) describe a Gaonic (eighth-ninth century) ruling that a master having sexual relations with a slave was to be flogged, be excommunicated for 30 days, and have his head shaved; the girl was to be sold and the money given to the poor. There were also repeated attempts by the Jewish religious authorities in Spain to completely end concubinage with Christian and Moorish women (see Chapter 4). Moreover, beginning in the ancient world, Jewish religious ideology developed the belief that disguised bastards and their offspring would be removed from the Jewish population by dying young (Baron 1952b, 222).[5] To the extent that Jews believed their religious ideology and acted on it (and there is every reason to suppose this), such a belief would discourage such deceptive efforts.

Such behavior is thus "accidental" from the standpoint of viewing Judaism as a group evolutionary strategy in the sense that the great majority of this gene flow occurred as the result of individual behavior by Jews in contravention of religious law and the wishes of community authorities. Because it was illicit behavior, it would have remained secret, and this is undoubtedly the reason we know so little about it.

# CONCLUSION

The most important conclusion is that the hypothesis of zero genetic differences between Jewish and gentile populations is, on the basis of the above data, essentially unthinkable. And it must be remembered that even very shallow genetic gradients between groups are consistent with group strategizing which would have important effects on gene frequencies. Virtually any group that segregates itself from another group is likely to vary genetically in some traits, if only because of the existence of random sampling effects.

Thus, in D. S. Wilson's (1989) examples of possible group structuring, it is theoretically possible for a subset of animals to separate themselves off from a larger group and pursue a group strategy. Such a group may have minimal genetic differences from the rest of the animals, but there would almost certainly be some genetic differences as a result of sampling effects. (These genetic differences from the original population may also involve traits that are important to following the group strategy. For example, in typical group selection models, the strategizing group is characterized by higher levels of altruism, and, in the case of Judaism, it is suggested in Chapter 8 that Jews were predisposed to their particular evolutionary strategy because of their relatively high level of ethnocentrism.)

Moreover, there is the strong expectation that genetic divergence between the segregating groups would occur after separation due to differential processes of selection and drift acting on the two populations over time. Thus even if there were almost no differences between the Jewish gene pool and the rest of the

Near-Eastern gene pool in, say, 586 B.C., such differences would be expected to occur increasingly over time, resulting, among many other possible reasons, from the Jewish eugenic practices described in Chapter 7. Indeed, John Hartung (personal communication, August 28, 1992) has suggested that modern Jews are less closely related to the ancient Israelites than to modern Palestinians—an ironic possibility to say the least.

Thus, any maintenance of cultural segregation over long periods of historical time between groups that are in resource and reproductive competition with each other (whether intrasocietal or intersocietal) is overwhelmingly likely to have evolutionary effects on gene frequencies in the population as a whole and therefore be of evolutionary interest. And it is the nature of these cultural isolating mechanisms that is the focus of the following two chapters.

Finally, although the data presented here indicate that Judaism is of importance to an evolutionist interested in interactions between different gene pools, there would be reason to pursue the present project even in the absence of genetic differences between Jews and gentiles. This is because the evidence reviewed in the following chapters indicates that in fact the religious ideology and the behavior of Jews constituted a group evolutionary strategy as outlined in Chapter 1 (with the exception that Judaism would not in fact be a fairly closed group evolutionary strategy). Even if, for example, Jewish communities in fact failed to control individually adaptive behavior, so that the genetic gradient between Jews and gentiles became non-existent, historic Judaism was a clearly articulated strategy in which there were great attempts to ensure compliance of all members of the Jewish community. If, in contradiction to all of the data presented in this chapter, the strategy nevertheless failed in genetic terms, it was a strategy nonetheless and therefore worthy of investigation. Moreover, since evolutionary mechanisms may well function on the basis of phenotypic rather than genotypic cues, even in the absence of genetic differences, one would still be justified in attempting to understand the remarkable phenomena of Judaism and anti-Semitism within an evolutionary framework.

# NOTES

1. Motulsky (1977a) suggests that the higher incidence of myopia in Ashkenazi Jewish populations could be the result of selection for higher verbal intelligence. Myopia and intelligence have been linked in other populations, and Jews tend to have higher intelligence and higher rates of myopia.

2. Patai and Patai (1989) argue against this proposition, and such a proposition is incompatible with Arthur Koestler's hypothesis that Ashkenazi Jews are Caucasians who derive for the most part from the remnants the Khazar Empire, which had converted to Judaism in the eighth century. These works are clearly apologetic in tone and are considered in *SAID* (ch. 4). On the other hand, recent data on intermarriage indicate the potential for a greater degree of genetic admixture between Jews and gentiles than in the past. These findings are discussed in *SAID* (ch. 10).

3. On the other hand, those forced to convert to Christianity were disproportionately wealthy. Many of these converts became crypto-Jews, and they and their descendants persisted in their Judaism for several centuries thereafter (see discussions in Chapter 5 and *SAID*, ch. 3 and 4).

4. The conflict between group and individual interests is a fundamental one in Jewish communities, discussed throughout this volume. We have already seen that poorer Jews were disproportionately likely to leave the group, presumably because their individual interests conflicted with group membership. There is also evidence that intermarriage following religious conversion occasionally occurred within the highest stratum of the gentile population (for traditional Poland, see Beauvois 1986, 89; for pre-19th-century England, see Bermant 1971, 14). These individual Jews have clearly defected from the group strategy to pursue individually adaptive strategies.

5. Baron (1952b, 222) recounts the Talmudic story in which Rabbi Ammi discovered such a deception and took credit for saving the bastard from an untimely early death. The bastard was advised to marry a gentile slave so that the offspring would be a slave who, upon liberation, could become a Jew. However, being a descendant of a slave was also a profound blot on one's genealogy. See Chapter 4.

# 3

# EVOLUTIONARY ASPECTS OF THE TANAKH

And ye shall not walk in the customs of the nation, which I am casting out
before you; for they did all these things, and therefore I abhorred them. . . . I
am the LORD your God, who have set you apart from the peoples. (Lev.
20:23-24)

There is a certain people scattered abroad and dispersed among the peoples
in all the provinces of thy kingdom; their laws are diverse from those of every
people; neither keep they the king's laws; therefore it profiteth not the king to
suffer them. (Esther 3:8)

This chapter has three purposes. The first is to show that the Tanakh (the Jewish
term for what Christians refer to as the Old Testament) shows a strong concern
for reproductive success and control of resources. The second purpose is to show
that there is also a pronounced tendency toward idealizing endogamy and racial
purity in these writings. Finally, it is argued that the ideology of Judaism as an
evolutionary strategy for maintaining genetic and cultural segregation in a
diaspora context is apparent in these writings.

# THE GENERAL IMPORTANCE OF REPRODUCTIVE SUCCESS AND THE CONTROL OF RESOURCES IN THE TANAKH

I will multiply thy seed as the stars of the heaven, and as the sand which is
upon the seashore. (Gen. 22:17)

The rich ruleth over the poor, and the borrower is servant to the lender. (Prov.
22:7)

Baron (1952a) notes that Judaism is often referred to as a "this-worldly" religion. While there is very little concern with an afterlife, "[b]oth early and later Judaism . . . continuously emphasized a firm belief in the survival of the group and in the 'eternal' life of the Jewish people down to, and beyond, the messianic age" (Baron 1952a, 9). Throughout the long history of Jewish writings, there is a strong emphasis on "the duty of marriage and the increase of family" (p. 12) and "a religious inclination toward aggrandizement of family and nation" (p. 31), as seen, for example, by numerous Biblical injunctions to "be fruitful and multiply" and injunctions to the effect that one will obtain reproductive success by following the precepts of Judaism.

The descriptions of the patriarchs return "over and over again to accounts of theophanies associated with blessings and promises of territorial possession and descendants" (Fohrer 1968, 123). For example, God says to Abraham: "'Look now toward heaven, and count the stars, if thou be able to count them.' and He said unto him: 'So shall thy seed be.' And he believed in the LORD; and He counted it to him for righteousness" (Gen. 15:5-6). Conversely, the result of not following God's word is to have diminished reproductive success: A portion of the extended curse directed at deserters in Deuteronomy states, "And ye shall be left few in number, whereas ye were as the stars of heaven for multitude; because thou didst not hearken unto the voice of the LORD thy God. And it shall come to pass, that as the LORD rejoiced over you to do you good, and to multiply you; so the LORD will rejoice over you to cause you to perish, and to destroy you" (Deut. 28:62-63).

This concern with reproductive success became a central aspect of historical Judaism. Baron (1952b, 210), writing of later antiquity, notes the "rabbis' vigorous insistence upon procreation as the first commandment mentioned in the Bible . . . and their vehement injunctions against any waste of human semen." Neuman (1969, II:53) makes a similar comment regarding Jews in pre-expulsion Spain, and Zborowski and Herzog (1952, 291) note the absolute obligation to marry and have children among the Ashkenazim in traditional Eastern European society, again based on the recognition that procreation is the first commandment of the Torah. "To be an old maid or a bachelor is not only a shame, but also a sin against the will of God, who has commanded every Jew to marry and beget offspring." Having many children was viewed as a great blessing, while a woman with only two children viewed herself as childless.

All of the Talmudic regulations regarding sexual behavior were aimed at maximizing the probability of conception (Zborowski & Herzog 1952, 312). Intercourse was prohibited during the woman's menstrual period and for one week thereafter so that it would occur during the woman's fertile period and at a time when the man had a high sperm count because of his abstinence. Friday evening was thought to be the most auspicious time because people were relaxed and festive during the Sabbath celebration.

Moreover, "the main stream of the Law sanctified daily pursuits performed in a spirit of service to the family or nation . . . approval, and not mere tolerance of economic activity, finds numerous formulations in the teachings of the rabbis" (Baron 1952a, 9; see also Baron 1952b, 256ff). Similarly, Johnson (1987, 248) notes the equation of economic success and moral worth in the Tanakh, the Apocrypha, and the Talmuds. He also points out that the Talmuds contain detailed discussions of business problems, so that Jewish education combined practical economic and legal education with what is more commonly viewed as religious.

Besides these general pronouncements regarding the importance of reproductive success and obtaining resources, there is good evidence for the importance of polygyny and sexual competition among males in the Tanakh.[1] Evolutionary anthropologists (e.g., Betzig 1986; Dickemann 1979) have noted a strong tendency for wealthy males in stratified societies to accumulate large numbers of wives and concubines and to have large numbers of offspring, while males with lesser wealth were restricted to one wife or none at all. Such behavior conforms to the theoretical optimum for individually adaptive male behavior.

On the basis of the presumptions of the law and the behavior of the leading personalities of the Tanakh, Epstein (1942) argues that polygyny is the primitive marriage form among the Israelites. Polygyny is assumed throughout the Tanakh (e.g., Exod. 21:10) and appears repeatedly in the behavior of Abraham, Isaac, and Jacob. For example, Jacob fathers 12 sons by four different women—two wives and two concubines.

While the early patriarchs engaged in the low-level polygyny made possible by their pastoral, nomadic life style, the settled agricultural society of Israel allowed for much greater differences in access to females and in reproductive success. Gideon is said to have had 70 sons, Jair the Gileadite 30 sons, Ibzan of Bethlehem 30 sons and 30 daughters, and Abdon 40 sons. King David clearly had a large number of wives and concubines, and at least 16 children, although it is difficult to determine their numbers. At 2 Samuel 15:16 he is said to have left 10 of his concubines in Jerusalem, with no implication that this was the total number.

King Solomon is the extreme example of this tendency for the wealthy and powerful to have large numbers of wives and children: "And he had seven hundred wives, princesses, and three hundred concubines" (1 Kings 11:3). Solomon's descendants also had very high reproductive success: Rehoboam is said to have had 18 wives, 60 concubines, 28 sons, and 60 daughters. Moreover, after the division of the kingdom, Rehoboam "dealt wisely, and dispersed of all his sons throughout all the lands of Judah and Benjamin, unto every fortified city; and he . . . sought for them many wives" (2 Chron. 11:23). Abijah, Rehoboam's son, is said to have had 14 wives, 22 sons, and 16 daughters (2 Chron. 13:21).

Reflecting the reproductive value of females, wives were considered legitimate spoils of war: Thus, King David obtains Saul's wives after his victory (2 Sam. 12:8), and the Syrian king Benhadad states his demands as follows:

"Thy silver and thy gold is mine; thy wives and thy children, even the goodliest, are mine" (1 Kings 20:3).

Competition among the wives in a polygynous household is expected and found. Elkanah has two wives—Peninnah and Hannah, but only Peninnah had children. As a result, Hannah received a lesser sacrifice during religious observances "and her rival vexed her sore, to make her fret, because the LORD had shut up her womb" (1 Sam. 1:6). The key to status and happiness for a woman in a polygynous household was to have children.

## The Importance of Consanguinity and Endogamy in the Tanakh

> And it came to pass, when they had heard the law, that they separated from Israel all the alien mixture. (Neh. 13:3)

There is an extremely strong concern for endogamy (i.e., marriage within the group) throughout the Tanakh. From an evolutionary perspective, endogamous marriage results in a relatively high average degree of genetic relatedness within the group as a whole, with implications for the expected degree of within-group cooperation and altruism (see Chapter 6). To the extent that a group prevents gene flow from outside the group, the fitness of individuals becomes increasingly correlated with the success of the entire group, and this is especially the case if the group has a high level of inbreeding to begin with. At the extreme, consanguineous marriage (i.e., marriage with biological relatives) results in the offspring being closely related to parents and each other, again with theoretical implications for familial and within-group solidarity. It is an extremely important thesis of this volume that Judaism has, at least until very recently,[2] been immensely concerned with endogamy—what is often referred to as racial purity; moreover, Judaism has shown relatively pronounced tendencies toward consanguinity, especially in comparison with Western societies (see Chapter 8).

Powerful tendencies toward consanguinity can be seen in the behavior of the patriarchs. Thus Abraham marries his half-sister (Gen. 20:12), and his brother Nahor marries his niece (Gen. 11:29).[3] Amram, the father of Moses and Aaron, married his aunt (Num. 26:59). Moreover, Abraham sires Ishmael by the Egyptian slave Hagar, but he makes his covenant with Isaac, the son of his half-sister Sarah, clearly a far closer genetic relationship than with Ishmael. When Sarah wants to cast out Hagar and Ishmael, Abraham is distressed, but God tells Abraham that Sarah is right and that he should indeed favor Isaac over Ishmael.

From an evolutionary perspective, God and Sarah are correct. It is in Abraham's interest to favor Isaac because Isaac shares more genes with him than does Ishmael. Later, it is stated that Abraham had six children by another woman, Keturah, and it is stated that "Abraham gave all he had unto Isaac. But unto the sons of the concubines, that Abraham had, Abraham gave gifts; and he sent them away from Isaac his son, while he yet lived, eastward, unto the east country" (Gen. 25:5-6). Thus, Abraham practiced the optimal evolutionary strategy of unigeniture, while favoring a child with a closer genetic relationship to one more distantly related. Clearly, his best strategy was to concentrate his resources in Isaac, who will then have sufficient resources to be polygynous himself, while allowing his other children to descend economically and hope for the best.

Similarly, Isaac is given an Egyptian slave as a wife in his youth, but his heirs are his children by Rebekah, the daughter of his first-cousin Bethuel (whose mother, Milcah, had married her uncle, Nahor [Gen. 11:29]).[4] Abraham makes very clear his desire not to have Isaac marry a woman of the Canaanites, whom he was presently dwelling with, but rather to return "'unto my country, and to my kindred, and take a wife for my son, even for Isaac'" (Gen. 24:4).

Esau, the elder son of Isaac, offends his parents by marrying two Hittite women: "And they were a bitterness of spirit unto Isaac and to Rebekah" (Gen. 26:35). Later, realizing that Isaac and Rebekah disapprove of his marriages, Esau makes a consanguineous marriage by taking Mahalath, the daughter of Abraham's son Ishmael,[5] as an additional wife (Gen. 28:9). Rebekah clearly abhors the thought of Jacob also marrying a local woman and sends him to her relatives with the advice of marrying a first cousin "of the daughters of Laban thy mother's brother" (Gen. 28:2). Jacob ends up marrying two of his first cousins, Rebekah and Leah. Although Esau was quite successful, the chronicler of Genesis ignores him to concentrate on the more consanguineous line of Jacob.[6]

The split between Esau and Jacob is theoretically significant. Because Jacob is denied any inheritance, he comes to marry his cousins without any bridewealth—quite unlike the situation where Abraham provided enormous bridewealth to the same group of kin in payment for Rebekah. As a result, Jacob must work many years and his relationship with his uncle Laban is filled with deception on both sides. When Jacob finally absconds with his family, Laban chases them, and they agree to remain separate.[7] After this point, there are no further marriages with Laban's branch of the family, and all of Jacob's sons have no choice but to marry foreign women. The consanguineous link with the other branch of Abraham's family is ended, and instead of concentrating the family within one highly inbred stem, Jacob's 12 sons become the founders of the 12 tribes of Israel.[8]

The importance of endogamy, at least from the standpoint of later redactors, can be seen in the treatment of the conquered peoples whom the Israelites displace after the Exodus (see also Hartung 1992, n.d.). The policy described in the Books of Numbers, Deuteronomy, and Joshua is to commit genocide rather than permitting intermarriage with the conquered peoples in the zone of settlement. The chronicler of Deuteronomy states as a general policy regarding the displaced peoples that the Israelites "shalt utterly destroy them; thou shalt make no covenant with them, nor show mercy unto them; neither shalt thou make marriages with them: thy daughter thou shalt not give unto his son, nor his daughter shalt thou take unto thy son" (Deut. 7:3).

As recorded in the Book of Joshua, this policy is then scrupulously followed when the Israelites cross the Jordan and eradicate the peoples there. Moreover, the emphasis on the need to exterminate other peoples in order to avoid intermarriage is repeated: "Else if ye do in any wise go back, and cleave unto the remnant of these nations, even these that remain among you, and make marriages with them, and go in unto them, and they to you; know for a certainty that the LORD your God will no more drive these nations from out of your sight; but they shall be a snare and a trap unto you, and a scourge in your sides, and pricks in your eyes, until ye perish from off this good land which the LORD your God hath given you" (Josh. 23:12-13). These instructions are carried out: "So Joshua smote all the land, the hill-country, and the South, and the Lowland, and the slopes, and all their kings; he left none remaining; but he utterly destroyed all that breathed, as the LORD, the God of Israel, commanded" (Josh. 10:40).

For peoples living outside the zone of settlement, the policy proposed in Deuteronomy is to kill only the males and to keep the women and children as spoils of war. However, although captured women can become wives, they have fewer rights than other wives: "[I]f thou have no delight in her, then thou shalt let her go whither she will" (Deut. 21:14). Moses is said to have commanded the Israelites to kill not only every male Midianite (including children), but also all non-virgin females. In light of a previous passage in which Moses condemns marriage between Israelites and Midianites (Num. 25:6), there is the suggestion that the captured females will be slaves and/or concubines for the Israelite males. Their children would presumably have lower status than the offspring of regular marriages, and, as pointed out by Patai and Patai (1989, 122), there is no mention of converting female slaves in the Tanakh.

There are two post-settlement instances in the Tanakh where children of foreign concubines rise to positions of power within the Israelite community. Both of these instances are instructive in showing the generally low status of such individuals. In the Abimelech story, the mother is from Shechem, and Abimelech succeeds to his father's inheritance only by killing his father's 70 legitimate children with the help of his mother's kinsmen, who are reminded of their blood relationship to Abimelech ("remember also that I am your bone and flesh" [Judg. 9:2]).

In the Jephthah story, a very salient fact is that he is expelled from the household by his half-brothers because he is viewed as having no inheritance (presumably also the fate of Abimelech, had he not taken matters into his own hands). As a result Jephthah is forced to live with a group of "vain fellows" (Judg. 11:3) with whom he eventually achieved military success. Moreover, it is not even clear that Jephthah's mother was a foreigner, since she is described only as a harlot. These stories hardly support the idea that the offspring of foreign concubines were readily absorbed into Israelite society.

Further indication of the low status of the offspring of foreigners comes from the very negative attitudes toward Solomon's many foreign wives. Solomon is cursed with the fragmentation of his kingdom after his death as a result of this practice (1 Kings 11:11; see also Neh. 13:26). Epstein (1942) notes that the offspring of Solomon's foreign wives had a separate status within Israelite society below the pure Israelite stock even into rabbinic times.[9]

Sexual relationships with the women of the surrounding peoples are invoked as a major source of evil within Israelite society. Thus, Moses orders the execution of Israelite men who consort with Moabite women (Num. 25:1-13). The men are executed and God also sends a plague because of the offense. Later, the Israelites are said to be living among a variety of peoples, "and they took their daughters to be their wives, and gave their own daughters to their sons, and served their gods" (Judg. 3:6). As a result of these practices, the Israelites were said to be dominated by the Mesopotamians for eight years.[10]

The origination of the Samaritans as a separate Jewish sect was also the result of a general abhorrence of exogamy. When the northern kingdom fell to the Assyrians and its elite were taken away, the remnant intermarried with the new settlers, creating a "mixed race" (Schürer [1885] 1979, 17). The intermarriage with aliens meant that "the Samaritans were not *ethnically* what they claimed to be" (Purvis 1989, 590), the Pharisees going so far as to refer to them as *kûtîm* (i.e., colonists from Mesopotamia). Their racial impurity was then "used to deny the Samaritans their original Israelite heritage. From that point onwards, their claim to be part of the chosen people . . . was never again acknowledged by the Jews" (Johnson 1987, 71).[11] The returning exiles rejected the offer of the Samaritans to help in rebuilding the Temple (Ezra 4:1-5), and intermarriage with the Samaritans was regarded with horror. Thus, Nehemiah comments on the marriage of the son of the high priest Eliashib to the daughter of the Samaritan Sanballat: "Therefore I chased him from me" (Neh. 13:28).

The apotheosis of the abhorrence of exogamy appears in the Books of Ezra and Nehemiah which recount events and attitudes in the early post-exilic period. The officials are said to complain that "'the people of Israel, and the priests and the Levites, have not separated themselves from the peoples of the lands, doing according to their abominations. . . . For they have taken of their daughters for themselves and for their sons; so that the holy seed have mingled themselves with the peoples of the lands'" (Ezra 9:2).

The use of the phrase "holy seed" is particularly striking—a rather unvarnished statement of the religious significance of genetic material and the religious obligation to keep that genetic material pure and untainted. The result was a vigorous campaign of what Purvis (1989, 595) refers to as "ethnic purification." Nehemiah states, "In those days also I saw the Jews who had married women of Ashdod, of Ammon, and of Moab; and their children spoke half in the speech of Ashdod, and could not speak in the Jews' language, but according to the language of each people. And I contended with them, and smote certain of them, and plucked off their hair, and made them swear by God: 'Ye shall not give your daughters unto their sons, nor take their daughters for your sons, or for yourselves" (Neh. 13:23-25).

All who have intermarried are urged to confess their guilt and give up their foreign wives and children. Ezra provides a list of 107 men who renounced their foreign wives and their children by these women.[12] These books also refer to genealogies that were used to deny access to the priesthood to some of the returnees from the Babylonian exile because there was a question regarding the racial purity of their marriages. The result was a hierarchy of purity of blood, at the top of which were those who could prove their status by providing genealogical records. This group married into priestly families, and its members were politically and socially dominant within the Jewish community. If doubt remained after genealogical investigation, the person could remain an Israelite, but was removed from the priesthood and no pure-blooded Israelite would intermarry with him. People with definitely impaired genealogies (including the offspring of mixed marriages) formed a third category. They married among themselves "and felt themselves fortunate if admitted to marriage with a Jewish family of doubtful record" (Epstein 1942, 164).[13]

The clear concern regarding intermarriage after the return from Babylon so evident in Ezra and Nehemiah may well be due to the fact that the returnees were forced to live among foreigners to a much greater degree than when they had political power. Prior to the exile, the issue of separation from neighbors could be treated relatively casually, since there were natural political and geographical barriers to intermarriage and the offspring of foreign concubines could be easily relegated to a low status. However, after the exile, the maintenance of genetic and cultural separatism created enormous problems, since the Israelites could not have complete political control over their area of settlement in Palestine. "Prohibitions against intermarriage, occasionally recorded and apparently fairly well enforced before the Exile . . . became an urgent necessity for the preservation of the Jewish people in Exile" (Baron 1952a, 147). The apex of concern for family purity among the Jews occurred in the Babylonian captivity and thereafter: "Purity of family was valued in Babylonia as never in Palestine before or after. For centuries the Babylonian Jews kept careful records of all significant family events so that they might be able to prove at any time pure descent from priestly or other distinguished stock. As late as the Talmudic age genealogical accounts . . . are frequently referred to. They must have been composed on the basis of records often covering a whole millennium" (Baron 1952a, 125). Thus, the data are compatible with the hypothesis that the almost obsessive concern with endogamy really coincides with the difficulty of maintaining genetic barriers within an exilic (diaspora) context.

Finally, as Neusner (1987, 37-38) emphasizes, it is important to note that Ezra was attempting to prevent intermarriage not only with foreign tribes like the Ammonites and Moabites, but even with the Israelites who had been left behind during the Babylonian exile. Although one can interpret this exclusion in purely ideological terms as a matter of the "cultic impurity" of these people who had been cut off from the aristocratic elite who had been exiled,[14] an evolutionary perspective suggests that it was the intermarriage of these settlers with surrounding peoples that was really the issue that determined their exclusion. As Purvis (1989, 597-598) notes regarding the Samaritans, some at least had undoubtedly retained a high level of cultic purity. The problem was that the ethnic purity of the Samaritans and the other *'am ha-ares* ("people of the land") was at best doubtful.[15]

After all, if doubts about religious practice had been the sole issue, it would have been easy to accept any individuals from any tribe (certainly including the non-exiled Israelites) into the cult if only they agreed to participate appropriately in the cult. One wonders why Ezra was so intent on forcing Israelites to abandon their alien wives and racially impure children if the only blemish on these individuals was cultic. Participation in cultic rituals without ethnic commonality is the basis for the ideology that conversion to Judaism would be possible at any stage in history. From the data described in Chapter 2, however, we know that Judaism has always retained its ethnic core, and we shall see in Chapter 4 that conversion to Judaism has always been problematic. In this sense, Ezra and Nehemiah are indeed the lawgivers to subsequent Judaism, and in fact Ezra has often been viewed by the Jews as "a virtual second Moses" (McCullough 1975, 49; see also Ackroyd 1984, 147).[16]

# THE EVOLUTIONARY IDEOLOGY OF THE TANAKH

For Thou didst set them apart from among all the peoples of the earth. (1 Kings 8:53)

For thou art a holy people unto the LORD thy God: the LORD thy God hath chosen thee to be His own treasure, out of all peoples that are upon the face of the earth. (Deut. 7:6; 14:2)

The root of Judaism—and of anti-Semitism—is in the very essence of the Ten Commandments ["I am the Lord your God"; "You shall have no other gods before me"]. (Arthur Hertzberg 1993b, 69).

## Israelite Monotheism as an Ideology of Separatism

The ideology of the separateness of the Jews is apparent throughout the Tanakh. Many of the statements encouraging separatism were inserted into the earlier passages by redactors during and after the Babylonian exile, and, indeed, recent scholars have emphasized that the entire Pentateuch[17] must be seen as a statement of the priestly group writing during the Babylonian exile (e.g.,

Neusner 1987, 35). The importance of circumcision and the Sabbath as signs of separateness were contributions of the Priestly (P) source stratum from the exilic or the post-exilic period, and the entire Book of Leviticus, which describes elaborate rituals that separate Jews from others, derives from this stratum (Ackroyd 1968; Fohrer 1968; Schmidt 1984). Schmidt (1984) also notes that the P stratum emphasizes the importance of reproductive success by the repeated use of the phrase "Be fruitful and multiply" and also shows a strong concern with genealogies. (After the exile, genealogies were used to determine who could be a member of the community and a candidate for the priesthood. See above and Chapters 4 and 8.)

Moreover, the P stratum is responsible for the exclusive covenant between God and Abraham's descendants (Gen. 17), complete with the mark of circumcision. There is thus an indication of an increased emphasis on the importance of practicing endogamy, maintaining separateness, and tracing purity of descent during and after the Babylonian exile. "The net effect of the Pentateuchal vision of Israel . . . was to lay stress on the separateness and the holiness of Israel while pointing to the pollution of the outsider" (Neusner 1987, 36). Neusner (1987) emphasizes that the elaborate regulations for holiness in the Pentateuch, and especially Leviticus 19:1-18, are really to be understood as means of separation from surrounding peoples. "Holiness meant separateness. Separateness meant life" (p. 43). Judaism had become an ideology of minority separatism.[18]

The nature of the Israelite God is also a mark of separateness and is closely linked with an abhorrence of exogamy and with aggression against foreigners.[19] The following passage from the P stratum links the jealousy of the Jewish god not only with aggression toward other gods, but also with cultural separatism and fear of exogamy:

> Take heed to thyself, lest thou make covenant with the inhabitants of the land whither thou goest, lest they be for a snare in the midst of thee. But ye shall break down their altars, and dash in pieces their pillars, and ye shall cut down their Asherim. For thou shalt bow down to no other god; for the Lord, whose name is Jealous, is a jealous God; lest thou make a covenant with the inhabitants of the land, and they go astray after their gods, and do sacrifice unto their gods, and they call thee, and thou eat of their sacrifice; and thou take of their daughters unto thy sons, and their daughters go astray after their gods, and make thy sons go astray after their gods (Exod. 34:12-16; see also Deut. 7:3-8).

The function of promoting separateness can also be viewed as an aspect of monotheism. The groups that surrounded Israel appear to have been polytheistic and the different gods served different human purposes (Johnson 1987; see also (Baron 1952a, 47). Indeed, at the time of the writing of the Tanakh, the religion of Israel was the only monotheistic religion (Goitein 1974).

For the Israelites, there was really only one purpose for God—to represent the idea of kinship, ingroup membership, and separateness from others. Supporting this view of Israelite monotheism, there is evidence that monotheism became more important in the exilic period—precisely the period in which barriers between Jews and gentiles were being created and enhanced. McCullough (1975, 14), discussing the writings of Deutero-Isaiah (i.e., Isa. 40-55) during the exilic period, states that "unqualified monotheism was to be a basic feature of Hebrew thought from this time on." Similarly, Soggin (1980, 317) finds that "it is not that Israel had not known monotheism before this period, but rather that only with Deutero-Isaiah was the faith changed to certainty," and there began for the first time to be a polemical attitude against polytheism. Schmidt (1984, 133) sums it up by stating that "the oneness of the people corresponds to the oneness of God . . . Yahweh Israel's God, Israel Yahweh's people." Or as a well-known rabbinic saying has it: "God, Israel, and the Torah are one" (see Baron 1973, 191).

Significantly, Ezra, whose abhorrence of intermarriage was a major influence on subsequent generations and who was revered among the Israelites as "a virtual second Moses" (McCullough 1975, 49), views intermarriage as a "great sin against Israel's God" (McCullough 1975, 48), a comment indicating the close connection between ethnic purity and the Israelite concept of God. In a very real sense, one may say that the Jewish god is really neither more nor less than Ezra's "holy seed"—the genetic material of the upper-class Israelites who were exiled to Babylon.

Unlike the gods of the Greeks and Romans, a major function for Israelite theology was not to interpret the workings of nature or to bring good fortune in various endeavors, but rather to represent the kinship group through historical time—clearly a unitary concept at least as an ideal, and especially so in a diaspora context. Israelite theology is intimately bound up with Israelite history. Moses "linked God with the fate of Israel in history in an inseparable way" (Baron 1952a, 47). There is a general lack of interest in cosmogony and anthropogeny, but "the history of man serves as a background for the still more significant history of Israel" (p. 47; see also Johnson 1987, 92-93). It is not Creation that is the most important event in early Hebrew history, but rather the Exodus, in which the Israelites successfully flee from Egypt after a successful sojourn as a minority in a foreign land.[20]

Finally, there are several allegories that stress the idea that separatist behavior resulting from worshiping the Israelite god may result in persecution, but there will eventually be rewards. In the Book of Daniel, Daniel and his three co-religionists remain faithful to the dietary laws, thus separating themselves from the other servants in the Babylonian court, and are rewarded by God with wisdom and understanding. Later, there are two incidents in which Jews are accused of not worshiping the gods of the Babylonians and the Persians. The Jews acknowledge these practices, but God saves them from punishment and improves their status so that, like Joseph and Nehemiah, they can use their status and power to help their co-religionists during their sojourn among the gentiles. As in the case of the Esther allegory, these stories clearly emphasize the idea that keeping the faith and remaining separate will eventually be rewarded. As Fohrer (1968, 479) notes, "the book seeks to strengthen the patience and courage of the devout who are suffering persecution, to give them new hope, and to exhort them, like Daniel, to remain loyal to their faith to the point of martyrdom."

## The Indestructibility of God as an Aspect of Diaspora Ideology

When the Israelites conquer other peoples (as recounted in the Books of Numbers and Joshua), they destroy the people and the representations of their gods. But Israel's enemies can never destroy representations of God because such images are forbidden. Israel's God is thus spiritual and can be understood as a representation of the continuation of the kinship group, even in the face of the destruction of all religious artifacts. Therefore, the destruction of the Temple does not destroy God. This aspect of religious ideology is thus ideal for sojourners with a precarious existence: The writers of Deuteronomy clearly anticipated that the Israelites would be subjected to oppression by others (e.g., Deut. 30:3, 31:21), but these oppressors could never destroy the Israelite God. Only the destruction of the Israelites themselves could accomplish that. Johnson (1987, 77) notes that Jeremiah emphasizes that the Israelite God is indestructible and intangible, and can thus survive defeat. Jeremiah "was trying to teach them how to become Jews: to submit to conquering power and accommodate themselves to it, to make the best of adversity, and to cherish the long-term certainty of God's justice in their hearts."

Related to this is the idea that there is no fixed abode for God. God is portable and resides in the Ark of the Covenant or inside a tent and can be moved from place to place. Fohrer (1968; see also Schmidt 1984, 183) notes that the idea of a transcendent god connected to a tent sanctuary is a product of the post-exilic P stratum of the Pentateuch. God is no longer to be associated with a specific site in the Temple—an assumption which presupposes a permanent settlement.[21]

The god of the diaspora had been created. Johnson (1987) notes that the concept of a movable, indestructible God easily accommodated to the period after the fall of the Temple and "reflects the extraordinary adaptability of the people, a great skill in putting down roots quickly, pulling them up and re-establishing them elsewhere" (p. 42).

## Understanding Evil: The Consequences of Straying

One of the unique aspects of Judaism long noticed by scholars has been the emphasis throughout much of the Tanakh on the idea that all of Israel's misfortunes come from rejecting God. The result is that being conquered or oppressed by another people with different gods is not viewed as a vindication of another god, but only as a sign that the Jews have been unfaithful to theirs. The Books of Deuteronomy, Judges, 1 Samuel, Joshua, Kings 1 and 2, and Chronicles 1 and 2, although they are clearly historical, also have a moral that is endlessly repeated: Worshiping other gods and straying from strict religious observance will lead eventually to destruction. For example, lack of strict adherence to religious orthodoxy is blamed for the destruction of the northern kingdom of Israel and for the Babylonian capture of Jerusalem. Fohrer (1968, 213) describes a "cycle of apostasy, punishment, conversion, and deliverance" imposed on the Book of Judges by the Deuteronomistic writers during the exile. "The whole pattern of history is seen portrayed in rebellion and forgiveness" (Ackroyd 1968, 75). "If Israel kept the Torah, God would bless his people, and if not . . . God would exact punishment for violation of the covenant" (Neusner 1987, 21; see also Ackroyd 1968, *passim*; Moore 1927, I:222; Schmidt 1984, 143).[21]

Reflecting the obsession with reproductive success characteristic of the writers of the Tanakh, the punishment for those who stray will ultimately be a lowered reproductive success: According to Hosea, "they shall commit harlotry [i.e., worship other gods], and shall not increase" (Hos. 4:10). Moreover, there is an implicit association between worshiping other gods and the crime of exogamy. When the returning exiles commit the crime of exogamy by intermarrying with the local people, Ezra states, "Since the days of our fathers we have been exceeding guilty unto this day; and for our iniquities have we, our kings, and our priests, been delivered into the hand of the kings of the lands, to the sword, to captivity, and to spoiling, and to confusion of face, as it is this day" (Ezra 9:7). Exogamy is a crime against God—a belief that makes sense if indeed, as argued above, God simply is another way of denoting an endogamous, unitary ethnic group, the holy seed of Israel.

Also reflecting the idea that exogamy is a crime against God, a particularly revealing and very common analogy for worshiping other gods is to "play the harlot." In Ezekiel 23, Jerusalem is compared to a harlot who has Assyrians, Babylonians, and Egyptians as lovers. In Egypt, she "doted upon concubinage with them, whose flesh is as the flesh of asses, and whose issue is the issue of horses" (Ezek. 23:20). Not only are the offspring of these alien lovers grotesque monsters, but also God out of jealousy turns the lovers against the Israelites, who then ultimately pay for their crime with lowered reproductive success: "[T]hey shall deal with thee in fury; they shall take away thy nose and thine ears, and thy residue shall fall by the sword" (Ezek. 23:25). "These things shall be done unto thee, for that thou hast gone astray after the nations, and because thou art polluted with their idols" (Ezek. 23:30).[22] Worshiping other gods is like having sexual relations with an alien—a point of view that makes excellent sense on the assumption that the Israelite god represents the racially pure Israelite gene pool.

The ideology attempts to increase group solidarity in the face of group failure. Recent psychological research on group identifications has indicated that group members may actually identify with the group even more strongly following group failure under circumstances in which there is a strong prior commitment to the group. But if prior commitment is weak, there is a tendency to identify with the group more strongly after success than after failure (Turner et al. 1984).

Given the virtual universality of anti-Semitism and the commonness of persecutions and expulsions in Jewish history, Judaism as a group strategy clearly requires a very strong prior commitment from group members. Interestingly, anti-Semitism is clearly anticipated in the Tanakh (e.g., Deut. 28: 64-67; see below). The ideology may be said therefore to be an attempt to rally group loyalties even in the face of the repeated disasters that were anticipated as a consequence of the strategy.

The expected outcome of the defeat of a group with very intense group identification is stronger group identification. In fact, defeat and persecution have not tended to result in Jews defecting from the group strategy. It has often been noted that the Jewish response to persecution has been increases in religious fundamentalism, mysticism, and messianism. "Judaism's response to historical events of a cataclysmic character normally takes two forms, first, renewed messianic speculation, and second, a renewed search in Scripture for relevant ideas, attitudes and historical paradigms" (Neusner 1986c, 26; see also Johnson 1987, 260, 267).

Thus, the rabbinic interpretation of the destruction of the Second Temple was that it was punishment for the sins of Israel (Alon 1989, 536), and Avi-Yonah (1984, 255) notes that the Jews regarded their persecution under the Byzantine Christians as a sign that the Messiah was coming. This was also the pattern in Yemen where persecution was particularly prolonged and intense. Following an expulsion in 1679, Ahroni (1986, 133; see also Nini 1991) comments, "As in all disasters, the Jews of Yemen responded to the Mauza calamity with an outpouring of self-flagellation. They saw in their sufferings trials imposed by God as a result of their sins. The note of Jeremiah's proclamation, 'Your ways and your doings have brought these [disasters] upon you' (5:18) rings through their poems, which call for penitence and repentance." The persecutions were followed by beliefs that the coming of the Messiah was imminent as well as by a powerful attraction to the mystical writings of the Kabbala.

Fischel (1937, 124-125)) notes that following the persecutions in Mongolian Iraq in the 13th century, "as so frequently happened in Jewish history, the destruction of political and economic influence led to a spiritual revival and to a period of internal growth. The birth of Hebrew-Persian literature falls in that gloomy political period . . . ." Kabbalistic writings, characterized by Johnson (1987) as "xenophobic, nationalist and inflammatory" (p. 195), became more common during the period of the persecutions of the 15th century (Johnson 1987; Neuman 1969, II:144).[24]

This phenomenon can also be seen in the modern world. For example, Meyer (1988, 338) notes that the response of liberal Reform Jews to the increased anti-Semitism of the Hitler years in Germany was increased identification with Judaism, increased synagogue attendance, a return to more traditional observance (including a reintroduction of Hebrew), and acceptance of Zionism. Following World War II, there were upsurges of religious observance and/or ethnic identification among American Jews in response to the Nazi holocaust and as a reaction to crises in Israel. The response to persecution is therefore a tendency to stress a unique Jewish identity, rather than to assimilate.

Throughout history, Jews who were less committed to the group undoubtedly had a tendency to worship the gods of their more powerful conquerors, neighbors, and persecutors. Indeed, Ackroyd (1968) emphasizes that the diatribes against idolatry in Ezekiel and Deutero-Isaiah are directed against Israelites who have begun to worship Babylonian gods during the exile, and Bickerman (1984) notes that some of the exiles had indeed begun the assimilation process. The ideology of the Tanakh can be seen as an attempt to lessen the normal tendency for such individuals to defect under these circumstances by blaming all sufferings on the fact that Jews have not adhered rigorously to the group strategy.

The ideology is non-falsifiable (and thus self-perpetuating) because it explains both success and failure in terms that imply continued allegiance to the group. Moreover, since adversity is always attributed to failure to obey religious practices, blame is always internalized. The result is to prevent a rational appraisal of the reasons for the adversity by examining the Israelites' behavior *vis-à-vis* their neighbors. Again, the typical response of Jewish populations to persecution has been a renewed intensity of religious fervor, often with strong overtones of mysticism.

## The Future Rewards of Faith: Judaism as a This-Worldly Messianic Religion

Unlike the Christian conception of an afterlife of happiness, the Tanakh makes clear that the rewards of keeping the faith and obeying religious regulations will be a high level of reproductive success, a return to power and prosperity in Israel, and the destruction and/or enslavement of Israel's enemies. (Recall Baron's [1952a, 9] discussion of Judaism as a this-worldly religion; see above.) As Neusner (1987, 41) states, the Torah presented the loss and recovery of land and political sovereignty as "normative and recurrent." "[T]he nation lived out its life in the history of this world, coveting the very same land as other peoples within the politics of empires" (p. 46). In the centuries following the Biblical period and the failed rebellions during the Roman era, the belief developed that "only by the immediate intervention of Almighty God could the might of the heathen kingdom be annihilated and the world made ready for the coming undivided and undisputed reign of God, or, in its national expression, the worldwide and eternal dominion of the holy people of the Most High" (Moore 1927, II:331; see also Schürer ([1885] 1979, 514ff).

A return to power in Jerusalem after being scattered is a prominent theme throughout the writings of the ancient period.[25] Often the enslavement or destruction of enemies is envisioned. "And the peoples shall take them, and bring them to their place; and the house of Israel shall possess them in the land of the LORD for servants and for handmaids; and they shall take them captive, whose captives they were; and they shall rule over their oppressors" (Isa. 14:2). Fohrer (1968, 384) states that Deutero-Isaiah "contains questionable nationalistic and materialistic traits." The relationship between Israel and foreigners is often one of domination: For example, "They shall go after thee, in chains they shall come over; And they shall fall down unto thee, They shall make supplication unto thee" (Isa. 45:14); "They shall bow down to thee with their face to the earth, And lick the dust of thy feet" (49:23). Similar sentiments appear in Trito-Isaiah (60:14, 61:5-6), Ezekiel (e.g., 39:10), and Ecclesiasticus (36:9).

Perhaps the epitome of worldly messianic expectations can be seen in the Book of Jubilees, where world domination and great reproductive success are promised to the seed of Abraham:

> 'I am the God who created heaven and earth. I shall increase you, and multiply you exceedingly; and kings shall come from you and shall rule wherever the foot of the sons of man has trodden. I shall give to your seed all the earth which is under heaven, and they shall rule over all the nations according to their desire; and afterwards they shall draw the whole earth to themselves and shall inherit it for ever' (Jub. 32:18-19).

Reflecting these messianic expectations, around 100 A.D. the *Shemoneh 'Esreh* prayer, said three times a day by traditional Jews in the following centuries, was finalized (see Schürer [1885] 1979, 456ff). It asks for a gathering of the dispersed in Jerusalem and the reestablishment of national authority.

## The Assumption of a Diaspora in the Tanakh

There are numerous references in the Tanakh to the scattering of the Israelites throughout the world. We have noted that the final form of the Pentateuch emerged during and in the period after the Babylonian exile. A prominent goal of these writings is to emphasize Israel's history as a sojourning people and those aspects of a religion that fit well with a sojourning life style while remaining separate from the host peoples (see also Chapter 8).

The Priestly (P) stratum, composed in exilic and post-exilic times, essentially prescribes a set of religious practices with no role for a state (Fohrer 1968). "P contains a program for the divinely willed reconstruction of the community after the Exile or for a reformation of the community in the postexilic period. This program is retrojected into the past in order to legitimize it and give it authority" (p. 184). In this new community, the priests become substitutes for earthly rulers: Schmidt (1984) notes that "anointing and other symbols of royalty now become distinguishing marks of priesthood (Exod 28f)" (p. 98).[26]

There are also a great many specific instances in the early history of the Israelites that involve sojourning among foreign peoples, most obviously the long sojourn in Egypt. In each case, the sojourn ends with the patriarchs or Israelites leaving the host society with great wealth and increased numbers.[27] There are also many sections in which there are positive attitudes toward living among strangers. Leviticus 25:23 states that the Israelites are sojourners with God. The land is God's and the Israelites are only sojourners. King David says, "For we are strangers before Thee, and sojourners, as all our fathers were" (1 Chron. 29:15), and the phrase is repeated in Psalms 39:13. Deuteronomy repeatedly states that God loves the sojourner and that the Israelites are expected to be kind to the sojourner, as they should be toward widows and orphans (e.g., Deut. 27:19).[28]

There is some indication that the authors of Deuteronomy did not believe that living among foreigners was ideal. Part of the curse on those who stray from the word of God is that they would be among foreigners, "[a]nd among these nations shalt thou have no repose, and there shall be no rest for the sole of thy foot" (Deut. 28:65). Nevertheless, provision is made for Israelites who are sojourning: By following the word of God, God will "return and gather thee from all the peoples whither the LORD thy God hath scattered thee" (Deut. 30:3). Indeed, Deuteronomy 31:18ff, written in the exilic period (Fohrer 1968) implies that disasters will happen to the sojourning Israelites because they fail to follow the word of God. Later, Nehemiah cites this passage, noting that God had told Moses that "[i]f ye deal treacherously, I will scatter you abroad among the peoples; but if ye return unto Me, and keep My commandments and do them, though your dispersed were in the uppermost part of the heaven, yet will I gather them from thence, and will bring them unto the place that I have chosen to cause My name to dwell there" (Neh. 1:8-9).

The reality of scattering (as well as the prediction of eventual reunification in a powerful state) is also assumed by the prophets. Isaiah speaks of recovering the remnant and gathering "the scattered of Judah From the four corners of the earth" (Isa. 11:12). "I will bring thy seed from the east, And gather thee from the west; I will say to the north: 'Give up,' And to the south: 'Keep not back, Bring My sons from far, And my daughters from the end of the earth" (Isa. 43:5-6).[29] Indeed, Baron (1952a, 107) cites this passage and notes that "[s]o many and so specific are the references to a really world-wide Diaspora, that they cannot be explained away as lavish interpolations. . . . Such utterances were no mere propaganda or eschatological wish dreams. They must have had some relation to actual facts. Even the 'back to Palestine' movement . . . could not check this steady, inevitable growth of the Diaspora." Moreover, the texts often use the plural, indicating that the authors suppose that the Israelites will eventually be scattered among many countries, not just Babylon.[30]

Finally, as described more fully in Chapter 8, a strong current of "Exodus ideology" in the exilic writings views the Babylonian Exile as analogous to the original sojourn in Egypt, with the expectation that God will provide for them in the end as He had done before. For example, Jeremiah writes, "Therefore, behold, the days come, saith the LORD, that they shall no more say: 'As the LORD liveth, that brought up the children of Israel out of the land of Egypt'; but: 'As the LORD liveth, that brought up and that led the seed of the house of Israel out of the north country, and from all the countries whither I had driven them'; and they shall dwell in their own land" (Jer. 23:7-8).

Indeed, Ackroyd (1968, 234) finds that during the Exile there was a general reworking of older materials so that all of Israel's previous history was seen from the standpoint of the Exile. The Exile was accepted as the result of turning away from God's ways and was viewed as part of a larger purpose. This larger purpose necessitated the establishment of elaborate legal codes, which separated Jews from gentiles, and the purification of the community: "[W]e are shown the community being purified, undertaking the response which testifies to the need for purity, purity of race, freedom from contamination with alien influence, so attesting its real nature as the people of God" (Ackroyd 1968, 236-237).

# CONCLUSION

The ideology of the Tanakh is a blueprint for an experiment in living in the sense utilized in Chapter 1. It was obsessed with the history of the Jewish people because one of its essential functions was to rationalize that history and provide a hope for a successful future. The religion of the Tanakh was greatly concerned with reproductive success, endogamy, and cultural separation from surrounding peoples within a diaspora context. It was a religion with powerful sanctions on individuals who worship other gods or stray from group goals, and one in which lowered reproductive success is the result of deviation from life within the confines of the kinship group, while those who continued in the kinship group would be rewarded with great reproductive success and eventual revenge and domination.

From an evolutionary perspective, the purpose of this ideology is to ensure the continuity of the kinship group, even within a diaspora context in which there are enormous pressures for assimilation and gradual loss of contact with other members of the group. The results have been extraordinarily effective: As indicated in Chapter 2, Jews have maintained a significant genetic distance between themselves and their host societies for centuries. Indeed, they are the only group that has successfully maintained genetic and cultural segregation while living in the midst of other peoples over an extremely long period of time. Johnson (1987, 3) calls them "the most tenacious people in history."

# NOTES

1. Evolutionists have also stressed the importance of paternity confidence and conflicts between kinship groups. Regarding the former, the Book of Numbers (5:11-31) describes a ritual used to induce a miscarriage in a woman suspected (but not known) to have committed adultery. If the woman is innocent, the potion will bring on the menstrual period; if guilty, the potion will "make thy belly to swell, and thy thigh to fall away" (Num. 5:22). Thus, the ritual will in any case ensure that the woman will not bear another man's child. Conflict and cooperation between kinship groups in Israelite society depending on genetic distance are discussed in Chapter 8.

2. Recent data on Jewish intermarriage and their implications are discussed in *SAID* (ch. 10).

3. See Goodman (1979, 2) for a diagram of the genealogy of the patriarchs from Terach to Jacob.

4. As described in Chapter 4, uncle-niece marriage came to be idealized in the Talmud and was extensively practiced by devout Jews in the ancient world.

5. Because Ishmael is only a half-brother to Isaac, Mahalath is only a "half-first cousin" (the coefficient of genetic relatedness r = 1/16) to Esau. Even if Esau made his covenant with the son of Mahalath, the line would be much less endogamous than the line of Jacob, who married his first cousin from a family that was already highly endogamous (including uncle-niece marriages).

6. The discrimination of others depending on the degree of genetic relatedness can be seen by the discussion of affective relationships. While the authors give no sign that Abraham mourns the deaths of his concubines, he is said to mourn the death of Sarah, his kinsman and principal wife. Similarly, while there is no mention that Isaac loves his Egyptian concubine, when his relative Rebekah becomes his wife, "he loved her" (Gen. 24:67). Jacob, too, loves Rachel (Gen. 29:20), but there is no mention of Esau loving his Hittite wife, and, indeed, this relationship is not approved by Isaac and Rebekah.

7. Johnson (1987), on the basis of recent archeological evidence, suggests that Jacob was adopted by Laban because he had no sons of his own and that when he later had sons, he attempted to go back on the arrangement. This accounts for the incident in which Rachel steals Laban's gods, since the household gods represent a symbolic title deed, which Laban had broken.

8. After the Exodus, kinship remains important. The Israelites are divided into 12 tribes, and at Numbers 26:52, the land is divided among the tribes according to their numbers, thus in effect rewarding the most prolific kinship groups. The importance of kinship can also be seen in that the tribes are expected to remain descent groups in which all land remains within the tribe. Thus, Moses rules that if a man has no sons, his daughters can inherit, but if so, they must marry within their tribe. Moreover, in the particular case recounted, the heiresses marry their first cousins, thus keeping the property not only within the tribe, but also within the immediate descent group (Num. 36:11). There are also several prescriptions in Deuteronomy enjoining cooperation within the kinship group and very different treatment of outsiders. This type of discrimination depending on group membership is a recurrent theme of historical Judaism and is a major theme of Chapter 6.

9. The tainted offspring of Solomon continued to provide a cautionary tale about the evils of exogamy long past rabbinic times. In the 15th century, Rabbi Moses Arragel stated that Solomon's foreign wives caused the woes of Israel, including the captivity. Solomon's poor example is then used to illustrate the general principle that Jews should not marry gentiles; see Castro 1971, 69.

10. Interestingly, Hartung (n.d.) emphasizes the idea that a major purpose of the Midrashic and Talmudic commentaries was to alter these stories in a manner that emphasized the idea that the Israelites had been seduced by the heathen women into betraying their religion. Despite the complete lack of evidence in the Biblical sources, Moabite women are depicted as engaging in deception and bribery in order to develop relationships with the Israelite men, who are depicted as innocent victims of these machinations. The moral is that gentile women are to be avoided at all costs, and Hartung notes that this conceptualization of the wily, immoral gentile woman intent on seducing Jewish men away from their families and religion has survived into modern times in the concept of the *shiksa.*

11. Schürer ([1885] 1979, 19) makes it clear that the issue between the Israelites and the Samaritans is the doubtful ancestry of the latter, not religious practice. They are "treated not simply as foreigners, but as a race of uncertain derivation. Their Israelite extraction cannot be taken as proved, but neither can it be a priori excluded. Their affiliation to the congregation of Israel is accordingly not denied but merely considered doubtful." When mainstream Pharisaic Judaism gradually triumphed, the religion of the Samaritans became increasingly different from that of the Israelites.

12. Without providing evidence for the claim, Fohrer (1968) states that the list is artificial, but, even so, at the very least the list is a powerful indication of negative attitudes toward exogamy.

13. Epstein (1942, 166) notes that Ezra's racialist motivation can be seen by his greater concern with Israelite men marrying foreign women because the children of such unions would be brought up in the Israelite community. The children of an Israelite female marrying a foreigner would be lost to the community. This suggests that the motivation for the tradition of tracing Jewish descent through the female line is the preservation of racial purity. A common pattern in the diaspora was for wealthy Jews to marry their daughters into the gentile nobility in return for a dowry payment (see *SAID*, ch. 3). This practice had no effect on the racial purity of the Jewish population.

14. The cultic uncleanness of the people remaining in Israel during the Babylonian captivity is a theme of the Book of Haggai. "'So is this people [unclean], and so is this nation before Me, saith the Lord; and so is every work of their hands; and that which they offer . . . is unclean . . .'" (Hag. 2:14). Haggai rejects the help of the non-Israelite settlers of the region in rebuilding the Temple because of their cultic impurity, "thereby inaugurating the sequestration that was to be typical of later Judaism" (Fohrer 1968, 460). Fohrer refers to rejection of help by foreigners "the birthday of Judaism" (p. 460)—an entirely appropriate designation from an evolutionary perspective in light of the importance of separatism for such a theory.

15. This exclusion of the people of the land also had a eugenic effect on the Jewish gene pool, since the Babylonians had exiled predominantly the wealthy aristocratic and priestly elements of Israel. In later periods down to contemporary times, the word *'am ha-ares* was a term of abuse, indicating an unlettered, ritually suspect individual. See Chapter 7.

16. There is wide agreement that the exclusivism promulgated by Ezra is fundamental to later Judaism. Thus, Schürer ([1885] 1973, 142) traces a continuous development of Judaism over six centuries from Ezra to its completion with the compilation of the Mishnah in 200 A.D. Schürer emphasizes the development of religious ritual during this period as central, and it is this body of ritual that effectively separated Jews from gentiles (see Chapter 4).

17. The Pentateuch is the first five books of the Tanakh.

18. McCullough (1975, 13) sums up these ideas by noting that "[i]t may be inferred, mostly from data found in Ezekiel, Ezra, Nehemiah, and the P document of the Pentateuch, that the exiles, to protect themselves against absorption by their environment, emphasized certain distinctive practices that could be followed in an alien land and would discourage assimilation, such as dietary habits, Sabbath observance, circumcision, marriage customs. These group mores seem to have acquired a new importance in the exilic community, and when, at a later date, some exiled Jews 'returned' to the homeland, they could be counted on to advocate such practices in Judah, as the careers of both Nehemiah and Ezra illustrate."

19. Ironically, the exclusivist nature of God as an expression of ethnic unity may have had long-term negative implications for diaspora Jews after the establishment of Christianity and Islam as official state religions whose monotheism derived directly from Judaism. The exclusivism of monotheism was retained in these religions, but it was a religious (and sometimes political and economic) exclusivism, rather than an ethnic exclusivism. Many historians have commented that the exclusivist nature of these religions tended to result in intolerance of other religions, and in particular Judaism. For example, Avi-Yonah (1984, 262) contrasts the relative tolerance of the Persian Empire, which was not based on religion, with the relative intolerance of Byzantine Christianity, and in Chapter 8, the exclusionary effects of Islam and medieval Christianity on Jews are discussed. In *SAID* (ch. 3) it is argued that Christianity in the late Roman Empire developed as an anti-Semitic movement which was a mirror image of several critical aspects of Judaism as a group evolutionary strategy, including monotheistic exclusivism.

20. Indeed, Hartung (n.d.) argues that the stated view of the Pentateuch and the Talmud is that non-Israelites are not fully human. In the Pentateuch, the term *adam* is often used to refer to humans in general, without regard to sex. However, Hartung argues that the term really refers only to Israelites because only the Israelites were created in God's image and are thus truly human, while contemporaries living in the land of Nod were not. While typically the Israelites are referred to with the term *adam*, the scriptures use other words to refer to non-Israelites. Similarly, in the Talmud, this term is specifically asserted to refer only to Israelites, and heathens are viewed as non-men: "*And ye My sheep of My pasture, are men;* you are called *men#* but the idolators are not called *men.*" The footnote states that "#. . . only an Israelite who, as a worshipper of the true God, can be said to have been like Adam created in the image of God. Idol worshippers, having marred the Divine image forfeit all claim to this appellation" (b. Yeb. 61a).

21. The prophet Ezekiel is important in this regard, since he advocated the separation of God from the Temple and Jerusalem, making him the "father of Judaism" in the eyes of some scholars (see Fohrer 1968). "It is no longer true that in one's native land encounter with God and real life are possible, while dwelling in a foreign land is like death; now life and death together lie in man's inward and outward conduct, wherever he may dwell and in whatever circumstances he lives" (p. 417). Schmidt (1984) notes that with Ezekiel "God's throne, which since the time of David and Solomon had been firmly fixed on Zion, becomes mobile, having wheels, as it were . . . and makes its appearance in a distant unclean land" (p. 253).

22. This ideology of the role of deviation from God's law in producing ill fortune was elaborated in the Talmud by the idea that the Messiah would come and restore Israel's fortunes as soon as Israel exactly obeyed the rabbinic laws to become a staple of later Judaism (Neusner 1987, 131). For example, "If Israel would keep a single Sabbath in the proper way, forthwith the son of David will come" (y. Taanit 1:1, quoted in Neusner 1987, 130).

23. It is very difficult to determine whether those aristocratic exiles in Babylon would have ultimately had a greater reproductive success if they had assimilated than if they had remained separate. Their reproductive success would necessarily have to be conceptualized as individual reproductive success because the endogamous, racially pure group would have disappeared. The assimilated groups in that part of the world were repeatedly conquered and reproductively exploited in later ages, often by alien ruling elites with their large harems (e.g., the Arab Moslems and the Mongols). Given this pattern, it may well be the case that the Israelite contribution to the gene pool of the Near East would have progressively diminished. The diaspora strategy was the only available opportunity to expand their numbers, while maintaining racial purity.

24. However, if mysticism is associated with failure, the response may be an even more rigorous legalism. Zborowski and Herzog (1952, 182) note that in the period following the collapse of hope in the false messiah Sabbettai Zevi in the 17th century (whose rise followed the Cossack persecutions), there was a trend for the rabbis to make an even greater number of regulations. Belief in the false messiah was attributed to irrational, emotional beliefs, and the rabbis reacted to the collapse of the movement by increasing their control via the further elaboration of the rules of appropriate behavior.

25. See the Books of Daniel, Isaiah, Jeremiah, Ezekiel, Joel, Haggai, Amos, Nahum, Obadiah, Zephaniah, Zechariah, and the apocryphal Books of Ecclesiasticus (36:1-17), Baruch (4:5-5:9), the Psalms of Solomon (8:34, 9:1-2, 11:1-9), Jubilees (23-32), 2 Esdras (13:39-50), and 4 Esdras (11:1-12). See also the discussion of restoration themes in the Book of Jeremiah in Ackroyd 1968, 58-61; and Sanders 1992, 290ff.

26. In Chapter 8, the unique role of priests in Israelite and early Jewish history will be emphasized as crucial in understanding the development of Judaism as an evolutionary strategy.

27. These examples are discussed extensively in Chapter 8.

28. However, strangers were expected to keep their lower status in Israelite society. In the prolonged curse upon Israelites who stray from the word of God (Deut. 28:15-68) there is the curse that "the stranger that is in the midst of thee shall mount up above thee higher and higher; and thou shalt come down lower and lower" (Deut. 28:43).

29. These passages come from both Isaiah and Deutero-Isaiah.

30. See Deut. 30:3; Isa. 43:5; Jer. 29:6, 29:14, 32:37, 23:3; Ezek. 11:16-17, 17:6, 20:34, 20:41, 36:19, 36:24, 37:21; Zech. 10:9.)

# 4

# GENETIC AND CULTURAL SEGREGATION OF JEWS AND GENTILES

Do thou, my son Jacob, remember my words, and observe the commandments of Abraham thy father: separate thyself from the nations, and eat not with them and do not according to their works and become not their associate; for their works are unclean and all their ways are a pollution and an abomination and uncleanness (Jub. 22:16)

When the nations of the world hear some of this [the glory of the Jewish God] they say, "Let us join hands with you," as it is written, "Whither is thy beloved gone, O fairest among women, whither is thy beloved gone that we may look for Him together?" Whereupon Israel says to the nations, Oh no! for it is written, "My beloved is mine and I am His . . . . " (Rabbi Akiba, *Mekhilta d'Rabbi Ishmael*, quoted in Alon [1980, 1984] 1989, 525, and dated by Alon to the later first century or early second century A.D.

Verily, this is the authentic religion of truth. It was revealed to us by the master of all the prophets, early and late. Through it, God has distinguished us from all the rest of mankind, as He has said: "Only the LORD had a delight in your fathers to love them, and He chose their seed after them, even you above all peoples" (Deut. 10:15). From Maimonides' Epistle to the Jews of Yemen [12th century]; reprinted in Stillman 1979, 235).

It was noted in Chapter 1 that in order to qualify as an evolutionary strategy, genetic segregation must be actively maintained by the strategizing group. There are sound theoretical reasons to suppose that a group strategy in a diaspora context could be maintained only by an ideology that emphasizes separation from the rest of society. If individuals are completely free to maximize self-interest, then membership within a kinship group is expected to be only one among several considerations affecting self-interest (MacDonald 1991), and, indeed, it has been suggested that individually adaptive behavior in contravention to the group strategy has been the source of at least some of the genetic admixture between Jewish and gentile populations over historical time (see Chapter 2). Mating on the basis of similarity in social class and assortative mating on a variety of valued phenotypic traits (e.g., intelligence) are expected to gradually break down rigid ethnic barriers in societies where there is free choice of a marriage partner (MacDonald 1991).

A genetically closed group strategy therefore depends on the development of social controls reinforcing group identity and preventing high levels of genetic admixture from surrounding groups. In addition, however, research on social identity theory (Hogg & Abrams 1987) indicates that the erection of very powerful cultural barriers between Jews and gentiles produces an intense identification with the ingroup and psychological distance from outgroups. As indicated in Chapter 3, this very powerful identification with the ingroup was necessary to maintain group cohesion in the face of disasters.

Among the factors facilitating separation of Jews and gentiles over historical time have been religious practice and beliefs, language and mannerisms, physical appearance and clothing, customs (especially the dietary laws), occupations, and living in physically separated areas, which were administered by Jews according to Jewish civil and criminal law. All of these practices can be found at very early stages of the diaspora, and in the ancient world, a *Mitzvoth* of 613 commandments evolved, including prohibitions that very directly limited social contacts between Jews and gentiles, such as the ban on drinking wine touched by gentiles and the undesirability of bantering with gentiles on the day of a pagan festival. Perhaps the most basic signs of separation, appearing in the Pentateuch, are circumcision and the practice of the Sabbath. The following material surveys these ideologies and behaviors with a concentration on the ancient world, the Sephardic Jews in Spain, and the Ashkenazi Jews in Eastern Europe. The chapter concludes by discussing Jewish cultural separatism since the Enlightenment.

From an evolutionary perspective, the uniqueness of the Jews lies in their being the only people to successfully remain intact and resist normal assimilative processes after living for very long periods as a minority in other societies. This unique resistance to assimilation dates from the period of the Babylonian exile and perhaps even the Egyptian sojourn described in Genesis. Bickerman (1988, 38; see also Cohen 1987) points out that in the ancient world there were voluntary diasporas of Greek, Aramaic, and Phoenician peoples, which eventually became assimilated into the surrounding societies. Moreover, it was a common practice of the Assyrians, Babylonians, and Persians to displace the peoples whom they had conquered, just as the Jews were displaced during the Babylonian exile. For considerable periods, it was common for these displaced peoples to live in separate communities and to continue to identify with the ethnic group and the religion that were left behind: "It could hardly be otherwise: the tribal organization of oriental peoples blocked the road to assimilation" (Bickerman 1988, 38). However, in the long run, these displaced peoples became assimilated, while the Jews did not.[1]

During the period of Greek hegemony, the Jewish religion was unique in forcibly resisting Hellenizing influences (Schürer [1885] 1973, 146), and the Jewish struggle with Rome was the most prolonged and violent of any of the peoples in the Empire. Indeed, one of the major results of the development of the Roman Republic and Empire was that the great diversity of ethnic groups, which characterized Italy and the rest of the Mediterranean region, was largely assimilated. For example, in Italy during the fifth century B.C., Etruscans, Samnites, Umbrians, Latins, Romans, and a variety of other groups were assimilated into a larger culture in which these ethnic divisions disappeared.

The Jews were the only ethnic group to survive intact after the upheavals that occurred at the end of antiquity. After the barbarian invasions and the collapse of the Roman Empire, there were further assimilative processes. The agricultural peoples of the Middle East, with the exception of the Jews, lost their identities in the early Islamic period (Goitein 1974). Moreover, Christianity steadily disappeared in parts of the Arab empire, but flourishing Jewish communities remained even after Jews were relegated to a subservient, humiliated status. Similarly, Lea (1906-07, I:39ff) notes the existence of Ostragoths, Visigoths, Celt-Iberians, and Romans in seventh-century Spain, but only the Jews survived as an independent ethnic group—the others presumably becoming completely assimilated via intermarriage. In general, after the barbarian invasions, Western Europe was a mixture of Roman and Germanic peoples whose ethnic identities, with the exception of the Jews, were eventually lost (e.g., Brundage 1987; Geary 1988). And there were a variety of national groups in medieval and post-medieval Poland besides the Poles and the Jews, particularly Scots, Germans, Armenians, and Tatars. Hundèrt (1986a) notes that by the end of the 18th century, these other groups had become assimilated and there were the beginnings of a Catholic bourgeoisie resulting from the amalgamation of these groups. The Jews, however, remained separate.

# JEWISH CULTURAL SEPARATISM IN THE ANCIENT WORLD

[The rulers of Alexandria] set apart for them a particular place, that they might live without being polluted [by the gentiles]. (Flavius Josephus, *The Wars of the Jews*, 2:487-488)

There is excellent evidence indicating that Jews actively maintained cultural separatism in the ancient world and that this cultural separatism acted to prevent exogamy. The following passage from 1 Maccabees (second century B.C.) illustrates the perceived connection between assimilation and intermarriage:

At that time there appeared in Israel a group of renegade Jews, who incited the people. 'Let us enter into a covenant with the Gentiles round about,' they

said, 'because disaster upon disaster has overtaken us since we segregated
ourselves from them.' The people thought this a good argument, and some of
them in their enthusiasm went to the king and received authority to introduce
non-Jewish laws and customs. They built a sports stadium in the gentile style
in Jerusalem. They removed their marks of circumcision and repudiated the
holy covenant. They intermarried with Gentiles, and abandoned themselves
to evil ways. (1 Macc. 1:11-15)

Assimilation was thus beginning to lead to intermarriage. However, the result
of the Hasmonean victory and the end of Greek domination "was to set up anew
walls of separation between Hebrew and heathen" (Epstein 1942, 168). The
Book of Jubilees,[2] written during this period, shows an extreme concern for
intermarriage. "If there is any man in Israel who wishes to give his daughter or
his sister to any man who is of the stock of the gentiles, he shall surely die, and
they shall stone him with stones . . . and they shall burn the woman with fire
because she hath dishonored the name of the house of her father and she shall be
rooted out of Israel" (Jub. 30:7). A variety of separatist practices derive from this
period, including prohibitions on feasting with gentiles, using wine or oil from
gentiles, and having any kind of sexual contact with gentiles.[3] Although Epstein
(1942, 170) notes that the racialism of Ezra was replaced by religious
nationalism as the basis for erecting barriers against intermarriage, it goes
without saying that the end result was the same from an evolutionary
perspective: genetic segregation of the Jewish gene pool from the surrounding
peoples.

In its final stage of development in the ancient world, following the Roman
conquest, the walls of separation were raised even higher as a response to
political dissolution: "[T]he antagonism to intermarriage enters upon its final
phase as a bulwark for group solidarity made the stronger as the political unity
of the people becomes the weaker" (Epstein 1942, 172). During this period, in
addition to the previous prohibitions on using wine and oil produced by gentiles,
Jews were not allowed to use wine or oil that was touched by a heathen, eat food
cooked by a heathen, or use products produced by heathens if Jewish rules had
not been followed in making the products. Gentiles, their houses, and all of their
belongings were regarded as unclean, and no observant Jew would eat with a
gentile. There were new sanctions against having any contact with heathen
religions, including any kind of business relationship. Chaperones were required
for contact between the sexes for Jews and gentiles, and flagellation was the
penalty for intermarriage. Capitalizing on a Roman concept, intermarriages were
ruled invalid.

In addition, Hegermann (1989, 158; see also Applebaum 1974b *passim*;
Sevenster 1975, 102ff) notes that self-imposed residential segregation in
diaspora communities governed by religious law became a clear policy among
the Jews by the middle of the first century B.C. Moore (1927-30, I:282) also
notes an increased concern on the part of the pharisees in the early Christian
period with educating Jews on religious practices and enforcing scrupulous

observance of ritual, much of which had separatist effects. Then, in the second century, there was increasing concern among Jews to expunge all Greek thought and emphasize knowledge of Hebrew in the period following the failure of the Bar Kocheba uprising (Baron 1952b, 142). This period was generally characterized by a "closing of the ranks" and the erection of barriers against the outside world, including in Baron's view, an increasingly indifferent or hostile attitude toward proselytes. On the Sabbath, Jews were to associate exclusively with other Jews, prompting Baron to comment, "No greater encouragement to the development of a voluntary ghetto was needed" (p. 149). Avi-Yonah (1984, 71ff) finds that even moderates in Palestine in the second and third centuries placed a great emphasis on separatism, but there were influential extremist preachers who advocated complete renunciation of Greek culture, including any knowledge of the Greek language or literature, use of Greek names, *et cetera*.

Neusner (1987, 56) makes the additional point that this trend toward separatism in a diaspora context can be viewed as imposing the cultic life of the priests on all Jews: "And ye shall be unto Me a kingdom of priests, and a holy nation" (Exod. 19:6). This was the program of the Pharisees and found its culmination in the writings of the Mishnah. The elaborate codes of uncleanness and holiness now applied to the everyday life of all Jews—"in kitchens, beds, marketplaces, whenever someone picked up a common nail" (p. 57). In virtually everything one did, one would be aware of the possibility of holiness—and the reality of separation from the rest of society.

Although the issue of cultural and genetic separatism in later periods is discussed in more detail below, it is worth mentioning at this point that there was a direct continuity between these ancient customs and the practices of succeeding centuries. Epstein (1942) notes that these walls of separation regarding intermarriage originating in the ancient world remained in place without controversy into the 19th century. Moreover, despite the attempts of some radical reformists in Western Europe, intermarriage continued to be condemned even by Reform rabbis well into the 20th century. Epstein notes that the emancipation of Jews in Eastern Europe had actually increased the fear of intermarriage and cultural assimilation:

> They saw the danger of extinction through assimilation, and therefore intensified their opposition to intermarriage even above the restrictions of traditional law. There was the intensity of a struggle against national doom. They considered intermarriage little less than apostasy. It was not unusual for parents to observe seven days of mourning with all its dramatized sorrow for a son or daughter who married out of the Jewish faith, and thereafter to consider that child as physically dead. Even in the new world, it is not unusual for congregations to write a clause in their constitutions to the effect that one married out of the faith cannot be admitted to or retain membership in the organization . . . even among people otherwise indifferent to tradition an intermarriage is considered a family tragedy. (Epstein 1942, 182-3)

# JEWISH PROSELYTISM IN THE ANCIENT WORLD

## Theoretical Issues

Although there is no question that Jews actively maintained barriers between themselves and their neighbors in the ancient world, it has been proposed that the Jewish community was in fact open to gentiles via conversion and that many gentiles overcame these barriers to become Jews. Such a possibility essentially envisages that the Jewish community in the ancient world had very high barriers, which were actively maintained, but that the community encouraged gentiles to overcome the barriers and become members of the Jewish community.

The issue of Jewish proselytism in the ancient world has received a great deal of attention from historians of Judaism, and often there is a clear apologetic tone in these writings. Several discussions of proselytism by Jewish historians, beginning with the studies of Bamberger ([1939] 1968) and Braude (1940), have developed a revisionist perspective, which attempts to show that Judaism has been a universalist religion at least since the Biblical period. However, they argue that, as a result of the hegemonic actions of governments or other religions (see also Eichorn 1965a; Raisin 1953; Segal 1988), Judaism failed to attract sufficient converts.

From an evolutionary perspective, the implicit argument would then be that the result of these hegemonic actions of other religions was an unintended genetic and cultural segregation from other peoples. Jewish actions facilitating this segregation were necessary in order to preserve a purely religious/ethical integrity whose correlation with genetic segregation was unintended and purely coincidental.

The idea that Jewish separatism fundamentally derives from a moral, even altruistic, stance has been common throughout Jewish history. Baron (1952a, 12) notes that an integral aspect of the ideology of Judaism has been that "segregation is necessary to preserve at least one exemplary group from mixing with the masses of others" who are viewed as morally inferior. Separatism not only is motivated by ethical reasons, but involves altruism: In being Jews, they were "living the hard life of an exemplar." And by serving as a morally pure exemplar, "they were being Jews *for all men*" (italics in text).

This sense that Judaism represents a moral ideal to the rest of mankind—"a light of the nations" (Isa. 42:6)—has been common throughout Jewish intellectual history, reflected, for example, in Philo, who depicts Israel "as a nation destined to pray for the world so that the world might 'be delivered from evil and participate in what is good'" (see McKnight 1991, 39); or "the Jewish nation is to the whole world what the priest is to the state" (McKnight 1991, 46). This theme also emerged as a prominent aspect of the 19th-century Jewish Reform movement and remains prominent among modern Jewish secular intellectuals (see below). Moore (1927-30, I:229) notes that in the ancient world the ideology contained the thought that "Israel is not only the prophet of the true religion but its martyr, its witness in suffering; it bears uncomplaining the penalty that others deserved, and when its day of vindication comes and God greatly exalts it, the nations which despised it in the time of its humiliation will confess in amazement that through its sufferings they were saved."

The implicit argument would then be that, even though the Jewish religion ended up denoting a highly endogamous, genetically segregated kinship group in which there was a great deal of within-group altruism and cooperation, combined oftentimes with successful competition with gentiles for resources (and sometimes with exploitation of gentiles; see Chapter 5), this fact is simply a consequence of its failure, despite its best efforts, to attract adherents, perhaps in conjunction with normative human tendencies for resource competition.

Apart from the difficult empirical question of whether Judaism was really self-consciously racialist and nationalistic in the ancient world (see below), the anti-voluntarist perspective is problematic from an evolutionary perspective. If indeed the present perspective that historical Judaism has often involved successful resource and reproductive competition with host population gene pools is correct (see Chapter 5), it is certainly reasonable to suppose that this behavior conforms to evolutionary expectations that humans often attempt to maximize biological fitness (reproductive success). One must then suppose that, even though historical Judaism often coincided with what one might reasonably suppose to be individual (and group) genetic self-interest, this result was a major departure from the original intention, since the original intention was to develop not only a religion that was theologically universalist, but also one in which ethnicity was theoretically irrelevant and in which there was an eager attempt to foster genetic assimilation with surrounding populations.

We must then suppose that only a pure sense of religious idealism prevented the Jews from abandoning this strategy once it failed in its universalist aims, *even though failure to abandon genetic and cultural segregation resulted repeatedly in resource and reproductive competition, accompanied by a great deal of intrasocietal violence and social division between genetically segregated groups.* For example, one would have to suppose that, despite the fact that religious and cultural segregation resulted in Jewish guilds competing with Christian guilds in both pre-expulsion Spain (Beinart 1981) and early modern Poland (Hundert 1992) and despite the fact that this competition led to a great deal of anti-Semitism and violence, this competition was merely an unfortunate result of a purely religious idealism and without interest from an evolutionary perspective.

At a very basic, common-sense level, such a view is extremely difficult to accept. But, more important, it undercuts any attempt to argue that Judaism represents an evolutionarily meaningful example of altruism or selfless moral idealism, since the evidence provided in Chapter 5 indicates that the historical instantiation of the ideology and practice of Judaism often resulted in intense resource and reproductive competition with gentiles in which there were genetic differences between these groups. If Judaism is fundamentally altruistic in an evolutionarily meaningful sense, it would be expected that Jews would characteristically engage in self-sacrificing behavior on behalf of gentiles—a thesis for which there is absolutely no evidence. On the other hand, if Jews wanted to avoid resource and reproductive competition based on the genetic segregation of Jewish and gentile gene pools, an obvious solution would be to adopt the religion of the host society and engage in an active program fostering exogamy.

From an evolutionary perspective, in the absence of actual genetic assimilation one is left to conclude that this Jewish sense of moral and religious idealism, which results in genetic segregation, is in fact a mask for a self-interested evolutionary strategy aimed at promoting the interests of a kinship group that maintains its genetic integrity during a diaspora.

Nevertheless, Bamberger's ([1939] 1968) view that Judaism is indeed a universalist religion that failed in its universalist aims bears scrutiny. If indeed Judaism is properly considered an evolutionary strategy, one might suppose that part of this strategy would be to prohibit conversion entirely. A complete ban on conversion and intermarriage would, after all, preserve the Jewish gene pool from foreign invasion.

However, such a conceptualization of the ideal evolutionary strategy ignores the context of human religious and intellectual discourse, at least in Western societies. Diaspora Judaism by necessity confronted a wide range of other religions as well as secular, rationalist ideologies. Moreover, the original confrontation occurred in the Greco-Roman world of antiquity, where there was a strong current of critical rationalism and where ethnic assimilation was the norm. Within this context, there is evidence that Judaism perceived a need to present itself in intellectually defensible terms. In the ancient world, "[t]he very survival of Judaism depended on working out a *modus vivendi* with the Gentile world" (J. J. Collins 1985, 184).

There appeared a large apologetic literature intended to present Jewish life, and particularly Jewish separatism, in a positive light and to present Jews as morally superior to gentiles by, for example, extolling their family life: "Most of the works which have been regarded as propaganda literature show little interest in proselytizing, but show a desire to share and be accepted in the more philosophically sophisticated strata of Hellenistic culture. Salvation is seldom restricted to membership of the Jewish people" (J. J. Collins 1985, 169).

Modern psychological research indicates that portraying Judaism as open to conversion would have important effects on gentile conceptions of Judaism. Consistent with the results of social identity research (e.g., Hogg & Abrams 1987), portraying Judaism as open to conversions would be expected to result in the perception among gentiles that Judaism is a permeable group, and this latter perception would be expected to reduce gentile hostility and perceptions of conflict of interest with Judaism. The perception that Judaism is a permeable group would also be expected to reduce the ability of gentiles to act in a collective manner in opposition to Judaism.

In fact, beginning with Hecataeus of Abdera (early third century B.C.) and culminating with Tacitus and others, Jewish intellectuals were confronted with a great many Greco-Roman writers whose basic criticisms centered around Jewish separatism, xenophobia, and misanthropy.[4] Given this context, there was a felt need among Jewish intellectuals to present Judaism as a universal religion. Thus, for example, in the *Letter of Aristeas* (written by a Jew masquerading as a gentile [Schürer (1885) 1986, 677]),[5] Judaism is presented as "most especially not an exclusive or closed fraternity. Rather Judaism is a gift to all humanity, since God's providence is universal" (Segal 1988, 349). Nevertheless, this document does not advocate proselytism, but rather separate Jewish and gentile religious rites, both of which are viewed as religiously beneficial.

In *Against Apion* (2:210), Josephus attempts to show that Jewish philosophers, lawgivers, and historians are at least equal to those of the Greeks, and he also notes that "our legislator admits all those that have a mind to observe our laws, so to do; and this after a friendly manner, as esteeming that a true union which not only extends to our own stock, but to those that would live after the same manner with us; yet does he not allow those that come to us by accident only to be admitted into communion with us."[6] As another example, Philo defends circumcision from the derision of pagan writers not as a symbol of ethnic/religious identity and separatism, as it was viewed among many contemporary intellectuals, but for its hygienic value and as a symbol of upright behavior—"in terms that will appear respectable to a Greek" (J. J. Collins 1985, 172).[7]

Social identity researchers have also emphasized the point that it is often in a group's interest to attempt to foster perceptions of group permeability even when actual permeability may be minimal or non-existent (Hogg & Abrams 1987, 56). As indicated above, it would appear that Jewish writers in the ancient world were well aware of the need to develop an ideology that Judaism was highly permeable, and that such a strategy had obvious perceived benefits.[8] It does not follow that Judaism was in fact highly permeable, and, indeed, the apologetic nature of this writing has long been apparent to scholars.

One might therefore reformulate the ideal strategy for Judaism as a fairly closed group evolutionary strategy as follows: Allow converts and intermarriage at a formal theoretical level, but minimize them in practice. This *de facto* minimization could occur as a result of failing to make strenuous, organized efforts to obtain converts or to encourage intermarriage; erecting imposing cultural barriers that would minimize social intercourse between Jews and gentiles and thus prevent the types of social contacts that would be the normal precursors of conversion and intermarriage; engaging in cultural practices that result in anti-Semitism, with the result that gentiles would be less likely to convert to a stigmatized religion; the existence of special Jewish taxes, such as the *fiscus Judaicus* imposed by the Romans; maintaining hostile and/or ambivalent attitudes to conversion, as well as hostile and/or ambivalent attitudes toward converts after they were admitted to Judaism, within a significant portion of the rabbinic leadership, as well as among the Jewish community as a whole; making the procedures of conversion highly unpleasant and demeaning (by, e.g., including requirements for the physically painful and dangerous rite of circumcision); reminding the convert of the dangers of being a Jew; relegating the convert to a lowered status within the community and giving the convert fewer rights than other Jews; making these disabilities continue for a number of subsequent generations before the convert's descendants could expect to attain full Jewish status; continuing the practices of endogamy among elite groups within the Jewish community and strictly keeping genealogies among these groups to ensure racial purity so that converts would be aware that marriage into these families would never occur, despite its theoretical possibility, even after many generations; continuing vestiges of Jewish national sovereignty, as represented by the existence of families that were reputed to be descended from the priests and kings of Israel and that retained prestige and authority among diaspora Jews; and keeping the messianic hope of a return to political power in a particular geographical area.

There is in fact evidence that Judaism has been characterized at all points in its diaspora history by at least some of these barriers, and, as indicated in the following, they were all present in the ancient Greco-Roman world, which, until the very recent spate of intermarriage in some Western societies, represented the apogee of Jewish proselytism.

## Jewish Proselytism in the Ancient World: Empirical Evidence

Bickerman (1988) notes that there is no evidence of conversions in the pre-Maccabean age (second century B.C.), "nor did they preach salvation to the gentiles" (p. 246). During this period, to be a Jew was to have a legal status as a member of a nationality, so that one would remain a Jew even if one failed to observe any religious laws. Conversely, a Greek who followed Jewish religious law could not legally become a Jew.

Conversions did occur in later times, but there is a large body of Christian and Jewish scholarship that depicts Judaism as hostile, ambivalent, or disinterested in converts from an early period or as changing to an attitude of hostility following the Hadrianic persecutions in the second century (see summaries in Bamberger [1939] 1968; McKnight 1991).

In the following, I will rely mainly on the views of several recent Jewish scholars, such as Bamberger ([1939] 1968; see also Feldman 1993; Rosenbloom 1978), because these authors have taken the position that Judaism has always been fundamentally positive toward converts, at least until external pressures forced them to abandon these practices. The point is that, even based on the views of this school, there is overwhelming evidence for ambivalence and hostility toward converts by some members of the Jewish religious hierarchy, for negative attitudes among the mass of Jews, and for a lowered social status for the convert within the community. Nevertheless, I will also summarize the views of several other scholars who appear to be much less apologetic.

While acknowledging that Ezra and Nehemiah present racialist doctrines, Bamberger ([1939] 1968) claims that Judaism became a universalist religion in the following period. Nevertheless, there are clear indications in his work that this view was far from unanimous either in theory or in practice.

There were many difficulties confronting converts. Converts were told, "Do you not see that Israel are now sick, shoved about, swept and torn, and that troubles come ever upon them" and that converts will be responsible for obligations to the poor. A prospective proselyte is repulsed three times, "but if he persists further, we receive him . . . one should repulse him with the left hand and draw him near with the right." Circumcision, clearly a very difficult barrier for an adult male, was mandatory for converts.[9]

Although only a theoretical possibility, converts had no right to any portion of Palestine, since this was reserved for the 12 tribes. Converts had a very low social status. If the community must choose among various members for compensation of property, redemption of captives, or saving lives, "the order is: priest, Levite, Israelite, *mamzer, Nethin,* convert, freedman" (Bamberger [1939] 1968, 64). Thus, the convert ranks below the offspring of illegitimate relationships (*mamzerim*)[10] and individuals from a foreign ethnic group who lived as servants among the Israelites (*Nethinim*). Baron (1952b, 409n) describes the extreme contempt in which rabbis in Talmudic times held *mamzerim*: "To be called *mamzer* was a superlative insult which the rabbis put under a more severe sanction (of thirty-nine stripes) than that of naming one a slave or an evildoer."

The Mishnah states that converts may intermarry with Israelites and Levites. While a priest could not marry a convert, it was controversial whether a priest could marry a convert's daughter.[11] (A convert could marry a daughter of a priest.) On the other hand, converts could marry *mamzerim, Nethinim,* foundlings, individuals who had been emasculated, and those with doubtful paternity, while native Jews could not. Israelites were forbidden to marry *mamzerim* or their descendants forever (Epstein 1942, 282; Jeremias 1969, 341). However, permission to marry *mamzerim* was extended to the descendants of converts for 10 generations (i.e., forever), and offspring between converts and *mamzerim* were considered *mamzerim*. (The only way to get rid of the stain of being a *mamzer* was to marry a female slave—obviously not an ideal solution, since the child would have the slave status of the mother (Epstein 1942, 285; Baron 1952b, 223), and being descended from a slave was also regarded with horror (see below). The implication is that if a proselyte married a *mamzer*, his/her children would forever be excluded from marrying legitimate Israelites. This "privilege" of marrying a *mamzer* or a *Nethin* is thus extremely derogatory, and there is a specific incident in which a group of converts was incensed when told of it (Epstein 1942, 200-201). Regarding the *Nethinim*, Alon ([1982, 1984] 1989, 27) states that they eventually were excluded entirely from the Jewish community.

The other categories of possible marriage partners are those in which Jewish ancestry is doubtful or in which the marriage will necessarily be infertile. Philo, who is perhaps the most universalist of all of the ancient Jewish authors, interpreted Deuteronomy as implying that *mamzerim* and those with crushed genitals could not enter the assembly of the Lord, and he had a very negative view of children who were offspring of Jewish men and gentile women (McKnight 1991, 44). Clearly all of these categories of people were highly stigmatized.

Moreover, the amount the husband had to pay for his convert wife's *ketubah* was only half the amount necessary for marrying a native Jewess, indicating a lessened value for such a woman. A further indication of the lessened value of convert women was that a man who violated a convert who became a Jewess after age three was freed from having to pay a fine to the woman's father. Also, a man who accidentally injured a pregnant convert would not have to pay damages under certain conditions. There were also restrictions on the testimony of converts in legal matters and formal requirements (as well as social practices) barring them from holding office in the community. Bamberger ([1939] 1968, 103), while generally attempting to de-emphasize bars to conversion, states that "converts were excluded in some localities, even where there was no legal impediment." While in theory they could hold some offices, there is no record of any ever holding office, and there are statements indicating that converts would not be appointed to supervise even the lowliest of community functions.

If a man and his sons converted and the man died, a Jew did not need to repay the children any outstanding debts to the man. Converts were viewed as having no blood relationships, with the result that relatives, including children, who were not Jews could not inherit. If the person had no Jewish relatives, his property went to the first Jew to appropriate it, by, e.g., obtaining physical access to the property. Bamberger ([1939] 1968) notes that there was much discussion of how such property could be obtained, with the general attitude being that such an expropriation was a fortunate windfall.

In conclusion, the convert was clearly a second class citizen according to Jewish religious law (*Halakah*). However, in addition to formal legal status, there is evidence that the actual marriage prospects of converts would be less than those theoretically available. As described more fully below, there was a powerful push toward endogamy within the various levels of Jewish society, so that Jewish society was in fact organized as a hierarchy of ever greater purity of blood ranging into the upper reaches of the priestly class. Even if converts could theoretically marry Israelites, these results indicate that Israelites who aspired to raise themselves or their children in this hierarchy of blood purity would be foolish to marry converts. Surely the existence of an unattainable, highly endogamous priestly class for whom family purity and genealogy were virtual obsessions would give pause to an ambitious person contemplating becoming a Jew. Under these circumstances, I am hard pressed to think of individuals for whom a decision to convert would be adaptive. The truly surprising thing is that anyone at all converted.

Bamberger ([1939] 1968) also considers the non-legal (aggadic) writings of the rabbis of the classical period. While there is no question that there are positive comments, there are also negative comments: "Beyond question, the Talmudic literature contains hostile remarks about proselytes" (Bamberger [1939] 1968, 161). The classic anti-convert statement in the Talmud, translated by Bamberger as "Proselytes are as hard on Israel as leprosy" (p. 163), is repeated five times, a statement that even Bamberger acknowledges as "unfriendly in tone" (p. 164), although he claims its exact meaning is vague, and he suggests that the author of the statement, Rabbi Helbo, is atypical in his animosity toward converts. Interestingly from the standpoint of the ideal strategy from an evolutionary perspective (see above), Rabbi Isaac is credited with the comment that "[e]vil after evil comes on those who receive converts" (p. 163), and the same author is credited with the view that Jews should "repulse the convert with one hand and draw him near with another" (Bamberger 1968, 287).

Even if these comments are atypical, they indicate hostility among some sections of the Jewish intellectual establishment, and this hostility, even if a minority viewpoint, would be highly salient to a potential convert. Moreover, there are several other negative statements and mixed opinions in the Talmud, summarized by Bamberger, that further indicate a far from unanimously positive official attitude toward converts. Segal (1988; p. 341) also notes that opinions regarding conversion were far from unanimous within the Jewish lay community, ranging from outright condemnation to acceptance on the assumption that the converts would represent a "fairly low number" (p. 365).

Although Bamberger ([1939] 1968) argues that these hostile comments can be interpreted in a benign manner or are obscure, they would surely give pause to a prospective convert. For example, the obvious interpretation of the statement "Converts and those who play with children delay [the coming of] the Messiah" (p. 162) is to lump converts with those who molest children (or, possibly, marry immature girls), and it states that such individuals delay the coming of the Messiah. A variant form is "Converts and nomads . . . ," which also lumps converts with a despised group whose existence is inimical to the goals of the Jewish people.

Bamberger ([1939] 1968) gives as an example of a "mixed opinion" the statement of Rabbi Eliezer: "Why . . . does the Torah warn us (against mistreating) the convert in thirty-six passages (and some say, forty-six passages)? Because his nature is evil" (p. 165). Bamberger states that Eliezer says this because converts, being relatively weak in their commitment to Judaism, may well relapse if they are mistreated. But even Bamberger acknowledges that the passage "reflects a poor opinion of the proselyte" (p. 166), and, indeed, to the extent that the fear of relapse was real (as it may well have been; see below), there is the suggestion that many converts did not persist in their new commitment and were thus lost to the Jewish gene pool. However, the clear implication of the passage is that converts are deficient in some manner. Indeed, Bamberger finds that in general "these 'mixed opinions' are the expression of teachers who were favorable enough to proselytism in theory, but who were dubious about the deep religiosity of the converts who were actually received in their own time" (p. 167). Again, there is the implication that converts were viewed as deficient and that Judaism, while theoretically permeable, was in fact quite impermeable.

Finally, as Bamberger ([1939] 1968) acknowledges, some of the positive comments must be construed as evidence that actual Jewish attitudes toward converts were often negative so that there was a need to remind the Jewish community to be friendly toward them: "*Among the people as a whole, there were certain prejudices against converts*" (p. 277; italics in text). The writers of the Talmud clearly felt a need to prevent particular practices that discriminated against converts, as shown by the following sayings: "If one sees a convert coming to learn Torah, he should not say: Look who comes to learn Torah! One who has eaten carcasses and torn things   .   .   . , reptiles and creeping things [i.e., forbidden foods according to Jewish religious law] . . . ," or "No one should say to a son of converts: remember the deeds of thy fathers" (p. 158).

Moreover, converts were apparently designated as such by appending the phrase "the proselyte" after their given names (Bamberger 1968, 295), a practice that would certainly emphasize their status in the community. Baron (1952b, 283) notes that synagogue services included a phrase to the effect that the blessing applied to proselytes and that "this extension was doubly necessary as there were recurrent attempts to segregate converts as a separate class of worshipers." Although Baron states that racial prejudice was characteristic only of a minority, such attitudes, even by a minority, would surely give pause to a prospective proselyte.

While Bamberger's self-consciously apologetic perspective is thus compatible with the view that there continued to be *de facto* genetic segregation, there are other recent examples of scholarship on this issue that are even more clearly compatible with the view that Judaism remained fundamentally impermeable in the ancient world. For example, Kraabel (1982) describes as a myth the idea that ancient Judaism was characterized by missionary zeal or that there were large numbers of converts (see also J. J. Collins 1985, 185). Jeremias (1969, 320ff) interprets the available data as indicating that it was quite difficult to find converts in the first century, at least partly due to ancient anti-Semitism. (Anti-Jewish attitudes of the Roman government following the failed rebellion of 66-70 A.D. resulted in the *fiscus Judaicus*, and Goodman (1989) emphasizes that gentiles would have been discouraged from conversion because they would have been subject to this tax.) Jeremias also notes the extremely debased position of the proselyte in the Jewish community. For example, all proselyte females who converted after the age of three years and one day, even married females, were suspected of having practiced prostitution, with the result that no gentile "knew his father."

In a more detailed presentation, McKnight (1991) notes abundant evidence for nationalistic statements and attitudes against intermarriage in the Tanakh/Old Testament, especially the Book of Ezra, and extending throughout the ancient period (see also the following section). Moreover, he notes that it was a common observation of gentiles in the ancient world that Jews were misanthropic, and there was a long history of gentile criticism of Jewish separatism. There are many writings from the Second Commonwealth period to the effect "that we [i.e., the Jews] might not mingle at all with any of the other nations but remain pure in body and soul" (p. 21). Israel is the "chosen race" and the "best of races" (p. 21). Moreover, "the list of derogatory comments about other nations is almost as long as there are nations" (p. 12) and spans a wide range of Jewish authors. McKnight notes that negative attitudes toward intermarriage are reiterated throughout Jewish literature of the period. For example, the Book of Tobit, whose plot revolves around marrying endogamously, contains the following statement: "Above all choose a wife from the race of your ancestors. Do not take a foreign wife who is not of your father's tribe, because we are the descendants of the prophets. Remember, my son, that Noah, Abraham, Isaac, and Jacob, our ancestors, back to the earliest days, all chose wives from their kindred. They were blessed in their children, and their descendants shall possess the earth" (Tob. 4:12). Segal (1988, 347) also points out the "ferocity of hatred directed against gentiles by some of the apocalyptic literature," as well as the themes of the inferiority of gentiles and the need for separation from the gentiles (e.g., Jub. 15: 26-27).

Although McKnight (1991, 27-29) explains these attitudes as the result of religious/moral conviction, such an explanation is meaningless from an evolutionary perspective, since the result is to create an ideology that, whether one terms it a moral/ethical idealism or a racialist nationalism, effectively resulted in the separation of gene pools. Moreover, McKnight proposes that there may have been some elements of the Jewish community who were indeed self-consciously motivated by "misanthropy and hate" (p. 28)—a feature unlikely to appeal to prospective proselytes.

McKnight (1991) also notes that many of the putative proselytes from ancient times are apocryphal and that the lists of proselytes suggest that converts were so few in number that individuals were remembered. We do not know the name of a single Jewish missionary, nor do we possess any Jewish missionary text. The evidence that there was any active Jewish proselytism at all is weak, and there is no indication of how common the practice was. Moreover, a major source of literature on conversion involves conversion of gentiles at the end of the world, after "God has subjugated Gentiles and drove them to admit the superiority of the Jewish nation" (McKnight 1991, 35); or God converts gentile nations that spare Israel. These are clearly views of conversion which are quite consistent with a nationalistic interpretation and in which the Jewish God, but not actual

Jews, is the agent of conversion. "A feature of this idea is the crushing defeat of Israel's foes, sometimes by the messiah, who will force submission on the part of the nations to Israel and its God" (p. 50), an idea sometimes combined with the idea that this conversion will happen after the ingathering of Jews from throughout the world. As indicated above, many authors (including Moore 1927-30, I:230; see also Chapter 3) have noted that Judaism's eventual triumph is conceived in nationalistic terms, with the overthrow of former enemies who will then become the servants of Israel.

Moreover, McKnight notes that positive attitudes toward converts do not imply that missionary activity actually occurred. The gentile is typically depicted as approaching the Jew, not the reverse (see also Goodman 1989, 176), as in the writings of Josephus who also had a consistently negative view of conversion (Feldman 1993, 290). Positive attitudes toward converts in the abstract are often mixed with negative beliefs about actual converts within the same author. For example, Philo, despite being perhaps the most universalist of ancient Jewish authors, notes that "to educate a disbeliever is difficult or rather impossible" (McKnight 1991, 43). Again, the data are quite consistent with the proposal that ancient Judaism developed an ideology of group permeability, but actively sought to minimize any actual permeability.

McKnight (1991) also notes that the rabbinic statement that proselytes are equal to Jews cannot reflect actual conditions, since there are many laws, reviewed above, showing the second-class status of converts. Moreover, "the very existence of a separate *halakot* for proselytes is a revelation in itself, which demonstrates that they were not seen as Jews in every respect" (p. 45). "The facts betray that Jews did not immediately accept converts as equals; in fact, the notion of three generations is probably closer to reality" (p. 45). Indeed, Jeremias' (1969, 301; see below) comment that Israelites were admonished not to marry anyone at a lower level of racial purity than themselves suggests that proselytes would not be accepted as full members of the Jewish community until all recollection of their origins had disappeared.

Converting to Judaism was really adopting another nationality: Segal (1988) notes that "[j]oining Judaism was primarily a decision to join another *ethnos*, which was not self-evidently possible to everyone, never taken lightly, and often viewed with some suspicion" (p. 346).[12] Conversion, when it occurred, was a long, gradual process and was never meant to overwhelm the group with pagan converts "because its message was for a sophisticated minority" (p. 346). Conversion to Judaism in the ancient world was really the adoption of another nationality with a geographic locus and a government in exile, while being a Jew in the diaspora was "somewhat like being a foreign national today" (Segal 1988, 348).

There is also some evidence for historical shifts in attitudes toward proselytes, albeit within a generally ambivalent, vacillating context. Based on his dating of the various rabbinic pronouncements, Avi-Yonah (1984, 81-83) argues that prior to the Bar Kocheba revolt (135 A.D.) there was a negative attitude toward proselytes (including that of a rabbinic authority who thought that converts were suspect until the 24th generation). In the following period (the first and second Amoraic generations), positive attitudes appeared to be in the majority, but this was followed, beginning in the third Amoraic generation, with an increasing representation of negative attitudes not only among the scholars, but also among the people and the popular preachers, and including the famous statement of Rabbi Helbo cited above. Avi-Yonah suggests that the Talmudic Tractate *Gerim* represents the final compromise, and it is clearly one of ambivalence: "Their ambivalent attitude may be summed up in the saying: 'Let your left hand always push [the proselytes] away and your right hand bring them near'" (1984, 83).

Finally, Goodman (1989) notes the following additional points:

1. There is a trend in Jewish writing throughout the ancient period that gentiles outside of the Holy Land are justified in worshiping their own gods, while on the other hand there is little concern about whether gentiles will join the Jewish community. In the second to fifth centuries, this trend was solidified by the development of the concept of the righteous gentile who observes the Noachide commandments. There is also "extremely indirect and allusive" evidence for rabbinic approval of attempting to win converts (Goodman 1989, 178). However, this notion was never explicitly developed. Interestingly, ideas hinting at approval of winning converts were developed at the same time and held by the same rabbis who also held what Goodman notes is the contradictory attitude of approval for precise requirements on being a righteous gentile. This is another indication that, although Judaism was permeable in theory, in practice Jews were quite happy to have gentiles go their own way.

2. The idea that Judaism was a universal religion that only ceased winning converts because of pressure from the Roman Empire is inadequate because such pressure did not stop Christianity or Manicheanism from actively seeking and winning converts. In these cases, opposition may have increased attempts to convert others. Moreover, the great majority of ancient cults did not seek converts at all, so there should be no presupposition that Judaism did.

3. The Roman opposition to conversion to Judaism must have been sporadic and/or theoretical, rather than implemented in practice, because inscriptions referring to proselytes were openly displayed by Jews.

How many proselytes were there? Not surprisingly, this is a controversial issue. The only substantial argument that Feldman (1993, 293) is able to provide that proselytism and missionary activity were widespread is that the Jewish population grew rapidly during the period from 586 B.C. to 70 A.D.[13] However, this is far from a conclusive argument, given the vagaries of population estimates in the ancient world (McKnight 1991, 29) as well as the ability of the Jewish population to expand rapidly in other historical eras (see Chapter 5). Indeed, the proposed increase in a Jewish population from 150,000 to 8,000,000 over a span of 656 years is well within demographic possibility, and the latter figure may well be inflated.[14] If one assumes that the entire increase came about from population growth, the 53.3-fold increase in 656 years would imply an annual growth rate of $r = \ln(53.3)/656 = 0.00606$ per year—much less than one percent, and not at all high for human populations.[15]

We have already noted that Kraabel (1982) describes as a myth the idea that there were large numbers of converts, and a similar view is held by J. J. Collins (1985, 185). Bamberger ([1939] 1968) provides a list of converts from the Talmudic period who are mentioned in the rabbinic literature and notes several other converts who are mentioned in non-rabbinic sources. Bamberger lists 45 instances of conversion, almost all of which involve conversions of particular individuals or families, and many of which are of dubious historical authenticity or known to be apocryphal (see also McKnight 1991). The only mention of a large group of converts is that of the converts of Mahoza, and the point of this incident was that they were insulted on being told they could marry a bastard (*mamzeret*).

There is also very little evidence for large-scale Jewish proselytism among the Romans. Leon (1960, 251) cites instances where aristocrats adopted some Jewish practices, but never converted, and full proselytism among prominent Romans was rare. Indeed, it is not even clear that the only two prominent Romans mentioned as possible proselytes were complete converts to Judaism: Fulvia, a senator's wife, practiced Jewish rites and was victimized by Jewish charlatans; Poppaea, Nero's wife, was known as a Judaizer, but this does not imply that she converted to Judaism. Among the non-aristocrats, Leon maintains that there are only 7 "indubitable" epitaphs of proselytes among the 534 Jewish inscriptions at Rome. Of these, one is that of a woman who converted at age 70 (apparently a wealthy benefactress of Jews whose property would revert to the Jewish community at her death); another is that of a woman who converted at age 41; a third is that of a female foster child who died at age three. Clearly, none of these individuals contributed to the Jewish gene pool, and the foster child is described as having two Jewish parents, but was reared in a non-Jewish household until adopted by a Jewish family. From a genetic standpoint, she was of pure Jewish stock. The other proselytes consist of two males and two females, but no ages of conversion are mentioned. At least two are former slaves of Jewish masters, and it is well-known from later periods that such individuals were not fully integrated within the Jewish community (see below).[16] In Italy as a whole, Kraabel (1982) notes that proselytes represent only one percent of the Jewish inscriptions. In Egypt there are no mentions of proselytes at all in 122 inscriptions or in 522 fragments of papyrus (Feldman 1993, 290).[17]

Apart from voluntary conversions, there were forcible conversions during Maccabean times. Interestingly, there is evidence that these converts were treated extremely badly by the Jews and not integrated into their community. Moore (1927-30, I:336), with a bit of tongue-in-cheek, terms these forced conversions accompanied by circumcision as "skin-deep." Indeed, Galilee, an area of forced conversion, was the origin of the main founders of Christianity, including Jesus.

Finally, Moore (1927-30) notes that proselytes may well have been the first to turn apostate at the first sign of trouble, as during the Hadrianic persecutions, or if there were any other advantages to be gained thereby. Baron (1952b, 148) and Segal (1988, 366) provide evidence that indeed the rabbis were convinced that proselytes were unreliable and potential informers. At the end of the second century Rabbi Hiyya the Great commented, "Do not have faith in a proselyte until twenty-four generations have passed, because the inherent evil is still within him" (quoted in Feldman 1993, 411). Given the low social status and poor prospects of proselytes within the Jewish communities and the importance of biological kinship ties to Jewish social behavior (see below), these results are not surprising. The implication would be that the long-term effects of ancient proselytism on the Jewish gene pool were minimal.

In the post-Talmudic period, Bamberger ([1939] 1968, XXIV-XXI); see also Seligson 1965; Eichorn 1965b; Schusterman 1965) lists several individual cases of conversions, but also notes a general reluctance to accept converts on the part of the entire Jewish community. Interestingly, Eichorn (1965b) describes a rabbinic responsum which states that it is not necessary to discourage returning Marranos (i.e., crypto-Jews persecuted by the Spanish and Portuguese in the 15th to the 18th centuries; see Chapter 5) from re-entering the fold, the implication being that others were indeed discouraged. Although in some cases such opposition may have been the result of possible retribution by non-Jews, he notes that "the opposition to which I now refer seems to have become more pronounced after such dangers had ceased to exist" (p. XXIX), and that "many authorities are exceedingly strict" (p. XXIX). The opposition to these restrictive attitudes is characterized by Eichorn as a "fairly small but vocal minority" (p. XXX).

Teitelbaum (1965, 213) notes that Jewish emancipation in the 18th century "failed to bring about any significant modification in the Jewish group attitude toward proselytism." Although the Reform movement dropped many aspects of cultural separatism, there was never any emphasis on proselytism. Interestingly, the prominent 19th-century American Reformist David Einhorn successfully opposed a proposal at a Reform conference that would have allowed male proselytes to forego circumcision. Einhorn stated, "The acceptance of proselytes, through which Judaism acquires many impure elements, must be made more difficult and it is precisely circumcision which can form a barrier against the influx of such elements" (quoted in Meyer 1988, 257). Not surprisingly, Einhorn was opposed to intermarriage because of its effect on racial purity.[18]

In the mid-20th century United States, "despite all social compacts between gentiles and Jews, the Jewish taboo against converting . . . remained largely in force as a social, if not as a legal or religious, measure. The various wings of Judaism may differ in degree but not in kind" (Teitelbaum 1965, 213). Indeed, in a 1965 survey of attitudes on whether Judaism should conduct missionary work among non-Jews, Teitelbaum found that the responses for laymen were 6 percent positive, 78 percent negative, and 17 percent indifferent or uncertain; for Reform rabbis, the figures were 30 percent, 36 percent, and 35 percent, respectively, and for Conservative rabbis, 10 percent, 63 percent, and 27 percent, respectively. Presumably the percentages for Orthodox rabbis would reflect an even more negative attitude about missionary work.

Moreover, even though more of the Reform rabbis expressed positive attitudes, there was no direct missionary effort even by this group. Clearly, attitudes toward proselytism remained at best ambivalent among both the leaders and the lay members of Jewish communities. Teitelbaum (1965, 222; see also Ellman 1987) also gives evidence for negative attitudes toward converts of many years standing, and concludes his survey by noting that "Jews have been exclusive as much as they have been excluded."

# JUDAISM AS A NATIONAL/ETHNIC RELIGION IN THE ANCIENT WORLD

> [Petronius] had also in mind the vast numbers of the Jewish nation, which is not confined, as every other nation is, within the borders of the one country assigned for its sole occupation, but occupies also almost the whole world. For it has overflowed across every continent and island, so that it scarcely seems to be outnumbered by the native inhabitants. (Philo, *Legatio*, 214)

Apologists for the position that Judaism aggressively sought and succeeded in obtaining large numbers of proselytes implicitly downplay the national/ethnic character of Judaism in the ancient world. However, there is overwhelming evidence that in fact Judaism was considered by both Jews and gentiles as a national/ethnic religion throughout this period. In a classic treatment, Moore (1927-30) states that Judaism developed as a national religion and that even after the dispersion, "they felt themselves members of the Jewish nation" (I:224). To those who had dispersed, even after many generations in alien cultures, "Judaism was in reality not so much the religion of the mother-country as the religion of the Jewish race; it was a national religion not in a political but in a genealogical sense" (I:225). As a result, conversion "was not entrance into a religious community, it was naturalization in the Jewish nation, that is—since the idea of nationality was racial rather than political—adoption into the Jewish race" (I:232). And despite instances of conversion, "the Jews . . . were, in their own mind and in the eyes of their Gentile surrounding, and before the Roman law, not adherents of a peculiar religion, but members of a nation who carried with them from the land of their origin into every quarter where they established themselves their national religion and their national customs" (I:233).[19]

Emphasizing the national character of ancient Judaism, both the Persian and the Roman empires recognized the offices of Exilarch (which traced its descent in an unbroken line from King Jehoiachin in the Babylonian exile) and Patriarch (*Nasi*) as symbols of former Jewish sovereignty. Both of these offices had great wealth and prestige, as well as authority and influence over Jews in the diaspora throughout the ancient period (Baron 1952b, 192ff; Avi-Yonah 1984, 38ff).[20] Moore points out that within Roman law the privileges granted to Jews applied only to born Jews, not converts, and the Patriarch of the Jewish religion "was treated as the head, not of a religious body, but of the Jewish people" (Moore 1927-30, I:234), at least in part because he exercised power over his people in the same manner as that of a king, including the ability to inflict corporal punishment and even death on his subjects.

Avi-Yonah (1984, 49ff) shows that it was the policy of the Patriarchate to gradually restore as much national sovereignty in Palestine as possible, including the ability to impose the death penalty, and that already in the third century Palestine was essentially a state within a state. The relationship with the homeland was also reinforced by pilgrimages, as well as by an obligation to mention the hope of a restored Temple in Jerusalem three times daily in one's prayers. There were also official contacts between the homeland and the diaspora, particularly via the office of Patriarch. "With the authority from the centre, the envoys supervised the administration of the communities, inspected the implementation of Law and Halakah, and levied taxes destined for the office of the Nasi" (Safrai 1974, 205). Within the homeland itself, there was a major effort to prevent the land from coming into the possession of gentiles and to discourage emigration (Avi-Yonah 1984, 27ff). Even in the fifth century, the patriarch administered an empirewide quasi-state and controlled well-organized legal and tax systems (Bachrach 1984, 413-414). It was only during this period that the Patriarchate was allowed to lapse due to the efforts of the newly powerful Christian Church, but even then another political body, the Sanhedrin, continued to function much as the Patriarchate had (Alon 1989, 10). In the seventh century, Jewish rule in Jerusalem was re-established briefly and it was only after their expulsion by their Persian overlords that realistic hopes for the re-establishment of a Jewish nation disappeared until the present century.

Clearly, Judaism retained its national character in the ancient world, and quite self-consciously so. Many Jews in the period believed in the imminent political restoration of Israel as prophesied in the Bible (Wilken 1984, 449-450), and even in periods of relative calm after the suppression of the Bar Kocheba rebellion, there were persistent attempts by zealots to restore complete national sovereignty in Palestine. Even the moderates had a highly developed sense of national allegiance (Avi-Yonah 1984, 67).

These beliefs were reflected in a strong national sense of messianism, which persisted among Jews long after the ancient period. Werblowsky (1968, 38) notes that "Jewish messianism, for the greater part of its history, retained its national, social, and historical basis whatever the universalist, cosmic, or inner and spiritual meanings accompanying it. One may, perhaps, speak of a spiritual deepening of the messianic idea in the history of Jewish religious thought, but these allegedly more 'spiritual' elements never replaced the concrete, historical messianism; they were merely added to it."[21] Outbreaks of messianism occurred sporadically throughout Jewish history—most notably the fiasco of Sabbetai Sevi in the 17th century—and always with the idea that the political restoration of Israel was at hand. Moreover, it was not uncommon for Jews throughout the centuries to settle in the Holy Land, and Werblowsky (1968, 40) states that these movements were often inspired by messianism.

As discussed below, this self-conscious conceptualization of Judaism as a national/ethnic religion persisted until the 19th-century Reform movement. Meyer (1988, 59) notes that the rejection of the Jewish doctrine of the messianic return to Zion by the Reform movement "cast doubt on a central principle of Jewish faith firmly grounded in all layers of Jewish tradition. To deny hope of Israel's reconstitution as a nation on its own soil and the rebuilding of the temple, it was felt, amounted to a denial of Judaism itself." However, this rejection of nationalism as the basis of Judaism was relatively short-lived, even within the Reform movement, since Reform Jews eventually embraced Zionism and a resurgence of Jewish tradition, and Orthodox Jews never abandoned the old conceptualization of Judaism. Moreover, as Werblowsky (1968) notes, Zionism is the most recent manifestation of the messianic/nationalist ideology of Judaism.

# CONSANGUINITY, ENDOGAMY, AND THE HIERARCHY OF RACIAL PURITY AMONG JEWS IN THE POST-BIBLICAL PERIOD

For our forefathers . . . made provision that the stock of the priests should continue unmixed and pure; for he who is partaker of the priesthood must propagate of a wife of the same nation . . . and take his wife's genealogy from the ancient tables, and procure many witnesses to it; and this is our practice not only in Judea, but wheresoever any body of men of our nation do live; and even there, an exact catalogue of our priests' marriages is kept . . . ; but if any war falls out . . . those priests that survive them compose new tables of genealogy out of the old records, and examine the circumstances of the women that remain; for still they do not admit of those that have been captives, as suspecting that they had conversation with some foreigners . . . ; we have the names of our high priests from father to son, set down in our records, for the interval of two thousand years. (Flavius Josephus, *Against Apion*, 1:30-36)

While different races base their claims to nobility on various grounds, with us a connection with the priesthood is the hallmark of an illustrious line. (Flavius Josephus, *Vita I*)

Up to the present, it has not been sufficiently recognized that from a social point of view the whole community of Judaism at the time of Jesus was dominated by the fundamental idea of the maintenance of racial purity. Not only did the priests, as the consecrated leaders of the people, watch anxiously over the legitimacy of priestly families, and weed out all priestly descendants born of an illegitimate union . . . ; but the entire population itself, in the theory and practice of religious legislation at the time of Jesus, was classified according to purity of descent. All families in which some racial impurity could be established were excluded from the pure seed of the community. (Jeremias 1969, 270)

## The Importance of Consanguinity in the Post-Biblical Period

As indicated in Chapters 3 and 8, the Jewish tendency toward consanguinity in marriage is of considerable theoretical importance. During the Second Commonwealth, the Pharisees attached special spiritual significance to marriages with nieces. Uncle-niece marriage was common during the Second Commonwealth (Epstein 1942, 250ff; Mitterauer 1991; Jeremias 1969, 218). While marriage to nieces was essentially tolerated by the Levitical rules, later it came to be viewed as desirable by the more devout, including priestly families whose concern with purity of blood and genealogy is a recurrent theme of this volume. Uncle-niece marriage was idealized in the Talmud: "One who married his sister's daughter—on him the Bible says: 'They thou will call and G-d will answer'" (b. Yeb 62b). The *Shulhan Arukh*, an authoritative legal compilation dating from the 16th century, also idealized uncle-niece marriage.

Goitein (1978, 26) notes that, despite its legitimacy and the elevated status of one's sister's children at the time, there were relatively few uncle-niece marriages recorded in the Geniza documents from the medieval Islamic period, quite possibly because of the influence of the Karaite sect during this period. However, first-cousin marriage was "extremely common" (p. 27). Grossman (1989) notes a clear trend toward consanguinity among the distinguished families of sages in Spain and Germany in the Middle Ages (see also Chapter 6). And Boyajian (1983, 46) finds frequent consanguineous marriages, including marriage between uncles and nieces, as well as between first cousins in the Sephardic international trading networks in the 16th to 18th centuries. Indeed, Beinart (1971a) notes that one of the criticisms of the New Christians by the Old

Christians during the period of the Inquisition was that they continued to intermarry—and did so within the degrees of relatedness prohibited by the Church.

In the United States, Jews have sometimes been exempted from laws prohibiting uncle-niece marriages (Epstein 1942) and from laws prohibiting first-cousin marriage (Goodman 1979, 463). Bermant (1971) shows that cousin marriage was common among wealthy Jewish families in England beginning in the 18th century.[22] Kaplan (1983, 298) shows that Jews in Germany between 1870 and 1930 were far more likely to engage in consanguineous marriages than gentiles, especially in the more traditional small towns and rural areas. In the 1920s, 18 percent of the Jews in one Hohenzollern town were married to first cousins, and the rate in another was 11 percent.[23] Generally, however, in recent times, the rate of consanguineous marriages, including uncle-niece marriages, has been declining among all Jewish groups, especially Ashkenazi Jews, although such marriages are not uncommon among some Oriental and Sephardic groups (Goodman 1979, 463-467). In one group of Oriental Jews, the Habbanites, the rate of first cousin marriage in modern times was 56% (Patai & Patai 1989, 230).

# The Maintenance of Racial Purity in the Post-Biblical Period

During the Restoration following the Babylonian exile, Ezra's racial doctrine legally prohibited any marriage with individuals with a taint of foreign blood, and there was an increased concern for tracing genealogies and separating the community into groups that varied in the purity of their blood. The result, as we have seen in Chapter 3, was that the community was divided into a hierarchy of racial purity.

While racialist ideology declined after Ezra's Restoration, racial exclusivity continued in practice: "Purity of stock continued as a token of aristocracy, family records were guarded jealously, and the separation of classes by blood taint as established by Ezra remained in effect for centuries after" (Epstein 1942, 167), even beyond the end of the Second Commonwealth. Intermarriage of those known to have foreign blood with those of doubtful status would not occur in practice until all memory and records of the foreign taint were lost (Epstein 1942, 186). And such persons could never intermarry with those whose genealogies were known, including especially the priests and the *meyuhasim* (those able to marry into priestly families) who were at the top of the hierarchy of purity of blood. The priesthood itself was "a closed circle which was not easily penetrated except by a few Israelitish families of exceptional distinction" (Epstein 1942, 309). Legitimacy within the priesthood was established by producing the appropriate genealogies, and, indeed, the common conceptualization of Jews in the ancient world (as seen by the epigraph from

Josephus quoted at the beginning of this section) was that priests could be traced directly back to Aaron, the brother of Moses.

Stern (1976) comments on the high level of consanguinity of the priests during the Second Temple period and notes the preponderance of these families in the Jewish aristocracy of the period.[24] As Mitterauer (1991, 312-313) notes, concerns for consanguinity and for racial purity dovetailed, because, by choosing a close relative for marriage, one could be more sure about his/her purity of descent. Other families that became prominent, such as the Tobiads and the Hillels, managed to marry into the priestly families.

Jeremias (1969, 213-221) and Schürer ([1885] 1979, 242) provide detailed accounts of Jewish practices related to racial purity in the ancient world. Genealogical examinations extending back at least four generations of mothers on each side (five if the prospective bride was a Levite or Israelite) were very carefully performed for all priests and for some Levites, as well as their wives. The extreme seriousness of these concerns can be seen from by the fact that priestly families typically went beyond the law by invoking draconian penalties on anyone whose sexual behavior might bring defilement on the family.[25]

Moreover, ordinary Israelites also knew the last few generations of their ancestors and which of the 12 tribes they belonged to. This was extremely important because only families of pure race were considered to make up the "true Israel" (Jeremias 1969, 275). Some lay people had genealogies that, like those of the priests, extended back to the time of King David. There is some suggestion that the priestly genealogies, along with the genealogies of the lay families who had married into the priestly class, were stored in an official archive at the Temple, which was destroyed early in the common era by King Herod out of jealousy because of his own lack of lineage.

Moreover, establishing one's genealogy was the ticket to success in the society and inclusion among the elect in the messianic world to come. It was the height of respectability to be able to say that one came from a family that could marry their daughters to priests or have sons who could serve in the Temple. All important honors and positions of public trust were dependent on establishing one's genealogy. Emphasizing the religious nature of the obligation to retain genetic purity, Jeremias (1969, 301-302; see also Mitterauer 1991, 312-313) notes that "[h]ere we have the most profound reason for the behaviour of these pure Israelite families—why they watched so carefully over the maintenance of racial purity and examined the genealogies of their future sons- and daughters-in-law before marriage. . . . For on this question of racial purity hung not only the social position of their descendents, but indeed their final assurance of salvation, their share in the future redemption of Israel."[26] The doctrine that only pure Israelites would share in the redemption brought about by the Messiah resulted in the belief that salvation itself depended on purity of blood.

Given the hierarchy of racial purity, it is not surprising that individuals at the lower levels of racial purity would attempt to remove rigid barriers between groups. Epstein (1942, 190) indicates that the pressure to remove most legal barriers to intermarriage came from the non-priestly classes whose power was increased following the collapse of the Jewish state and the establishment of a hierarchy based on learning.

However, the evidence indicates that the priestly class did not abandon its concern with genealogy when legal barriers to marriage were lessened. Jeremias (1969, 274; see also Epstein 1942, 190) emphasizes that the priestly class adopted "an inexorably rigorous stand" on issues related to marriage and racial purity—far more restrictive than that prescribed by the scribes. Even though it was legally possible for a priest to marry any Israelite of legitimate descent, in fact high priests almost invariably married members of other priestly families (Jeremias 1969, 155). This continuing concern with genealogy, despite the lack of legal restrictions, was typical of the community as a whole, not only priestly families: Epstein notes that "Israelites of distinction thought it socially improper to marry a half-Jew, despite the leniency of the halakah" (Epstein 1942, 196).[27]

In the diaspora, it was common for priestly genealogies to be publicly displayed well into the medieval period (e. g., Ahroni 1986, 74). And genealogies continued to be of great importance among the scholars and other elite Jewish families in 12th-century Babylon (Grossman 1989, 120). Descent in these families was traced back to the original tribes of Israel.[28] Similarly, Goitein (1978, 4-5) describes the reading of genealogies at funerals in the medieval Islamic period, in which ancestors were commonly traced back 10 or more generations. Levite families were able to trace their ancestry to the Biblical tribe of Levi, suggesting a continuing concern with maintaining the purity of lines of descent over a period of at least 1,000 years. Goitein notes that in the 20th century even common Jewish emigrants from Yemen knew their ancestors for six or more generations and suggests that this represents a continuity with previous practices.

A continuing concern with genealogies and purity of blood can also be seen by considering with writings of Maimonides in the 12th century. Johnson (1987, 183) notes that Maimonides himself could list six generations of his father's ancestors and 14 generations for his father-in-law's family through the illustrious female side. He also notes that most Jews could trace their lineage through at least seven generations. Reflecting the supreme importance of scholarly ability within the Jewish community (and the high level of reproductive success of scholars; see Chapter 7), the genealogy typically began with the name of a well-known scholar.

Maimonides' concern with genealogy is also apparent in his codification of Jewish law in the 12th century.[29] Priests were liable to be flogged for any intercourse with a heathen woman. A priest caught in the act of intercourse with a heathen woman was liable to be put to death: "[S]hould zealots fall upon him and slay him, they are worthy of commendation for their zeal" (p. 81). A child born from such a union was not admitted to the fold of Israel, and, indeed, the heathen woman "is liable to be put to death, because an offense has been committed by an Israelite through her, just as in the case of an animal" (p. 83).

At this point Maimonides relies on Numbers 31:16-17, in which Moses commands the killing of the non-virgin Midianite women captured in the war of the conquest of Canaan.

Maimonides notes that the rules of the Torah and the Sages are fairly lenient regarding intercourse with a slave woman. He states, however, "[n]evertheless, let not this transgression be esteemed lightly in your eyes, just because the Torah does not prescribe a flogging, for this also causes a man's son to depart from following after the Lord, since the bondswoman's son is likewise a slave, and is not of Israel" (p. 83). The offspring of a concubine/slave is thus not admitted to the community, and, indeed, intercourse with such a woman is compared to sodomy, citing Deuteronomy 23:18. Conversion of the bondswoman removes these difficulties,[30] but Maimonides reiterates the general distrust of proselytes typical of the ancient world, citing the Talmudic dictum that "'[p]roselytes are as hard to bear for Israel as a scab upon the skin,' since the majority of them become proselytes for ulterior motives and subsequently lead Israel astray, and once they become proselytes it is a difficult matter to separate from them" (p. 91). The latter comment indicates that the community would attempt to remain separate from proselytes.

The Maimonidean code reiterates the discriminatory regulations on the marriage of proselytes. Interestingly, the descendants of the proselyte continue to be impaired until all memory is lost of a person's impaired origins. Thus, the offspring of two proselytes (but not the offspring of a proselyte and an Israelite) is permitted to marry a bastard, "[a]nd so on until his proselyte descent sinks into oblivion, and the fact that he is a descendant of proselytes is no longer known. After that he is forbidden to marry a bastard" (p. 99). Presumably the requisite length of time would be at least seven generations, since it was common to know one's genealogy at least to this extent (see above).

Maimonides describes rules for ascertaining the purity of descent of a family. If two witnesses testify that a bastard, an unfit priest, or a slave is in a family's ancestry, people are advised not to marry into the family until there is an investigation of the eight maternal relatives on each side (including great-great-grandmothers). If the family is Levitical or Israelite, the investigation is to proceed to the great-great-great-grandmother level because there is said to be a greater danger of pollution in non-priestly families. Interestingly, despite the concentration on investigating female relatives to assure family purity,[31] the goal is to maintain the purity of the male line—Ezra's "holy seed." Females can marry men of invalid descent, but not the reverse, and, in a previous passage, Maimonides notes that in intermarriages among priests, Levites, and Israelites, the child retains the status of the father, "as it is said, *and they declared their pedigrees after their families, by their fathers' houses* (Num. 1:18)" (pp. 124-125; italics in text).

Maimonides then presents a discussion of the necessity of proving genealogy for the priests in his day. Pedigree must be traced back to a priest who ministered at the altar in the Temple or was a member of the Sanhedrin prior to the destruction of the Temple in 70 A.D., "since only priests, Levites, and Israelites of proven genealogy were appointed to the Sanhedrin" (p. 127). Priests of proven genealogy must produce witnesses that their sons are indeed their sons and that the women they marry are of valid descent. There is a long section on determining whose testimony is to be believed, on preventing fraud, and on ensuring that the father was a priest by classifying as doubtful priests those children born to a woman who remarries within three months of the birth of a child. If a child is born out of wedlock, he cannot be a priest, "as it is said, *and it shall be to him and to his seed after him, the covenant of an everlasting priesthood* (Num. 25:13): so long as his seed traces its proven genealogy from him with assurance" (p. 132; italics in text).

All of these concerns indicate that in the 12th century genealogy, and especially the genealogy of the priestly group, was still of great concern. Moreover, being of priestly descent still resulted in considerable social respect. Maimonides describes a child recounting his immersion and eating of the priestly heave offering who states that his companions "kept their distance from me and called me 'Johanan, the eater of dough offering'" (p. 130).

The elevated status of individuals from the tribes of the Levites and the priests (*Kohanim*) continued as an element of synagogue service into modern times and persists among Orthodox Jews and Haredim (Heilman 1992; Mintz 1992). The first two men to read from the Torah at the traditional Ashkenazi synagogue service were required to be from the tribes of the Levites and the Kohanim (Zborowski & Herzog 1952, 56). The rules requiring Kohanim to refrain from marrying widows or divorced women were also observed, as was the rule that the Kohanim must have no contact with the dead (pp. 272, 282). The birth of one's firstborn son was the occasion for a contribution to a member of the Kohanim (p. 320), a practice that dates back to the idea that the firstborn son was obligated to serve in the temple unless redeemed by a payment to the priesthood.

Genealogy was also of great importance in the traditional Jewish *shtetl* communities of Eastern Europe. There was a strong concern for *yikhus*, defined as referring to the purity of one's lineage, but also including the scholarly credentials and economic success of one's ancestry. Mayer (1979, 82) notes that yikhus is "a sort of credit rating. One's rating is presumed to be known until proven otherwise. But proof of one sort or another must be furnished in the form of recognizable credentials." In the Eastern European shtetl, "the yikhus of every member is generally known down to the last detail, and to recite one's yikhus to a new acquaintance is an integral part of an introduction (Zborowski & Herzog 1952, 78). Moreover, "the family with yikhus will strive to maintain it, to keep its purity unsullied, and if possible to augment it. Many a girl has been forced to renounce her beloved because to marry beneath her yikhus would 'put a spot on the family name'" (Zborowski & Herzog 1952, 78). Although an illustrious pedigree was not a necessary condition for yikhus, it appears to be a sufficient condition, since the best type of yikhus depends on the number of wealthy and learned ancestors. It was common to refuse marriage with any family whose yikhus did not extend back seven or eight generations. In the 20th century, some families were able to trace their ancestry back to the medieval period, as, for example, the family of 20th-century Zionist Nathan Birnbaum, who traced his roots back to the medieval scholar Rashi (Birnbaum 1956, 11).

There is a powerful continuing concern with yikhus among groups of Orthodox Jews in contemporary America and Israel (see Heilman 1992; Mayer 1979; Kamen 1985). Kamen (1985) describes one such community of Hasidic Jews in 20th-century America. The *tzaddikim* (righteous men) who lead the community are regarded as having "holy seed" (p. 3) and inherit their positions—what Kamen terms "hereditary saintliness" (p. 3). Hasidic rebbes typically trace their genealogy to the founder of Hasidism, Baal Shem Tov, or one of his disciples (Zborowski & Herzog 1952, 169). Mayer (1979) describes the followers of one Eastern European rebbe who re-established his lineage in 1963 by locating his grandson. Clearly, genetic linkages are an extremely important aspect of legitimacy in these communities.

# GENETIC AND CULTURAL SEGREGATION AMONG THE SEPHARDIC JEWS IN THE MEDIEVAL PERIOD

Baer (1966, vol. I) emphasizes the continuity of Sephardic customs and beliefs from practices originating in the ancient world. There remained a consistent trend in Jewish religious thought in the Middle Ages that depicted Jews as a chosen people living among hostile nations from whom they must remain separated, while remaining tied to their ancestral homeland (e.g., Judah Halevi [12th century]). Beginning in the 13th century, a long series of cabalistic writings created "a new, mystically clothed, ethnic concept" in which the non-Jewish world was viewed as evil, and any compromise or assimilation with it was rejected. The worst behavior of all was to enter into intimacy with gentile women (Baer 1961, I:246). "Jewish pietism, with its overtones of mysticism deepened the sense of 'foreignness' imbedded in the consciousness of a people living in exile in strange lands" (Baer 1961; I:248). Later, in the 15th century and beyond, the records of the Iberian Inquisitions "breathe a nostalgic yearning for the national homeland, both earthly and heavenly—a yearning for all things, great and small, sanctified by the national tradition" (Baer 1961, II:425).

## Maintaining Racial Purity among the Medieval Sephardim

The medieval Sephardic Jewish community was greatly concerned with providing and enforcing communal sanctions aimed at preventing gentile contamination of the Jewish gene pool. We have already noted that Maimonides, whose views were authoritative, had a very negative attitude regarding having sexual intercourse with gentile slaves and/or converting them. Baer (1961) gives many examples of rabbinic writings that indicate disapproval of sexual relationships with gentiles, as in the following: "Intercourse with a slave woman is a capital sin . . . for the sinner defiled the holiness of God by loving and possessing 'the daughter of an alien god' (Mal. 2:11). His alien offspring will be a snare to him and a reminder of his sin" (quoted in Baer 1961, 256). Cabalistic writers, citing Hosea 5:7, railed against those who "have betrayed the Lord by begetting alien offspring"; and further, "He who lies with a Gentile woman . . . of this it is written, 'and the people began to have illicit relations with the daughters of Moab . . . and the anger of the Lord blazed against Israel'" (Num. 25:1,3) (from the *Sefer ha-Zohar*; see Baer 1961, I:262).

Neuman (1969) provides an opinion of a medieval Jewish court in Spain that two individuals were "of pure descent, without any family taint, and that they could intermarry with the most honored families in Israel; for there had been no admixture of impure blood in the paternal or maternal antecedents and their collateral relatives" (II:6). In this case, two brothers had been accused of having a slave as an ancestor, and the charge was so serious that the accused "could not rest with the verdict of the local rabbis" and invoked the aid of all the prominent rabbis in their vicinity, begging them to confirm with the weight of the authority the sentence already pronounced. "The entire responsum is charged with deep emotion. The fact that a blemish had been cast on an innocent family in Israel was regarded with horror as an act of monstrous villainy" (II:7). Notice also that even collateral relatives were examined. Having impure blood cast a shadow over the entire family, not only on the direct line of descent.

Offspring of female slaves received "grudging social recognition and tolerance," the master freeing the slave, converting her to Judaism, and then engaging in a "semi-marriage" (Neuman 1969, I:11), presumably similar to concubinage. The opinions of Maimonides and the responsum discussed above indicate the descendants of such unions were not accepted as full members of the Jewish community, and this was certainly the case for the mixed offspring of Sephardic masters and their gentile slaves immigrating into the Ottoman Empire during the period of the Inquisition (Shaw 1991, 47).

Neuman (1969) also finds that the Jewish authorities were greatly concerned with discouraging any sexual relationships between Jews and gentiles. They dealt severely with the Jewish offender. In one instance, when a Jewish woman gave birth to a child by a Christian man, two rabbis concurred that her nose should be cut off. Reformists periodically removed non-Jewish women from the Jewish quarter. The mystic Don Todros "rose and expelled the alien women from the Jewish quarter" (Baer 1961, I:257), and regulations were adopted such that Jews were required to refrain from intimacy with Moslem women and to sell their Moslem slave girls on pain of excommunication.

Neuman (1969, II:12) notes that some Jewish communities established Jewish prostitution in order to ensure that young men would not consort with Christian prostitutes. Brundage (1987) notes that Mosaic law forbade Jewish women from prostitution, but that foreign prostitutes were tolerated. However, this stricture was not always obeyed, and some authorities distinguished between prostitution within the Jewish community and outside it: "Some later authorities argued that even a priest might marry a Jewish harlot, provided that in the course of her career she had not had sexual relations with any gentiles, slaves, members of her own household, or married men of any kind" (Brundage 1987, 56).[32]

## Community Enforcement of Separation Among the Medieval Sephardim

In Chapter 1, it was noted that an essential feature of any group evolutionary strategy is to develop mechanisms that prevent individuals from self-interested behavior which conflicts with group goals. As noted above, Jewish diaspora communities beginning in the ancient world were characterized by powerful internal governments, which aggressively monitored individual behavior and ensured conformity with group interests.

In Spain prior to the expulsion of 1492, there was a strong separation between the Jewish *aljamas* and the rest of society. This residential segregation was not rigidly maintained or legally imposed until after the destruction of many Jewish communities in 1391, after which residence in a *juderia* became compulsory in some areas (Neuman 1969, I:166; Gampel 1989; Leroy 1985). Nevertheless, even in the absence of residential segregation, all Jews were under the authority of the *aljama* government.

As was also the case in Poland (e.g., Weinryb 1972), besides the physical separation, the aljamas were fiscally separate from the surrounding communities and were governed by Jewish religious law, rather than the common law of the land, "*imperia in imperio.*" As the rabbis said, "God forbid that the holy people should walk in the ways of the gentiles and according to their statutes. . . . Would they teach their children the laws of the gentiles and build themselves altars of the uncleanliness of the heathen?" (Neuman 1969, I:14).

The judicial and legislative powers of the aljamas represented a potent means of social control within the community. Any Jew who attempted to avoid the Jewish courts in proceedings against other Jews was viewed as an informer and was subject to severe discipline, including excommunication and heavy fines. Even the death penalty could be imposed against informers after getting approval from the authorities.[33] The courts, often in conjunction with the royal authorities, prosecuted violations of religious practices, such as the regulations concerning the Sabbath.

There were less-formal mechanisms of social control as well. A particularly interesting aspect of community control over individual behavior relates to the prevention of apostasy. Writing of 13th-century Spain, Baer (1961) notes that measures were taken to protect converts to Christianity from abuse by their former co-religionists.[34] The interesting thing is that conversion was "a blot on the family. The disgrace of one convert in a family was enough cause to warrant the disruption of the wedding engagement of an innocent relative. His former brethren regarded him as a renegade and ostracized him" (Neuman 1969, II:190).

This type of social control in which relatives were penalized for individual behavior in contravention of group norms was common throughout Jewish history. Goitein (1978, 33, 45), writing of medieval Islamic times, notes that the responsibility of the extended family was recognized by public opinion, although it was not a formal part of Jewish law. Hundert (1992; see also Katz 1961a) notes that in traditional Ashkenazi society the son of a convert was ostracized and ridiculed because of his father's apostasy, indicating that conversion had negative effects on the entire family even beyond the immediate generation. And Deshen (1986) describes a 19th-century Moroccan case in which a man was allowed to break an engagement with a woman whose aunt had given birth out of wedlock. The decision was based on a precedent in which a man was allowed to break an engagement with a woman whose sister had converted to Islam. The following takhanan of the Synod of Frankfort (1603) illustrates well how community controls over individual behavior related to cultural separatism were linked to penalties on other family members: "If it is proven that any Jew has drunk wine in the house of Gentile, it shall be forbidden for any other Jew to marry his daughter, or to give him lodging, or to call him to the Torah or to allow him to perform any religious function" (quoted in Finkelstein 1924, 260). The same synod established penalties for avoiding Jewish charity, which included the exclusion of children from the community.

These social controls on individual behavior facilitated the group strategy because an individual contemplating apostasy or other major breaches of the rules would realize that the consequences of such an act would accrue not only to himself, but also to the relatives left behind—thus raising the stakes considerably. There is, of course, an excellent evolutionary logic embedded in such controls: Individuals are implicitly assumed to take into account the costs of their actions on their relatives.

## The Practice of Cultural Separatism among the Sephardim

Interestingly, the Sephardic Jews are credited by Roth (1974) with pioneering the discarding of external signs of Jewish separateness such as clothing and language,[35] and Castro (1971) notes that Jews often lived among non-Jews, rather than in exclusively Jewish quarters (*Juderia*). Nevertheless, the Sephardic lack of concern with external signs of separateness was highly compatible with a strong sense of exclusivity. The dietary laws, circumcision, the practice of the Sabbath, and the *Mitzvoth* of 613 commandments in general would be expected to result in a profound sense of being a Jew and being separated from gentile society.

It should be noted that the Sephardic sense of exclusivity and superiority is legendary even among the other branches of Judaism (e.g., Patai 1977, 381-383; Chapter 8). After the expulsion, the Sephardim continued to use a dialect of archaic Spanish (*Ladino*) in their communities in other parts of the world, so that in the 19th century most Sephardic Jews living in the Turkish Empire could understand neither Turkish or other local languages such as Greek and Romanian. In Morocco, the Sephardic Jews continued to speak a Castilian dialect which differed from Ladino until the 19th century.

Benardete (1953) emphasizes that, in addition to this "secretive language for communication among coreligionists" (p. 59), there was a wide variety of other religious customs, gestures, celebrations, and culinary laws that separated them from gentiles and even other Jews living among them. Benardete cites observations indicating that the Sephardim in the United States considered themselves "a people apart" with "hermetic groupings" and superior to Ashkenazi Jews, even though they were of lower social class than the latter (whom they referred to with the derogatory term *tedesco*) (1953, 145-146; see also Patai 1977, 381-383; Sachar 1992, 63; Baron 1973, 36). In Morocco, the Sephardim remained separate for the most part from the native Jews for whom they used the disdainful term *forasteros* (aliens) (Patai 1986).

This is perhaps an appropriate place to mention the general phenomenon of linguistic separatism among the Jews. Patai (1971) notes that from the Middle Ages to at least the 19th century there has been a strong trend for linguistic separatism characterized typically by Jews clinging to archaic native languages to which they added Hebrew words (e.g., Ladino, Yiddish, Judeo-Persian, Hebrew-Aramaic-Arabic). The result was that in many areas, such as Poland on the eve of World War I (Lichten 1986), the great majority of Jews could not communicate in the language of the gentiles. In addition, Hebrew ("the holy tongue" [Patai 1971, 131] remained throughout the ages as a language of written and often oral communication among Jews. Hebrew was a prominent sign of Jewish separatism in the medieval period—viewed by Christians as a "hidden language" all the more mysterious because of the rabbinic prohibition on teaching the language to gentiles (Gilman 1986, 25-26). Clearly, linguistic separatism has been an important force for maintaining genetic and cultural separation between Jews and gentiles over a very long period of historical time.

# GENETIC AND CULTURAL SEGREGATION AMONG THE ASHKENAZIM IN THE TRADITIONAL SOCIETIES OF EASTERN EUROPE

[Russian Jews] never seem for an instant to lose the consciousness that they are a race apart. It is in their walk, their sidelong glance, in the carriage of their sloping shoulders, in the curious gesture of the uplifted palm. (Harold Frederick, *The New Exodus: Israel in Russia* [London, 1892], 79-80); quoted in Lindemann 1991, 129)

As I began to reconstruct the life of my grandfather's family . . . , I received the distinct impression that the life of my grandfather and that of the Hungarian peasants of Pata had almost nothing in common. . . . The contact between my grandparents and the peasants of the village was confined to the occasions when the latter stopped by the store to make their small purchases. . . . [A]part from this, my grandfather lived entirely in the world of Jewish tradition, primarily that of the Talmud. He knew almost nothing of the cultural traditions of the Pata peasants. . . . [B]oth grandfather's and grandmother's clothing was different; so were their hair styles and the food they ate, and, because of the strict separation of milk from meat dishes, even the arrangement of the kitchen. If one adds the differences between the intellectual interests of a learned and traditional Jew and those of a Hungarian peasant, and between the ethos of the one and of the other, one reaches the conclusion that this Hungarian Jew lived in practically complete cultural isolation from his purely Hungarian environment. (Patai 1971, 136-137)

There is no question that there was a powerful tendency toward cultural separatism among the Ashkenazi Jews. The principal barriers included physical appearance, attitudes, language, residential propinquity, and social relationships. Jews tended to live in the same neighborhoods, whether in the ghetto imposed by the authorities or in self-chosen segregated neighborhoods near the synagogue (Hundert 1992; Katz 1961a). As was the case throughout the diaspora from ancient times, Jews lived under their own laws derived from the Talmud and organized their own communities.

Indeed, even when the ghetto was imposed by the gentile authorities, "[m]any rabbis would have liked the walls of the ghetto higher" (Johnson 1987, 238). Any contact at all between Jew and Gentile was more or less deemed a departure from a theoretical ideal: "[H]ad it been practically feasible, complete segregation from the outside world would have been desirable. . . . [T]he Jewish quarter lived a life of its own in which society-at-large had no part" (Katz 1961a, 33).

Jewish education was "introverted and singular, devoted exclusively to Jewish studies" (Weinryb 1972, 98; see also Chapter 7). Jews spoke a different language, Yiddish, at least among themselves, and, as noted above, on the eve of World War I the Jewish masses of Poland did not understand Polish (Lichten

1986). Those least likely to know the language of the gentiles were those with the highest prestige in the Jewish community, the rabbis (Zborowski & Herzog 1952, 160). An edict of the Russian government that every rabbi learn the Russian language was avoided by several subterfuges, including abandoning the distinctive hat of the rabbi in public. In 19th-century Lithuania, "the study of European languages was seen as unnecessary and even dangerous" (Etkes 1989, 167).

Regarding physical appearance, Weinryb (1972, 83) notes that "Jews in Western countries mostly wore clothes that distinguished them from non-Jews, possibly at first for religious reasons: as a barrier against the outside world." Besides clothing, Katz (1961a, 13) also notes that men and women wore their hair differently, and there were perhaps even differences in their physiognomy, "which was somehow more distinctive than during periods of social rapprochement."

Regarding attitudes, the Jews viewed themselves as separate even from the land: Many rabbis viewed Poland itself as defiled and unclean, and not the permanent habitat of the Jews (Weinryb 1972). Reflecting this sense of sojourning, the burial service in traditional Ashkenazi shtetl communities included depositing a small amount of soil from Palestine under the head of the deceased (Zborowski & Herzog 1952).[36] Katz (1961a) notes that Jews were conscious of being only temporary resident aliens and were considered in this manner by gentiles. There was also a powerful sense of separation from gentiles. Katz (1961a, 26ff) describes the common philosophical belief among Jews that Judaism and Christianity differed not merely in matters of ritual and belief, but also in essence. Moreover, this essential difference was often viewed as ultimately the result of racial differences, with Jews descending from Abraham, Isaac, and Jacob, while the gentiles descended from Esau.

Social contacts between Jews and gentiles were to remain "strictly business-like. No encouragement whatsoever was given to sociability as such, to cultivation of personal attachments, entertainment, and fraternization" (Katz 1961a, 22)—practices that were even more strictly enforced later than they were in the medieval period. Dietary laws prevented Jews from eating at gentile homes, so that "only on rare formal occasions did Jew and gentile invite each other. Religious authorities inveighed against even these occurrences, however exceptional" (Katz 1961a, 22).

These barriers had the expected effect of preventing marriage with non-Jews. Fraikor (1977, 120; see also Weinryb 1972, 96) characterizes the Ashkenazi Jews as an "extremely religious, cohesive, endogamous group who were extremely selective in choosing marriage partners according to Biblical, Talmudic, and rabbinical precepts," including, as already noted, a preference for uncle-niece marriage.

Throughout the Jewish settlement in Poland, there was a very low level of assimilation via conversion and especially forced conversion. Voluntary conversions were small in number and most involved poor and obscure Jews

(Weinryb 1972, 94). During persecutions, particularly during the 1648 massacres, there were forced conversions as well as conversions of convenience of Jews in Poland. However, there were also laws preventing reconversion to Judaism of those who had converted to Christianity, suggesting controls on "conversions of convenience" and an attempt to prevent crypto-Judaism. However, many of these converts succeeded in returning to Judaism after the danger had passed, and some converts continued to maintain their relationships with their Jewish relatives and other Jews after conversion, suggesting crypto-Judaism.

There are indications that when Jews converted to Christianity, they were able to rapidly intermarry with Poles, indicating that the barriers to intermarriage were mainly erected by the Jews.[37] For example, Ciechanowiecki (1986) describes a wealthy Jewish family that converted and attained important places in the aristocracy and was able to make very good marriages with other aristocrats. Intermarriages, though rare, were not scandalous (Kieniewicz 1986). Indeed, as was the case in England at least until the end of the 18th century (Bermant 1971, 14), there is evidence that intermarriage following religious conversion tended to occur only within the highest stratum of the gentile population.[38]

Jews in Poland actively resisted assimilationist attempts by non-Jews resulting from the ideology of the Enlightenment. Enlightenment intellectuals advocated giving Jews complete access to economic activity, including state service, but called for an end to the "damaging Jewish monopoly in trade and finance" (Kieniewicz 1986, 72). These ideas were rejected by Jewish and Polish conservatives alike, the latter advocating emancipation of Jews only after they had assimilated. Emancipation "did not initiate a marked assimilation trend" (Kieniewicz 1986, 76). "The assimilative trend, which grew noticeably among Polish Jews in the second half of the nineteenth century, slackened, or even came to a halt in later times (p. 77; see also Lichten 1986, 128).[39]

Moreover, from the present perspective, the precise meaning of assimilation is important. Barriers such as clothing and language are important to viewing Judaism as a fairly closed group evolutionary strategy only insofar as they are means toward the end of genetic segregation. However, it is quite possible that these barriers could fall, but that genetic segregation (as well as resource and reproductive competition between ethnic groups) could continue. Indeed, Lichten (1986) notes the broad range of Jewish assimilationist positions in Poland from the late 19th century to the pre-World War II period, the vast majority of which were consistent with continued genetic segregation and resource competition.

For example, an assimilationist organization in 1937 expressed patriotic sentiments for the Polish state as well as support for the idea that all citizens be treated according to their personal accomplishments, regardless of religion or national origin (see Lichten 1986, 124). By themselves, these proposals would clearly not be sufficient to end genetic segregation and resource competition based on ethnicity. In fact, if such a program (which essentially corresponds to the official position of Reform Judaism [see below]) had been implemented, it is quite possible that the result would have been to intensify ethnically based resource competition on the assumption that complete emancipation of the Jews would result in their being better able to compete with gentiles. Evidence for this latter proposal is presented in Chapter 5.

# CONFRONTING THE MODERN WORLD: THE IDEOLOGY AND PRACTICE OF GENETIC AND CULTURAL SEPARATION SINCE THE ENLIGHTENMENT

It is not an overstatement to claim that the European Enlightenment has been the most traumatic event in the history of Judaism as a group evolutionary strategy. We have seen that in traditional societies over nearly two millennia the separation between Jews and gentiles was more or less complete, with the result that "nobody would have doubted at the end of the eighteenth century that the Jews were an ethnic unit, separate from the local inhabitants in any place where they may have built a community. Similarly, the unity of these communities all over the world was also taken for granted" (Katz 1986b, 90). The barriers erected to restrict the normal intercourse among individuals were very high indeed, and Jews generally organized themselves as a state within the larger gentile political organization.

However, with the Enlightenment all this changed. Jews were expected to take their place as citizens like any other in nation-states, and the powerful centralized Jewish governments disappeared as a condition of Jewish citizenship. Judaism was forced to come to grips with the fact that the intense cultural separatism characteristic of Jews in traditional societies was widely viewed as incompatible with life in a modern nation-state. Judaism of necessity became a voluntary association, and there was no way for any central authority to prevent intermarriage or complete defection from Judaism.

The problem, then, was whether separation could be maintained in this radically new environment. Jews were forced to walk a very fine line between two unacceptable alternatives: On the one hand Jews were strongly motivated to avoid the traditional hermetic Jewish separatism because of its perceived incompatibility with citizenship in a modern state and its tendency to provoke anti-Semitism. On the other hand, there was a powerful fear that abandoning these traditional practices would result in true assimilation into gentile society and the end of Judaism as fundamentally a cohesive national/ethnic entity.

Theoretically, there is no reason to suppose that the voluntary nature of post-Enlightenment Judaism is incompatible with Judaism continuing as a group evolutionary strategy as outlined in Chapter 1. One need only suppose that some subset of group members will actively attempt to continue Jewish separatism even in the face of powerful assimilatory pressures and that those who fail to adhere to this separatism will simply be excluded (or exclude themselves) from the group. Under conditions of voluntarism, it is expected that Jewish education and socialization will become even more important for maintaining group commitment than in traditional societies where the possibilities of changing group membership were severely limited.

In the following, several modern reformulations of Judaism will be discussed because they illustrate how Jewish *de facto* separatism can persist even when the basis for group cohesion was forced to change. In each of these cases, the intention has always been to continue Jewish cultural and genetic separatism, although different mechanisms, including ideological rationalizations, have been used to achieve this goal. Moreover, the mechanisms have differed in their success in achieving the twin goals of accommodating to the modern world while maintaining group cohesion and *de facto* separatism from the gentile world.

## Reform Judaism as a Response to the Enlightenment

> We are not a *people*, we are a *religion*. (French rabbi Lazare Wogue [1843]; quoted in Meyer 1988, 170; italics in text)

> We recognize in the modern era of universal culture of heart and intellect the approaching of the realization of Israel's great Messianic hope for the establishment of the kingdom of truth, justice and peace among all men. We consider ourselves no longer a nation, but a religious community, and, therefore, expect neither a return to Palestine, nor a sacrificial worship under the sons of Aaron, nor the restoration of any of the laws concerning the Jewish state . . . We are convinced of the utmost necessity of preserving the historical identity with our great past. (From the Pittsburgh Platform [1885]; reprinted in Meyer 1988, 388)

> The definition of the Jewish community as a purely religious unit was, of course, a sham from the time of its conception. (Katz 1986, 32)

The Reform movement of Judaism beginning in the 19th century was an attempt to integrate Jews into the modern Western European nation-state. In Germany, the *font et origo* of the Reform movement, the goal was political emancipation. From the standpoint of the Jewish reformers, there was no intention to end separatism, but only to find a new basis for voluntary separatism now that the old powerful, centralizing force of Jewish autonomous communities had disappeared (Sorkin 1987, 101). On the other hand, the entire purpose of emancipation from the perspective of Christian countries was "to put an end to the anomaly of Jewish existence, offering Jews of every country the chance to be absorbed into the local population" (Katz 1986b, 143).

In the event, Jews were not simply absorbed into German society: "The experience of certain individuals notwithstanding, the entrance of Jewry as a *collective* into the body of German society did not mean integration into any part, stratum, or section of it. It meant, rather, the creation of a separate subgroup, which conformed to the German middle class in some of its characteristics" (Katz 1985, 85; italics in text; see also Katz 1986, 143-144). In fact, emancipation led to a new kind of German-Jewish subculture: "Assimilation—as intermarriage, conversion, or the denial of connection with and separation from other Jews—was not the experience of the majority of the new bourgeoisie but a marginal phenomenon. The bulk of the bourgeoisie shared a specifically German-Jewish life: they were members of a minority group who constituted a community" (Sorkin 1987, 6).

A crucial aspect of this transformation was the development of institutions that served many of the functions of the old *Kehilla* system and served to reinforce the internal cohesion of the community in the absence of powerful central controls—what Volkov (1985, 196; see also Sorkin 1987, 113) refers to as a post-emancipation "intimate culture" composed of specifically Jewish associations. By 1900, there were 5,000 Jewish associations in Germany, which formed a society parallel to the gentile society, including a vast array of charitable services (see Chapter 6). Even by 1840, there had developed a homogeneous German Jewish subculture based now on voluntary association, rather than rigid centralized control. This fundamental homogeneity transcended religious differences among the Jews: "The manifest discrepancy between the ideologues' vision that the Jews would be distinguishable by religion alone and the actual social situation of German Jewry led to a fundamental paradox. What eluded German Jewry was that at the very moment that religious practice and belief became a divisive factor within the community, a secular ideology had become a new structural factor of cohesion" (Sorkin 1987, 123).

While emancipation led to no structural changes in Germany, there were major ideological changes. The principle change was the attempt to recast Judaism as a universalist missionary religion whose mission was to continue to remain separate from the gentiles while showing them the true religion and leading them to more elevated ethical behavior—the ancient idea that Judaism represents "a light of the nations" (Isa. 42:6).[40] In the words of Nachmam Kochmal in the early 19th century, Judaism had survived "so that it might become a Kingdom of Priests, i.e., teachers of the revealed absolute faith to the human race" (quoted in Meyer 1988, 155). Sorkin sums up this broad intellectual trend by noting that "[t]he ideologues thus effected a theoretical reconciliation of the inherent paradox: universal values could sustain the Jews' particularism, were indeed integral to it, since Jews had a role to play on the stage of universal moral history" (Sorkin 1987, 103; see also Endelman 1991, 196; Neusner 1987, 187; Patai 1971, 46).[41]

Reform Judaism explicitly rejected nationalistic aspirations of a return to Israel. During the French Revolutionary period and the Napoleonic period, French Jews attempting to obtain equality of economic and political rights "went out of their way to state publicly that their religion did not conflict with the duties of citizenship" (Meyer 1988, 27) by de-emphasizing the messianic return to Palestine. An assembly called by Napoleon explicitly declared that the Jews were no longer a separate people or, as Napoleon believed, a "state within a state."[42] Similar sentiments appeared in the Pittsburgh Platform of 1885.

Patai (1971, 43) notes that as a result of these ideas, the traditional prayers referring to the chosenness of the Jews, "Jewish peoplehood," a return to Jerusalem, and even almost all mention of Zion or Jerusalem were expurgated from the prayer books of Reform Judaism or at least modified in order to be less incompatible with citizenship in a secular nation-state. Prayers asking God to protect Israel were changed to ask God to protect all oppressed people. "By means of such devices the *Union Prayerbook* actually succeeds in transforming the Jewish synagogue service from a family colloquy between the Children of Israel and God their Father—which was its character throughout Jewish history—into a formal audience in which the Jewish worshipers appear before the Lord in their capacity of a self-appointed delegation to present to Him the petitions of all mankind" (p. 45).

Given the *quid pro quo* of Jewish emancipation in Germany, the reforms served the function of making gentile political leaders more willing to grant Jews complete political and economic emancipation (Meyer 1988, 144). However, the ideological rationalizations also served the same functions as they did in the ancient world: to provide an ideological basis intended to appeal to gentile intellectuals during an era in which Judaism was beset by lack of respect from gentile intellectuals (Meyer 1988, 204)[43] and to shore up morale within the Jewish community, which was badly in need of a new basis for internal cohesion after the decline of Jewish political autonomy (Sorkin 1987, 102).

As early as the beginning of the 20th century, there was a trend among American Reform Jews to reverse the entire process and re-introduce elements of Jewish particularism (Meyer 1988, 295), including the celebration of traditional religious feasts and a greater appreciation of Orthodox Judaism as essential to the continued existence of Reform Judaism, rather than simply an outdated relic of the past. By mid-century, educational efforts had been extended, and the goal "was no longer simply to make Jewish young people into better human beings, but to make them also into dedicated members of the Jewish people" (Meyer 1988, 299). Reform Judaism became increasingly less differentiated from Conservative Judaism, where ethnic identification and religious rituals continued to retain a prominent role.

Moreover, there was an increasing attempt to make Reform Judaism compatible with Zionism. The issue of Zionism was extremely difficult for Reform Jews because of the issue of dual loyalty. But, in 1937, the Columbus Platform officially accepted the idea of a Palestinian homeland and shortly thereafter accepted the idea of political sovereignty for Jews in Israel.[44] As Sachar (1992, 510) comments in his discussion of this statement: "Was the statement, then, ethnicity reflecting itself as Zionism, or Zionism as ethnicity? In fact, each reinforced the other." Reform Judaism had clearly made its peace with Jewish ethnicity and the ideology of Jewish nationhood.[45]

Reform Judaism was therefore not intended to end Jewish cultural separatism (see also Woocher 1986, 5). Nor was it intended to end Jewish genetic segregation. According to Katz (1985, 85; see also Levenson 1989), the clearest sign of continuing separatism in post-emancipation Germany was endogamy: Jews continued to marry almost exclusively among themselves. The small percentage of Jews who married exogamously (and their children) were lost to the Jewish community. Moreover, "[a]s far as actual and active kinship was concerned, Jews remained almost exclusively bound to their own kind—a fact that more conspicuously than any other set them apart from the population at large" (Katz 1985, 86). Sorkin (1987, 111) notes that there was very little defection from Judaism in the 19th century in Germany despite the disappearance of powerful community controls. The annual rate of apostasy among Jews is estimated at no more than 6 or 7 per 10,000, and intermarriage is described as "not a significant factor."

The vast majority of those attending the Reform conference of Brunswick (Germany) in 1844 were opposed to mixed marriage, but many of the participants felt a need to make some accommodation on the issue in order to avoid charges of Jewish misanthropy. The conference resolved to state that mixed marriages were valid, but that there was "a lack of sympathy" for them (Meyer 1988, 135) because of the stated fear that mixed marriage would decimate the Jewish community. Indeed, the conference included the provision that the children of mixed marriages should be raised as Jews, and since this was impossible in Germany, there could be no practical effect of this resolution.

The Reform attitude toward intermarriage parallels the Jewish response to conversion in the ancient world, reviewed at the beginning of this chapter. In both cases, there appears to have been a gap between rhetoric, in which intermarriage or conversion was theoretically tolerated in order to appeal to the gentile community, and actual practice, which strongly discouraged these activities. Levenson's (1989, 321ff) discussion indicates that throughout the 19th century and into the 20th century in Germany, the Reform policy was to affirm the validity of intermarriage in principle in order to avoid charges of misanthropy and intolerance, but also to strongly oppose intermarriage in practice. In the words of Ludwig Philippson, a major Reform leader, whose opposition to intermarriage became stronger as time went on, "The reason lies simply in that one feels in part not entirely at one with one's self on this matter, and in part one fears, by giving a decisively negative answer, the reproach of intolerance . . ." (quoted in Levenson 1989, 324).[46] And in fact levels of intermarriage remained extremely low.

Levenson (1989, 326) notes that the public opposition to intermarriage was stronger among Reform thinkers in the United States than in Germany because intermarriage in the United States was more likely and the costs of an intolerant policy were lower (because of lower levels of anti-Semitism). The American thinkers were thus able to be much more forthright in their condemnation of intermarriage and even engaged in anti-Christian polemics, which would have been unthinkable in the German milieu.

While official ideology is undoubtedly a poor guide to private attitudes, it is worth noting that the Reform opposition to intermarriage in the United States officially avoided framing the reasons in racialist terms (Levenson 1989, 327ff). For example, the prominent Reform rabbi Samuel Schulmann explicitly rejected the racialist arguments against intermarriage put forward by the German Zionist Arthur Ruppin, arguing instead that intermarriage would destroy the Jewish community. However, explicitly racialist considerations for opposing intermarriage did appear among prominent Reform intellectuals. The prominent 19th-century Reform leader David Einhorn was a lifelong opponent of mixed marriages and refused to officiate at such ceremonies, even when pressed to do so (Meyer 1988, 247). Einhorn was also a staunch opponent of conversion of gentiles to Judaism because of the effects on the "racial purity" of Judaism (Levenson 1989, 331). The influential Reform intellectual Kaufman Kohler was also an ardent opponent of mixed marriage, as well as a believer in the hereditary genius of the Jewish people in the area of religion. The election of Israel is due "to hereditary virtues and to tendencies of mind and spirit which equip Israel for his calling" (Kohler 1918, 328). Kohler goes on to note that the idea of the election of Israel is closely linked in Deuteronomy to negative attitudes regarding intermarriage. The conclusion is that Israel must remain separate and avoid intermarriage until it leads mankind to an era of universal peace and brotherhood among the races (Kohler 1918, 445-446). Moreover, Israel's mission is not to convert others, but to be an altruistic martyr who provides a shining example of morality to the rest of mankind who will eventually acknowledge the truth represented by the Jewish God (pp. 339-340, 375).

The negative attitude toward intermarriage is confirmed by survey results. A 1912 survey indicated that only seven of 100 Reform rabbis had officiated at a mixed marriage, and a 1909 resolution of the Central Council of American Rabbis declared that "mixed marriages are contrary to the tradition of the Jewish religion and should be discouraged by the American Rabbinate" (Meyer 1988, 290). In 1947, a resolution to ban officiating at mixed marriages was narrowly defeated, and a 1973 resolution actually strengthened the language of the 1909 resolution opposing intermarriage (Levenson 1989, 331). Even in the 1970s "virtually all" Reform rabbis opposed mixed marriage in principle (Meyer 1988, 371) and a majority of Reform rabbis refused to officiate at such marriages.

Meyer (1988, 144) makes the interesting point that in Europe Reform Judaism was most successful in societies, as in 19th-century Germany, where there was a realistic hope of political and economic gains by de-emphasizing the national/ethnic character of Judaism. "Had German Jews been totally without hope of full acceptance, as in eastern Europe, or already achieved it entirely, as in France, they would not have felt as self-conscious about the prayers for return to the Land of Israel." Similarly, it was noted above that, because of differing political situations Jewish rhetoric against intermarriage could afford to be much more strident in the United States than in Germany. This suggests that in the absence of perceived necessity, there is an inertial tendency to return to an ideology of ethnic and cultural separatism. The following explores several modern formulations in which the national/ethnic character of Judaism remains salient.

## Zionism, Conservative Judaism, and Neo-Orthodox Judaism as Responses to the Enlightenment

While Reform Judaism rationalized a limited cultural assimilation between Jews and gentiles by de-emphasizing the national/ethnic character of Judaism, the reverse process is apparent in Zionism and the recent upsurge in Neo-Orthodox and Conservative Judaism. It is important to note that Zionism must be viewed as one of the responses of Judaism to the Enlightenment, and, indeed, Woocher (1986, 9) describes it as the most important response of Eastern European Jews to modern times—as a mechanism that, along with Reform, Conservatism, or Neo-Orthodoxy, would "enable Jews to live in the modern world on its terms, but as Jews" (p. 9).

Zionism openly accepted a national/ethnic conceptualization of Judaism that was quite independent of religious faith. As Theodore Herzl (1988, 76) stated, "We are a people—one people." In words highly compatible with the theoretical perspective developed here, the Zionist Arthur Hertzberg stated that "the Jews in all ages were essentially a nation and . . . all other factors profoundly important to the life of this people, even religion, were mainly instrumental values" (quoted in Neusner 1987, 203).

Interestingly, Endelman (1991, 196) argues for a link between the development of Zionist ideology and the perceived failure of the Reform movement due to the fact that many Jews became completely assimilated, including especially a substantial incidence of conversion and intermarriage. "Zionist ideologues and publicists argued that in the West assimilation was as much a threat to the survival of the Jewish people as persecution was in the East" (Endelman 1991, 196). Zionists, such as Moses Hess ([1862] 1918, 124), early on noted that the Reform conceptualization of Judaism as a religion with no national basis "fostered only indifference to Judaism and conversions to Christianity." As early as 1862, Zionism was thus seen by its proponents as an attempt to retain the national/ethnic character of Judaism in the face of the corrosive assimilative forces of the modern Western world. In terms of the group strategy idea, Zionism is therefore an attempt to continue Judaism as a fairly closed group evolutionary strategy.

Similarly, the recent revival of Neo-Orthodox Judaism in the United States is attributed by Danzger (1989) to a rejection of Reform Judaism because the relative assimilation of these Jews had resulted in high rates of intermarriage and conversion and a complete lack of religious or ethnic identification by some Jews. This movement is essentially an "ethnic return" (p. 7) and implies a return to the traditional manners of observing the laws of family purity, the Sabbath, and ritually prepared food, as well as minimizing the importance of secular education or even banning it altogether. Kaplan ([1934] 1967, 149) notes the importance of cultural isolation, which "demands racial purity and precludes intermarriage," for Neo-Orthodoxy. Mayer (1979, 92), describing contemporary Neo-Orthodox groups, states that "[t]he value of separateness and the closed or exclusive structure of the Orthodox and Hasidic community needs little further elaboration. Whether in the ghettos of Eastern Europe or in the low-status ethnic enclaves of New York City, the world of the Orthodox Jew has been woven out of a special language (Yiddish) and particular values, along with specialized religious paraphernalia (clothes and institutions) which perpetuate the values."

Neusner (1987, 189ff) also shows that Neo-Orthodox Judaism, although remaining much closer to the original separatist formula than Reform Judaism, also made accommodations to the modern world, and one wing of Neo-Orthodoxy accepted the legitimacy of secular education (see also Mayer 1979, 72ff). Orthodox Judaism accepted enough of the gentile customs to "lessen the differences between the Holy People and the nations" (p. 196). However, as Patai (1971, 47ff) points out, many Orthodox (and Conservative) Jews have continued to accept the ideology of a nation in exile, while still attempting to better their lot in the countries of the *galut* and with no intention of emigrating to Israel.

A resurgent sense of ethnocentrism and cultural separatism is also a factor in the increasing importance of Conservative Judaism. A 1990 survey found that over 40 percent of American Jewish households considered themselves Conservative, approximately the same as the percentage identifying themselves as Reform (Kosmin et al. 1991). While Conservative Judaism is more liberal in rejecting some Orthodox requirements (e.g., mixed-sex seating at synagogue) and has attempted to become "fully American" (Elazar 1980, 105), there is far more emphasis on traditional ceremonies and practices that promote separatism, including a strong stand against intermarriage. Sachar (1992, 685) notes that "[t]here was little pretense to prophetic universalism among the Conservatives. . . . From beginning to end, their focus was on Jewish peoplehood." Woocher (1986, 7) notes that for the Conservative movement ideology was far less important than "the primordial affinity of Jews for one another . . . ."

Indeed, Elazar (1980, 107) notes that it was common for Conservative Jews to have theological doubts, but to rationalize the continuation of religious rituals "for the sake of Jewish peoplehood"—clearly a position not much different from the practices of Judaism as a civil religion, described in the following section. The clear commitment to peoplehood as central to Judaism attracted to the Conservative movement a considerable number of Zionists, Jewish educators, and others who were intensely committed to Jewish life. Sachar (1992) notes that since the mid-1970s Conservative Judaism has declined somewhat, but this decline does not indicate an overall decrease in Jewish separatism and a declining concern with ethnicity, since there has been a corresponding upsurge of Orthodox Judaism, and Reform Judaism has become more traditional. In the end, Reform, Neo-Orthodoxy, and Conservatism, despite elements of disagreement about ideology and practice, "were in fact ideological allies. All affirmed the possibility and necessity of maintaining Jewish identity and communality in the modern world (Woocher 1986, 8).

The example of Zionism shows that Jewish cultural separatism can be maintained independent of religious organization, and this is also the case for secular re-interpretations of Judaism.[47] Indeed, Elazar (1980) describes the "religious" nature of contemporary American Judaism as a "protective coloring" (p. 9), adopted because "it is a legitimate way to maintain differences when organic ways are suspect" (p. 23)—a comment itself indicative of the tensions arising from conceptualizing Judaism in ethnic terms in the post-Enlightenment intellectual world.[48] Consistent with such a perspective, he notes that philanthropy has become far more important to identification with Judaism than religious worship. "Rightly or wrongly, secretly or openly, Jews function as Jews in response to their needs as a collectivity first and foremost—in other words, as a polity . . ." (p. 10). "Even their Jewish concerns . . . tend to be 'tribal' in character, not motivated by any hope for the redemption, individual or collective, traditionally associated with the Jews' covenant with God, but by the comforts derived from the association of like with like, or, with renewed importance, fears for survival" (p. 17).

Moreover, support for Israel, rather than any set of traditional religious beliefs, has become the litmus test of being a Jew: Elazar (1980) notes that "Israel has become the keystone to the entire Jewish belief system" (p. 92), so that individuals who fail to support Israel's claims are "more or less written off by the Jewish community and certainly are excluded from any significant decision-making role" (p. 91). Thus, for example, the "committed Jewish left" is forced to straddle a fine line between support for Israel and, because of its general sympathy with Third World causes, support for Palestinian self-determination.

## Judaism as a Civil Religion in the Contemporary World

The result is that the best characterization of contemporary Judaism is what Woocher (1986) calls a "civil religion." As described by Woocher (1986, 12-13), the civil religion of Judaism has been firmly in place at least since the 1960s.

This civil religion is a vehicle for unity among the different religious and national ideologies that have grown up within Judaism since the Enlightenment. The focus of civil religion is on the civic political institutions of the society, not on what are traditionally thought of as religious beliefs. The Jewish civil religion acknowledges the tension between integration into American life and the survival of Judaism as a distinct group, but denies that there is any inherent conflict and actively attempts to promote the continuation of a powerful sense of group identity in the face of constant threats of assimilation emanating from the wider society. "The civil religion's commitment to Jewish continuity constitutes a clear response to the threats to Jewish survival which have become manifest in recent decades" (Woocher 1986, 65).

Once again, as in the "light of the nations" concept so common throughout Jewish history, the proposed moral nature of Judaism is utilized as a rationale for maintaining the perpetuation of the group: "The identification of Judaism with applied morality has been a primary Jewish civil religious strategy for vindicating both its embrace of America and its support of Jewish group perpetuation" (Woocher 1986, 28). The belief gradually emerged that "the Jewish community qua Jewish community had an important contribution to make to American life, and the Jewish tradition had helped to shape America's values" (p. 45). In a manner that recalls the rationalization of the Reform movement for continued separation (see above), the continuation of Jewish group identity and a measure of cultural separatism were thus viewed as quintessentially true to American ideals because of their moral, civilizing influences on American life. Within the confines of Judaism as a civil religion, "[t]he survival of the Jewish people is a consuming passion because the Jewish people plays a unique role in history as the bearer of Jewish values. In the work to insure the perpetuation of these values, the survival of the Jewish people and the Jewish community becomes a value in its own right, a crystallization of all that is being defended" (Woocher 1986, 76).

The acceptance of mutual responsibility and within-group charity (*tzedakah*) are basic tenets of Judaism as a civil religion and are central to the perceived moral nature of Judaism. As in traditional Judaism (see Chapter 6), charity is conceptualized primarily as directed within the group. Thus, Woocher (1986, 125) finds that 51 percent of a group of American Jews in Jewish leadership development programs agreed that providing social and welfare services for Jews was a high priority, and only 2 percent viewed it as a low priority. However, only 4 percent agreed that providing social and welfare services for anyone in need was a high priority, compared to 70 percent who viewed it as a low priority.

Within-group charity has become a primary mechanism for maintaining group cohesion and separation in contemporary American society. Indeed, Woocher (1986) finds that voluntary within-group altruism has become a primary criterion for who is a Jew (see also Chapter 6). The result is that "Jewish involvement in nonsectarian fundraising and social service was thus integrative, but not assimilatory in its impact" (Woocher 1986, 37). Fund raising on behalf of group interests, rather than the common acceptance of religious dogma, became a basis for unity: "[F]ederation [i. e., secular communal organization centered around fundraising for communal causes] has become, in effect, religion" (Woocher 1986, 54). "The communal enterprise not only expressed Jewish values, it became a source of meaning in life, the meaning that flows from being united with others in an unquestionably great task" (p. 56).

Woocher's (1986) data indicate that the leaders of civil Judaism in the 1970s had a strong sense of Jewish ethnicity and were greatly concerned about Jewish intermarriage. A strong sense of ethnic pride and a sense of Judaism as making a unique, irreplaceable contribution to human culture are characteristic of these individuals, as indicated by agreement with the following statements: "The Jewish contribution to modern civilization has been greater than that of any other people" (over 60% agree or strongly agree); "The Jewish people is the chosen people (over 60% agree or strongly agree). Regarding the latter, Woocher (1986, 145) notes, "Civil Judaism, like many modern Jews, often finds the traditional language of chosenness, and the implications of that language discomforting. For this reason, it is possible to lose sight of how critical the myth of chosenness really is, to fail to recognize that it is the glue which holds together the pragmatic ethos and the transcendent vision of civil Judaism." In addition, 72 percent agreed that intermarriage was a "very serious" problem, and an additional 21 percent viewed it as "moderately serious."

Several other authors have noticed an upsurge recently in an ethnic rather than a religious conceptualization of Judaism (e.g., Elazar 1980; Neusner 1987, 198). Indeed, in 1972, only 18 percent of Jews in the United States viewed being Jewish as primarily religious, while 61 percent perceived Judaism as denoting an ethnic/cultural group (Sachar 1992, 699-700). Reflecting this trend, Sachar (1992, 746) notes that in recent years "[t]he emergent music, drama, poetry, and prose of American Jews, even their religious expression, all laid increasing emphasis on ethnic Jewishness, on Jewish peoplehood in its widest contours." There was also a rejection of the melting pot conceptualization of the United States in favor of a cultural pluralism model developed originally by Horace Kallen (1915, 1924) early in the century as a mechanism for preserving Jewish separatism within American society.

Whatever the ideology underlying separatism, the attempt to remain separate in the United States was largely successful, at least until very recently. Goldstein (1974) found that, among the Jews of Los Angeles, close personal relationships were with other Jews, even though synagogue attendance was low and secular interests and other signs of assimilation were high. Writing of the 1970s in the United States, Sachar (1992, 688) states that "the Jewish family's principal 'religious' 'philosophic' concern was simply the in-group marriage of its children. It was to ensure that immemorial endogamy that Jewish education acquired its unique importance in the postwar years." "Well into the 1980s, even with all doors swinging open, Jews still joined, visited, and married largely among their own" (Sachar 1992, 863).

Finally, data on intermarriage from the last few years indicate a significant rise in the rate of intermarriage for Jews in the United States as well as increases in the numbers of gentiles converting to Judaism in conjunction with marriage to a Jewish spouse (e.g., Ellman 1987; Kosmin et al. 1991). These data present difficult problems of interpretation, and the long-term implications of these trends are much in doubt. Nevertheless, there is the *prima facie* possibility that these events could have a major impact on the conceptualization of Judaism within an evolutionary framework. From an evolutionary perspective, intermarriage is the only form of assimilation that really matters, and if it occurred to a sufficient degree, it would effectively end Judaism as an evolutionary strategy. The issues raised by these very recent events are deferred to *SAID* (ch. 10).

# NOTES

1. See, for example, Dandamayev's (1984, 339) description of the gradual assimilation of Egyptian exiles in Babylon during the same period when the Israelite exiles developed their ideology of retaining genetic and cultural separatism in a diaspora. While the other exile groups in Babylon were gradually assimilating genetically and culturally, Bickerman (1984, 348), on the basis of the material in the Book of Tobit, states that members of the exiled Israelite aristocracy were marrying their kin and were greatly concerned with genealogy.

2. The Book of Jubilees generally exhibits a powerful concern with separation of Jews and gentiles, as does the Mishnah, particularly the tract *Avoda zarah*. Bickerman (1988) describes the Book of Jubilees as "ultraorthodox" (p. 250).

3. Josephus (*Antiquities of the Jews*, XII:4, 6) tells the story of Joseph the tax collector, who plotted to have a sexual relationship with a heathen, but, because of his brother's chicanery, ends up marrying his niece—the epitome of a consanguineous relationship.

4. These writings are reviewed in *SAID* (ch. 2).

5. The attempt at deception is significant. There was a large Jewish apologetic literature in antiquity, and a common technique was to masquerade as a gentile in order to achieve greater credibility. See *SAID* (ch. 4).

6. Interestingly, Baron (1952b, 195) notes that Josephus never mentions the existence of the "princes of captivity" (i.e., the Patriarch of Palestine and the Exilarch of Babylon) in his apologia for Judaism intended for Western audiences, clearly because these offices pointed to the national character of the religion.

7. Similarly, the European Enlightenment resulted in a powerful upsurge of intellectual work by Jews, intended to show that Judaism could be made intellectually, esthetically, and socially acceptable as a universal, ethical religion, while still maintaining cultural and genetic separatism—a project that continues to draw intense interest from Jewish intellectuals (Meyer 1988, 62ff; see below and *SAID*, ch. 4). As in the ancient world, there have been attempts to show that Judaism could be rationalized in the presence of powerful intellectual critiques emanating from gentile philosophers such as Kant, Hegel, and Schleiermacher and in the context of Darwinism and modern Biblical scholarship.

This enormous intellectual energy in the service of developing self-justifying ideologies is an excellent testimony of the critical importance of ideology in an evolutionary account of human affairs.

8. The intensity and clear apologetic tone with which Jewish scholars such as Bamberger ([1939] 1968) and Eichorn (1965a) have approached these issues are also testimony that there is a continuing interest in fostering the belief that Judaism has always been a permeable group. See *SAID* (ch. 4).

9. Simon ([1948, 1964] 1986, 486) states that circumcision was "physiquement pénible et, pour un païen de l'époque, moralement humiliante." Circumcision also may have a rather potent symbolic function that would exclude gentiles: Discussing circumcision in the ancient world, Boyarin (1993, 233) states "It was not that the rite [circumcision] was difficult to perform . . . but rather that it symbolized the genetic, the genealogical moment of Judaism as the religion of a particular tribe of people. . . . [B]y being a marker on the organ of generation, it represents the genealogical claim for concrete historical memory as constitutive of Israel." Besides circumcision, converts were baptized by immersion in water up to the genitals in the Gerim version, a ceremony that may reasonably have been perceived as symbolizing the cleansing of the genetic material on admission to the fold. Alon (1977, 148) argues that the immersion of proselytes is, like other immersions described in the Torah, intended to "purify a person from his bodily defilement." Moreover, a prominent legal aspect of conversion was that the convert had no blood relationships with non-Jews and had no father. Both of these principles suggest that conversion involved a complete break with membership in a different gene pool. In a sense, therefore, these phenomena attest to the self-conscious belief that indeed converting to Judaism was essentially an act of entering a different gene pool.

10. Baron (1952b, 409) notes that the word *mamzer* originally referred to the offspring of prohibited unions with foreigners, but in Talmudic times came to mean the offspring of any adulterous or incestuous relationship.

11. Amazingly, Bamberger ([1939] 1968) claims that the restriction on priestly marriage with converts does not betray a negative attitude toward converts because of the priestly emphasis on genealogy: "No matter how friendly one might be toward a convert, one could not regard him as of the aristocracy of Israel" (p. 85). The comment reveals Bamberger's awareness that genealogy was in fact a highly valued resource in Jewish society. However, it was clearly a resource that a convert and his descendants could never possess.

12. Segal's (1988) remarks suggest that converts would have come disproportionately from the more successful classes of gentiles. This fits the general patterns of what we know about converts in other ages (see Chapters 2 and 7).

13. This is a surprising argument, given that over the great majority of this time span Judaism had no pretensions at all of being a universal religion and concerns with racial purity and rejections of gentile culture were highly salient. Apologia intended to portray Judaism as universalist did not appear until the first century and were intended to counter gentile beliefs in Jewish exclusivism. (As is typical of his methods, Feldman (1993, 432ff) interprets Jewish religious apologia and the large literature which glorifies Jewish culture and accomplishments as evidence for actual missionary efforts and large-scale conversion to Judaism. For a contrary view of this literature, see J. J. Collins 1985, 169.) In order to be viable, the demographic argument must suppose that there was a mass conversion of gentiles toward the end of this period. Such an event would certainly have been noted, but there is no evidence at all for large-scale conversions to Judaism at this time, and indeed Goodman (1989) emphasizes the almost complete lack of interest in converts at least to the end of the first century.

14. Safrai (1974, 122) suggests a population of around 6-8 million *circa* 70 A.D.

15. I am indebted to Alan Rogers, Department of Anthropology, University of Utah, for these calculations. They are based on the formula for the rate of natural increase of populations: $r = \ln(n_2/n_1)/T$, where $n_1$ is the original population size, $n_2$ is the later population size, and T is the number of intervening years. The populations of Kenya and Kuwait have recently been growing at $r = 0.04$, or 6.6 times the rate suggested by Feldman's data on Jewish population size. Supposing that one might justify an inference of conversion with $r = .05$, the Jewish population of 70 A.D. would need to be about 2.6 x $10^{19}$ (10 billion times larger than the current population of the world) to warrant such an assumption. Obviously, no human population can sustain such growth, but the point is that human populations can grow very quickly. Without some data about survivorship and fertility, Feldman's proposal is meaningless. Weinryb (1972, 137) notes that the Jewish population of Poland increased by a factor of 40 or 50 in a period of 250 years, reaching a population of about 500,000 and indicating a growth rate of between .0148 and .0156. Although these estimates include immigration, the data indicate that Jewish populations can grow very quickly. In the modern era, Johnson (1987, 356) notes a Jewish population growth rate of 2 percent per year in Europe in the period from 1880 to 1914. See also Chapter 5.

16. Feldman (1993, 392) notes that converting slaves was a religious obligation at least partly because conversion would allow slaves to perform their duties (such as food preparation) in a manner consistent with Jewish religious law. Thus, one source of proselytism may well have been forcibly converted slaves. As indicated below, the descendants of slaves were not considered as marriageable by other Jews.

17. If the 1 percent figure is extrapolated to the entire Roman Empire, given a Jewish population in the Roman Empire numbering several million, the proselytes would number in the tens of thousands. This range for the number of proselytes would surely be sufficient to include the numbers of proselytes known from the sources, but, clearly, a conversion rate of 1 percent would not have a major effect on the genetic makeup of the Jewish population, especially given the fact that non-reproductives and slaves appear to be overrepresented among converts.

18. Nineteenth- and 20th-century attitudes on intermarriage, including Einhorn's, are considered in more detail below.

19. See also Alon (1980, 1984) 1989, 86-87; Baron 1952b, 103-104; Kraabel 1982; Neusner 1987, 141; Safrai 1974, 185.

20. The Patriarchate was abolished by the Church in the fourth century. However, Benjamin of Tudela (see Adler 1909, 39-42) describes the great power and influence of the Exilarch over Jews in Muslim lands in the late 12th century. The Exilarch's authority as the Head of the Captivity was officially recognized by the Muslim authorities.

21. Interestingly, some ancient rabbis stated that in the messianic age all ritual prohibitions would be suspended (Werblowsky 1968, 37-38), a comment that suggests a self-conscious awareness of the necessity of maintaining the law as a wall of separation during the *galut* (exile).

22. See also Chapter 6. In the case of the Rothschilds, there was a dramatic increase in consanguinity as their economic fortunes improved. Prior to becoming an extremely wealthy and powerful family, the first two sons of Mayer Amschel Rothschild married undistinguished Jewish females. As the family prospered, the next two sons married the daughters of the most prestigious Jewish families in England and Germany, respectively. However, the youngest son, whose marriage occurred after the family had become the wealthiest in Europe, married his niece, and in the next generation, no less than 9 of the 12 marriages consummated by the sons were with first cousins in the male line (an

additional marriage was to a cousin in the female line, Juliana Cohen). Moreover, five of the six marriages of daughters were with other Rothschild family members (including Betty, who married her uncle James) (see genealogy in Morton 1961). Morton finds that of the 58 weddings contracted by the descendants of Mayer Amschel Rothschild, fully half were with first cousins.

23. During this period, it was common to attribute any ailment putatively associated with Jews, such as hysteria, to the practice of consanguineous marriages (Gilman 1993, 108, 116), suggesting a common perception even among Jewish scientists of the period that consanguineous marriages had been common.

24. The general rise of the tribe of Levi to the point where its members dominated the aristocracy of the Second Temple period paralleled the rise to power of the Hasmoneans who were from that tribe, and there was a corresponding decrease in the status of the tribe of Judah (Stern 1976, 581). Such a result, in conjunction with the data on endogamy, represents a good example of the persistence of the importance of kinship for Judaism during this period.

25. For example, a young girl who had been given as hostage was refused marriage even though all attested that she had retained her virginity and even though hostages were not considered prisoners of war (for whom marriage to a priest was illegal).

26. Jeremias refers here to passages in b. Qidd. 70a and 70b. The following are relevant (Neusner's [1992] translation; italics in text):

> And said Rabbah bar R. Adda said Rab, and some say, said R. Sela said R. Hamnuna, "Whoever marries a woman who is not genealogically suitable to him—Elijah binds him to the stock and the Holy One, blessed be He, administers the flogging." *And a Tannaite statement:* In regard to all of them, Elijah writes and the Holy One, blessed be He, signs: "Woe to him who invalidates his seed and does injury to his family's genealogy. Elijah binds him to the stock and the Holy One, blessed be He, administers the flogging."

> Said R. Hama b. R Hanina, "When the Holy One, blessed be He, brings his divine presence to rest on Israel, he will bring it to rest only on families of proper genealogy in Israel: 'At that time says the Lord will I be the God of all the families of Israel' (Jer. 31:1)—not to 'all Israel,' but to 'all the families of Israel,' 'and they shall be my people.'" Said Rabbah bar R. Huna, "This is a distinguishing point that separates Israelites from proselytes, *for in the case of Israelites it is written,* 'and they shall be my people,' *while with reference to proselytes,* 'for who is he who has boldness to approach me,' says the Lord. 'You shall be my people,' then 'I will be your God.'" Said R. Helbo, "Proselytes are as hard for Israel as a scab: 'And the stranger shall join himself with them and they shall cleave to the house of Jacob' (Isa. 14:1). Here we find the word 'cleave,' and elsewhere, using the same letters, it is written, 'This is the Torah for all kinds of signs of the plague of the skin ailment: And for a rising or for a scab' (Lev. 14:56)."

In these passages, therefore, God's favor is reserved for racially pure Israelites, and proselytes are viewed as a temporary affliction, which will be removed eventually in a process of racial purification. At b. Qidd. 71a, there is a discussion of God purifying the tribes of the genetically tainted, and there are several repetitions of the following statement implying a hierarchy of racial purity: "All other countries are like gross dough [not fine flour] in comparison to the Land of Israel, and the Land of Israel is like gross dough by comparison to Babylonia." The Babylonians were known to be extremely concerned about purity of descent. The Babylonian Rabbi Zeiri refused to marry the daughter of Rabbi Yohanan despite the latter's accomplishments as a scholar because of the relative impurity of his descent. Yohanan states, "Our Torah is valid, but our daughters aren't valid?" (b. Qidd. 71b).

27. A high priest could not marry a woman who had been captured in war, presumably because such women might be raped by their captors and even give birth to genetically tainted children. Jeremias notes that this rule was taken very seriously by the Pharisees, who rebuked both John Hyrcanus and his son on these grounds.

28. Benjamin of Tudela describes two heads of the Babylonian academies as tracing their pedigrees back to Moses and Samuel, respectively. There is also reference to two different lines of Exilarchs descending from King David, one through the scholar Hillel (see Adler 1907, 39-40).

29. References are from *The Code of Maimonides, Book 5: The Book of Holiness*, ed. L. Nemoy, Yale Judaica Series (New Haven and London: Yale University Press, 1965), ch. XII.

30. Epstein (1942, 299) describes the Talmudic law as prohibiting the marriage of a Jew to a former slave with whom he has had sexual relations (while a slave) and who has converted. This would also tend to minimize such conversions.

31. Maimonides claims that the focus is on females because any blemish among the males would have been used as a slur in the quarrels among men, while women seem less interested in using such accusations. As a result, any blemish in the male line would have been well known (p. 126).

32. The importance of purity of descent also emerged in questions related to the status of the New Christians after the forced conversions of 1391. See *SAID* (ch. 3).

33. Castro (1954) relates the story of the execution of Don Juzaf Pichon in 1379 as a result of a conspiracy among other Jewish courtiers. The subsequent scandal resulted in the removal of the power of capital punishment from the aljamas. Castro states that the episode was "a drama characteristic of life in the *aljama* with their dense, indeed choking, atmosphere of passion" (p. 533n).

34. Hostility directed against apostates has been a common phenomenon in other times and places as well. For traditional Poland, see Weinryb 1972; Zborowski & Herzog 1952, 231; for medieval France, see Chazan 1973, 23; for Arab countries in the 20th century, see Stillman 1991, 21; for 16th-century France, see Davidson 1987, 26.

35. It should be noted that lack of linguistic separatism among the Jews living in Spain was not without its critics: Neuman (1969) notes that it was common for Jewish intellectuals in Spain to deplore the fact that most Jews had only superficial knowledge of Hebrew. Moreover, "(t)hey decried the fact that Hebrew was no longer the spoken tongue of the Jews and pleaded passionately for the study of Hebrew grammar and philology" (Neuman 1969, II:98).

36. The uncleanness of gentiles and gentile land in particular is enshrined in Jewish religious ideology. See, for example., *The Code of Maimonides, Book 10, The Book of Cleanness*.

37. In some cases, barriers to intermarriage were also maintained by gentiles. Nevertheless a common pattern in both pre-expulsion Spain and other parts of Europe was for wealthy Jews to marry daughters into the gentile nobility in return for providing a substantial dowry. In these cases, the stem family remained Jewish. See discussion in *SAID* (ch. 3).

38. While conversion followed by intermarriage appears to have occurred occasionally at the top of society in England and Poland, it should also be noted that there is evidence

(summarized in Chapters 2 and 7) that in general poor Jews have been most likely to defect. This suggests a bi-modal situation in which defection has been more likely to occur at either the very top or the bottom of Jewish society.

39. Similarly, Lindemann (1991) notes that Jews in 19th-century Russia were typically viewed as a stubborn, compact mass. Most of them remained, by their own image of themselves, "a people apart," not only in religion, but also in language, dress, culture, and economic activity. They were not "Russians," and most resisted the idea of ever becoming Russians. Danzger (1989, 149) recounts the story of a *yeshiva* in Russia in 1893 that closed rather than agree to a demand by the authorities that Russian be taught.

40. The "light of the nations" conceptualization of Judaism was also invoked by secular Jewish intellectuals in the 20th century. See *SAID* (ch. 4).

41. The claim that Judaism was nothing more than a religion often proved difficult to maintain. Patai (1971, 39) notes that Jews were considered by both Jews and gentiles as ethnic minorities in non-Western countries. "Nevertheless, all individuals who followed the Jewish religion . . . were considered by the assimilationist Western Jews as members of a purely religious community to which they applied the term Diaspora." Ragins (1980, 85) focuses on the tension between the statements of liberal Jews that Judaism was nothing more than a religion and their recognition that traditional Judaism had been far more than simply a religion. The claim that Judaism was nothing more than a religion also conflicted with the reality that "there was a sense of relatedness and cohesiveness among Jews which seemed to extend beyond the lines drawn by religious factions, uniting Orthodox and Reform." Recognizing this, the Centralverein, a self-defense committee representing liberal Jews in Germany beginning in 1893, at times acknowledged that Judaism was more than simply a religion and should be defined by a "consciousness of common descent *(Abstammung)*" (p. 85) or race (p. 86).

42. Interestingly, Napoleon advocated mixed marriages as a means of eventually assimilating the Jews into French society. The assembly tactfully stated that intermarriages were not forbidden by Jewish law, but that they had no religious status. Epstein (1942, 180) describes several historical inaccuracies in the Jewish position intended to present Jewish attitudes toward intermarriage in a favorable light.

43. Meyer (1988, 201) points out that the entire Reform movement faced a crisis in Germany when the changes in ideology and liturgy failed to result in respect from gentile intellectuals and failed to end general anti-Semitism. While the Reformers had hoped that science would vindicate the role of Judaism in establishing the moral basis of Christianity, gentile scholars during the period developed the view that in fact rabbinic Judaism and Christianity really had very little relationship. Gordon (1984, 24) provides a long list of German gentile intellectuals described as "respectable anti-Semites," some of whom focused on the ethnocentric nature of Judaism. See *SAID* (ch. 2-3). The entire Reform project may have been considered deception by many anti-Semites. Writing of the upsurge in anti-Semitism in Germany in the late 19th century, Meyer (1988, 202) notes that anti-Semites focussed their hatred most on the non-Orthodox Jews, "since they were the least conspicuously Jewish, yet persisted in maintaining a purposeful religious differentiation."

44. The 1937 Columbus Platform illustrates some of the intellectual tensions of Reform Judaism and indeed Judaism in general in the modern world. The statement attempts to continue the conceptualization of Judaism as a religion, while nevertheless affirming the importance of deeper ties among Jews. And there is an attempt to reconcile Zionism with loyalty to the modern nation-state:

Though we recognize in the group loyalty of Jews who have become estranged from our religious tradition, a bond which still unites them with us, we maintain that it is by its religion and for its religion that the Jewish people has lived. The non-Jew who accepts our faith is welcomed as a full member of the Jewish community.

In all the lands where our people live, they assume and seek to share loyally the full duties and responsibilities of citizenship and to create seats of Jewish knowledge and religion. In the rehabilitation of Palestine . . . we behold the promise of renewed life for many of our brethren. We affirm the obligation of all Jewry to aid in its upbuilding as a Jewish homeland (From the Columbus Platform: "Guiding Principles of Reform Judaism" [1937]; reprinted in Meyer 1988, 389)

45. While the 1937 Columbus Platform still regards Judaism primarily as a religion (see note 44 above), the San Francisco Platform of 1976 speaks openly of the Jewish people and again shows the tensions between Zionism and loyalty to the modern nation state:

The State of Israel and the diaspora, in fruitful dialogue, can show how a people transcends nationalism even as it affirms it, thereby setting an example for humanity which remains largely concerned with dangerously parochial goals . . . Until the recent past our obligations to the Jewish people and to all humanity seemed congruent. At times now these two imperatives appear to conflict. We know of no simple way to resolve such tensions. We must, however, confront them without abandoning either of our commitments. A universal concern for humanity unaccompanied by a devotion to our particular people is self-destructive; a passion for our people without involvement in humankind contradicts what the prophets have meant to us. Judaism calls us simultaneously to universal and particular obligations. (From the San Francisco Platform: "Reform Judaism—A Centenary Perspective [1976]; reprinted in Meyer 1988, 393-394)

46. Reflecting the deceptive nature of the Reform rhetoric on intermarriage, Levenson (1989, 322) notes that in 1807 the Paris Sanhedrin "gave Napoleon a qualified 'no' which they hoped he would take as a qualified 'yes.'"

47. There is good reason to view most manifestations of the Jewish left, which originated in the late 19th century, as a secular form of Judaism. See *SAID* (ch. 6).

48. As also noted by Katz (1986, 32) and Woocher (1986, 8), the attempt to portray Judaism as a religion must be seen as a rationalization for a movement that has remained at its core an national/ethnic group strategy. Indeed, Elazar (1980, 23) notes that, while a religious conceptualization of Judaism retains its usefulness in the contemporary United States, in Latin America Jews are viewed as an ethnic minority with their own mother country (Israel).

# 5

# RESOURCE AND REPRODUCTIVE COMPETITION BETWEEN JEWS AND GENTILES

One type of Moroccan Muslim folktale depicts the Jews as evildoers who seek to inflict harm upon the Muslims and Islam, but whose nefarious machinations are thwarted. Another type consists of humorous stories in which the Jew tries to get the better of a Muslim, but is outwitted by the latter . . . .

The Moroccan Jewish folktales present a reverse image of the Jewish-Muslim contest of wits: in them it is not the Muslim, but the Jew who wins. They tell of rivalry between a righteous Jewish and a wicked Muslim courtier, of clashes between a Jew and a Muslim in which the clever Jew triumphs over the foolish Muslim, of kings of Marrakesh favorably disposed to the Jews. (Patai 1986, 126-127)

The preceding chapters indicate that throughout its history Judaism may be conceptualized as a group that has maintained genetic and cultural separatism from gentile societies, while living as a diaspora among them. As indicated in Chapter 1, this state of affairs may be conceptualized as a pseudo-speciation, and the evolutionist must then attempt to characterize the ecological relationship between the pseudo-species.

We have seen that an important aspect of traditional Jewish religious ideology has been that Judaism has an altruistic role to play vis-à-vis the gentile world (e.g., Kohler [1918] 1968, 339-340, 375; Moore 1927-30, I:229). An evolutionary perspective suggests rather that all humans possess adaptations that motivate them to attempt to control resources and achieve reproductive success. The present chapter indicates that not uncommonly Jews and gentiles have had conflicts of interest over control of resources and that these conflicts have had implications for differential reproductive success between Jews and gentiles. Further, although resource competition is clearly not the only factor involved in anti-Semitism, data reviewed here support the proposition that resource competition has often exacerbated anti-Semitism.[1]

# JEWS AS INTERMEDIARIES IN TRADITIONAL SOCIETIES

It must be noted at the outset that there has been a recurring situation related to Jewish economic and reproductive competition: In traditional societies, Jews have commonly been utilized as an intermediary group between a ruling elite (and especially alien elites) and the native population. In these situations, the elite gentile group has often actively encouraged Jewish economic interests to the detriment of other sectors of the native population.

Thus, Baer (1961, I:33) notes that Jews tended to become prominent in autocratic societies, rather than in those in which there was a powerful aristocracy: "In a republic headed by aristocratic families there was no room for Jewish statesmen. On the other hand, a monarch or other autocrat, the absolute ruler over an unfriendly native population, would attract to his service Jews—the perpetual 'aliens'—on whose loyal support he could count in securing his regime. This phenomenon, in varying forms, manifested itself time and again also in the history of Christian Europe." Thus, for example, in medieval England, the Jewish population was utilized as a source of revenue for the king, while very hostile attitudes toward Jews developed among the aristocracy and the peasants (Roth 1978). Ultimately the increasing power of the aristocracy was an important factor in the eventual expulsion of the Jews, and the expulsion was also highly popular among the peasants and the clergy.[2]

Using foreigners as intermediaries is an example of a general phenomenon noticed by Balch (1986), who finds that despotic rulers have often attempted to develop a bureaucracy made up of individuals with no family or kinship ties (and thus no loyalty) to the people who were being ruled. The evolutionary aspects of this situation are obvious. Jews were the ideal intermediary for any exploitative elite precisely because their interests, as a genetically segregated group, were maximally divergent from those of the exploited population. Such individuals are expected to have maximal loyalty to the rulers and minimal concerns about behaving in a purely instrumental manner, including exploitation, toward the rest of the population.

Katz (1961a, 55) expresses it well when he notes in his comments on the economic position of the Ashkenazi Jews in 16th-18th century Europe that "[s]ince Jewish society was segregated religiously and socially from the other classes, its attitude toward them was likely to be almost purely instrumental. . . . The non-Jew had no fear that the Jew would take a partisan stand in the struggle between the rulers and the ruled, who bore the economic yoke of the political privileges enjoyed by the rulers." The corollary of this is that anti-Semitism has tended to have strong popular roots in traditional societies and that autocratic rulers and aristocratic elements who were least in competition with Jews have often been forces against anti-Semitism. Writing of the period after the Thirty Years War, Israel (1985) notes that in central Europe the trend was for princes to develop Jewish policies that were completely contrary to the interests of the populace and the clergy. Repeated instances are given in which the nobility extended invitations to Jewish merchants and traders despite the vehement objections of native commercial interests.

These findings are congruent with cross-cultural research indicating that elites around the world tend to be far more individualistic and have less loyalty to the group than lower-status individuals (Triandis 1990, 1991). Elites are unlikely to identify with the interests of the society as a whole, and they are relatively eager to agree to arrangements that are personally beneficial, even if they negatively impact other groups of the society.

This phenomenon is therefore not restricted to Jews, but Jews as "perpetual aliens" have often been utilized in this role. Shibituni and Kwan (1965, 191-192) note many such examples, including East Indians in Burma, the Chinese in several areas of Asia, Middle Easterners (Greeks, Syrians, Lebanese) serving as middlemen between colonial Europeans and Africans, Indians in East Africa, and Arabs in Indonesia. In all of these cases, the middlemen were highly vulnerable, since their power came from a dominant elite, and especially so in times of stress. "In effect, the price the minority pays for protection in times of minimal stress is to be placed on the front lines of battle in any showdown between the elite and the peasant groups (Blalock 1967, 82).

In the present chapter, evidence will be provided for this phenomenon both in Sephardic Spain under Christian and Moslem rulers and among the Ashkenazi Jews in Europe dating from the early modern period in Poland and echoed in alliances between Jewish financiers and the ruling aristocracy in 19th-century Western Europe. However, this type of relationship between Jewish and gentile populations has been found even in antiquity at the very dawn of diaspora Judaism. Baron (1952a, 117) notes that the Jews had special status as imperial clients of the Persian government in the fifth century B.C. in the Elephantine province in Egypt. However, "this governmental favoritism brought about a natural resentment in the native majority" (p. 116; see also Sevenster 1975, 49, 182). Later, during the Hellenistic period, Seleucid and Ptolemaic rulers settled Jews in Osroene, Cyrenaica, Egypt, Syria, Parthia, and throughout Western Anatolia (Bickerman 1988, 91; A. Y. Collins 1985, 193-194). These colonists typically were allowed to live according to their own laws (i.e., in a culturally separatist manner). The Jews had a status midway between citizens and resident aliens, and they acted as a counterforce to the local Greco-Asiatic populations. When the power of the Hellenistic kings declined, tensions between Jews, living in their separated communities, and the citizens increased, and there were attempts to abolish Jewish privileges. Baron (1952b, 103) also suggests that the diaspora Jews were useful to the authorities in the Roman Empire because of their lack of interest in the nationalistic strivings of local populations.

Similarly, Stillman (1979) notes several such instances in the Muslim world in which foreign rulers used Jews as intermediaries over subject populations. For example, Jews prospered during the Fatimid occupation of Tunisia (10th century); during and following the Arab conquest of Spain (8th-11th centuries; see also Castro 1954); during the early period following Mongol rule in Iraq (13th century; see also Fischel 1937); during the Merinid occupation of Morocco (13th-15th centuries); during the early Ottoman period (16th century); in 20th-century Morocco, where after 1912 they formed a layer between the French colonial government and the Muslim population as part of the French government's "*diviser pour régner*" colonial policy in which minorities, including Jews, were actively encouraged in a role over subject populations; and in the regime of the "outsider" King Faysal in 20th century Iraq. Finally, in the post-World War II era Jews were useful to the Soviets in establishing anti-popular satellite governments in Eastern Europe (Ginsberg 1993, 33).

In Iraq (1291), Spain (1066), Tunisia (1012), Morocco (1276, 1465), and Jewish settlements in Ottoman areas (end of the 16th century and during the 19th century following the civil emancipation of the Jews), these interludes of prosperity were punctuated by violent popular anti-Jewish uprisings occurring concomitantly with the decline of control by the central government.

Co-incident with this role as intermediary between ruling elites and the rest of the population has been a strong tradition in which Jews who were prominently placed among the gentile power structure furthered the aims of their co-religionists—a phenomenon that is intimately related to the Jewish emphasis on elitism in education and marriage (see Chapter 7), as well as the importance of altruism and cooperation within the Jewish community (see Chapter 6). The archetype of the well-placed courtier who helps other Jews, while oppressing the local population, is Joseph in the Biblical account of the sojourn in Egypt. Joseph intercedes with the pharaoh on behalf of his family: "Then Joseph settled his father and his brothers, and gave them a possession in the land of Egypt, in the best of the land . . ." (Gen. 47:11). However, the account also emphasizes Joseph's role in oppressing the Egyptians on behalf of the king. Joseph sells grain to the Egyptians during a famine until he has all of their money. He then requires the Egyptians to give their livestock for food and finally their land. "The land became the Pharaoh's; and as for the people, he made slaves of them from one end of Egypt to the other" (Gen. 47:20-21). However, regarding the Israelites, the section continues: "Thus Israel dwelt in the land of Egypt, in the land of Goshen; and they gained possessions in it, and were fruitful and multiplied exceedingly" (Gen. 47:27).

The prototypical Jewish role as an instrument of governmental oppression has been that of the tax farmer.[3] This phenomenon appears to have begun in ancient times: Although the details of the account are disputed by some historians (see Sevenster 1975, 67), Josephus describes Joseph, a Jew in the court of the

Ptolemies, who was an extremely effective tax farmer whose bid was twice as high as the bids of the local principle men and rulers of the areas where the taxes were collected. "The king was pleased to hear that offer; and, because it augmented his revenues, said he would confirm the sale of the taxes to him" (XII:177). Joseph obtained compliance by killing prominent citizens and confiscating their property in areas that refused to pay their taxes, thereby stripping Syria "to the bone" (Bickerman 1988, 120). However, Joseph became very wealthy and was instrumental in aiding his co-religionists. Josephus concludes that Joseph "was a good man, and of great magnanimity; and brought the Jews out of a state of poverty and meanness, to one that was more splendid" (*Antiquities of the Jews* 12:224).

However, while it has generally been true that Jewish populations in traditional societies existed at the sufferance of gentile elites who benefited from them in some way, the economic role of Jews often extended far beyond that of being merely agents of princely oppression. It will be seen that, with the exception of primary (agricultural) production and in the absence of powerful controls on Jewish economic behavior, Jewish-gentile resource competition extended throughout the economy to include trade, merchandizing, moneylending, manufacturing, and artisanry. This generalized resource competition between foreign ethnic groups and native populations is also not unique to the relationships between Jews and gentiles. Zenner (1991, 75) describes a wide range of restrictions enacted against diaspora Chinese as a result of resource competition with native populations. For example, the Chinese were prohibited from owning land in Java and California and were expelled from Sonora in the 1920s. Pogroms against Chinese residents occurred in Indonesia in the 1950s, and in Sumatra, the nationalist government attempted to replace Chinese traders with natives.[4]

# THE SEPHARDIC JEWS IN THE IBERIAN PENINSULA

Baer (1961) notes repeatedly that the kings of Spain throughout the period of Reconquest viewed the Jews as performing indispensable functions, especially the collection of taxes via tax farming (see also Castro 1954; Lea 1906-07, I:98; Neuman 1969, II:221).[5] "Barring temporary fluctuations caused by war, anarchy or civil strife, it was the fixed policy of Spanish rulers for over five hundred years to conserve and increase the number of Jews in their provinces, and to protect their interests against the encroachments of the other elements of the Spanish population" (Neuman 1969, I:6).

Moreover, Baer (1961; see also Castro 1954) describes repeated attempts by kings to prevent anti-Semitic laws and behavior in Spain prior to the Inquisition. Or he shows that kings agreed to anti-Semitic measures only as a result of pressure from other classes in society, including the nobility, the clergy, and the popular masses. Even on the eve of the Inquisition and only 10 years prior to the expulsion, King Ferdinand in 1481 wrote letters condemning anti-Semitic actions to the prelates of Saragossa, but did not send them on the advice of his counselors, who told him of the popular hatred and violence against Jews in that city. Castro (1954, 504) suggests that Ferdinand's reluctant actions against the Jews stemmed from the fact that the kingdom had become ungovernable in view of the hatred of the lower clergy and the masses, "especially if it was necessary to use the people to wage wars in distant lands."

Supporting the thesis of a general alliance between the king and the Jews, Baer notes a tendency such that "every interregnum was likely to bring disaster down upon [the Jews]," including the disaster of 1391 in which there were widespread persecutions and forced conversions of Jews (Baer 1961, II:17). "The lower classes, not the upper, were behind the expulsion of the Jews, who were protected by the upper classes for centuries against all manner of attack and abuse" (Castro 1954, 618).[6]

Resource competition (and anti-Semitism) therefore came from the non-royal estates of Spain. Thus, for example, in 1283, the clergy, nobility, and burghers attempted to end the Jewish influence in government, each estate having its own interests in competition with the Jews (Baer 1961, I:115). Hillgarth (1976) notes that the resulting limitations on Jewish competition resulted in an expansion of opportunities for the non-Jewish bourgeoisie. Early in the 14th century, the king reappointed Jewish tax farmers with the result that "The old rivalries between the Christian and Jewish courtiers thereupon flared up anew" (Baer 1961, I:308; see also I:326). "Every important post held by a Jew was deeply resented by the many disgruntled noblemen who coveted the office" (Neuman 1969, I:226).

Besides rivalries among Jewish and non-Jewish courtiers, there was a gradually increasing tide of popular anti-Semitism dating from at least the 11th century, which culminated in the anti-Jewish riots of 1391, the anti-Converso[7] riots of the 15th century, and eventually the Inquisition itself (Beinart 1971a; Haliczer 1987; Lea 1906-07; Roth 1974). Even in the latter part of the 13th century, Baer (1961) writes of "deep and widespread unrest" resulting in anti-Semitic actions (I:167). Neuman (1969 I:13) describes the "ever-present danger from the surrounding population" and the bitter economic rivalry between the Jews and the burghers who "sought to impose legal restrictions on them in order to cripple them in the competitive struggle," including restrictions on engaging in handicrafts and trade and even barring Jews from entering into contracts of any kind with Christians (Neuman 1969, I:185).[8]

In the 1370s, anti-Semitism was strongest among the urban lower classes: "the artisans who aspired to wrest control of the municipalities and the mendicant friars who mingled with the poor" (Baer 1961, II:86). Indeed, regarding the riots of 1391, the king made active efforts to defend the Jews, prosecute the offenders, and rehabilitate the Jewish communities after the riots. The rioters, on the other hand, were mainly "little people," although "in every locality noble families and even priests had been involved in the crimes" (Baer 1961, II:99). Castro (1971 339-340) writes of the conflicting interests of the opposed castes (i.e., Spaniards, Muslims, and Jews)—a conflict that "was translated into the enmity of the lower classes toward the bourgeoisie of the cities, who were qualified for leadership by their culture, their economic power, their administrative and technical efficiency, and who were, irremediably, Hispano-Judaic."

Besides direct competition among artisans and over jobs in public administration, several authors have noted that popular anti-Semitism derived from Jewish moneylending, and especially tax farming. Neuman (1969, II:226) notes that, "as the Jews were conspicuously identified with the collection of the royal revenue, and the people groaned under the burden of taxes, the Jewish officials were hated by the populace as tools of oppression" (see also Lea 1906-07, I:100; H. Kamen 1985). In the event, the anti-Jewish activities of the Inquisition had "near unanimous" popular support throughout the Iberian peninsula (Baron 1973, 261).

The popular uprisings against the Jews in the 14th and 15th centuries were often fomented by the Church, which was also in competition with the Jews. For example, Jewish domination of the Castilian king Pedro the Cruel was used as a political weapon by his victorious enemies in a fratricidal civil war ending in 1369, with the result that the power of the Church increased and the power of the Jews decreased at the royal court (Baer 1961, I:190). Castro (1954, 511) notes that from the Church's point of view the alliance between the government and the Jews in the area of fiscal affairs and tax farming deprived the Church of revenue. "A permanent abyss was carved between the people and the government, and also between the state and the Church, because in the Jew the kings had a convenient source of income and in the Church a rival that was taking it away from them." Castro (1954, 512) also notes that "[c]hurchmen of lesser rank never ceased complaining of the favor shown the Jews by the Spanish monarchs." In the long run, the government was unable to oppose this ecclesiastical-popular alliance. Ultimately, it was the clergyman Ferdinand Martinez who fomented the popular discontent that resulted in the massacres of 1391 (and ultimately led to the Inquisition).

Castro (1954, 539) notes that "[i]n the thirteenth and fourteenth century the Jew had dreamed of the possibility of dominating Castile, the new promised land. He had in his hands the promotion and administration of wealth of the kingdom as well as the technical and scientific knowledge possible at that time." Resource competition and the belief that the Jews were intent on dominating Spain intensified in the period following the forced conversions of 1391, since there were no longer any restrictions on the upward mobility of the Conversos as there had been on the Jews.[9]

In the period following the riots of 1391, Jews who had been forcibly converted "continued to maintain the hold of their class and race on trading and capital" (Kamen 1965, 7). Johnson (1987), Roth (1974), and Salomon (1974) write of the conflict between the Spanish masses and the Conversos that developed when the latter had entered Spanish society in the 15th century, "quickly penetrating the ranks of the Castilian middle and upper classes and occupying the most prominent positions in the royal administration and the Church hierarchy" (Salomon 1974, IX). The economic progress of the Conversos and their descendants was "phenomenally rapid. . . . The law, the administration, the army, the universities, the Church itself, were all overrun by recent converts of more or less questionable sincerity, or by their immediate descendents. They thronged the financial administration, for which they had a natural aptitude, protest being now impossible. They pushed their way into the municipal councils,[10] into the legislatures, into the judiciary. They all but dominated Spanish life. The wealthier amongst them intermarried with the highest nobility of the land" (Roth 1974, 21).[11]

Indeed, Walsh (1940, 144) describes a common belief during the period that the New Christians "were planning to rule Spain, enslave the Christians, and establish a New Jerusalem in the West."[12] These beliefs were abetted by two tracts written by the Converso Selemoh ha-Levi, formerly a highly respected rabbi, but later the Bishop of Burgos, in which he declared that the Jews were attempting to rule Spain. Another common belief was that the Conversos had infiltrated both the aristocracy and the Church and were attempting to destroy Spanish society from within (H. Kamen 1985).

Resource competition appears to be an important factor in the anti-Converso activities of the 15th century. Thus, the anti-Converso riots of 1449 in Cuidad Real, like those in Toledo and elsewhere, were the result of the increasing political and economic influence of the Conversos at the municipal level, with the result that "it was the notaries, *alludes*, and other office-holders and notables who were the first to be hit" (Beinart 1981, 58; see also Kamen 1965, 22). The riots of 1474 were "concerted actions by local inhabitants" (Beinart 1981, 63). Guilds were organized along ethnic lines during the Converso period prior to the Inquisition (H. Kamen 1985), so that economic competition between Jews and gentiles continued even after surface religious-group membership ceased to differentiate the two groups. Moreover, the legal exclusion of Conversos from some craft guilds and city offices prior to the Inquisition (Beinart 1971a; Haliczer 1987) suggests Jewish competition with the gentile non-aristocracy was an issue.

Since the Church was an important avenue of upward mobility, another source of competition between the New and Old Christians was access to the ecclesiastical administration. Many authors have noted the penetration of the Conversos into high positions in the Church, and Kamen (1965, 23) notes the struggle between the Conversos and the Old Christians over access to the ecclesiastical administration. The Old Christians "resented sharing power with men of mixed race and doubtful orthodoxy." The clergyman Fray Alonso, a major instigator of the Inquisition, is depicted as angered by seeing the large number of Conversos filling important posts in the court of Queen Isabella. When Archbishop Siliceo, a man of humble origin, advocated *limpieza* (i.e., purity of blood) statutes to deny Conversos access to the Church, he was in effect making a brief for privileged access to resources for his social class.[13]

Similarly, the Portuguese New Christians in the 16th century moved up socially even more rapidly than did the Spanish New Christians in the previous century. "Their wealth was enormous. . . . They almost monopolized commerce" (Roth 1974, 76), and they became well established in politics, literature, medicine, the military, and even the clergy. "They grew rich and prosperous, they intermarried with the noblest houses, and they largely entered the Church . . . much of the active capital of the kingdom was in their hands" (Lea 1906-1907, III:238-239).

There is also evidence of a contemporary concern with Jewish reproductive success. Andrés Bernáldez, a defender of the Inquisition and self-conscious spokesman for the viewpoint of the masses, noted that the Conversos had risen "to the rank of scholars, doctors, bishops, canons, priests and priors of monasteries, auditors and secretaries, farmers of Crown revenues and grandees. They had one aim: to increase and multiply" (quoted in Beinart 1981, 21-22; see also Longhurst 1964). Indeed, the Bull of Pope Sixtus IV of 1478 establishing the authority for the Inquisition noted not only that there were crypto-Jews, but also that "their numbers increase not a little" (quoted in Walsh 1940, 149). Concerns about the reproductive success of Jews and their descendants extended well beyond the beginning of the Inquisition: Baron (1973, 186, 241) refers to widespread concern about the reproductive success of the New Christians in early-17th-century Spain and Portugal. For example, Baron notes that a conference of theologians concluded in 1629 that the descendants of Jews proliferated like "the sands of the sea."[14]

Resource competition between New Christians and Old Christians also continued long after the establishment of the Spanish and Portuguese Inquisitions. Boyajian (1983) recounts the opposition of Spanish merchants to the increasing influence of Portuguese New Christians at the Madrid court, beginning in the 1620s as a result of the New Christian involvement in financing the Spanish monarchy. In order to obtain the cooperation of the New Christians, the monarchy supported granting the demands of the New Christians, including relaxing the Inquisition, giving them the right to participate in Spanish trading ventures, and allowing them to enter military orders of the aristocracy, which had been closed off by *limpieza* laws. However, these interests conflicted with the interests of the Old Christian merchants in Seville and elsewhere in the Spanish Empire, and the latter found powerful allies in the Churches and the Inquisitions of Spain, Portugal, and the New World. Although the monarchy advanced these causes and protected the New Christians for a considerable period, the Old Christian courtiers, urban patricians and merchants, and churchmen eventually prevailed, and the Inquisition and its concern with *limpieza* were reinvigorated, especially in the period following the independence of Portugal in 1640.[15]

A very interesting case involving Sephardic Jews after their emigration from the Iberian peninsula is represented by Venice in the 16th century. In Venice, Jews competed successfully against the local merchants and "aroused great jealousy" (Roth 1974, 210), leading to a temporary expulsion. Davidson (1987, 24) finds that anti-Semitic sentiments in 16th-century Venice "were often inspired by economic rivalry" and notes the development of Christian sources of credit by wealthy families attempting to avoid Jewish moneylenders. In the words of two contemporary Venetian patricians, Jewish moneylending is the means by which they "consume and devour the people of this our city" (p. 24).

It is of interest, however, that the Venetian authorities eventually developed very precise and minutely detailed regulations on Jewish economic activity, which appear to have minimized anti-Semitism because the Jewish economic role was intended to "complement, rather than compete with, the activities of long-established Venetian nobility and citizenry" (Pullan 1983, 146). Jews were forbidden to own land, could not become artisans or engage in manufacturing, and could only charge 5 percent interest on loans.[16] The result was that "Venetians in general could not be relied upon to despise or detest them, save perhaps at certain seasons of the year such as carnival or Passiontide" (p. 159). The role of this intensive regulation of Jewish economic activity in minimizing anti-Semitism was recognized by a contemporary rabbi who, describing the causes of anti-Semitism elsewhere, noted that

> Usury makes them unpopular with all the orders of the city; engaging in crafts with the lesser people; the possession of property with nobles and great men. These are the reasons why the Jews do not dwell in many places. But these circumstances do not arise in Venice, where the rate of interest is only 5 percent, and the banks are established for the benefit of the poor and not for the profit of the bankers. The Jews cannot engage in crafts or manufacture, nor can they own real property. Hence they do not seem burdensome or threatening to any estate or order within the city. (Quoted in Pullan 1983, 159)

However, these restrictions did not prevent continuing hostility centering around Jewish competition in trade, and there was concern that Jews would emigrate to the Levant with the great wealth obtained by trading in Venice and that this wealth would eventually benefit the Turks in their wars with Venice.[17] Eventually, the government allowed Jews to dominate trade at the expense of gentile traders and was content to profit from the taxes generated by this economic activity. However, despite the decline of Venetian gentile traders, the gentile community as a whole may have continued to benefit from the international Jewish trading network, since, besides taxes, the exported goods and the goods and services consumed by the Jewish community were manufactured by gentiles.

The example is instructive because it indicates that in traditional societies a sort of "win-win" economic situation could exist in which Jewish economic activity benefited the society as a whole. However, the example also shows that this type of situation occurred only when there were very powerful, rigidly enforced controls on Jewish economic activity. In the absence of such controls, the evidence from this chapter indicates that there is a general tendency for resource competition with most sectors of the gentile economy in traditional societies.

# ASHKENAZI JEWS IN EARLY MODERN POLAND

There is excellent evidence for resource competition between Jews and non-Jews throughout Polish history, as well as for the hypothesis of a significant alliance between the Jews and the aristocracy. In the post-medieval period in Poland most Jews lived in privately owned towns, and the owners often encouraged Jewish settlement. The Polish nobility welcomed Jews as estate managers and toll farmers, bankers, and moneylenders. They also encouraged Jewish trade and commerce because, as a consuming class, they benefited from the lower prices brought on by competition (Weinryb 1972; see also Hundert 1986a; Katz 1961a; Tollet 1986).

The preponderance of Jewish economic activity was ultimately the result of franchises derived from the nobility, but eventually, due to increasing numbers, Jews began engaging in non-franchised economic activity such as artisanry—activity that brought them into direct competition with other sectors of the Polish population. There was competition between gentile and Jewish craftsmen, such as butchers, tailors, blacksmiths, and shoemakers, in which non-Jewish guilds attempted to eliminate Jewish craftsmen (Katz 1961a; Weinryb 1972, 64-67). Moreover, non-Jewish merchants often viewed Jews as competitors, and there were periodic attempts to restrict Jewish trade and business, especially in areas where Jews lived on lands owned by the king. For example, in 1485, there was an agreement between the Jewish community and the city council of Cracow in which the Jews agreed to give up trade and most selling, and in 1764, Jews were barred from trade in cattle, grain, and horses. In the 16th century, Jewish rights of commerce were limited in several cities, and other cities were granted the privilege of excluding Jews altogether. In the late 19th century, the Galician government organized an economic boycott of Jewish businesses with a slogan of "buy from your own kind" (Litman 1984, 7), with the result that the Jewish population suffered an economic decline and many emigrated.

Nevertheless, despite recurrent restrictions and exclusions, Jews had essentially won this competition in the areas of trade and artisanry by the time of the 1764 census (Klier 1986, 10). Hundert (1986a) notes that Jews increasingly dominated small-scale domestic commerce and, by the 18th century, they dominated trade with the West as well. The Jewish share of commerce "increased dramatically" (p. 57) from the 16th to the 18th century. Beauvois (1986) notes that there were 12,285 Jewish merchants compared to 1,790 Christian merchants in previously Polish provinces of the Russian Empire in 1840. Moreover, there is considerable evidence that some Jewish families obtained great wealth. "Jews in Poland . . . were building tax farming, estate leasing, and commercial empires; erecting large houses to live in; and trying to amass (to some extent successfully) large fortunes to leave to their children" (Weinryb 1972, 168).

These trends are well captured in the case study of the town of Opatow from the 17th through the 18th century (Hundert 1992). Jews began settling there in the 16th century, and even in 1569, there is an indication of concern by Christian merchants about Jewish competition. In the 17th century, there was a gradual rise in the percentage of trade controlled by Jews in the region, and Jews began to lease the estates of the nobleman who owned the town. Already in the 17th-century, Jews were reluctant to join Christian guilds, and there were anti-Semitic incidents. By the end of the 18th century, Jews dominated almost all areas of trading, manufacturing, and estate managing, and they had become dominant among the artisans as well. Competition was most intense between Jewish and Christian artisans, and there were constant complaints that Jews refused to join Christian guilds, that they controlled the trade in raw materials, that they imported finished products into the town, and that they encouraged Jews not to buy from Christians—complaints that were common throughout Poland at the time. By the end of the 18th century, there were Jewish guilds for butchers, furriers, and hatmakers, and Christians had been almost completely displaced as butchers, bakers, tailors, furriers, and goldsmiths. Corresponding with these developments, Christians increasingly abandoned artisanry in order to work in agriculture.

Similarly, in the area of commerce, Jews were accused of not participating in Christian guilds, and "there were complaints . . . that Jews had pushed Christians entirely out of commerce" (Hundert 1992, 54), with the result that Christian merchants were forced to move elsewhere. Reflecting the separate worlds of Jew and gentile in the town, Jewish merchants complained when a Greek merchant hired a Jewish agent to promote business, with the result that the Greek was forced to hire someone of his own religion. Following this, "Jewish domination of the town's commerce . . . was almost complete" (p. 57). Finally, Jews came to dominate all phases of the alcoholic beverage business, including manufacture, distribution, and retail.[18]

The Jewish community generally prospered not only economically, but also reproductively during this period. The Jewish expansion into almost all phases of the economy supported a Jewish population of Opatow that increased dramatically from the late 17th century until about 1770. Although the Jewish population then stagnated or declined somewhat, there was increasing emigration to surrounding towns and to Warsaw by Jews who could not be supported in the local economy. Clearly, the economic success of the Jews had translated into a high level of reproductive success as well.

This increasing Jewish economic domination resulted in clashes with the gentile population most affected by this competition. Weinryb (1972, 140) notes that "[i]n all these attempts to limit or exclude Jews and other minorities from trade and crafts, as in the staged violence, it was the lower strata of the city, the small trader, the artisan, and the mob, who were in the forefront of the struggle. The urban elite, the wealthy merchants, were generally less apt to fear Jewish (or any other) competition." Writing of the 19th century, Kieniewicz (1986, 75) notes that mistrust and hatred were common between Jewish and Christian shopkeepers, pedlars, and middlemen.

Finally, despite the general alliance between the Jews and the nobility, there was significant competition at least some of the time between Jews and all except the very highest levels of Polish society. Weinryb (1972, 60; see also Tollet 1986) notes that in the 15th century, the lower nobility competed with the Jews in the areas of agricultural export and toll farming. Laws were made to prevent Jews from lending money, to restrict the interest rates charged by Jews, and to prevent Jews from farming tolls. Weinryb (1972, 121) also describes a concern among the nobility for the "huge increase" in the Jewish population (and their "fabulous wealth"), which resulted in various restrictions on Jews.

# RESOURCE COMPETITION BETWEEN JEWS AND GENTILES IN EUROPE FOLLOWING JEWISH EMANCIPATION

The post-Enlightenment period generally ended the formal alliances between Jews and gentile elites so characteristic of traditional societies. Nevertheless, as indicated in Chapter 4, this did not end *de facto* Jewish separatism, and the evidence provided below indicates that Jewish-gentile resource competition continued and perhaps actually increased during this period.

Jews had a very powerful advantage in this competition. As indicated by the data presented in Chapter 7, Jews, because of their long history of eugenic practices and emphasis on education, were uniquely suited to upward mobility in the newly developing industrial economies of the period. Sorkin (1987, 108) makes the interesting point that the German advocates of Jewish emancipation envisioned Jews as fitting into an agrarian society by entering "productive" occupations such as farming and artisanry (see also Katz 1986, 68ff). The hope among the pro-emancipation forces of the period was that the Jewish economic, educational, and occupational profile would be similar to that of the gentiles. However, Jewish emancipation resulted in marked differences in the economic, educational, and occupational profiles of Jews and Germans.

Lindemann (1991, 10) notes that "[i]n the long history of the Jews, the rise of the Jews in the nineteenth century has few parallels in terms of the rapid transformation of the condition of the Jews—in absolute and relative numbers, wealth, in fame, in power, and in influence." The extraordinary rise of Jews in Germany in the period from 1870 to 1933 following emancipation was a general phenomenon. Jews were concentrated in urban areas and in particular occupations. In general, they were vastly overrepresented in areas requiring a high level of education (business, professions, public service) and underrepresented in agriculture and domestic service—a pattern that Gordon (1984) finds had existed since the Middle Ages. In 1871, when the Jews became fully emancipated in Germany, 60 percent were already in the middle- and upper-income brackets (Sorkin 1987, 110).

Mosse (1987, 204) estimates that despite representing less than 1 percent of the population, Jews controlled 20 percent of the commercial activity in Germany in the period from 1819 to 1935, as indicated by percentages of Jews among the economic elite. Moreover, Jewish involvement in the largest companies was even more substantial than this figure might indicate. For example, Mosse (1987, 273-274) finds that in 1907 Jews had a dominant position in 33 of the 100 largest companies and in 9 of the 13 companies with share capital over 100 million marks. Jews occupied a similar position through the Weimar period (pp. 357-358). In some areas where Jews were concentrated, the overrepresentation of Jews was far higher. Thus, in the capital of Berlin, Jews accounted for nearly 45 percent of the official government *Kommerzienrat* awards given to outstanding businessmen, and in Prussia in 1911 44 percent of the 25 richest millionaires were Jews, as were 27.5 percent of the 200 richest millionaires and 23.7 percent of the 800 richest. In Berlin, as in the Hesse-Nassau area, 12 of the 20 wealthiest taxpayers were Jews.

In the period from 1928 to 1932, Jews controlled 25 percent of retail sales and had a dominant position in certain areas, such as metal businesses, textiles and clothing, grain trade, and department stores (Gordon 1984). Jews also had a prominent position in private banking, so that, for example, in Berlin in 1923, there were 150 Jewish banks and 11 non-Jewish banks. And Jews were also prominently involved in the stock market, the insurance industry, and economic consulting firms. In 1923 Jews occupied 24 percent of the supervisory positions in joint-stock companies. Gordon (1984) also shows that Jews were vastly overrepresented in the legal and judicial system, among university faculty, and as physicians.

At times, the competitive benefit of Jewish group membership was decisive. Thus, in attempting to account for the almost complete absence of gentile banking enterprises in Prussia in the late 19th century, Mosse (1987, 117) emphasizes the competitive advantage enjoyed by Jewish banking firms resulting from the patronage of the Rothschilds, who provided them with capital and higher credit ratings. Jewish banks also had a competitive advantage because, as emphasized in Chapter 6, they were able to take advantage of international Jewish contacts, which were not available to their gentile competitors.[19] In the era after 1900, all of the large joint-stock banks had a prominent representation of Jews on their boards of directors (Mosse 1987, 158). The result was the development of a separate "Jewish sector" of the German economy in which there were "virtually two separate economies" (Mosse 1987, 275).[20]

However, the largest overrepresentation of Jews in Germany during this period was in the media: the theater, arts, film, and journalism. In Berlin in 1930, fully 80 percent of the theater directors were Jewish, and Jews wrote 75 percent of the plays produced. Jews edited leading newspapers and were vastly overrepresented among journalists (Gordon 1984; see also Laqueur 1974). Not surprisingly, average Jewish income was considerably higher than average gentile income, with tax return data suggesting that the Jewish/gentile income ratio was at least 2 to 1, and more probably in the range of 4 to 1.[21]

This prosperity was associated with higher aggregate reproductive success than the gentile population: In the period from 1820-1871 in Germany the Jewish population increased faster than the Christian population (74 percent to 63 percent), despite the fact that Jews entered the demographic transition a full generation earlier than the rest of Germany. Jews had a lower fertility than Christians, and the men married later, but marriage restrictions on Jews had been lifted, and the infant mortality rate among Jews was lower.[22]

Jewish economic success was associated with anti-Semitism throughout Europe. Lindemann (1991, 10) describes the "rise of the Jews" during the 19th century in Europe as a necessary condition for the modern forms of anti-Semitism that began to appear in the latter part of the century. Lindemann shows that Jews were encroaching on traditional economic and social areas that were formerly exclusively Christian; that Jews were vastly overrepresented in professional occupations, which represented a common means of upward mobility for Jews and gentiles; and that they had attained considerable political influence, thereby diminishing the power and control emanating from traditional sources.

There is evidence that anti-Semitism in Germany in the period after 1870 was strongest among those most in competition with Jews.[23] Bracher (1970, 38) makes the general statement that in the period following 1870, "Anti-Semitism as a separate movement or as part of an increasingly popular race theory generally flared up in times of economic and political crisis." Gordon (1984, 44) notes that "it is difficult to reject these [economic] differences out of hand as non-existent or unimportant, and they probably continued to contribute to anti-Semitism because they fostered group tensions . . . ."

Massing (1949) shows that a concern with disproportionate Jewish representation in education[24] and the occupational profile of Jews was a common ingredient of the wave of racial anti-Semitism that occurred among urban Germans during the period from 1870 to 1895. The anti-Semitic press and anti-Semitic politicians routinely called attention to Jewish overrepresentation in higher education, business, and the professions and to their underrepresentation among artisans and farmers (see also Ragins 1980, 69). Their agitation struck a responsive chord among the upwardly mobile members of the German lower middle classes:

> Insecurity and instability were the dominant notes of their existence. Taking advantage of easier access to higher education, members of the lower middle classes vigorously pushed their way up into new occupations which had only a limited absorptive capacity. Competition was bitterly intense and the competitors were frequently Jewish. That aspirants from the lower middle classes, unsure of their prospects, were particularly sensitive to this fact is testified to by numerous, recurring complaints about the disproportionately high ratio of Jewish high school pupils and university students, lawyers, and physicians. (Massing 1949, 76)

Calls for restrictions on the economic and political roles of Jews were characteristic of the many unsuccessful anti-Semitic political movements dating from the 19th century in Germany (Bracher 1970, 44; see Massing 1949, *passim*). Gordon (1984, 199) notes that during the Nazi era, "the majority of Germans appeared to approve the nonviolent exclusion of Jews from German life, as indicated by their general acceptance of quotas, the elimination of Jews from the civil service and the professions, and the Nuremberg laws [which penalized sexual contact between Jews and gentiles]." This general approval of non-violent exclusion is highly compatible with a widespread concern among Germans about Jewish competition.[25]

Anti-Semitism was typically more characteristic of the lower middle class and urban petty bourgeoisie in Western and Central Europe, while in Eastern Europe, anti-Semitism also occurred among the gentry threatened by the rise of the Jews. In the former areas, anti-Semitism was most common among artisans, clerks, shopkeepers threatened by Jewish-owned department stores, and those who felt deprived of the opportunity of upward mobility because of Jewish overrepresentation in professional schools.[26] On the other hand, Lindemann (1991, 46) notes that anti-Semitism was relatively muted in Hungary where the native middle and lower classes were small, so the arrival of Jews did not displace an already existing group. However, as Jews began to dominate economic life in Hungary, and increasingly bought up land previously owned by the aristocracy and gentry, anti-Semitism became more common among these classes as well, and there were efforts to halt Jewish immigration from Russia.

In Russia, restrictions on Jews were justified by the authorities because they feared that the Slavic peasants could not compete with the Jews in the newly industrializing economy—fears made more intense because of the tremendous growth in Jewish population in the 19th century (Lindemann 1991, 135-137). Jews were viewed as more intelligent, more educated, and more able to compete economically than the mass of Russians by a broad range of political opinion,[27] with the result that the authorities viewed completely free economic competition with considerable trepidation. "There was, in short, a rather widespread consensus in Russia that Jews were a separate, somehow superior race, stubbornly resisting assimilation, and steadily working to dominate those among whom they lived" (Lindemann 1991, 138-139).

The Russian pogroms of 1881 were associated with Jewish population growth and increased Jewish immigration into towns, and some of the rioting was instigated by businessmen attempting to compete with Jews (Lindemann 1991, 140). Later, there was competition between middle-class Jews and gentiles in Russia (e.g., the physicians of Kishinev [p. 158], so that by the turn of the century, "[a]s in western Europe, modern racist anti-Semitism linked to nationalism seems to have been most pronounced in those urban areas where elements of the Jewish and Gentile middle classes found themselves in harsh competition" (Lindemann 1991, 144).

Anti-Semitism was relatively muted in France, where, despite the rapid rise of a Jewish bourgeoisie and a somewhat more rapid population rise than for the population as a whole, the Jewish population never exceeded 0.2 percent of the total. Nevertheless, Jews were overrepresented in the professions, finance, middle- and top-level government positions, academia and the military, and as students at elite secondary schools. Anti-Semitism occurred among several groups threatened by this rise, including French Catholics concerned about the decline in political power and patronage associated with their religion; nationalists concerned about the financial power of Jews as a foreign element, often with German origins; shopkeepers and small businessmen threatened by larger stores or factories disproportionately owned by Jews; and butchers in direct competition with Jews. The relative success of Jews was psychologically very salient to the French. A successful Jewish student (Julien Benda) recalled that his triumph in the *concours général* "appeared to me one of the essential sources of the anti-Semitism we had to bear fifteen years later. Whether the Jews realized it or not, such success was felt by other French people as an act of violence" (quoted in Johnson 1987, 382).[28]

Finally, Lindemann (1991) stresses that the rise of the Jews in 19th-century Europe not only was a matter of increased wealth and social prestige, but also involved a population explosion, especially in Eastern Europe. As indicated below, the rate of population increase among Jews during this period in Eastern Europe was much higher than that of non-Jewish populations (i.e., as a community, they had greater reproductive success). The result was that there was increasing social differentiation within the Jewish population (including considerable poverty), as well as emigration to Western Europe and America, especially in the late 1870s and 1880s. Lindemann (1991) emphasizes the contribution of the population explosion of Jews in Eastern Europe (e.g., Russia [pp. 133-135]) to anti-Semitism in a Western Europe that was inundated by Jewish immigrants (pp. 28-29).

There were also large population movements within countries from rural to urban areas. After emancipation in Austria, a great many Jews from rural areas settled in Vienna, leading to gentile perceptions of an "invasion" by an alien group (Lindemann 1991, 25), especially because gentiles were being driven out of their occupations by this large group of immigrants. Gay (1988, 20) notes that "[f]eeling beleaguered by this ever-growing Jewish presence, Austrian gentiles worried over it in humor magazines, social clubs, and political meetings. They made anxious jokes, pleaded for the assimilation of the 'alien' invaders, or, some of them, issued strident calls for their expulsion."

Before concluding this section, it is worth making a brief comment on Jewish-gentile competition in the United States in the early 20th century. As noted above in the case of France, there was concern that Jews would "overrun" prestigious private universities if intellectual merit were the only criterion (Sachar 1992, 328). As a result, quota systems were developed to restrict Jewish competition not only in private universities, but also in professional schools, although in most cases the percentage of Jewish students was still well above their representation in the population.[29] As expected, the diminished resources available during the Great Depression exacerbated these attempts to limit Jewish access to elite schools and high-status professions, or indeed other jobs. Numerical quotas in the professions became more restrictive, and employment advertisements carried an unprecedented number of restrictions on Jews. These quotas were lifted following World War II, and by 1952, Jews constituted 24 percent of the students at Harvard, 23 percent at Cornell, 20 percent at Princeton, and 13 percent at Yale despite constituting only 3 percent of the population (Sachar 1992, 755).

There are a number of other indications that Jews very rapidly achieved a highly disproportionate representation in several key areas of American society in the post-World War II era, and especially after 1960. Rothman and Lichter (1982) summarize data on the extraordinary representation of Jews in the American academy in the 1960s and 1970s. A 1968 survey found that 20 percent of the faculty at prestigious schools were Jewish, and there was a strong concentration in the social sciences, with fully 30 percent of the most productive faculty in social science departments at elite universities being Jewish. Similarly, Jews constituted 20 percent of the legal profession during this period and represented fully 38 percent of the faculty at elite law schools. Sachar (1992, 755) notes that in 1957, Jews constituted 32 of the 70 most eminent intellectuals in a list compiled by *Public Interest*, and in 1973, Jews were overrepresented by 70 percent in the *Directory of American Scholars*.

More informally, Patai and Patai (1989) found that in 1972, 6.5 percent of a sample from *Who's Who in America* were Jewish although, they represented only 2.7 percent of the population. Similarly, Weyl (1989, 21), using the Jewish last name method, found Jews overrepresented on several indices of achievement, including *Who's Who in America, American Men and Women of Science, Frontier Science and Technology, Poor's Directory of Directors, Who's Who in Finance and Industry, Directory of Medical Specialists,* and *Who's Who in American Law.*

Rothman and Lichter (1982) note that academic social science departments are an important source of social influence, and this disproportionate Jewish influence on society extended also to the media during this period. A quarter of the Washington press corps were found to be Jewish in a 1976 study, and 58 percent of the television news producers and editors at the ABC television network in a 1973 study were Jewish. A 1979 study found that Jewish background was characteristic of 27 percent of the staff at the most influential news media. During this period, half of prime-time television writers were Jewish, and 32 percent of influential media critics were Jewish.

Jewish representation in academia and the media may well have increased in recent times. Ginsberg (1993, 1) notes that as of 1993 the percentages of Jewish representation at elite academic institutions were undoubtedly higher than in the late 1960s. Ginsberg also states that despite the fact that Jews comprised only 2 percent of the population, almost half of American billionaires were Jews as were approximately 10 percent of the members of the U. S. Congress. Jewish overrepresentation continues to be apparent in the media. Kotkin (1993, 61) notes that "[t]he role of Jews within Hollywood and the related entertainment field remains pervasive." Ginsberg (1993, 1) notes that the owners of the largest newspaper chain and the most influential newspaper (*The New York Times*) are Jews, as are the chief executive officers of the three major television networks and the four largest film studios. Rothman and Lichter's (1982, 98) conclusion would appear to be accurate: "Americans of Jewish background have become an elite group in American society, with a cultural and intellectual influence far beyond their numbers."[30]

# REPRODUCTIVE COMPETITION BETWEEN JEWS AND GENTILES

As noted above, Beinart (1981, 21) cites the view of historian Andrés Bernáldez, who, writing during the period of the Inquisition, noted that the purpose of the crypto-Jews was to "increase and multiply," a comment that clearly indicates that the Old Christians were concerned about reproductive competition between themselves and the crypto-Jews of the 15th century. Baer (1961) points to the increasing Jewish population as well as the concomitant social differentiation and class conflict among the Jews from the late 13th to the 15th century. Baer cites a 14th-century observer who noted that, whereas previously the Jews were few in number and wealthy, there was now a great deal of social differentiation within the Jewish community and the Jewish quarter was densely populated. Baer also infers an increasing Jewish population from the development in the 13th century of a growing class struggle and from the growth of executive bodies within Jewish communities. Roth (1937) mentions their "rapidly increasing descendents" (p. 26) in the 15th century prior to the

Inquisition, and Lea (1906-07, I:86) notes that the number of Jews increased "until they formed a notable portion of the population."

Nevertheless, although there is agreement that the Jewish population was increasing rapidly prior to the expulsion, I have been unable to find explicit comparisons between Jewish and Christian population changes in pre-expulsion Spain. Hillgarth (1978) notes that there are no good population estimates for Castile before 1528, but suggests that the population of Aragon did not grow in the period from 1300 to 1500 and may actually have decreased, a finding that, given the Jewish demographic data discussed above, would indicate that the Jewish population increased at a greater rate than did the gentile population during this period.

There is wide agreement that at least until the demographic transition Jews in Eastern Europe had a much greater rate of natural increase than gentile populations (Deshen 1986, 46; see also Ritterband 1981; A. Goldstein 1981). Johnson (1987, 356) notes that in the period 1880-1914, the Jewish population of Europe grew at a rate of 2 percent per year, "a rate of increase that exceeds all other European peoples for this period" (Katz 1986, 4).

For Poland, Abramsky, Jachimczyk, and Polonsky (1986; see also Hundert 1986a; Hundert 1986b; Hundert 1989; Israel 1985, 163) find that the percentage of Jews in Poland increased from 0.6 percent at the end of the 15th century to 5 percent by the mid-17th century and to 10 percent by 1920.[31] Similarly, in Russia from 1820 to 1880, the Jewish population increased by 150 percent, while the non-Jewish population increased only 87 percent (Lindemann 1991, 133-134). The increase in certain areas was even more remarkable (e.g., increasing by 850 percent from 1844 to 1914 in the southern provinces, compared to 250 percent for non-Jews), and most of the increase was in urban areas. The phenomenon of the "village Jew" occurring in the 16th to the 18th century in Poland (Weinryb 1972) suggests that the Jews had reached the limit of the urban economy during this period, with the result that there was increasing colonization outside the traditional Jewish urban economic sphere.

On the basis of Polish data, Plakans and Halpern (1981) attribute greater Jewish fertility primarily to the young age at which females married, and to the fact that virtually all females married. Both of these attributes of Jewish families contrast strongly with the general European pattern in which significant numbers of females remained unmarried during times of economic hardship. Since the usual interpretation of the European pattern of delayed marriage and female celibacy reflects economic constraints (e.g., Wrigley & Schofield 1981), the results suggest that there were fewer economic constraints on Jews regarding marriage than was the case for gentiles.[32] However, there are also indications that the mortality rate among Jews was significantly lower than that for surrounding populations (Gitelman 1981), a finding related to the high-investment parenting typical of most Jewish communities throughout history (see Chapter 7).[33]

It is quite possible that anti-Semitism has been a significant factor in Jewish demographic history. Although Jews appear to have had a more rapid rate of increase in Spain prior to the Inquisition and expulsion, the ultimate result of the Spanish Inquisition and the expulsion was probably far different, since the great majority of the Sephardic refugees eventually ended up in the Moslem world, where there was a long-term demographic and cultural decline of Judaism resulting ultimately from anti-Semitism on the part of the local populations.[34]

Fraikor (1977) describes the boom-and-bust nature of Ashkenazi population growth, growing quickly due to very high fecundity, but then dropping back as the result of persecution and massacre. As reconstructed by Fraikor, the Ashkenazi population increased rapidly until the period of the Crusades, when anti-Semitic massacres and expulsions occurred throughout Western Europe, with the Jewish population reaching a low point in the 14th century.[35] This was followed by a rapid rise during the "Golden Age of Jews" in Poland, followed by a demographic crash as a result of the Cossack massacres and other wars in the 17th century. This pattern has continued into the 20th century, and not only with the Nazi holocaust. Gitelman (1981, 45) notes that in Russia the events from 1914 to 1945, including over 2,000 pogroms between 1918 to 1921 and the Stalinist purges of the 1930s, had a devastating demographic effect on Jews.

A particularly interesting gentile response to reproductive competition with Jews in traditional societies was to place restrictions on the fertility of the Jewish population. This appears to have been particularly common in Germany. Lowenstein (1981, 98) describes regulations in parts of pre-emancipation Germany that prescribed that the number of Jewish families in each town was not to increase and that Jews could not settle in other towns without special permission. Families could only be started if there was emigration or death of a head of household. However, exceptions were made in the case of wealthy merchants or industrialists, craftsmen, and farmers.[36] Alice Goldstein (1981, 118), writing on the basis of 18th-century German data, finds communities restricting marriage to only one child per family and restricting the number of marriages per year out of fear "that the Jews would become too populous and then too powerful."

These laws continued in some parts of Germany in the 19th century and were especially strong in Bavaria, where the population of Jews decreased from 52,908 to 50,648 in the period from 1818 to 1871. There was some indication that these legal restrictions resulted in a later age of marriage in these areas than in areas without the restrictions. In some areas, however, illegal marriages and high rates of illegitimacy occurred as a result of the restrictions.

These data clearly indicate that resource and reproductive competition occurred between Jews and gentiles in traditional societies. In at least some cases, there is very good evidence that Jews won this competition, especially by squeezing out competitors in the urban economy—i.e., the economy that was midway between the primary production of the peasantry and the ruling gentile elite. Moreover, there is evidence that Jewish population growth, undoubtedly in conjunction with Jewish control of economic resources, was viewed negatively by gentile communities and was associated with attempts to control the Jewish population, as well as attempts to limit Jewish control of resources, which made possible the Jewish demographic increases.

Finally, the generalization that the rate of population increase among Jews was higher than that of gentiles in many traditional societies and the industrializing societies of Eastern and Central Europe does not extend beyond these societies. Data reviewed in Chapter 7 indicate a decline in Jewish fertility in contemporary Western societies to a level below that of gentiles.

# NOTES

1. In *SAID* (ch. 1) I develop a theory of anti-Semitism based on social identity theory. From this theoretical perspective, resource competition is expected to exacerbate anti-Semitism, but other factors (e.g., cultural separatism) are expected to be important as well.

2. During the civil war leading to the Magna Carta, Jews were often the first target of the aristocratic forces, and the Magna Carta itself contains two clauses that restrict the lending practices of Jews by ensuring that widows and orphans had first claim on the estate before debts owed to Jews (Roth 1978, 36-37). In the following period, Jews were tolerated only if they could show they were of financial benefit to the king, and when, as a result of royal depredations of Jewish wealth, this ceased to be the case, the Jews were expelled entirely. Jordan (1989, 182) indicates that Christian merchants were also instrumental in the expulsion of the Jews as a means of removing a source of competition.

3. A tax farmer is one who promises to pay the governmental authorities a certain sum for the right to collect taxes in a particular area .

4. Although these data suggest resource competition between overseas Chinese and host populations, Zenner (1991, 78ff) also notes that the Chinese did not maintain rigid cultural or reproductive barriers between themselves and the host society. There are other indications that the overseas Chinese did not really constitute a closed group strategy. Thus, the evidence that Chinese merchants favored friends and relatives (Zenner 1991, 80), is compatible with essentially individual/family strategies where the Chinese businessman conceptualizes his relationships in terms of kinship and reciprocity, rather than in an ingroup/outgroup manner where the ingroup includes all diaspora Chinese. Also compatible with this interpretation is Zenner's (1991, 81; see also Yee 1993) comment that the locus of ethnocentrism and group identification among the Chinese was the extended family unit (as indicated, e.g., by ancestor worship as the primary religious manifestation). Jews, on the other hand, developed a highly elaborated diaspora ideology in which the locus of group identification included all members of the dispersed group, no matter how distantly related. One's family was simply a part of this much larger group. Reflecting this group, rather than a familial sense of identification, Jews typically communicated regularly and often engaged in altruistic behavior toward co-religionists in distant parts of the world (see Chapter 6). This did not occur with the Chinese.

5. The Jews were also viewed as indispensable to the Muslim rulers of Spain, even during periods characterized by considerable anti-Semitism. Fischel (1937) notes that despite many *de jure* restrictions on Jews during the 'Abbasid caliphate, Jews were

utilized in the civil services where their services were indispensable, especially in the roles of physician and banker.

6. The Jews were well aware of the protection provided by the king, and grateful for it. Baer (1961) notes that laws on Jewish informers generally prohibited actions that would benefit Christians. The exception, however, was the king. "If anyone would tell the king (whom God save!) or the lords of council a thing to his [the king's] advantage and for his well-being—even if the information was directed against a Jew—that man shall not be stigmatized as an informer or slanderer, since all Jews are in duty bound to seek the king's welfare" (quoted in Baer 1961, II:266).

7. Many Jews were forced to convert to Christianity as a result of the riots of 1391. Forced converts and their descendants are termed *Conversos* or New Christians (or sometimes the derogatory *Marranos*) in contrast to gentiles or Old Christians.

8. Brief mention should be made regarding Jewish competition with gentiles in the Muslim world (see also Chapter 7). Stillman (1979) notes the exclusion of Jews from a wide range of economic activities by Muslim guilds in medieval Morocco and from government service in 14th-century Egypt (p. 273). In Morocco, Jews were restricted to certain crafts and moneylending, which were prohibited or viewed negatively by Muslims for religious reasons, and Sephardic Jewish artisans formed their own guilds and professional societies there. A commentary on the Jews of Tunis in the late 19th century notes that Jews were displacing Arabs in trade and industry because they were protected by the authorities. Their newly acquired status enabled the Jews to successfully compete with the native Arab population and resulted in fear and jealousy by the displaced Arabs. "This fear and jealousy is added to the hatred of centuries, and the old 'Dshifa, ben Dshifa' (carrion, sons of carrion), is still the usual designation when they speak of Jews" (see Stillman 1979, 416-419).

9. As discussed in *SAID* (chs. 3 and 4), the Converso community remained highly cohesive and endogamous over a time span of several hundred years. Many of its members became crypto-Jews, often openly returning to Judaism after emigrating from the Iberian peninsula.

10. Even after the establishment of the Inquisition and well into the 16th century, the Conversos retained control of the municipal councils (Castro 1971, 340).

11. As discussed in *SAID* (ch. 3), intermarriage into the nobility tended to occur as a result of Jews providing dowries so that their daughters could marry into the gentile nobility. Such marriages therefore did not affect the racial purity of the Jewish gene pool, since the children were reared as gentiles. Moreover, there was no intermarriage at all in the lower social classes.

12. These beliefs may well have been exaggerated, but they certainly indicate that perceptions of resource competition were important psychologically to the Old Christians. The social identity theory of anti-Semitism developed in *SAID* (ch. 1) is highly compatible with the importance of false, exaggerated beliefs in the development of anti-Semitism.

13. As discussed in *SAID* (ch. 3), racial purity (*limpieza*) became a prime consideration for competition for resources during the period of the Inquisition, resulting in upward mobility of the lower classes because they were much less likely to have any Jewish ancestry.

14. The comment is undoubtedly intentionally reminiscent of God's promise to Abraham at Genesis 22:17: "I will multiply thy seed as the stars of the heaven, and as the sand which is upon the seashore."

15. The persecution, however, occurred within the context of continued New Christian financing of the Spanish monarchy, since there was no effective alternative to New

Christian participation in the royal finances. Eventually, however, all except the most powerful New Christians increasingly looked elsewhere for their future and eventually settled in diaspora Portuguese communities and northern mercantile centers such as Amsterdam, where they reverted to their Jewish identity.

16. The very precisely defined economic role of Jews in Venice required policing. The main activity of the Inquisition of Venice was to prevent deception by crypto-Jews posing as Christians in order to circumvent the restrictions on Jewish economic activity. Crypto-Jews who declared their Judaism upon entering Venice did not come under the purview of the Inquisition. But individuals were investigated if they were believed to have remained crypto-Jews in Venice and continued to conduct business as Christians (Pullan 1983, 315).

17. Concern with Jewish ties to the Turks is an example of the loyalty issue—a consistent theme of anti-Semitism. See *SAID* (ch. 3).

18. The only exception was the wine business, which was perhaps due to ritual reasons. However, Jews were active in the wine business in other areas of Poland (see Katz 1961a).

19. Mosse (1987, 131ff) also describes intense competition in the wire-making industry between a Jewish group and a gentile firm, which eventually resulted in amalgamation. However, he points to a continuing ethnic aspect of the episode. The Jewish group, although unrelated, retained its central core of Jewish managers over four generations and retained close commercial ties with other Jewish firms. Similar examples are discussed in Chapter 6.

20. For example, in 1931, of the 100 largest companies, 31 were predominantly Jewish, 58 were predominantly gentile, and only 10 were a mixture (Mosse 1987, 357).

21. Data summarized by Gay (1988, 19-20) indicate a similar pattern in Vienna during this period, where by 1880 Jews made up 10 percent of the population. There are clear associations between resource competition and the rise of anti-Semitism emanating from the gentile society. Regarding the extent of Jewish cultural dominance in *fin de siècle* Vienna, Gay (1988, 21) quotes the German Jewish novelist Jacob Wasserman as writing that "nearly all the people with whom I came into intellectual or cordial contact were Jews. . . . I soon recognized that all public life was dominated by Jews. The banks, the press, the theater, literature, social functions, all was in the hands of the Jews."

22. In Chapter 7, these demographic tendencies among the Jews are viewed as general aspects of Judaism as an evolutionary/ecological strategy.

23. As indicated in note 1, resource competition is not expected to be the only factor involved in anti-Semitism (see *SAID*, ch. 1). Gordon (1984) notes that German anti-Semitism was strongest in areas with the greatest numbers of unassimilated Eastern European Jewish immigrants, suggesting an independent effect of negative attitudes engendered by cultural separatism. The restriction of Jewish immigration was a common theme of anti-Semitism in Germany (e.g., Bracher 1970, 40).

24. Katz (1985, 91) finds that by 1860 the percentage of Jewish children attending secondary school was 3 to 4 times that of the gentile population and that this ratio increased in later years.

25. There is no question that Hitler's perception that Jews and "Aryans" were locked in an intense competition was central to his world view (Bracher 1970; Gordon 1984; see discussion in *SAID* [ch. 3]). These perceptions of economic competition and Jewish economic domination, although clearly having a basis in reality, may well have been exaggerated—a not uncommon aspect of anti-Semitism and one that is highly compatible with an evolutionary perspective (see *SAID*, ch. 1). However, when the Nazis ultimately achieved power, anti-Semitism became a top-down movement in the sense that its

direction was determined by the leaders of the party and was quite independent of popular support: "Nazi victory meant that Hitler and the radical anti-Semites in the Nazi party, not the German electorate in general, would determine Jewish policy" (Gordon 1984, 90).

26. Carlebach (1978, 60) notes that all classes in Germany (nobility, merchants, small shop keepers, and laborers) feared they would be negatively affected by the emancipation of the Jews. Jews established close links with the ruling aristocracy and the aristocracy often became financially dependent on Jews (Lindemann 1991, 13, 37, 43-45). Carlebach (1978, 60) also notes that the nobility in Prussia opposed the emancipation of the Jews because they feared that Jews would purchase all of the land. There was no fear that emancipating the gentile peasants would similarly alter the old social order.

27. These opinions are supported by modern research (see Chapter 7).

28. In addition, Lindemann (1991) shows that Jews were also overrepresented among those responsible for major financial scandals, such as bank failures, large-scale fraud, and stock market panics. These incidents often had disproportionately adverse effects on gentiles, and gentiles attributed them to Jews. Although these incidents do not involve direct competition, they involve an exploitative Jewish-gentile relationship in the sense that individual Jews were overrepresented among those who benefited by these affairs, so that resources are moving from the gentile community to the Jewish community without proportionate reciprocity.

29. For example, while 58 percent of the graduates of City College of New York who applied to medical school were accepted in 1925, only 15 percent were accepted in 1939; the percentage of Jews in medical school at Columbia University declined from 47 percent in 1920 to 8 percent in 1940 (Dinnerstein 1991).

30. Ginsberg (1993) shows that Jewish economic and cultural success since 1960 in the United States has the potential to result in anti-Semitic repercussions. For example, Jews were predominant among those involved in hostile corporate takeovers and insider trading scandals during the 1980s, and gentile reactions to these activities often had anti-Semitic overtones (Ginsberg 1993, 189-199). Moreover, African-Americans with the highest level of anti-Semitism are elite professionals who are in competition with Jews for positions in the public and quasi-public sectors of the economy (p. 181). There are also suggestions that non-Jewish White liberals may sometimes welcome African-American anti-Semitism as a means of decreasing Jewish influence (p. 180).

31. These percentage increases occurred despite the existence of considerable emigration, which began in the 17th century following the Cossack uprisings.

32. Notice that, within this perspective, celibacy does not play an independent role in limiting population growth among gentiles. Rises in celibacy are a result of economic constraints.

33. In at least one instance, greater Jewish fertility occurred despite later marriage. Alice Goldstein (1981) finds that, although Jews were indeed more fertile than gentiles prior to 1880 in a German sample, they actually married later than gentiles.

34. See Chapters 7 and 8 and *SAID* (ch. 2).

35. Fraikor (1977) also notes that the plague contributed to the demographic low point in the 14th century.

36. The latter two categories were encouraged as part of government policy to get the Jews to adopt these occupations, rather than the more typical occupation of petty trade.

# 6

# COOPERATION, ALTRUISM, AND COMMUNITY CONTROL OF GROUP INTERESTS AMONG JEWS

It must not be forgotten that although a high standard of morality gives but a slight or no advantage to each individual man and his children of the same tribe, yet an increase in the number of well-endowed men and advancement in the standard of morality will certainly give an immense advantage to one tribe over another. A tribe including many members who, possessing in a high degree the spirit of patriotism, fidelity, obedience, courage, and sympathy, who were always ready to aid one another, and to sacrifice themselves for the common good, would be victorious over most other tribes; and this would be natural selection. (Charles Darwin [1871, 500], *The Descent of Man and Selection in Relation to Sex*)

[We face] death on behalf of our laws with a courage which no other nation can equal. (Flavius Josephus, *Against Apion*, 2:234)

Nowhere are the poor of that nation [i.e., Jews] seen abandoned without assistance to become a burthen to the country; and while those very men, who regard as barbarians those who are strangers to the world and to its ways, reluctantly give a trifling portion of their superfluity to the wretched victims of misery, a people whose name is held almost synonymous with ferocity, would really think they should deserve the appellation, if they could hesitate to share their moderate resources with the unfortunate who surround them. Those who delight in affixing guilty intentions to praise-worthy actions will see nothing in this union but a dangerous association; but the sentimental observer will never hold back his just approbation. (*An Appeal to the Justice of Kings and Nations* [1801]; quoted in Tama [1807] 1971, 72-73)

A principle conclusion of the discussion of Chapter 1 is that human group evolutionary strategies are conceptualized as "experiments in living," rather than the determinate outcome of natural selection acting on human populations. It is therefore an empirical question to determine the position of any putative strategy on several theoretically important independent dimensions. One of these theoretically important dimensions ranges from high levels of within-group altruism and submergence of individual interest to group interests at one extreme to complete within-group selfishness at the other. Human group evolutionary strategies may be conceptualized as falling anywhere on this dimension, and the purpose of this chapter is to show that historical Judaism can be characterized as near the altruistic end of the dimension, although we shall see that in fact there have been important limits on altruism within historical Jewish communities.

It would be difficult to overestimate the theoretical importance of altruism in evolutionary accounts of behavior. Altruism is deeply problematic because it implies that individuals engage in self-sacrificing behavior in the interests of others. Genes for altruism are therefore always selected against within groups, and many theorists have concluded that the evolution of altruism by natural selection is unlikely to be a major force in evolution.

Nevertheless, there is every reason to suppose that humans can develop altruistic groups that rely ultimately on human abilities to monitor and enforce group goals, to prevent defection, and to create ideological structures that rationalize group aims both to group members and to outsiders (MacDonald 1988a, 290ff; Wilson & Sober 1994; see also Chapter 1). Thus, while it may well be that group-level evolution is relatively uncommon among animals due to their limited abilities to prevent cheating, human groups are able to regulate themselves via social controls so that theoretical possibilities regarding invasion by selfish types from surrounding human groups or from within can be eliminated or substantially reduced.

Whatever the nature of the evolved machinery of the human mind, the thesis here is that human groups are able to impose altruism, cooperation, and acceptance of group goals on their members. A primary mechanism for the development of within-group altruism and the maximization of group rather than individual interests is proposed to be culturally invented community controls on individual behavior. Such controls can ensure that "cheaters" (i.e., non-cooperators, non-altruists) can be excluded from the group. Social controls also result in the reasonable expectation that the burdens of altruism will be fairly and impartially distributed within the community.[1]

However, social controls are not the only important mechanism influencing altruism, cooperation, and acceptance of group goals among Jews. Evolutionary models imply that the threshold for within-group altruistic behavior is markedly lowered when the group members are biologically related (Wilson 1991; Wilson & Sober 1994), and the data summarized in Chapter 2 indicate that indeed there is significant genetic commonality among even widely dispersed Jewish groups, combined with a genetic gradient between Jewish and gentile populations. Moreover, these data indicate that, with the exception of non-Jewish Middle Eastern populations, all Jewish groups are more closely related to each other than to any non-Jewish group. Thus, unlike universalist religions such as Christianity and Islam, Judaism over its history has fundamentally been a large kinship community in which the threshold for altruistic behavior toward group members was markedly lower than for altruistic behavior toward outgroup members.

In addition, the degree of biological relatedness within the many small and scattered Jewish diaspora communities was undoubtedly much higher than the degree of biological relatedness characteristic of the Jewish population as a whole. This is especially so since these communities were often founded by a very few families, so that the actual level of biological relatedness within particular Jewish communities may well have been very high indeed. Several authors (e.g. Chase & McKusick 1972; Fraikor 1977; Mourant, Kopec, & Domaniewska-Sobczak 1978) have emphasized the importance of founder effects and inbreeding in the population genetic history of the Jews, stemming ultimately from the fact that Jewish communities were often founded by very few individuals who married endogamously and consanguineously, including relatively high levels of uncle-niece and first cousin marriage (see also below). The point here is that this phenomenon would also have increased the level of biological relatedness within Jewish communities and lowered the threshold for altruism. Moreover, as indicated below, immigration from other Jewish communities was often strongly discouraged by the Jewish community itself. Such a policy would also have the effect of keeping the level of biological relatedness within the Jewish community relatively high.

The relatively high level of biological relatedness both within and among Jewish communities is therefore expected to be a powerful force in facilitating altruism and the submergence of individual interests to those of the entire group. An important aspect of the following treatment will therefore be to provide evidence that relationships of kinship were important to Jews themselves and figured prominently in Jewish economic activity, marriage decisions, and Jewish charity. From an evolutionary perspective, an important role of kinship in these activities is not expected to be restricted to Jews. However, its establishment as being an important principle among Jews is highly compatible with the thesis that Judaism is an altruistic group evolutionary strategy.

Another force expected to facilitate altruism and a group orientation among Jews derives from the typical role of Jews as a minority group in the midst of an often hostile gentile society. A perennial problem for Jewish communities was to prevent individuals from engaging in behavior that would threaten the entire group. Thus, Katz (1961a, 40-41) notes that life in a hostile world required high levels of community control over individual behavior: "The danger threatening the group as a result of individual misconduct operated as the most forceful check. Reiterated warnings and admonitions that were issued by public institutions and communal leaders stressed the fact that the life and death of the whole community rested in the hands of its individual members. The security of the Jewish community constituted a supreme and essential value . . . ."[2]

As described more fully in Chapter 1, in situations of external threat, individual self-interest increasingly coincides with an interest in preserving the group. Indeed, external threat may well provide a cue that triggers evolved altruistic, group-oriented psychological mechanisms.[3] Moreover, because anti-Semitism has been virtually universal throughout Jewish history, altruism may come to verge on anticipated future reciprocity. Reflecting these realities, the *Shulhan Arukh* advised that "[o]ne should also consider that the wheel of fortune is ever revolving, and that he himself or his son or his grandson will eventually have to beg for charity" (quoted in Zborowski & Herzog 1952, 198). Such sentiments were common beginning in the ancient world (Baron 1952b, 270).

A high level of within-group charity may also have benefited the group strategy because it provided a safety net in traditional societies where economic success can be ephemeral for anyone. The ephemerality of economic success is likely to be particularly salient to Jews since they have often been subject to capricious seizures of property, expulsions, and confiscatory taxation.

Interestingly, a medieval German synod enacted a law that required the entire Jewish community to pay when the king required a Jew to pay a capricious contribution, the only exception being in cases where the Jew was at fault (Finkelstein 1924, 60). In other words, if a Jew was penalized capriciously because of his group membership, the entire group was expected to pay. Regulations such as this could be an important concomitant of a group strategy, since the risks of group membership were spread throughout the entire group and individuals who were subject to such capricious acts were less likely to defect because their individual losses were minimized.

Hundert (1992) notes the perception among Jews in Poland that wealth was ephemeral, and Katz (1961a) notes that Jewish capital in traditional Poland was always precarious, since it was liable to expropriation by the authorities. Jews often specialized in obtaining forms of wealth that could be concealed and that "could be quickly switched from a point of danger to a point of resettlement" (Johnson 1987, 246).

Moreover, in traditional societies the economic basis of wealth among gentiles has often been the control of large areas of land—a relatively stable source of wealth. But, among Jews, the economic basis of wealth has been much more likely to depend on trade and commerce—occupations which are more prone to economic fluctuations—and Jews were often prohibited from owning land. Economic success in trade and commerce would also be facilitated by a safety net, which would encourage Jews to take economic risks. Engaging in economically risky behavior has been noted by many writers as being characteristic of Jewish economic activity throughout history (e.g., Johnson 1987; Mosse 1987, 314ff).

The diaspora situation itself also facilitated within-group cooperation among Jews. The diaspora resulted in Judaism being essentially a large kinship group in which internal divisions were de-emphasized and in which the major division was between Jews and gentiles, rather than within the Jewish community. As discussed below, by shifting to a diaspora context, economic oppression of Jews by other Jews was minimized, and Judaism itself developed a relatively homogeneous set of interests. Economic cooperation within the community was maximized and economic exploitation minimized, but conflict and competition with the gentile societies among whom they lived remained.

A principal theme of this volume is that Judaism is a collectivist culture in the sense of Triandis (1990, 1991; see also Chapters 7 and 8). Collectivist cultures (and Triandis [1990, 57] explicitly includes Judaism in this category) place a much greater emphasis on the goals and needs of the ingroup than on individual rights and interests. Ingroup norms and the duty to cooperate and submerge individual goals to the needs of the group are paramount. "Collectivists are concerned about the results of their actions on others, share material and nonmaterial resources with group members, are concerned about their presentation to others, believe in the correspondence of outcomes of self and ingroup, and feel involved in the contributions and share in the lives of ingroup members" (Triandis 1990, 54). Collectivist cultures develop an "unquestioned attachment" to the ingroup, including "the perception that ingroup norms are universally valid (a form of ethnocentrism), automatic obedience to ingroup authorities, and willingness to fight and die for the ingroup. These characteristics are usually associated with distrust of and unwillingness to cooperate with outgroups" (p. 55). Each of the ingroup members is viewed as responsible for every other member, and relations with outgroup members are "distant, distrustful, and even hostile" (Triandis 1991, 80). In collectivist cultures, morality is conceptualized as that which benefits the group, and aggression and exploitation of outgroups are acceptable (Triandis 1990, 90). These themes will be apparent in the following.

Besides its obvious relevance to an evolutionary account of Judaism, it should be noted that within-group altruism and submergence of individual interests to those of the group result in an extraordinarily powerful competitive advantage against individual strategies. The competitive advantage of altruistic group strategies has always been obvious to evolutionists. The difficulty has been to conceptualize how altruistic groups could evolve as the result of natural selection. In the case of Judaism, however, the argument of this chapter will be that there has been an extraordinary confluence of forces that have resulted in relatively high levels of within-group cooperation and altruism and a de-emphasis on individual interests.

# ECONOMIC COOPERATION AND PATRONAGE AMONG JEWS

> And for our duty at the sacrifices themselves, we ought in the first place to pray for the common welfare of all, and after that our own; for we are made for fellowship one with another; and he who prefers the common good before what is peculiar to himself, is above all acceptable to God. (Flavius Josephus, *Against Apion,* 2:196)

In Chapter 7, I will discuss the importance of eugenics and the conscious development of an intellectual, entrepreneurial elite among Jews. However, this development must be seen within the wider context of Judaism as an national/ethnic strategy that emphasizes the rights and obligations of the entire community of Jews. This sense of community involvement and kin-based altruism can be seen as an aspect of the basic ideology of Judaism. Baron (1952a, 10) notes that "Judaism stresses the general aims of the Jewish people. . . . to this day orthodox Jewish ethics has remained in its essence national rather than individual, and this accounts, incidentally, for the otherwise incomprehensible legal theorem of the common responsibility of *all* Jews for the deeds of each." The Law therefore is an "instrument of history" to which the individual is subservient, and "what really matters in the Jewish religion is not the immortality of the individual Jew, but that of the Jewish people" (Baron 1952a, 12). "The nation's future and not that of the individual remained the decisive objective" (Baron 1952b, 40; see also Alon 1989, 524; Bickerman 1988, 270-271; Johnson 1987, 159; Moore 1927-30, II:312). There was also a sense of corporate rather than individual merit—a sense that individuals inherited some merit from their illustrious ancestors (Bickerman 1988, 270-271).

In the period following the Destruction of the Second Temple (70 A.D.), organized systems of social welfare and mutual assistance developed among Jews (Alon 1989, 534). These systems of social welfare had their antecedents in the early history of Israel as a kinship group in which the social ideal was to eliminate within-group exploitation (see also Chapter 8). Deuteronomy 15:1-18 clearly articulates the obligation to develop systems of welfare for poor Israelites. However, Israelite society often failed to live up to the ideal of a relatively egalitarian group in which within-group exploitation was minimized (see also Chapter 8). Israelite society was rife with class distinctions and the oppression of the poor during the period of national sovereignty, despite the disapproval of many prophets. Often the language used by the prophets reflects the language in the sections of Deuteronomy that emphasize the importance of social welfare among the Israelites, as when Ezekiel notes that among the sins of Israel "the fatherless and the widow are wronged in you" (Ezek. 22:7). The Maccobean period also had its share of despots, and sharp social divisions persisted through the Second Commonwealth Period.

Oppression within Jewish society would tend to lead to a lack of social solidarity among Jews and a loss of the fundamental kinship structure of Jewish society. However, when living as a minority in the diaspora, these trends were greatly lessened: "Before the battle for ethnic-religious survival, the inner class struggle receded" and a common economic front *vis-à-vis* the rest of the world developed (Baron 1952b, 241). "The Jewish minority community, placed on the defensive by a hostile world, could never develop those sharp internal conflicts which had characterized the Second Commonwealth" (pp. 242-243). In the diaspora context, even vast differences in wealth within the Jewish community would be less likely to be the result of poor Jews being exploited by wealthier Jews, since Jewish wealth would tend to primarily derive from economic transactions carried on with the gentile community. Rather than the exploitation of poorer Jews by wealthier Jews, the emphasis was on cooperation and patronage within the Jewish community, while economic relationships with the gentile community could be, using Katz's (1961a, 55; see Chapter 5) felicitous phrase, "purely instrumental."

Reflecting this, several writers have noted the high degree of commonality of interest and lack of class conflict in traditional Jewish diaspora societies. Weinryb (1972) writes of traditional Poland that "[t]heir communications and interests were similar, as were their fears and hopes, despite increasing socioeconomic stratification" (p. 96). And Israel (1985, 171), referring to European Jewish society in the 17th and 18th centuries, notes that "[g]enerally speaking, [Jewish society] conformed hardly at all to the Marxist notion of class differentiation and struggle. Almost always, the vertical ties which lent Jewish society its inner cohesion—commercial collaboration and the patronage network implicit in Jewry's institutions, charities, and welfare system—were of much greater significance than any occasional friction between rich and poor."

The emphasis on minimizing within-group conflict is apparent in Jewish religious writing from the ancient period. The writers of the Talmud placed a high value on class harmony among Jews, as well as a strong sense of collective economic responsibility (Baron 1952b, 251; see also Alon [1980, 1984] 1989, 521ff). Neusner (1987, 161) finds that a major theme of the Babylonian Talmud is the imposition of community norms on individual behavior. Oppression of Jews was sharply enjoined, and individual economic rights were sharply curtailed in the interests of communal and family solidarity.

Reflecting these trends, there is excellent evidence that Jewish economic activity has historically been characterized by high levels of within-group economic cooperation and patronage. Jewish elites overwhelmingly tended to employ other Jews in their enterprises. In Chapter 5, the importance of highly placed courtiers in the general fortunes of the entire Jewish community was noted, the relevant point here being that there was a strong tendency for these individuals to help their co-religionists. Baer (1961, I:31) finds that the prosperity of Jewish communities in Spain under both Spanish and Moorish rulers depended on the influence of Jewish courtiers: "In the courts of princes,

Jews rose to positions of eminence and influence. The fate of Jewish communities was closely bound up with the political fortunes of these Jewish courtiers, whose personal rise or fall often carried with it the prosperity or ruin of their community." Similarly, Stillman (1979) notes the role of Jewish courtiers in extending patronage to other Jews in a variety of Muslim societies and the fact that "the fall of a Jewish courtier was a cause of deep anxiety for his brethren until the storm had passed" (p. 62; see also Patai 1986; Ahroni 1986, 138). During the early period of Mongol domination in Iraq, the Jew Sa'd ad-Daula filled his administration with "his brothers, kinsmen, and coreligionists" (Fischel 1937, 107). His fall resulted in violence directed at the entire Jewish community.

There are numerous examples of high-placed Jewish courtiers or capitalists employing co-religionists in their economic activities. During the period of increasing dominance by the New Christians in 15th-century Spain, Roth (1974) notes that when Diego Arias Davila was appointed treasurer, other New Christians quickly achieved similar high positions as a result of his influence. Roth (1974) also describes a general pattern in the New World in the 16th century in which the Sephardim controlled all imports and exports, with distribution throughout the country also performed by other Sephardim.

Israel (1985) shows that the Court Jews of 17th-century Europe overwhelmingly employed their relatives and other Jews in their operations on behalf of various governments. Jewish economic activity during the period is described as a complex interdependent pyramid in which all classes benefited from each other's activities: "From Court Jew to pedlar these divergent groupings penetrated and depended on each other economically . . ." (p. 171). For example, when Samuel Oppenheimer (1630-1703) obtained the right to settle in Vienna, he brought with him around 100 other Jewish families who were directly dependent on him. Oppenheimer also organized a vast network of co-religionist agents and suppliers; "he secured for them charters and passes, contracts and monopolies, and obtained for them permission to settle in cities from which Jews had been excluded for centuries" (Stern 1950, 28). Stern comments that this pattern occurred not only in Austria, but also throughout the German states.

In Poland, Jews went into partnership as moneylenders, merchants, and toll farmers on a large scale, and the employees in these business enterprises and in toll and tax farming were Jews over whom the entrepreneur often exercised judicial rights (Weinryb 1972, 97). Indeed, Katz (1961a) notes that there was an entire Jewish working class among the 16th-18th-century Ashkenazim who "engaged in production, transport, and the management of enterprises financed by Jewish capitalists" (p. 49). Like the dependents of Jewish courtiers, this Jewish working class was entirely dependent on the success of the capitalist, and the capitalist in turn was absolutely dependent for his position on his being useful to the gentile authorities. Weinryb (1972, 97) notes that "[s]olidarity and contacts played a considerable role in economic activity. The strength and structure of an enterprise, firm, or partnership were conditioned by group solidarity."

This basic pattern continued into the 19th and 20th centuries: Lindemann (1991) describes wealthy Jewish capitalists employing other Jews in 19th-century Russia, and Sachar (1992) and Liebman (1979) find a similar pattern in the United States in the early 20th century. Indeed, Howe (1976) describes a sort of self-contained economic world of immigrant Jews in the early 20th century in which the vast majority of economic transactions for products and services were carried on with other Jews. Kotkin (1993) describes the continuing importance of what one might call "tribal economics" among far-flung Jewish groups in the contemporary world.

Beginning in the ancient world, Jews also tended to form protective trade associations (guilds) with other Jews (Baron 1952a, 261). Neuman (1969) describes numerous merchant and artisan guilds among the Jews of pre-expulsion Spain. Groups of Jewish traders and craftsmen organized "for purposes of self-defense and for regulating the industries in which they were engaged," and there were intense, bitter rivalries with Christian guilds in the municipalities (Neuman 1969, I:182ff). As indicated in Chapter 5, competition between guilds organized around ethnicity continued even after the forced conversions of 1391 and even though the New Christian guilds were nominally Christian. Similarly, Benardete (1953, 111-112) cites a 19th century observer of Sephardic Jews in Salonica "who was shocked to learn that the solidarity among them is so great that in the business world trade-union practices . . . prevailed." There was a "religious significance attached to the protection of one's livelihood" (p. 112).

In addition, Jews formed Jewish unions and other types of Jewish socialist labor movements in which the entire membership was Jewish (e.g., the Polish and Russian Bunds and, in the United States, the Union of Hebrew Trades and the Jewish Socialist Federation) (Levin 1977; Liebman 1979). These specifically Jewish labor movements, which typically combined socialism with a strong sense of Jewish cultural separatism, often conflicted with the internationalist, assimilationist tendencies of the wider socialist movement and ultimately with the Communist government in the Soviet Union (Levin 1977, 97-112; Pinkus 1988, 49ff). Indeed, Levin (1977, 213) describes the Jewish labor movement in the United States as a sort of "sub-nation" in which "Jewish laborers worked for Jewish employers, and the class conflicts between them were carried on in a Jewish ethnic culture . . . ."

Interestingly, the class conflict appears to have been much muted because the employers were also Jewish: Because the Jewish socialist leaders retained strong ties to the Jewish community, they were less hostile toward the Jewish bourgeoisie and often obtained charity for Jewish workers from Jewish capitalists. "Assistance, common interests [especially combating anti-Semitism], and relationships of this kind contributed to the muting of the Socialist union leaders' class hostilities. They also significantly diminished their intracommunal class hostility and helped to make these Socialists more broadly Jewish in their orientation" (Liebman 1979, 263).

On the other hand, Liebman (1979, 267-268) suggests that the Jewish union leaders became more conciliatory toward management when the ethnic composition of the unions changed toward being predominantly gentile. Moreover, union-management relations became more formal, rather than a communal affair, when the unions became predominantly gentile. The suggestion is that ethnicity had a powerful effect on all of these relationships.

This powerful communal sense can also be seen in immigration patterns. Aid was forthcoming not just from family members, but also from other Jews emigrating from the same town or region. Jewish employers often recruited preferentially from particular regions, with the result that "families, neighborhoods, and towns would be transported almost intact and set down again in a tenement, block, or small neighborhood in a city in the United States" (Liebman 1979, 142). Once in the United States, Jews developed extensive mutual aid societies, including the *Landsmanshaft* societies, based on kinship ties and/or a common place of residence in Europe. Describing the function of the *Landsmanshaft,* Wirth (1956, 222-223) notes that

> a stranger who is able to call himself a *Landsman* not only loosens the purse-strings of the first individual he meets, but also has access to his home. Not only do the *lanslite* belong to the same synagogue, but as a rule, they engage in similar vocations, become partners in business, live in the same neighborhood and intermarry within their own group. A *Landsmanshaft* has its own patriarchal leaders, its lodges and mutual aid associations, and its celebrations and festivities.

Communication was also an element of Jewish economic cooperation. Katz (1961a, 151) emphasizes the fact that Jewish economic unity in the face of dispersion was important for its economic success: "The possibility of constant communication with people living in other countries, with whom there existed a kinship of language and culture, gave an economic advantage to the Jews, who were scattered over many lands." For example, writing of the Court Jews during the period from 1640 to 1740 in Europe, Stern (1950, 18-19) notes that "the Jew seemed to be better qualified for the position of war commissary than the Christian. He was in close contract with his coreligionists throughout Europe. He was therefore able to maintain agents and correspondents in all countries and could receive through them necessary goods and important news."

Stern (1950, 137) also notes that Jews were also ideally suited to function as financial agents to gentile princes because of their contacts with foreign banking firms. Ties of language were especially advantageous, since Jews from widely dispersed areas could easily communicate with each other.[4] Shaw (1991, 94) also describes a system of bills of exchange that were honored by other Jewish traders and bankers and that gave Jewish traders a competitive advantage over Christian and Muslim traders.[5]

Such ties continued well into the modern era: Mosse (1987, 399), writing of the period from 1820 to 1935 in Germany, notes that "Jewish commercial activities outside Germany were facilitated by a strong sense of Jewish solidarity and mutual trust, often reinforced by kinship ties. Later with a weakening of the ties of social solidarity based on traditional Jewish observance, Jewish contacts across national frontiers persisted on a basis of common networks of acquaintance, of apprenticeships, of long-standing commercial relations occasionally reinforced by kinship ties." These commercial networks were much more extensive than those typically available to gentiles.

There were other benefits as well: Sorkin (1987, 122) notes that a function of one of the many voluntary Jewish associations that sprang up in Germany in the 19th century was to provide loans to Jewish businessmen. Moreover, Mosse (1987, 36) finds that a large network of lesser Jewish bankers developed under the aegis of the Rothschilds. Mosse also provides several examples of "Jewish banks" in which the partners and directors tended to be Jewish even when there were no familial connections. And Jewish entrepreneurs in a wide range of industries often were financed by banking firms owned by Jews (e.g., Mosse 1987, 152, 155, 249). Moreover, Jews tended to do business with other Jews throughout this period "almost certainly beyond the call of 'purely economic necessity'" (Mosse 1987, 403).

Finally, in the era of joint stock companies after 1900, a "Jewish sector" of the German economy developed, characterized by interlocking directorships among commercial and industrial enterprises and their financial institutions (Mosse 1987, 257). In a statement which would also serve as a rough summary of Jewish economic behavior throughout history, Mosse (1987, 17) notes that one theory of the remarkable Jewish economic success, particularly in the banking industry (Mosse 1987, 382) in Germany throughout the period from 1820-1935 was based on

> an internal dynamic of dynasty formation, personal relations, kinship ties, socialization processes, and, in general, the operation of a variety of informal networks. At least until mid-[19th] century Jews tended to transact business mainly with fellow Jews, in part because Jewish ritual laws impeded, if they did not completely inhibit between Jew and Gentile the social intercourse almost inseparable from sustained business relations. . . . [W]hether through kinship ties, greater confidence and sympathy, feelings of solidarity, or recommendations, there would be a marked tendency for Jews to employ fellow-Jews in positions of trust, as men having *prokura*, and eventually to raise them to a partnership. Close and harmonious business relationships reinforced by personal friendship, the friendship of families, and common leisure pursuits would, not infrequently, contain also an element of common 'Jewishness.'

# THE GROUP ETHIC OF JUDAISM AND ITS ENFORCEMENT WITHIN THE JEWISH COMMUNITY

A heathen cannot prefer charges of overreaching because it is said "*one his brother*" (Lev. 25:14). However, if a heathen has defrauded an Israelite he must return the overcharge according to our laws (in order that the rights of) a heathen should not exceed (those of) an Israelite. (*The Code of Maimonides, Book 12, The Book of Acquisition*, ch. XII:1, 47)

It is permissible to borrow from a heathen or from an alien resident and to lend to him at interest. For it is written *Thou shalt not lend upon interest to thy brother* (Deut. 23:20)—to thy brother it is forbidden, but to the rest of the world it is permissible. Indeed, it is an affirmative commandment to lend money at interest to a heathen. For it is written *Unto the heathen thou shalt lend upon interest* (Deut. 23:21). (*The Code of Maimonides, Book 13, The Book of Civil Laws*, ch. V:1, 93)

*Nesek* ("biting," usury) and *marbit* ("increase," interest) are one and the same thing. . . . Why is it called nesek? because he who takes it bites his fellow, causes pain to him, and eats his flesh. (*The Code of Maimonides, Book 13, The Book of Civil Laws*, ch. IV:1, 88-89)

The group ethic of Judaism is also apparent in the formal rules and regulations of Jewish diaspora communities in traditional societies. The present section reviews evidence indicating that Jewish economic behavior was highly conditioned on group membership and that the interests of individual Jews were consistently subordinated to the interests of the group. From the standpoint of the group strategy, the goal was to maximize the total resources of the community, not to allow each individual member to maximize his interest. These regulations were enforced by the powerful centralized Jewish governments that existed throughout the diaspora.

Business and social ethics as codified in the Bible and the Talmud took strong cognizance of group membership in a manner that minimized oppression within the Jewish community, but not between Jews and gentiles. Perhaps the classic case of differential business practices toward Jews and gentiles, enshrined in Deuteronomy 23, is that interest on loans could be charged to gentiles, but not to Jews. Although various subterfuges were sometimes found to get around this requirement, loans to Jews in medieval Spain were typically made without interest (Neuman 1969, I:194), while those to Christians and Moslems were made at rates ranging from 20 to 40 percent (Lea 1906-07, I:97).[6] Hartung (1992) also notes that Jewish religious ideology deriving from the Pentateuch and the Talmud took strong cognizance of group membership in assessing the morality of actions ranging from killing to adultery. For example, rape was severely punished only if there were negative consequences to an Israelite male.

While rape of an engaged Israelite virgin was punishable by death, there was no punishment at all for the rape of a non-Jewish woman. In Chapter 4, it was also noted that penalties for sexual crimes against proselytes were less than against other Jews.

Hartung notes that according to the Talmud (b. Sanhedrin 79a) an Israelite is not guilty if he kills an Israelite when intending to kill a heathen. However, if the reverse should occur, the perpetrator is liable to the death penalty. The Talmud also contains a variety of rules enjoining honesty in dealing with other Jews, but condoning misappropriation of gentile goods, taking advantage of a gentile's errors in business transactions, and not returning lost articles to gentiles (Katz 1961a, 38).[7]

Katz (1961a) notes that these practices were modified in the medieval and post-medieval periods among the Ashkenazim in order to prevent *hillul hashem* (disgracing the Jewish religion). In the words of a Frankfort synod of 1603, "Those who deceive Gentiles profane the name of the Lord among the Gentiles" (quoted in Finkelstein 1924, 280). Taking advantage of gentiles was permissible in cases where *hillul hashem* did not occur, as indicated by rabbinic responsa that adjudicated between two Jews who were contesting the right to such proceeds. Clearly this is a group-based sense of ethics in which only damage to one's own group is viewed as preventing individuals from profiting at the expense of an outgroup. "[E]thical norms applied only to one's own kind" (Katz 1961a, 42).

There was also keen concern for restricting competition within the Jewish community in order to maximize the economic benefits to the entire community even at the expense of individual Jews. Finkelstein (1924) summarizes the Talmudic law regarding economic competition among Jews. An early Tannaitic (second century A.D.) source forbade Jews to undersell each other. However, this regulation was overruled by later sages in the interest of competition inside the Jewish community—i. e., competition that would benefit Jewish consumers. A later authority ruled that, if all the trade among the gentiles is in Jewish hands, "it is forbidden for a newcomer to undersell a fellow-Jew, and therefore all competition is prohibited" (p. 377), and this ruling was upheld by later commentators. Thus, there could be free trade within the Jewish community in order to protect the buyer, but monopolistic practices outside the Jewish community were sanctioned. Finkelstein notes that the French and German commentators supported the proposition that Jews should not compete with each other, but the point was clearly to prevent competition among Jews in trade with gentiles, not in trade with Jews. Thus Rabbi Eliezer b. Joel Ha-Levi ruled that "[i]f the *Gentile* cannot come to the house of R. except by passing the house of S. (the newcomer) then R. (the original shopkeeper) may object in accordance with the view of R. Huna" (quoted in Finkelstein 1924, 377; italics in text).

Katz (1961a, 61) finds that there was a large literature on preventing competition between Jews doing business with gentiles among the Ashkenazim. Jews were not allowed to underbid other Jews for franchises, nor were Jews allowed to interfere with monopolies held by other Jews, the point being "not to lose the money of Israel." Similar practices occurred among Jews in the Ottoman Empire (Shaw 1991, 64f).

Among Italian Jews in the 16th century there were regulations providing for exclusive monopolies on lending money to gentiles (see Finkelstein 1924, 312-313).[8] And even in the Jewish-dominated banking industry in Germany in the late 19th and early 20th centuries, Mosse (1987, 383) finds that, although there were some rivalries among Jewish financial institutions, "on the whole, a co-operative spirit (based on a philosophy of 'give and take' and 'fair shares for all') prevailed."

Jews were prohibited from bringing non-Jewish customers into a non-Jewish store or helping non-Jews with business. Partnerships and even temporary agreements between Jews and Christians were forbidden by Jewish law, and such laws were repeatedly enacted and re-enacted by the Jewish authorities: "There were constant condemnations and bans of excommunication against those who 'reveal the secrets of Israel', to merchants or noblemen" (Hundert 1986, 61).[9] Among the Sephardim, it was a major crime to cause a fellow Jew to lose property to a gentile. A Spanish synod of 1432 ruled that in such cases the culprit was subjected to extreme forms of punishment, including branding on the forehead, whipping, and execution (see Finkelstein 1924, 363).

# CLOSE KINSHIP TIES AS ELEMENTS OF JEWISH ECONOMIC BEHAVIOR

> I did many acts of charity for my kinsmen, those of my nation who had gone into captivity with me at Nineveh in Assyria. (Tob. 1:3)

There is evidence that close kinship ties have been an important aspect of Jewish economic activities. Zborowski and Herzog (1952, 304-306) document the general importance of kinship as implying an obligation to provide assistance. The obligation for relatives to provide assistance is simply assumed and taken for granted not only within the immediate family, but also within the extended family. "Kinship ties, even distant ones, entitle an individual to food, lodging and support when he comes to visit. In a strange town or city you seek a relative to stay with . . . . He may be your uncle, your seventh cousin, or the nephew of your brother's mother-in-law. If a man needs a job, a wealthy relative must give him one if it is at all possible. If not, he must help him to find one" (p. 306).

In addition, besides the general patronage of wealthy Jews toward their co-religionists, close kinship relations were of great importance in cementing business ties. Leroy (1985) notes that Jewish business and commerce in medieval Navarre were facilitated by intermarriage and family solidarity. This pattern was not significantly altered by the severe persecution that began in the 15th century and continued well into the 18th century. Round (1969) notes the high degree of endogamy among the 15th-century New Christian office-holding families, despite their (often nominal) conversion to Christianity, and notes the role of these alliances in facilitating professional solidarity and the pursuit of patronage. Boyajian (1983; see also Baron 1973 108-109; Beinart 1971b; Benardete 1953; Finkelstein 1924, 11; Haliczer 1987; Roth 1974) shows that the Sephardic international trading network and the commercial credit it depended on were facilitated by religious and kinship ties among these families. Within these families, "frequent consanguineous marriages . . . , matching cousins and cousins, uncles and nieces, reinforced kinship and recombined capital for enterprise. . . . The same pattern of kinship and intermarriage among the participants extended to the Diaspora and to correspondent bankers in Antwerp and Venice, or even overseas in Brazil and Spanish America" (Boyajian 1983, 46).

Similarly, as Johnson (1987) emphasizes, the Court Jews of 17th- and 18th-century Europe married exclusively among themselves and developed a large network of financial families whose resources could be organized to support particular goals. For example, Samuel Oppenheimer (1630-1703) was able to organize the resources of a "vast network" of such families, virtually all of whom were interrelated. "It became rare for Court Jews to marry any other kind" (p. 257), so that they in effect became a separate endogamous class within the Jewish community. In particular, Stern (1950, 28) notes that Oppenheimer's son served as his general representative in the Empire and that his two sons-in-law were stationed in the important trading center of Frankfort; his brother Moses was the principal agent in Heibelberg, and, in Hanover, he was represented by another close relative (Leffemann Behrens) and his son; in Italy, his interests were supervised by his grandson, and, in Amsterdam and Cleves, his relatives, the Gumperts family, were in charge.

In Arab lands, Goitein (1974) notes that Jews entered into partnerships with other Jews and that these business relationships were cemented by marriage alliances. The Geniza documents from the medieval period indicate numerous business relationships among close relatives (Goitein 1978, 40ff), including fathers and sons, brothers, brothers-in-law, cousins, and uncles and nephews. Fischel (1937) also notes this kinship solidarity among Jews in Arab lands, a solidarity "which economic historians have long recognized as a characteristic feature of Jewish participation in economic life" (p. 30; see also references therein). Deshen (1986), writing about traditional Moroccan practices, notes that individuals were enmeshed in extensive kinship networks in which kin were responsible for debts and businesses and homes were shared among close kin, and Shaw (1991, 94) makes a similar comment regarding Ottoman Jewry.

Among the Sephardim in 18th-century America, highly consanguineous marriages often cemented commercial arrangements, as among the Hendricks, Tobias, and Gomez families (Sachar 1992, 33).[10] Hyman (1989) notes that through the 19th century "Jewish family firms were often founded by brothers, and family contacts sustained the mercantile success of Jewish entrepreneurs in both Europe and America" (p. 185). Moreover, if business partners were not related to begin with, they typically arranged to become related: Solomon Loeb and Abraham Kuhn married each other's sisters, and in the firm of Goldman and Sachs, two Sachs sons married two Goldman daughters (Kaplan 1983, 298).

This pattern of consanguineous business relationships also occurred among the German Jewish merchant bankers in the 19th century (see Sachar 1992, 92, for a variety of examples). Perhaps the apotheosis of the Jewish tendency for consanguinity centered around a successful business is the behavior of the Rothschild family during the 19th century. After consolidating their family's position as the wealthiest in Europe, the youngest son of Mayer Amschel Rothschild married his niece, and Morton (1961) finds that of the 58 weddings contracted by the descendants of Mayer Amschel Rothschild, fully half were with first cousins.[11]

## Interim Conclusion

The data presented in the foregoing sections are highly compatible with an evolutionary account: The social (and its correlative genetic) gulf between Jews and gentiles was associated with profound differences in economic behavior. Economic behavior in communities with Jews and gentiles cannot be understood as the atomized transactions of individual actors. Group membership was critical, and especially so for the often large percentage of Jews who were entirely dependent on a "Jewish" sector of the economy created and maintained by co-religionists.

The data also show that genetic variation within the Jewish community was viewed as a very important resource. The concentration of economic resources coincided to a significant extent with the concentration of genetic variants.

The conclusion must be that genetic distance is important for understanding Jewish economic behavior. As will be seen in the following, this is also true in the case of Jewish charity: While there are high levels of economic cooperation (and charity) within the entire Jewish community and almost no charity between Jews and gentiles, even higher levels of economic cooperation (and charity) are associated with the close kinship ties created by connections of biological relatedness between specific families.

# JEWISH CHARITY AS AN ASPECT OF JUDAISM AS A GROUP EVOLUTIONARY STRATEGY

You shall not harden your heart or shut your hand against your poor brother, but you shall open your hand to him, and lend him sufficient for his need, whatever it may be. Take heed lest there be a base thought in your heart, and you say, 'The seventh year, the year of release [of debts], is near,' and your eye be hostile to your poor brother, and you give him nothing, and he cry to the LORD against you, and it be sin in you. You shall give to him freely, and your heart shall not be grudging when you give to him. (Deut. 15:7-10)

Whatever sum is decided on by us as necessary shall be collected each year, and each person shall pay the sum assessed against him. If any Jew fail to give their share and disobey the agent of the General Community, their names shall be announced in every community in Germany. The announcement shall take this form: "The following men, who are mentioned by name, have been separated from the remainder of the Dispersion, they may not mingle or intermarry with us, neither they nor their children, and no person may recite from them the benediction of marriage. If any one transgresses this order and does marry them, whether he act willingly or under compulsion, the marriage is declared void." (Takkanan of the Synod of Frankfort [1603]; reprinted in Finkelstein 1924, 263-264)

There is no question that Judaism has been characterized by high levels of within-group altruism. The general importance of charity within the Jewish community dates from Biblical times and is strongly emphasized in the Talmud: "an undying spirit of common responsibility of each individual for the whole group and of the group for the individual" (Baron 1952b, 270; see also Johnson 1987, 158). Emphasizing the group nature of this responsibility, Woocher (1986, 85) notes that the traditional term *tzedakah* implies "an obligatory act of justice, not a noblesse oblige expression of personal beneficence. *Tzedakah* is a collective communal responsibility, one aspect of the larger command to the Jewish people that they pursue justice as a society."

The extent to which charity was emphasized within the Jewish community is truly remarkable. Writing of the traditional shtetl communities of Eastern Europe, Zborowski and Herzog (1952) show that the requirement for charity fairly pervaded life in the group; "at every turn during one's life, the reminder to give is present" (p. 193). Charity was "a badge of group membership [which] has been so worked into the structure of society that it serves as a channel through which property, learning and services are diffused" (p. 194).

Every celebration and holiday included gifts to the poor, and, indeed, any event that was out of the ordinary elicited a contribution to one of the several tin cups that each family had for placing coins intended for various charitable causes. It was not only the wealthy who were expected to be charitable, but everyone—even those who were the recipients of charity. Children were socialized early regarding the importance of charity, partly by being used as go-betweens between donors and donees. Women contributed by visiting the sick and providing them with food and clothing.

There was also a variety of official community charitable organizations, including separate organizations for providing clothes for the poor, dowries for poor girls, support for orphans, medical expenses for the poor, support for itinerant beggars, support for the aged, and support for burial expenses. There was also a community association that gave interest-free loans for starting businesses, and individual charity that helped others enter business was very highly regarded.

Penalties for avoiding Jewish charity were severe. The Spanish Synod of 1432 imposed the "stringent herem of ten maledictions" against tax evaders (Finkelstein 1924, 371). Goitein (1971, 67), writing of practices during medieval Islamic times, notes that payments for charitable purposes were viewed as a major religious obligation, analogous to membership dues in a modern religious congregation. Resident foreigners were also forced to pay toward the support of the community poor under threat of being banned. The passage from the Frankfort synod of 1603 quoted at the beginning of this section is also an excellent example of social controls that resulted in altruism among Jews: Individuals were assessed a certain sum of money, and they and their children were threatened with expulsion from the community if they did not comply.

But the greatest negative sanction was simply that of public opinion—the "cold shoulders, wagging tongues, and raised eyebrows" of other community members (Zborowski & Herzog 1952, 209). The social cost of avoiding contributions was "so severe that few would brave it" (Zborowski & Herzog 1952, 209). Wealthy men who were called to read the Torah at Sabbath services had to contribute to the community in return for this privilege. The amount contributed was announced to the congregation in advance of the reading. Wealthy men who developed a reputation for not being sufficiently charitable were called to read the Torah for the explicit purpose of providing group pressure on the individual to contribute.

In addition to these negative sanctions against those who fail to contribute, there was a strong emphasis on positive reinforcement. A principal source of one's reputation in the community depended on commitment to group goals. Being rich in itself brought far less prestige than being known as generous to the community. The rewards of charity were "so far-reaching and on so many levels, that they are almost irresistible" (Zborowski & Herzog 1952, 209). Charity is second only to learning in creating prestige for an individual (p. 75). But even so, being a scholar logically implied that one would not be miserly (p. 206), a result indicating the extent to which the scholar was expected to embody all of the social ideals of Judaism. A man who is *sheyn* (beautiful) "is a man of social conscience, fulfilling his responsibility to the community by service to the group and its individuals. His accepted obligation is to succor and protect those who are less wealthy, less privileged than he" (p. 75). Such a person receives *koved* (deference) from others.

It was customary to donate within the Jewish community for education as the first priority (e.g., for the medieval period among the Ashkenazim, see Kanarfogel 1992, 51). Charity for education served a group function because it would assist poor, but talented Jews to be an economic asset to the entire Jewish community in economic transactions with gentiles. However, by supporting the education of poor Jews, the economically self-sufficient Jews were also facilitating the development of the skills of children who would compete with their own children within the Jewish community. As discussed in the following chapter, the Jewish community was an intellectual meritocracy in which the ultimate payoff was reproductive success.

Charity for the poor was also of great importance. Obligation to the poor was proportional to one's wealth, and all of the poor were to be supported, although we shall see below that in fact there were important limits on Jewish charity. Goitein (1971), writing of practices during the medieval Islamic period, shows that the burden represented by the poor was heavy at times—estimated by Goitein as amounting to one relief recipient to every four donors. Shaw (1991) notes that in the Ottoman period individuals with means were expected to give between one-tenth and one-fifth of their wealth to the poor, including especially dowries for poor brides.

A particularly interesting aspect of community support for the poor was the practice of supporting the marriages of poorer members of the community by providing dowries for poor girls—a practice that dates from at least the second century (Baron 1952b, 221). This type of charity is rather directly associated with the reproductive success of individuals whose own resources were insufficient to support a marriage. And because it is so intimately associated with attaining evolutionary goals, it is precisely this type of charity that would be expected to lead to high levels of commitment to the group.[12]

There are many examples of Jewish charity among widely dispersed groups. Neuman (1969, I:171) notes that "a Jewish wayfarer was assured of protection and welcome among his brethren in any part of the world. The essential unity of Jewish life in the Middle Ages transcended geographical boundaries and rendered Jews one sympathetic community in which the Oriental, African, Spanish, Italian and German brethren were perfectly at home with one another." Goitein (1971, 94ff) gives numerous examples of Jews supporting the poor in distant Jewish communities in the medieval Arab world. "Gifts were sent to localities in which the need was greatest" (p. 95), so that, for example, Jews in Cairo contributed to ransoming Jews in Byzantium, Spain, and other parts of Europe. Weinryb (1972) notes that during the anti-Semitic uprisings of the 17th century in Poland, Jews were welcomed as refugees in other Jewish communities in Poland and were ransomed by other Jewish communities from Italy, Constantinople, Amsterdam, and Hamburg. Israel (1985) describes taxes imposed on the communities of central Europe during the 17th century intended to free captives in the Mediterranean area, and Shaw (1991, 74) states that Jewish communities in the Ottoman Empire "taxed themselves very heavily" in order to ransom Jewish slaves in the entire period from 1300 to the 19th century.

Another aspect of this far-flung effort was to contribute to the support of scholars and scholarly institutions in distant countries, and especially the academy in Palestine (Goitein 1971, 94). Israel (1985) describes the institutionalization of charity intended to prop up Jewish communities in the Holy Land among both Sephardic and Ashkenazi communities in Europe during the 17th century.

In Chapter 4, the general point was made that emancipation led to the decline of rigid forms of centralized community controls among Jews, but did not lead to an end to Jewish cultural and genetic separatism as an important aspect of Judaism as an group evolutionary strategy. Within-group altruism continued as an important aspect of Judaism in this period as well. In Hamburg in 1815, this voluntary rather than community-imposed system of support "provided a network of support from the cradle to the grave," which amounted to a sort of parallel universe of social support outside gentile society, including every aspect of social welfare, loans for businessmen, dowries for poor girls, and support for artisans and students (Sorkin 1987, 122). Moreover, Lindemann (1991) notes the numerous active attempts by Jews to help other Jews in different countries in late-19th- and early-20th-century Europe (e.g., French Jews helping Syrian Jews during the Damascus blood libel trial, the charitable and educational activities of the Alliance Israélite Universelle, Western European Jews helping Russian Jews during the pogroms that occurred between 1881 and 1914).

Similar tendencies, especially notable during the period of immigration from 1880 to 1920, were evident among Jews in the United States (e.g., Sachar 1992, 151). Woocher (1986, 25-26) points out that charitable work is a very central aspect of contemporary American Judaism as a "secular religion" and in fact constituted the main force for Jewish unity beginning early in the 20th century. Indeed, in the absence of social controls enforcing within-group charity, voluntary financial contribution to Jewish causes became a defining feature of being a Jew. The obligation to aid other Jews had become "a primary expression of the meaning of Jewishness" (Woocher 1986, 28), the primary means for achieving a Jewish identity, for recognizing someone as a Jew, and for maintaining group cohesion in the face of powerful assimilatory pressures. Jewish charity became a mechanism where all involved could participate in the Jewish tradition, including the administrators, the volunteers, the professionals, and the recipients of aid. And, in particular, this mutual responsibility came to entail a deep commitment to Israel: "Jewish unity, mutual responsibility, and Jewish survival all come together in Israel; it is the symbolic center of the civil Jewish universe . . ." (Woocher 1986, 77).

The evidence therefore indicates that Judaism was able to continue as a homogenous, highly endogamous subculture separated from the host society even after the demise of the *kehilla* system of self-government in the diaspora.

As in traditional Judaism, Jewish charity is obligatory, but in the post-emancipation world there are no formal sanctions against those who do not contribute. However, by ceasing to participate in Jewish charity, one in effect ceases to be a Jew. Woocher notes that by maintaining such an obviously moral requirement, Judaism also gains a sense of moral justification—an important aspect of the ideology that Judaism represents an ethical "light of the nations".

Finally, in reading treatments such as that of Zborowski and Herzog (1952, 191ff) and Woocher (1986, 26ff), one gets the impression that charity has always functioned to make each individual aware of the group nature of Judaism. At all turns, one is reminded that all Jews had a common fate and that the group, not the individual, must come first in one's thoughts. As Zborowski and Herzog (1952, 194) note, charity is a badge of commitment to group goals—the best sign that one has adopted the group ethic of Judaism.

On the one hand, the clear evidence for a very powerful set of institutional controls and strong cultural pressures toward charity is testimony that group strategies must overcome considerable evolutionary inertia that biases people away from high levels of altruism, even within a group that has retained a fairly high level of biological relatedness. On the other hand, the evidence implies that people can accept such a powerful group orientation and that quite high levels of altruism can develop within human group strategies. The importance of Jewish charity as a badge of group membership is particularly good confirmation of the fundamental thesis of this volume: that Judaism is a group evolutionary strategy characterized by high levels of within-group altruism.

## Limitations on Jewish Charity as an Aspect of Judaism as a Group Evolutionary Strategy

> If we have been reproached at one time with want of industry, indolence, and aversion to labour, let us now avoid such reproaches, which might have been unjust formerly, but which we should now deserve. Let us exert all our influence to accustom our poor, who, till now, have been fed by our alms, to prefer the gains of labour, even at the sweat of their brows. (Letter of M. Berr-Isaac-Berr to his Brethren, in 1791, on the Rights of active Citizens being granted to the Jews; reprinted in Tama [1807] 1971, 28-29)

Despite the evidence that within-group altruism is an important component of Judaism as an evolutionary strategy, there were important limits on this altruism. As noted in Chapter 1, there are theoretical reasons to suppose that a successful altruistic group strategy must develop ways to protect against "freeloaders," and in the case of Judaism, charity toward the poor was neither complete nor unconditional.

In the traditional shtetl societies of Eastern Europe, orphans and the very poor supported by the community had a very low status and only very minimal provisions were made for their education (Zborowski & Herzog 1952, 102-104).

These children attended the *Talmud Toryeh*, and they were dressed very shabbily. On the other hand, children attending the *yeshiva* might be equally poor, but they had much more status because of their future prospects in the community. The Talmud Toryeh children were well aware of their low social status and were the butt of children's hostility.

More importantly, the Talmud Toryeh children were apprenticed to a trade and had no opportunity to ascend the ranks of scholarship. This gap between the religious ideal and actual practice appears to have resulted in a sort of communal guilt: "Uneasiness seems to be associated with the Talmud Toryeh which, although it fulfills the shtetl standard of helping the needy, nevertheless countenances a merging of sacred and worldly teaching that violates the traditional spirit of study" (Zborowski & Herzog 1952, 104).

Despite the Talmudic injunction regarding the obligation to provide dowries for poor girls, the Ashkenazim consistently regulated the marriages of the lower classes (Hyman 1986; Katz 1961a; Weinryb 1972), and Hundert (1986b) notes that the marriages of poor and indigent Jews came under special scrutiny by community officials. (The poor were also prevented from voting in *Kehilla* elections [Katz 1961a]). For example, it was common for the Jewish communities of Poland to have a quota of marriages of individuals with less than a certain dowry. Hundert cites a community regulation of 1595 to the effect that "no betrothal may take place in which the bride gives under 150 zlotys before there has been an investigation establishing that they will not become a burden on the community" (p. 23). In 1632 a couple was allowed to marry on condition that they not receive any community support for five years, and in 1679 and 1681 in Poznan a regulation was passed prohibiting no more than six marriages in which the dowry was less than 400 zlotys. Other communities had a lottery for poor girls allowed to marry.

There is some indication that at times the community regulation of marriage was motivated by a concern for an overpopulation of Jews. Katz (1961a, 140) notes that "(t)he *kehilla* was often responsible for the postponement of marriages in its wish to limit the number of breadwinners in the locality." If correct, this attempt to gauge the carrying capacity of the environment and regulate the population according to group interests would be a remarkable example of a group-level adaptive response involving altruism on the part of individual Jews.

In evolutionary terms this community control of reproduction is an extraordinary example of the triumph of group interests over individual interests. Although this type of group-selectionist thinking about population regulation has long been derided as a general principle of evolution since the writings of Williams (1966), there is no theoretical reason whatever to suppose that a human group strategy could not develop this type of ability and be able to enforce it.

Finally, despite the general tendency to minimize social class conflicts within Judaism, highly salient social class divisions did develop at several periods of Jewish history and did indeed result in conflicts of interest. These social class divisions within the Jewish community occurred especially in areas, such as

19th-century Eastern Europe, where a very large increase in the Jewish population was accompanied by economic and social diversification within the Jewish community. Lindemann (1991, 143) notes that in Russia Jewish capitalists sometimes used Christian employees as strikebreakers against their Jewish employees, and there was a great deal of labor agitation by immigrant Jewish employees working for Jewish employers in the garment industry in early-20th-century New York (Levin 1977; Liebman 1979; Sachar 1992).

There are other indications of conflict of interest within the Jewish community. The Hasidic movement was supported primarily by "poor, rough people" (Johnson 1987, 297)—less-educated Jews who felt disenfranchised within the Polish Jewish community, which was dominated by "an intermarried oligarchy of rich merchants and lawyer-rabbis" (Johnson 1987, 294; see also Zborowski & Herzog 1952, 166-188). Moreover, it is a salient fact that throughout Jewish history there has been a tendency for the relatively poor and obscure to defect from Judaism (see Chapters 2 and 7), suggesting that within-group altruism is insufficient to overcome the pull of assimilation for these individuals. Nevertheless, Jewish charity has certainly been a very salient feature of Judaism and has certainly contributed to its internal solidarity.

Limits on charity are also suggested by the fact that charity has tended to be stronger with more closely related individuals. This direct correlation between altruism and biological relatedness is quite common in human societies (see Alexander 1979) and is certainly predicted by evolutionary theory. This type of gradation was recognized by the ancient sages. Baron (1952b. 271) notes, "In the hierarchy of philanthropic values they taught, 'your own poor come before those of your city, those of your city before strangers.'" Thus, among the Ashkenazim, there was the expectation that one's own poor relatives should receive priority, especially with regard to the duty to provide dowries to the daughters of poor relatives (Katz 1961a). Indeed, Goitein (1978, 45) notes that wealthy individuals in medieval Islamic times had a duty to keep poor relatives from being a burden to the community.

The diminution of Jewish charity with genetic distance can also be seen from the fact that Jewish communities deriving from different areas have often segregated themselves from each other and prevented foreign Jews from entering. Thus, beginning in the medieval period, European Jews developed the institution of the *herem ha-yishuv* to deny admittance to newcomers (Goitein 1971, 68). Ben-Sasson (1971, 215) describes the ideals of the medieval Hassidim of Ashkenaz (Germany) as attempting to marry completely among themselves and exclude other Jews completely from their communities. Israel (1985) notes a community regulation in England requiring Jews who were admitted to prove that they were financially independent. While such formal institutions did not develop in the Arab world during this period, there is evidence that newcomers who represented competition with local Jews were discouraged from entry.

Beginning in the late 19th century into the early decades of the 20th century, there was a major split in the United States between the older German-American

Jewish community and the more recently arrived immigrants from Eastern Europe. We have seen that the German-Jewish community did provide charity for the immigrants, but there are indications that it was resented and, to some extent, minimized. Liebman (1979, 152) quotes a Yiddish newspaper of the period as follows:

> In the philanthropic institutions of our aristocratic German Jews you see beautiful offices, desks, all decorated, but strict and angry faces. Every poor man is questioned like a criminal, is looked down upon; every unfortunate suffers self-degradation and shivers like a leaf, just as if he were standing before a Russian official. When the same Russian Jew is in an institution of Russian Jews . . . he feels at home among his own brethren who speak his tongue, understand his thoughts, and feel his heart.

Liebman suggests that these negative attitudes on the part of the German-American Jews resulted in attempts among the new immigrants to build up their own charitable organizations. Moreover, Liebman (1979, 153) describes "numerous occasions when the philanthropy of the German Jews coincided with their economic interests to the detriment of the needy Eastern Europeans," including using their positions in charities to recruit cheap labor or to break strikes. It is of interest that the mutual animosity between these two communities of Jews lessened in times of external threat: Pogroms and other threats to Jews in Eastern Europe tended to soften the attitudes of the German-American Jews toward their co-religionists (Liebman 1979, 155)—another indication of the importance of external threat in facilitating group cohesion and altruism.

The importance of a gradation in Jewish charity depending on degree of genetic relatedness is also indicated by the descriptions of the *Landsmanshaft* societies among Jewish immigrants in the United States presented earlier in this chapter. Mutual aid was a direct function of the physical proximity of the other members of the group, and this physical proximity was closely bound up with endogamous marriage practices.

These findings not only show the importance of Jewish charity, but also show that Jews were often highly selective in their charity: The examples suggest that, when a choice was necessary because of limited resources, they favored the Jewish individual or group that was more closely related genetically. Thus, the idea that Judaism is simply a religion, rather than a national/ethnic movement, breaks down even when thinking about relationships within Judaism: Despite sharing the same religion, charity is preferentially directed to more closely related individuals.

# CONCLUSION

The material summarized in this chapter indicates that historical Judaism can be characterized as a group evolutionary strategy in which individual self-interest was significantly submerged in the interests of group goals. This group orientation does not imply the absence of competition within the Jewish community. On the contrary; in the following chapter, it will be shown that competition for social and economic status within the Jewish community (and its correlative reproductive success) was intense. However, the data reviewed here indicate that this intense competition within the group was not allowed to compromise group goals. From the standpoint of the group, it was always more important to maximize the total resource flow from the gentile community to the Jewish community, rather than to allow individual Jews to maximize their interests at the expense of the Jewish community. Within the Jewish community, however, there was a significant redistribution of wealth, so that in the end decrements to individual interests resulting from these community social controls were minimized.

The material reviewed in Chapters 2, 4, and 6 can be viewed as a summary of the main centripetal forces binding Jews to the community and preventing defection from the group strategy: the maintenance of high levels of genetic commonality within the group and a genetic gradient between Jewish and gentile populations; the development of powerful cultural barriers between Jews and gentiles; extremely severe sanctions on defectors ("informers") and their families; a high level of economic cooperation and a relative lack of class conflict within the group; and a high level of altruism within the group, which benefited lower-status members and provided a safety net for all. In the following chapter, it will be shown that traditional Jewish society was to a significant extent a meritocracy, so that lower-status Jews could hope that they or their children could rise in status. Presumably this also cemented allegiance to the group.

# NOTES

1. Mechanisms that result in equality of risk imply selection at a higher level than the units undergoing risk. At the genetic level, meiosis evolved as a random process for excluding some genetic variants. Wilson and Sober (1994) note that this implies that meiosis (apart from meiotic drive) must be conceptualized as a group-level phenomenon, since fitness differences are eliminated at the genetic level. This is also presumably the reason why "drawing straws" and other random determinations are sometimes used as a mechanism for determining who should engage in dangerous work for the benefit of the community (e.g. military draft lotteries)—implying selection at the group level. It is also the reason why social controls at the community level that significantly level reproductive success and access to resources within groups, as proposed here for Judaism, imply

group-level processes. Combined with data indicating group differences in fitness (see Chapter 5), this implies selection at the group level among humans.

2. The theory of anti-Semitism developed in *SAID* (ch. 1) implies that in cases of group conflict examples of immoral behavior by individuals tend to be uncritically generalized to the group. Community control over individual behavior has therefore been a major aspect of efforts to combat anti-Semitism.

3. As discussed in *SAID* (ch. 4), in addition to high levels of real danger resulting from anti-Semitism, Jewish groups have often exaggerated external threats with the result that group allegiance is heightened.

4. In 1618, a French diplomat noted that Jews

> are numerous and influential in Amsterdam and have exceedingly intimate relations with the State, because they are equally attentive to foreign news and to commerce. . . . In both matters they obtain their information from the other Jewish communities with which they are in close contact . . . . By this means the Jews in Amsterdam are the first and the best informed about foreign commerce and the news of what is going on in the world . . . . These practices are the source of their riches. (Quoted in Baron 1973, 48)

Baron (1973, 49) states that these remarks may be exaggerated, but "they undoubtedly contain a grain of truth."

5. Shaw (1991, 95) also notes that because Jews controlled the customs in the Ottoman Empire, they charged non-Jews more money on their goods, another competitive advantage of ethnic solidarity.

6. The Deuteronomic law of interest has been variously interpreted throughout Jewish history, and an apologetic historiographical literature has developed (see, e.g., Stein 1955). These issues are discussed in *SAID* (ch. 4). (See also note 7.)

7. The ethical double standard *vis-à-vis* gentiles has been a very prominent theme of anti-Semitism (see also *SAID*, ch. 2). During the Middle Ages, there were several disputations between Jews and Christians centering around the permissibility of Jewish moneylending to Christians and other examples of ethical double standards (Maccoby 1982; Rabinowitz 1938, 90; Rosenthal 1956; Stein 1955, 1959). For example, one disputed passage, b. B. K. 38a, states that if a Canaanite ox gores an Israelite, damages must be paid, but damages need not be paid if an Israelite ox gores a Canaanite. The passage also recounts an incident in which Roman agents investigating the ethics of the Talmud disagreed with this passage, but did not tell their government. During the medieval period, several prominent Jewish apologists vigorously defended the differential treatment of Jews and Christians regarding moneylending. There were also attempts to argue that Talmudic references to heathens or idolators (*'akum*) in matters of differential ethics did not apply to Christians. Rosenthal (1956, 68; see also Rabinowitz 1938, 90) notes that despite this type of argument, the Jewish masses "did not differentiate between the non-Jew in the Talmud and the non-Jew of his time." And Stein (1959, 58; see also Katz 1961a) notes that the idea that gentiles were not idolators (and thus not subject to an ethical double standard) continued to be controversial among Jewish thinkers. Maimonides, for example, explicitly viewed all Christians as idolators. Maccoby (1982, 33) argues that, since medieval Christians behaved savagely toward Jews, it was reasonable that they be viewed as *'akum*.

8. Interestingly, the text of the regulation notes that the non-Jewish nobility often attempted to make the owner of the monopoly give up his exclusive rights in favor of competition that would tend to lower interest rates to the advantage of the gentiles.

9. These practices were a potent fuel for anti-Semitism (see *SAID*, ch. 2). Anti-Semitic writers often condemned Jews for proscriptions on doing business with Christians. Non-Jews attempted to respond to the competition represented by Jews by using many of the same tactics, so that monopolistic-exclusion principles operated on both sides (Weinryb 1972, 159).

10. Indeed, Sachar (1992, 33) suggests that the strong tendency toward consanguinity resulted in a tendency toward mental retardation among the Gomez family.

11. This percentage would undoubtedly have been higher had first cousins always been available. The four sons born to James and his wife/niece Betty all married exogamously, the marriages occurring between 1905 and 1913 at a time when marriage to first cousins was impossible because of lack of availability. As noted in Chapter 4 (note 22), the Rothschild marriage strategy shifted from establishing attractive alliances to consanguinity after the Rothschilds became the wealthiest family of Europe.

12. Herlihy (1991) makes this point in assessing the importance of the ability to marry in explaining the powerful group orientation of the early Mediterranean city-states in Greece and Rome: "Under conditions of acute competition, it was necessary to maintain the moral commitment and physical energies of the citizens. Such conditions favored the development of democratic and republican, rather than despotic institutions. The citizens whose moral commitment was essential for the welfare of the state had to be granted some participation in it. But another, equally crucial means of maintaining commitment and morale was to offer all citizens access to marriage. Not only would they gain the satisfactions of sexual union, but the rearing of the family and the acquisition of heirs would give them a large stake in the *salus populi*" (pp. 14-15). Similarly, the ability to marry would be a highly salient force that would tend to create allegiance to group goals among Jews.

# 7

# JUDAISM AS AN ECOLOGICAL STRATEGY: SELECTION FOR PHENOTYPIC TRAITS RELATED TO INTELLIGENCE, HIGH-INVESTMENT PARENTING, AND SOCIAL COHESION

[The law] commands us to bring . . . children up in learning and to exercise them in the laws. (Flavius Josephus, *Against Apion,* 2:204)

The evidence reviewed in the first several chapters indicates that Judaism may be viewed as an evolutionary strategy that has often involved intrasocietal resource competition with host gene pools. In particular, in Chapter 5 the extraordinarily rapid rise of Jews in Western societies after emancipation was noted, as was their success in competing with gentiles in a wide variety of areas ranging from business to the sciences and the arts. The purpose of the present chapter is to describe evidence related to the question of whether these high levels of achievement can in any sense be viewed as an aspect of Judaism as an evolutionary strategy.

As throughout this volume, in order for a particular practice to be considered an aspect of an evolutionary strategy, there must be evidence of a conscious purpose, rather than passive imposition. The proposal here is that Judaism represents an ecologically specialized group evolutionary strategy. The data presented in Chapter 5 indicate that Jews have competed with gentiles in a very wide range of economic activity and aspects of social status, ranging from artisan guilds to positions of influence with the government. These findings make generalization difficult. However, one very common feature of Jewish economic activity, noted, e.g., by Lindemann (1991, 146) is that Jews have often been overrepresented among middlemen as conduits for gentile primary production, as well as in relationships of manager over gentiles or employer to gentiles. We have also noted a strong tendency for Jews to compete successfully for positions that require education, literacy, and intelligence. In ecological terms, the generalization is that Jews tended to concentrate at the top of the human energy pyramid in prototypical societies throughout their history.[1]

In this regard, Jews are typical of several other "middleman minorities" that have occupied a similar ecological role in a variety of human societies (e.g., the Chinese in Southeast Asia; see Sowell 1993; Zenner 1991). The point here is that Jews, and undoubtedly other middleman minorities as well, tend to have a suite of traits that enable them to attain this ecological position above other groups in the society, the most important being intelligence and certain traits related to what personality psychologists refer to as "conscientiousness."

The purpose of this chapter is to show that Judaism as an evolutionary strategy has emphasized education and high-investment parenting, as well as eugenic practices and cultural supports related to intelligence and resource acquisition ability. In addition, however, there is evidence for the development of traits conducive to the group cohesion that is so essential to Judaism as a group evolutionary strategy.

# EDUCATION AND INTELLECTUAL ABILITY AS ASPECTS OF JUDAISM AS AN EVOLUTIONARY STRATEGY

Take fast hold of instruction, let her not go; Keep her, for she is thy life. (Prov. 4:13)

Death and life are in the power of the tongue; and they that indulge it shall eat the fruit thereof. (Prov. 18:21)

If you discover a wise man, rise early to visit him; let your feet wear out his doorstep. (Ecclus. 6:36)

A poor man with wisdom can hold his head high and take his seat among the great. (Ecclus. 11:1)

Schoolchildren may not be made to neglect their studies for the building of the Temple. (b. Shabbath 119b)

There is evidence in the ancient world for an intense interest in education among the Jews. The Jewish religious law was incredibly elaborated in the first centuries of the Christian era, culminating with the writing of the Mishnah and the Palestinian (Yerushalmi) and Babylonian (Bavli) Talmuds. These documents not only contain an extraordinary amount of sheer information, but also are presented in an extremely complex rhetorical style, so that thorough mastering of Jewish law requires an extremely high level of literacy, the retention of voluminous detail, and the ability to follow highly abstract arguments.

The proposal here is that Torah study as the *summum bonum* within the Jewish community had four important benefits relevant to the present perspective on Judaism as an evolutionary strategy: (1) Most obviously, scholarly study resulted in knowledge of an incredibly wide ranging set of laws and customs, which constituted an important source of the barriers between Jews and gentiles and therefore was important for facilitating genetic and cultural segregation. There is also a long scholarly tradition that holds that the Pharisees and their successors utilized their knowledge and practice of the law to separate themselves from lower-class Jews—the *'am ha-ares* (Sanders 1992, 428; see discussion below). (2) Training in the Jewish law would result in a relatively high level of education for the Jewish population as a whole compared to surrounding populations. This training would then be useful in resource competition with surrounding populations. (3) However, apart from the general level of Jewish education compared to surrounding populations, the educational system was geared to producing a highly educated elite. We have seen that the prosperity of the Jewish community in traditional societies often depended on the actions of a highly educated, wealthy elite of courtiers, capitalists, and lessees who in turn employed other Jews and thereby advanced the fortunes of the entire Jewish community. (4) Scholarly study became an important arena of natural selection for intelligence by serving as a vehicle of upward mobility within the Jewish community, as well as providing access to resources and reproductive success.

It should be noted that knowledge of barriers between Jews and gentiles could be obtained by means of oral communication of the law to the masses. As emphasized by Bickerman (1988, 170), if the only goal were to ensure that the people were aware of the large number of segregative rituals, there would be no need to develop a highly educated elite or to emphasize universal education for a high level of literacy within the Jewish community as a whole. Nor would it be necessary to develop a system that resulted in a large overlap among intelligence, education, resource control, and reproductive success. However, beginning around 200 B.C., perhaps with the writings of Ben Sira (Bickerman 1988, 170), there was an attempt to develop an intelligentsia separate from the priestly clans in which wisdom was identified with knowledge of the Torah and there was a concomitant effort to make some level of education available to the entire community of Jews.

## The Importance of Education

Moore (1927-30 I:281) notes that the attempt to educate all Jews in their religion was unique in the ancient world. Moreover, "[i]n its singular adaptation to the religious education of the whole people it seems rather to give evidence of intelligent purpose" (I:286). Religious study and teaching became "fundamental institutions of Judaism" (I:311), long preceding the Christian era, and organized schools date from shortly before this period.

Bickerman (1988) describes the development of the scribes as an educated, literate class beginning at least by the second century B.C. During this period, there was an idealization of "wisdom" defined as knowledge of the law of Moses, as represented by the writings of Ben Sira: "The Torah of the priest and the scribe was to be the foundation and the fulfillment of secular, liberal education" (p. 170), and this "Torah-centric" education (p. 172) was no longer restricted to the hereditary priestly class. This new scholarly elite, a sort of union between scribes and priests, would rise to their positions of social prominence on their own merits (Neusner 1987, 66). From this period on, the scholarly class became dominant in the Jewish community, and the entire community was expected to become "a nation of priests" and familiar with the law (Baron 1952a, 142; Baron 1952b, 276).

Bickerman (1988) stresses the idea that this concern with education was based on contemporary Greek interest in education: "The study of law was a Hellenistic innovation in Jerusalem" (p. 173). This suggests that the Jewish response was self-consciously motivated by a need to develop an educated intelligentsia able to compete in the Greek world. Indeed, Bickerman suggests that being a sage or a student of a sage was a necessary preparation for success in the Greek world, and by the end of the second century the author of pseudo-Aristeas could say that the ideal Jew not only was learned in the Torah, but also could impress Greek philosophers, with the result that "the myth of Jewish intellectual superiority began to take shape in Jewish thought" (p. 175). On the other hand, in Egypt and Babylon, native religious knowledge continued to be the province of a narrow class of priests and gradually disappeared.

As expected from this functionalist interpretation, the importance of education increased when it became increasingly clear that hopes for national independence were dashed. Baron (1952b, 120) notes that "[i]n the period following the failed rebellions in the second century [A.D.], the study of the Torah now became the very core of survival" (Baron 1952b, 120). The rabbis "declared the acquisition of a good education to be one of the primary duties of each individual, and provision for it a major responsibility of the community" (Baron 1952b, 274; see also Stern 1976, 946). "Torah study was not confined to the legal experts and the priests, but became a general community matter" (Stern 1976, 946). This requirement that all Jewish children be educated was quite unlike the practices in the surrounding Greco-Roman culture, where education was never intended to be available for everyone (Safrai 1968, 148).

Safrai (1968) finds the first reference to universal education for Jewish children in the beginning of the first century B.C., but proposes that the process began earlier and was completed only somewhat later. Stern (1976) cites a first century baraita that requires Jewish communities to have schools (b. Sanhedrin 17b), and the custom of measuring the greatness of a town by the number of schools. "A town which did not employ teachers of the written and oral Law had no right to exist" (p. 947). Reflecting this supreme importance, the Talmuds contain much discussion of methods of instruction and educational facilities.

"Judaism attached unique social recognition, in accord with its supreme evaluation of the all-human, indeed cosmic importance of Jewish education" (Baron 1952b, 276).

In keeping with the general segregationist thrust of Judaism, only Torah was taught in these schools: "The general Jewish school system dealt neither with Greek culture nor with their language" (Safrai 1968, 153). Nevertheless, as has probably been the case throughout subsequent Jewish history, the result even in the ancient world was that the average level of education among Jews was significantly higher than among the surrounding populations.

Apart from community-wide elementary education, there was an even stronger emphasis on education of an elite group of scholars. The emphasis on a scholarly elite can be seen in Ecclesiasticus 38:24–39:11, written in the second century B.C. This passage contrasts those who work with their hands with the scholar who preserves ancient knowledge, is of service to rulers, and is a source of sound advice for the community. Whereas the scholar has the most noble profession, those who work with their hands "are not in demand in public discussions or prominent in assembly. . . But they maintain the fabric of this world, and their prayers are about their daily work." The emphasis on elitism among the ancient Jews can also be seen in the exalted status Josephus attaches to wealthy, successful individuals (Sevenster 1975, 19-21). Individuals who remained without education and in ignorance of the law came to be regarded as of low status, and called by the pejorative term *'am ha-ares*. As indicated below, there is excellent evidence for social, economic, and genetic discrimination against this group by the scholarly elite.

Corresponding to the very high social status attached to success as a scholar, there were economic as well as ultimately genetic benefits to being a successful scholar. From the origins of Judaism in the ancient world, rabbis were given special privileges, such as freedom from taxes, and there was a meritocracy such that family connections and money counted for little in attaining high status (Baron 1952b, 279). As early as the end of the second century and certainly by the third century, the practice developed that each community would provide economic support for a "resident spiritual leader-scholar-judge" (Alon [1980, 1984] 1989, 498). Moreover, as elaborated below, success as a scholar was valuable because it allowed the scholar to contract a desirable marriage, often to a woman from a wealthy family. At the very center of Judaism, therefore, was a set of institutions that would reliably result in eugenic processes related to intelligence and resource acquisition ability.

## The Jewish Canon as an Arena and Product of High Level Intellectual Competition within the Jewish Community

Given the high social status accorded to scholars, as well as their ability to make good marriages, it is not surprising that the Jewish religious canon became extremely elaborated and complex, with the result that aspiring to a position of scholarly prominence required a great deal of intelligence and prolonged study. Regarding the substance of higher education, "[e]ven a moderate proficiency in it was not to be attained without long and patient years of learning; mastery demanded unusual capacity. The method of the schools developed not only exact and retentive memory and great mental acuteness, but an exhaustive and ever-ready knowledge of every phrase and word of Scripture" (Moore 1927-30, I:319-320). In the language of modern research on intelligence, there is a strong emphasis in the traditional Jewish curriculum on verbal knowledge, rote memory, verbal concept formation, and comprehension of abstract ideas (Levinson 1958, 284).

It is important to note that the vast literature of the Mishnah, the Yerushalmi and Bavli, Midrashic collections, and subsequent commentary actually "contributed relatively little to the fundamentals of Judaism. All the essentials had been laid down by the Pharisaic scribes with an astounding finality, and Talmudic Jewry adhered to them with unswerving fidelity" (Baron 1952b, 310). Although there was a definite need for a body of civil and business law and other aspects of life as a self-governing community in the diaspora covered by the Mishnah and Talmuds, evidence provided here indicates that these documents contain a vast amount of material for which there are no practical functions at all. The incredible elaboration of Jewish religious law in these writings suggests that this mass of material is the result of intense intellectual competition within the Jewish community and that the resulting Torah then provided an arena for intellectual competition within the Jewish community.

To begin with, these writings are extremely difficult to understand without a great deal of study. There is no attempt to develop an easily comprehensible code of law or religious ideology that would be comprehensible to an individual who did not have an extraordinary degree of education and commitment to study.

> *What* is said in the Mishnah is simple. *How* it is said is arcane. . . . Its deep structure of syntax and grammatical forms shapes what is said into an essentially secret and private language. It takes many years to master the difficult argot . . . . (Neusner 1988b, xxv; italics in text).

Neusner notes that although the Mishnah may be described as a law code, a schoolbook, and a corpus of tradition, it is best described as a work of philosophy in the Aristotelian tradition. The Aristotelian nature of much of this work is well illustrated by Neusner's (1988a, III:204-205) analysis of Tractate Terumot, a tractate concerned with designating a portion of agricultural crops for heave-offering for priests, which is an expansion of six verses from the Book of Numbers (18:8-13). The tractate contains extremely complex discussions of the classification of mixtures and things that fall into different classes. The differences between potential and actual and between intentional and unintentional are important for classification, and the tractate discusses cases that involve several principles of classification. "I cannot imagine a more profoundly philosophical reading of a topic that, in itself, bears no philosophical interest whatever" (Neusner 1988a, III:205).

As in the case of Aristotelian philosophy, there is a great concern with classification and logical relationships among categories. Notice, however, the last sentence in this comment. The topic itself is without philosophical interest. Moreover, although the topic of heave-offering concerns a religious obligation with considerable practical concern to the authorities (see below), it becomes elaborated far beyond any practical usage here, and to characterize the tractate as religious is to strain the usual meaning of the term.

Indeed, many tractates have no foundation in Scripture at all and yet contain elaborate regulations. Thus, Tractate Tohorot concerns the cleanness or uncleanness of animals and raises a host of highly abstract issues involving classification.[2] Neusner (1988a, 209) interprets one section to state that "if pieces of food are joined together and one of them is made unclean, all are affected and remain so. . . . But if we have an unclean piece of food and join others to it, while, when joined, all fall into the same remove of uncleanness as has affected the original, when separated, the pieces are unclean only by virtue of their former contact with that original piece and fall into a diminished remove of uncleanness."

Obviously, this is a very high level of casuistry indeed, and although these regulations may indeed alter the way in which an educated Jew would look at the world, there is a patent "made up," unnecessary quality about the entire tractate. Much of the material deals with issues that could not possibly have been of relevance to anyone at all apart from those who were discussing these issues. Moore (1928, II:74) says it well when he notes, regarding the elaborate regulations on which animals may be eaten, that "inasmuch as most of them were creatures that no civilized man would eat anyhow, these restrictions on diet belonged to learning rather than to life." Moreover, Neusner (1988b, xxvi), notes that, although there is a myriad of rules and regulations, it is difficult to see the Mishnah as a law book because no punishments are prescribed: "The Mishnah hardly even alludes to punishments or rewards consequent upon disobedience or obedience to its laws." Thus, hundreds of examples of how one can become unclean or clean are presented in an extremely difficult logic, but that is pretty much the end of the story.

Many of the problems appear to involve intellectual disputation for its own sake. The Mishnah is thus not constructed in order to produce a logically organized, easily grasped set of laws for purity and legal codes for self-government during the exile. Rather, "[t]he Mishnah begins nowhere. It ends abruptly. There is no predicting where it will commence or explaining why it is done. Where, when, why the document is laid out and set forth are questions not deemed urgent and not answered" (Neusner 1987, 87-88). Sanders (1992,

471) says simply that the Mishnah "does not consist of set rules that governed society. It consists of debates."

Yet the Mishnah is "the initial and definitive statement of Judaism" (Neusner 1988a, I:5)—an integral part of Jewish canon. Moreover, and this is the point, the mastery of this canon was the *summun bonum* of a religion whose elite were not a group of celibate intellectuals, but rather a group of individuals with a great deal of social status and control of resources and whose first religious obligation was to "be fruitful and multiply."

This massive set of writings is therefore substantially *unnecessary* in terms of fulfilling any purely religious or practical legal need. Although, as indicated above, much of the Mishnah itself appears to exist only for the sake of intellectual disputation, this is even more true of the massive set of later writings. Neusner (1986a) shows that the majority of the material in the Yerushalmi and the Bavli is exegesis, including a great deal of expansion, of the Mishnah. Thus, it is common to generalize from the Mishnaic rules and to raise further questions, or establish entirely new lines of inquiry within the overall framework of the Mishnaic tractate. The consistency of rules from the Mishnah (and sometimes between the Mishnah and Tosefta) is explored.

Moreover, the Yerushalmi and the Bavli provide largely non-redundant commentaries on the Mishnah (Neusner 1986, 48ff), so that the sequence from the Mishnah—Yerushalmi—Bavli must be seen as one of ever greater elaboration of material that was already highly abstract and unnecessary to begin with. For example, the Mishnah Tractate Sukkah provides an elaboration on the rites performed in connection with the feast of Tabernacles based on three passages of the Pentateuch. While the scriptural passages only allude to a general obligation regarding the feast, the Mishnah provides prolonged discussions on the validity of particular structures, precisely who has the duty to perform the rite, and "a vast amount of [other] information in neat patterns" (Neusner 1988a, III:164). The Yerushalmi and the Bavli then expand on these issues and resolve disputes arising from positions arising in the Tosefta. For example, sukkahs are said to be valid only if exposed to the firmament, but this raises the issue of whether one sukkah can be on top of another one and of what happens when valid forms of roofing are intertwined with invalid forms. While the Mishnah never came up with a rule for this situation, it is now decreed that combinations of valid and invalid are valid and, moreover, that if no one is living in the upper one, the bottom one is valid. Many other questions are raised, but there is no indication that any of this discussion arose out of any practical need to resolve real disputes arising from the celebration of the feast.

Moreover, not only are the Yerushalmi and the Bavli non-redundant and essentially independent, but there is no suggestion that the latter has an identifiable interpretive ideology or message that might provide a credible rationale for such a massive undertaking. As Neusner (1986, 73) notes, "they wish to do much the same thing, which is to subject the Mishnah to a process of explanation and amplification." The differences are differences of detail and taste: "The genus is the same, the species not" (p. 76). Some tractates, such as b. Qiddushin, add nothing to previous writings on the subject (Neusner 1992, 1).

These linkages between the Mishnah and Scripture provide a sort of intellectual justification of the Mishnah—considered as without autonomous authority—and the latter—viewed as authoritative—but the conclusion must be that the massive Talmudic commentaries on the Mishnah add little or nothing that is new, but serve the purely intellectual function of rationalizing and legitimating previous writings: "[T]heirs was a quest for a higher authority than the logic of their own minds" (Neusner 1987, 105).

Now such a purely intellectual endeavor is certainly understandable without supposing any grand evolutionary function. Within the Western tradition, there have been many purely intellectual attempts to show that religious beliefs are justified on the basis of reason or science or, more recently, that scientific research is compatible with Scripture. For example, during the Middle Ages, the Scholastic philosophers such as Thomas Aquinas attempted to deduce the existence of God, the nature of the soul, and the nature of evil by the use of human reason in conjunction with Scriptural revelation. Their work is at a similar level of complexity, and mastering it would require a similar level of intellectual ability.

There are at least three major differences, however, between the purely intellectual endeavors of these medieval philosophers and the work that resulted in the massive set of writings produced by Judaism in later antiquity—and indeed beyond. In the case of Judaism, mastering these writings was a key to success in the community and ultimately was linked rather directly with control of economic resources and reproductive success. Success in mastering these purely intellectual pursuits was thus important not only as a means of satisfying intellectual curiosity, but also as a key to achieving evolutionary ends. In the case of the scholastic philosophers, there may indeed have been psychological and even some material rewards for their activities, but the activities of these monks were hardly the key to enhanced reproductive success.

Moreover, mastery of these works, or at least familiarity with them, was a major goal for the entire community—indeed, its *summum bonum*. The entire Jewish community—not simply an intellectual elite—was enjoined to become familiar with these works at some level. In a sense every Jew was being graded on the level of his intellectual ability and his knowledge of what had become an overwhelmingly vast and extremely complex scholarly tradition. This was certainly not the case with gentile communities, at least in traditional societies, and certainly never as a matter of religious practice.

Finally, the writings of the sages as a whole came to be viewed as part of the religious writings that, along with Scripture, constituted the Torah. While scriptural exegesis and philosophical and scientific approaches to religion were not uncommon in Christianity, they hardly became part of the sacred tradition itself. For Judaism, however, there was an enormous expansion of sacred writings, so that being a full participant in the religious community required enormous intellectual effort and ability.

We have seen that the vast majority of these writings are without any function in terms of establishing religious and legal practice within the Jewish community; nor, for the most part, are they spiritual or religious in the usual sense of those terms. The present perspective hypothesizes that this mass of written material is, however, profoundly functional as an aspect of the establishment of Judaism as a eugenic/high-investment strategy for intrasocietal, intergroup resource competition. Mastering this immense mass of material is important because such mastery is an extraordinarily good indication of a high level of intellectual ability. The rabbis who contributed to this corpus had to be intimately acquainted with the massive Mishnah as well as the relevant opinions of the Tosefta. They also had to have an enormous knowledge of Scripture and be able to bring particular statements from Scripture to bear on particular problems. By any standard, this requires a high level of intellectual ability, and there is no question that modern psychological research supports the proposition that this high level of intellectual ability would generalize to competence in fields seemingly far removed from the scholarly study of ancient writings. Research on psychometric intelligence clearly shows that there is a strong general component to intelligence (Spearman's $g$ factor). Being able to master this vast mass of writings is thus an excellent indication of a high level of *general* intelligence, and, as indicated below, especially verbal IQ.

One need not suppose that there was a conscious intent on the part of the rabbis to develop a Torah that could serve as a forum for high-stakes intellectual competition. Once scholarship was established as the *summum bonum* and the key to social status, resource control, and reproductive success within the Jewish community, there would be intense competition to develop an intellectual reputation. The writings produced as a result of this competition therefore become increasingly complex and inaccessible to those with less intellectual ability. Within a fairly short time, one could not hope to enter the arena without a very long period of preparation, a firm dedication, and persistence, as well as (I would suppose) native intellectual ability.

Similarly, in contemporary professional sports, the high salaries, social status, and fame of a successful athlete ensure that the competition to achieve success will be extremely intense. The level of play will be the highest available at the current time because the level of rewards ensures a very high level of participation in the competition and no defections from those who are successful. Viewed in this manner, the development of this massive corpus of material is more a consequence of the development of the strategy than a consciously intended aspect of the strategy. In either case, reaching a position of influence and respect in the Jewish community would now require a keen intellect and long, diligent preparation.

This proposal for the function of the massive Jewish canon is compatible with the canon fulfilling other purposes. As indicated above, at an obvious level, there was a need for developing a legal system for a self-governing group living in the diaspora. Also, given the extremely robust separatist thrust of Judaism, these elaborations served to isolate Jews from their surrounding environments and were thus functional not only in a self-consciously religious sense but also in a genetic sense. Moreover, Neusner (1987, 120) takes the view that the Yerushalmi attempted to confront the newly triumphant Christianity and re-interpreted recent history, and especially Roman power, from the standpoint of Judaism. There is also speculation on the possibility of a Messiah. These elaborations of the basic diaspora ideology may well have been functional in cementing the resolve of the community.

However, the point is that, even if there are other purposes for the incredible elaboration of the canon during this period, it is clear from the above that practical concerns are not the whole story. And there is no question that the canon was elaborated to the point that only long and patient study by a very intelligent person could possibly hope to master it. Indeed, the Jewish canon is an open canon, so that the task of mastering it continues to grow even now. Yet mastering this canon was for many centuries the *summum bonum* of the religion, and all Jews were expected to become at least somewhat knowledgeable regarding it. It is this latter unique phenomenon that must be explained by any competing theory.

Finally, it is worth commenting on the philosophical status of the basic Jewish canonical writings. Although, as emphasized by Neusner (1988a, I:*passim*), there are important commonalities between these canonical writings and the formal philosophical methodology deriving from Aristotle and Stoicism, it should be noted that the arbitrariness and unpredictability of many of the topics chosen by the Mishnah, as well as the arbitrariness of the distinctions made and the common appeals to authority of particular rabbis, differentiate this work from the Aristotelian tradition in Western philosophy. Regarding the importance of received authority, Neusner (1986a, 43) in discussing the Yerushalmi notes that "[f]ar more common are instances in which the deed of a rabbi is adduced as an authoritative precedent for the law under discussion. It was everywhere taken for granted that what a rabbi did he did because of his mastery of the law . . . . So on the basis of the action or practice of an authority, a law might be framed . . . ." Because of the essential arbitrariness of the rules, appeals to authority may have been necessary in order to provide an aura of legitimacy to the entire enterprise.

Thus, although I agree with Neusner that the Mishnah shares a concern with taxonomy and relationships among qualities with Aristotelian philosophy, in the case of this latter tradition there is the attempt to use this method to unravel the secrets of reality, including the physical and natural world and the nature of humans and their societies. The topics chosen are thus certainly far from arbitrary, and the authors are clearly attempting to understand a reality perceived by them to be not of their own making. The canonical writings of Judaism are, very self-consciously I believe, a man-made system of categorization with a great deal of arbitrariness in the topics chosen and in the manner of their treatment.

In addition, although the Mishnah is extremely complex and thus demands a keen intellect to master, it is fundamentally irrational. Principles are often simply enunciated and expanded on or shown to require further principles or distinctions in order to apply to particular cases. The Mishnaic procedure resembles much more that of an abstract, *a priori* set of laws in which one attempts to develop principles that apply to every conceivable (not necessarily actual) possibility. Any legal system inevitably comes up against cases that are difficult to decide because more than one law may be applicable or because the law is not precise about what it applies to. However, the attempt to specify every possible eventuality in advance quickly becomes, as in the case of the Mishnah (as well as similar exercises in the Talmuds), an intellectual exercise whose purpose must be sought beyond the need to develop a practical legal system, much less an attempt to understand the world in rational terms.

Indeed, John Hartung (n.d.) describes the logic of the Talmudic references to Biblical passages as follows:

> The criterion for using Biblical passages seems to have been that it should be possible to construe the words cited, when taken out of their original context, to be not obviously incompatible with the argument being made. Even then, in most cases, the Sages perceived themselves as having the authority to patch disparate phrases together and add or subtract text in order to make the meaning of works, as perceived by them, not a *non sequitur* to others. "Arguments" like this were deemed especially cogent if other Sages asserted their agreement and/or supplied additional totally irrelevant references. (p. 43)

Despite the logical veneer, the point was not to make a rational, scholarly argument. A great deal of intelligence was required, but ultimately there was no attempt to seek truth, religious or otherwise. These writings are thus ultimately irrational. And as is inevitable with irrational undertakings, acceptance of the Jewish canon was essentially an act of authoritarian submission.[3]

# JEWISH EDUCATION AMONG THE SEPHARDIM AND ASHKENAZIM

> Do not neglect the studies of the learned, but apply yourself to their maxims; from these you will learn discipline, and how to be the servant of princes. (Ecclus. 8:8)

> The world endures only for the sake of the breath of schoolchildren. (b. Shabbath 119b)

*It is better to give charity so that youngsters may study than to give charity to the synagogue.* (Motto of German Jewry in the medieval period; quoted in Kanarfogel 1992, 17; italics in text)

Religious study was of central importance among the Sephardic Jews in Spain. Parents were expected to provide education for their children, although elementary and secondary education was often supplemented by communal assessments, and the *kehilla* typically provided for Talmudic study. "The motive was never lost sight of that the study of the Torah was a religious precept for which no sacrifice was too great" (Neuman 1969, II:69).

Study of the complexities of the Mishnah and the Talmud began as early as age seven or eight. Higher education in the Talmud and Jewish law was the province of the local rabbi, and there was great prestige attached to this role. The rector of the *yeshiva* "was the living embodiment of their highest ideal. . . . Outside the walls of the academy, in the community at large, he was the custodian of Judaism and a regenerating moral and spiritual force among his people . . . he was a dominating moral figure in the community and he wielded considerable legal powers" (Neuman 1969, II:81-82).

The scholar was free from communal taxes, and his government taxes were paid by the communal treasury. This special treatment was not because these scholars were impoverished, but occurred even if the scholar was wealthy, as a sign of reverence. The scholar was also protected from personal abuse by use of the *herem* (ban) and fines, and he was accorded a prominent place of burial.

These trends are also clear in work on traditional Ashkenazi societies. During the medieval period rabbinical rulings required fathers to hire a *melammed* (tutor) for their sons (Kanarfogel 1992, 19). Torah study was viewed as the noblest pursuit (Kanarfogel 1992, 30). During this period, scholars, while not supported by the community as in Spain, were revered, and efforts were made to ensure that they would be able to make a living effortlessly. Thus, for example, Kanarfogel (1992, 45) describes a ruling that scholars are allowed to retain monopolies in trade with gentiles, while such monopolies are not allowed for other Jews: "The community is mandated by Talmudic law to protect and aid this scholar, whose work is the work of heaven . . . and who teaches Torah without compensation, in order that he not be distracted from his studies." By the 14th and 15th centuries, as the Ashkenazi communities became larger, formalized community support for scholars became the rule.

Katz (1961a), writing of the 16th-18th centuries, notes that all Jewish children were expected to obtain schooling at a *heder* (elementary school, for children up to ages 12-13), even those in remote villages and poor children. Schooling occurred in public institutions under the supervision of the *kehilla*, and the *kehilla* also supported the education of poor children. The *kehillot* in turn were strongly pressured to maintain their educational institutions by super-*kehilla* organizations, and small villages who could not afford a *yeshiva* were obligated to contribute to the support of those in larger towns.

There was a keen interest in ensuring that the children actually made progress in school by having the rabbi make periodic examinations. There was also close supervision to ensure that there were not too many pupils per teacher or that the teacher did not lower the hours of instruction or engage the children in extraneous pursuits. Zborowski and Herzog (1952, 58) describe the custom of having the teacher visit on Sunday afternoon while the student was being quizzed by his father to determine his progress in school. For the teacher, it was an important moment because his livelihood depended on the performance of the child.

We have noted the historical importance of a highly educated, wealthy elite for the fortunes of the entire Jewish community. Corresponding to this circumstance, Jewish education among the Ashkenazim was highly elitist. The ultimate aim of education was to create scholars in Jewish law, and for this task *yeshivot* were created. Teachers at the *heder* level were poorly paid, and there was little prestige attached to this occupation, while the head of the *yeshiva* had immense prestige and was often wealthy and connected by marriage to other wealthy families (see below). Katz (1961a) makes the claim that education in the *heder* was intended not so much to provide a broad basic education for the masses as to provide the minority of children who were capable an opportunity to study the Talmud (Katz 1961a, 191). In this arena of extreme importance, the free market reigned supreme: The rabbi who ran the *yeshiva* obtained his position solely via the approbation of the students and the scholars.

Regarding the education received at the *yeshivot*, Katz (1961a) states that "[t]he scholarship of yeshiva students reached such a stage of complexity and acuteness that no one who had not devoted several years to intensive study could follow a lecture on their level or a learned discussion between them" (Katz 1961a, 194). Argumentation was highly abstract, "an exaggerated casuistry (*pilpul*)" that was "divorced from reality" (Katz 1961a, 195). A major activity consisted of attempting to logically resolve contradictions in the Talmud by engaging in dialectical Talmudic discourses termed *halukim*. Consistent with the present functionalist hypothesis, it was an activity that demanded "penetration, scholarship, imagination, memory, logic, wit, subtlety" (Zborowski & Herzog 1952, 98). Besides the abstract casuistry, part of the school year was devoted to developing a knowledge of the precise meaning and analysis of the Talmud. Katz (1961a) notes that "the method of precise analysis of the meaning of the early codifiers was also sufficiently complicated so that only several years' study would equip a person to follow such a course" (p. 195).

Students who completed their studies and received the titles of *haver* and *moreinu* obtained a variety of privileges within the community, and the rabbi of the *yeshiva* "could expect to gain prestige which would carry over to [his] other fields of [economic] activity. . . . The honor accorded the rabbi as head of the *yeshiva* and as disseminator of learning among the people, values that were universally esteemed, strengthened his hand as he carried out his function as arbiter of the values of the entire community" (Katz 1961a, 197-198). The *talmid hakam* (scholar) was "the living embodiment of the law;" "the terrestrial realization of the divine image" (Sorkin 1987, 45-46).

"Study was identical with all of the religious virtues, then, including morality" (Sorkin 1987, 46), and being a scholar was a route to prestige and a good livelihood. Indeed, ranking within the traditional Eastern European shtetl community corresponded closely with scholarly ability (Zborowski & Herzog 1952, 80). Seating arrangements in the synagogue were in order of learning, with the rabbi and other *mizrakh*, as the most learned, nearest the eastern wall and next to the Ark where the Torah was housed, while those near the western wall were the most illiterate, ignorant members of the community (Zborowski & Herzog 1952, 73). Having illustrious scholars in one's pedigree was an important component of one's *yikhus* (family background; see Chapter 4), an essential aspect of social status in the community and known to all. While wealth could compensate for learning, a man with no money who was nevertheless learned, could achieve the highest status. However, it was unlikely that such a learned man would remain poor, since he would be sought by wealthy men as a son-in-law. Even very poor *yeshiva* students were accorded great respect because their prospects for wealth and high social status were good. Further, if a person with yikhus lost his money, he was the object of discreet charity, indicating that his pedigree continued to be a resource even during times of adversity.

On the other hand, an illiterate *amorets* (from *'am ha-ares*, meaning "ignoramus"; see below) was at the absolute bottom of the hierarchy, despised as not really a complete Jew. Zborowski and Herzog (1952, 152) show that the dichotomy intellectual/non-intellectual was more or less coincident with Jew/non-Jew, and persons without intellectual ability were constantly confronted by the social superiority of those who had intellectual ability. Persons without intellectual ability were also morally suspect—suspected of being more likely to beat their wives and engaging in other horrible deeds (p. 82). Parents scolded their recalcitrant children with the prospect that if they continued to fail to excel at scholarship, they would descend to the depths of being an *amorets*.

Hundert (1992) shows that the income from rabbinic duties obtained by the rabbi of the small town of Opatow at the end of the 18th century placed him at the very top level of income for the entire community, below only the top estate managers. Goitein (1971, 95), writing of the medieval Islamic period, shows that scholars were often the recipients of gifts from other Jews in distant countries.

There is no question that Jews tended to be far more educated than the populations they lived among, and this was not only true in traditional societies. Even in the early stages of emancipation in Germany, Jewish families increasingly shifted to an emphasis on secular education as a means to ensure upward mobility and compete on equal terms with gentiles (Carlebach 1978, 28). By 1840 Jews had established their own school system through high school and teacher training colleges, and an increasing number of Jewish students attended secular universities. The eventual result was that Jews were vastly overrepresented among university students between 1870 and 1933 (Gordon

1984, 13-14). Despite consisting of less than 1 percent of the population, Jews comprised 25 percent of students in law and medicine and 34 percent of graduate students in philosophy. Even in grammar schools, Jewish children were overrepresented by a factor of over 6 to 1 in Berlin in the early 20th century. Jewish overrepresentation was a prominent theme of anti-Semitic rhetoric in Germany during this period (see Chapter 5 and *SAID*, ch. 2).

# EDUCATION AND EUGENICS AMONG JEWS

A man should sell all he possesses in order to marry the daughter of a scholar, or marry his daughter to a scholar or other man of character, because he may then rest assured that his children will be scholars; but marriage to an ignoramus will result in ignorant children. (b. Pesachim, 49a)

For a learned man to marry the daughter of an ignoramus (*'am ha-ares*) is like planting a vine tree among thorns. (b. Pesachim, 49a)

If one sees that scholarship is dying out in his children, one should marry his son to the daughter of a learned man. (b. Pesachim, 49a,b)

An unlettered Israelite should not marry a woman of priestly descent, since this constitutes in a way a profanation of the seed of Aaron. Should he marry her nevertheless, the Sages have said that the marriage will not prove successful, and he will die childless, or else he or she will come to an early death, or there will be strife between them. On the other hand, it is laudable and praiseworthy for a scholar to marry a woman of priestly descent, since in this instance learning and priesthood are united.

A man should not marry the daughter of an unlettered person, for if he should die or be sent into exile, his children would grow up in ignorance, since their mother knows not the crown of the Torah. Nor should a man marry his daughter to an unlettered person, for one who gives his daughter in marriage to such a husband is as though he had bound her and placed her in front of a lion, seeing that the beast's habit is to smite his mate and have intercourse with her, since he has no shame. A man should go so far as to sell all his possessions in order to marry a scholar's daughter, for should he die or go into exile, his children would grow up to be scholars. Similarly, he should marry his daughter to a scholar, since there is no reprehensible thing or strife in the house of a scholar. (*The Code of Maimonides, Book 5: The Book of Holiness*, ch. XXI: 31-32, 140)

Eugenicists such as Hughes (1928) and Weyl (1963, 1989) have long emphasized Jewish eugenic practices as resulting in high levels of intelligence among Jews. Although there are major differences between an evolutionary perspective and a eugenics perspective on Judaism,[4] the evolutionary perspective is highly compatible with the supposition that eugenic practices have been an important aspect of Judaism as an evolutionary strategy. From this perspective, not only did the Jewish canon perform an educational function, but also there is evidence that the Talmudic academy often functioned as an arena of natural selection for intelligence.

The first major eugenic effect occurred when the Babylonian exiles returned to Israel (now a part of the Persian Empire) in the fifth century B.C. The Babylonian exiles were disproportionately wealthy compared to the Israelites left behind, and in Chapter 3 data were presented indicating that these relatively wealthy and aristocratic exiles returning from Babylon refused to intermarry or associate with the "people of the land" (*'am ha-ares*)—both the Samaritan remnants of the northern kingdom and the former Israelites of the southern kingdom. The main reason given for this exclusion was that these groups had not preserved their ethnic purity, but Ezra's policy of removing all individuals of foreign taint from the Israelite community would also have had a eugenic effect.

Dating the origins of eugenics as a conscious policy among Jews is difficult. The evidence described in this chapter indicates that concern with education originated at least by the second century B.C., and there is evidence for social, economic, and genetic discrimination against the less educated classes at least from the period following the Second Commonwealth (70 A.D.). Moore (1927-30, II:157ff; see also Alon 1977; Safrai 1968) suggests that, following the destruction of the Temple in 70 A.D., the new class division was between an educated, religiously observant elite called "associates" (the *haverim*; sing. *haber*; i.e., members of the fellowship) and the *'am ha-ares*, who were either characterized by a withdrawal from Torah education and knowledge or suspected of being careless in the performance of the religious law. The appellation *'am ha-ares* itself is significant, since it is the term used for the racially mixed, religiously impure native population inveighed against by Ezra and Nehemiah during the Restoration in the fifth century B.C. It is thus a derogatory term, and the animosity between these groups was rather intense, especially during the second century A.D.[5]

Avi-Yonah (1984, 63f, 108f) notes that after the destruction of the Second Temple, the highly observant, exclusive *haberim* were the only group available to reconstitute a national authority, and they quickly assumed power as magistrates and used their authority to enforce rigorous observation of a very strict interpretation of the religious law, including the agricultural laws, which impacted so heavily on the *'am ha-ares*. (For example, during the economically difficult times of the third century, the *haberim* strongly opposed the relaxation of the sabbatical year law, in which fields were to remain fallow in the seventh year despite the hardship this caused to the *'am ha-ares*.) The rabbis had power in the towns, but they were freed from taxes while at the same time being dependent ultimately on the *'am ha-ares* for support. The freedom from taxation was especially resented during economic crises, as during the third century. The result was the development of an elite class of scholarly rabbis whose status was based on intellectual ability and who were supported by a relatively illiterate and poor peasantry.

There were a variety of methods of social discrimination against the *'am ha-ares*. The *'am ha-ares* were ritually unclean, so that any contact with them was fraught with difficulty. For example, Mishnah Tractate Tohorot (7:1-9—8:1-5) goes into great detail on how *'am ha-ares* impart uncleanness to virtually everything they come in contact with, including the space surrounding them.[6]

Moore (1927-30 II:159) summarizes these prohibitions by noting that "the presumption of uncleanness was a serious bar to social intercourse, and indeed to friendly relations of any kind." Because of their ignorance of the law, the *'am ha-ares* may not have paid the requisite tithes on agricultural produce to the authorities, with the result that business relationships were also highly problematic. Moreover, the *'am ha-ares* were prevented from testifying in legal proceedings, could not be entrusted with a secret, and could not be appointed guardian of an orphan or be in charge of the poor rates. During the economic troubles of the third century, the Patriarch only reluctantly and belatedly opened his storehouses to the *'am ha-ares* after originally opening them to "students of the Bible, of the Mishnah, of the Gemera, of the Halakah and the Haggadah" (quoted in Avi-Yonah 1984, 110).

These comments indicate that the policies of the *haverim* would have had negative economic effects on the *'am ha-ares*, and the social discrimination might reasonably be supposed to result in defections of the *'am ha-ares* from Judaism. Of particular interest here is that "marriage between the two classes was condemned in terms of abhorrence" (Moore 1927-30, II:159-160). Thus, the Talmud states that

> A Jew must not marry a daughter of an *'am ha-ares*, because they are unclean animals [*sheqes*] and their women forbidden reptiles [*sheres*] and with respect to their daughters the Scripture writes: "Cursed be he that lieth with any manner of beast [Deut. 27:21]! . . . Said R. Eleazar: one may butcher an *'am ha-ares* on a Day of Atonement that happens to fall on a Sabbath [when any kind of work constitutes a violation of a double prohibition]. His disciples said to him: Master, say "slaughter" [instead of the vile word, butcher]. But he replied "slaughtering requires a benediction, butchering does not require a benediction." (b. Pesachim 49b)

In the words of Hillel, "No ignorant man (*'am ha-ares*) is religious" (cited in Moore 1927-30, II:160). Being religious meant having knowledge of an enormously complicated code of laws, many of which "from our point of view seem of the smallest religious significance" (Moore 1927 II:160). Thus, a great deal is made of the regulations on agricultural tithing to priests (perhaps because many of the *'am ha-ares* were peasants), even though the priests no longer had any religious function. There is an extraordinary interest in the Mishnah in the regulation and taxation of agriculture, resulting in thousands of regulations (Avi-Yonah 1984, 20) elaborated to a truly amazing level of complexity.

Regarding the general system of agricultural taxation, Moore comments that

> the system, with its numerous and various payments in kind, was complicated, while the method of collection, so far as there was such a thing, had the semblance—and doubtless the substance—of extortion by the beneficiary.
>
> It is small wonder that the peasant earned the reputation of being very "untrustworthy" in acquitting himself of his religious obligations in this sphere. Even the most scrupulous of the class doubtless followed in this as in other matters the prescriptive usage of their fathers, heedless of the stricter interpretation of these laws in the schools and of the refinements of the oral law. (Moore 1927-30, II:72).

The clear animosity between these groups, the emphasis on elaborate regulation of the economic behavior of the *'am ha-ares* by an intellectual, and non-agricultural elite, the elaborate set of rules regulating social contact between the groups based on the uncleanness of the *'am ha-ares*, and the extreme importance of not marrying into the family of an *'am ha-ares* are highly compatible with a eugenic interpretation in which community controls facilitating eugenic mating among the scholarly rabbinic class were highly salient to members of both groups. Moore indicates that the barriers between the *'am ha-ares* and the *haverim* were not absolute, since an individual could be admitted to the educated class if he accepted instruction during a probationary period. However, the response of many of the *'am ha-ares* was to flaunt their lack of knowledge and literacy and to thumb their noses at the *haverim*.

Nevertheless, Avi-Yonah (1984, 107, 110, 238) states that by the third century the rifts between these classes had receded and in the sixth century wealthy *'am ha-ares* could achieve positions of power and influence in the community. There is the clear suggestion, however, that assortative mating based on intelligence and active avoidance of intermarriage with the unlettered was characteristic of the scholarly class beginning at least during the first century. Minimally, there is the suggestion that marriage would only be within-group, and even after the disappearance of this class distinction, only wealthy, intelligent *'am ha-ares* would be able to have influence in the towns and *connubium* with the rabbinic class.

Moreover, it is apparent from this material that the *'am ha-ares* would have had maximum motivation to leave the group. It has been mentioned that the poor and obscure have always been the most likely to leave Judaism, and this must have been particularly so during this period. From an evolutionary perspective, the exclusionary behavior and economic disabilities imposed on the *'am ha-ares* by the *haberim* are absolutely incompatible with supposing that both of these groups were at that time members of the same evolutionary strategy. Quite clearly there is the indication of maximal divergence of interest here, rather than the impression of a unified, corporate type of Judaism in which there were high levels of within-group altruism and the consequent strong group cohesion. The image presented by this ancient conflict is highly discordant with the image of Judaism apparent from the material discussed in Chapter 6.

## Theory and Practice of Eugenics Among the Jews

The Talmuds show a strong concern with eugenics. Marriage with a scholar or his children is highly recommended: "For marriage, a scholar was regarded . . . as more eligible than the wealthy descendent of a noble family." The Tannaim did not tire of reiterating the advice that "under all circumstances should a man sell everything he possesses in order to marry the daughter of a scholar, as well as to give his daughter to a scholar in marriage. . . . Never should he marry the daughter of an illiterate man" (Baron 1952b, 235).

Feldman (1939) shows that the authors of the Talmud, like the other ancients, believed that heredity made an important contribution to individual differences in a wide variety of traits, including physical traits (e.g., height), personality (but not moral character), and, as indicated by the above quotations from the Talmud, scholarly ability. "Every care was taken to prevent the birth of undesirables by a process of selective mating" (p. 32). Individuals contemplating marriage are enjoined to attend to the family history of the future spouse: "A girl with a good pedigree, even if she be poor and an orphan, is worthy to become wife of a king" (Midrash Num. R.i, 5; quoted in Feldman 1939, 34). A prospective wife should be scrutinized for the presence in her family of diseases believed to be inherited (e.g., epilepsy), and also the character of her brothers should be examined, suggesting an awareness of the importance of sex-linked factors. Physical appearance was not to be a critical resource for a woman: "For 'false is grace and beauty is vain.' Pay regard to good breeding, for the object of marriage is to have children" (Taanith 26b and 31a; quoted in Feldman 1939, 35).

Feldman interprets the *k'tsitsah* (severance) ceremony, described in b. Kethuboth 28b, as intended to show the extreme care the rabbis took to ostracize anyone who had contracted a marriage not made according to eugenic principles.[7] A barrel of fruit was broken in the market place in order to call attention to the event, and the following words spoken:

> "Listen ye our brethren! A. B. married an unworthy wife, and we fear lest his offspring mingle with ours; take ye therefore an example for generations to come that his offspring may never mix with ours."

In his authoritative 12th-century compilation of Jewish law, Maimonides states that "A man should not marry a woman belonging to a family of lepers or epileptics, provided that there is a presumption based on three cases that the disease is hereditary with them" (*The Code of Maimonides, Book 5: The Book of Holiness*, ch. XXI:30, p. 140). The advice, therefore, in the Sephardic community was to carefully scrutinize the family of a prospective mate for heritable diseases, and there is an implicit theory that the more commonly the disease is found among family members the more likely it is to be heritable—advice that makes excellent sense from the standpoint of modern genetics.

These writings were not without practical effect. There is evidence that the practice of intermarriage between daughters of wealthy men and males with high ability in scholarship dates from the very origins of Judaism as a diaspora religion. Baron (1952b, 221) notes that in Talmudic times wealthy men selected promising scholars as sons-in-law and supported them in their years of study.

Interestingly, Johnson (1987, 183) notes that most Jews during medieval times could list at least seven generations of ancestors. The main purpose of the genealogy was to show that one had illustrious scholars in one's lineage, and the list usually began with a famous scholar. Maimonides himself listed four important scholar/judges as ancestors (Johnson 1987, 184). The implication is that having illustrious scholars in one's pedigree was an important resource in social interactions (including marriage) within the Jewish community.

These practices also occurred among the Ashkenazim from an early period. Grossman (1989) notes that in medieval Germany it was the custom among *yeshiva* heads (themselves members of distinguished families) to choose their best pupils as sons-in-law. The son-in-law would then succeed him in his leadership within the community. In the shtetl societies of Eastern Europe, the Talmudic commandment to attempt to marry a scholar was taken very seriously to the point that there was a very direct correlation between the amount of the dowry and the number of scholars in the family tree (Zborowski & Herzog 1952, 82).

> Parents dream of marrying their daughter to a learned youth or their son to the daughter of a learned father. The matchmaker, who is a very important institution in the shtetl, has in his notebook a list of all the eligible boys and girls within range. Under each name is a detailed account of his yikhus, in which the most important item is the number of learned men in the family, past and present. The greater the background of learning, the better the match. (Zborowski & Herzog 1952, 82)

There was also a concern with mental disorders in the genealogy of prospective mates in traditional shtetl society and at least until very recently, among Hasidic Jews in contemporary New York (Mintz 1992, 216ff; see also Chapter 4). A person with a psychiatric disorder was a blot on the marriage prospects of the entire family for generations, with the result that families made every effort to prevent psychiatric disorders from being known to the wider community.[8]

There is also very clear evidence for eugenic practices among the 19th-century Ashkenazim. Etkes (1989) finds that, although a variety of traits were important in the choice of sons-in-law, including appearance, health, and temperament, particular value was placed on the perceived potential for Torah study. In other words, marriage with the daughter of a wealthy man and consequent support of study during the years of adolescence (the *kest* period) were conditioned primarily on scholarly ability, and, indeed, the prospective father-in-law would give the future son-in-law an examination prior to agreeing to the marriage. The father-in-law would then support the couple for a specified period of years and provide a large dowry, which would secure the financial future of the couple.

Katz (1961a) shows that scholarly ability was the *summum bonum* within the Jewish community—the ultimate resource when contemplating marriage. Wealthy individuals who were not themselves scholars could obtain scholarship indirectly by providing large dowries so that their daughters could marry scholars: "If an unlettered person married into a family of scholars, he would bask in the reflection of their glory" (p. 206). Moreover, in some cases, scholars could become wealthy simply as a result of their incomes and the many gifts they received. Individuals, such as the Court Jews of the 17th and 18th centuries, provided gifts and support for scholars. They thereby developed "the reputation of 'cherishing the Torah,' and the merit so acquired was equivalent to that achieved by study itself" (p. 206).

Beginning in the ancient world, wealthy men would marry their daughters to promising scholars and support the couple until adulthood (Baron 1952b, 221). This practice became a religiously sanctioned policy and persisted among both the Ashkenazim (Katz 1961a) and the Sephardim (Neuman 1969).[9] Katz (1961a) notes that this pattern of early marriage, and the associated period of prolonged dependency on adults (the *kest* period referred to above), was assured only to the wealthy: "Only members of the upper class who were outstanding in both wealth and learning could afford the luxury of an early match without lessening their prospects. They were assured of a 'good match' by their very position" (p. 142). The poor, even when allowed to marry, would be forced to marry later, and there was a group of both sexes that was forced to remain unmarried—a clear marker of sexual competition within the Jewish community. On the other hand, upwardly mobile individuals would often defer marriage until they had obtained status, whether in the business world or by developing a reputation as a scholar.

As noted in Chapter 6, the officials of the Jewish community acted to regulate the marriages of the lower classes (Katz 1961a; Weinryb 1972), and the marriages of poor and indigent Jews came under special scrutiny by these officials (Hundert 1986b). These regulations included minimum dowry payments, foregoing Jewish charity for a certain period, and numerical limits on the marriages of poor Jews.

The result of these practices was a large overlap among scholarship, control of economic resources, social status, and, ultimately, fertility. Hundert (1992) notes that rabbis were often wealthy, socially prominent merchants, manufacturers, or traders. Throughout most of the 18th century, there was a Jewish aristocracy in Poland-Lithuania consisting of a small number of prominent families who "held an astonishing number of rabbinical and communal offices" (p. 117).

As in all traditional European societies (see, e.g., Herlihy & Klapische-Zuber 1985), Hundert (1992) finds that there was a positive association between wealth and numbers of children in Jewish households in the 18th century, and Weinryb (1972) notes that there were marked differences in fertility among Jews, with successful business leaders, prominent rabbis, and community leaders having a large number of children reaching adulthood, while families of the poor were small. Vogel and Motulsky (1986, 609) note that in mid-18th-century Poland prominent Jews had 4-9 surviving children, while poorer Jewish families had 1.2-2.4 surviving children. As is typical in pre-industrial societies, wealthy families also benefited from having adequate food and were better able to avoid epidemics. Similarly, Goitein (1971, 140) notes that the families of wealthy Jews in the Medieval Islamic world were much larger than those of poor Jews.

Katz (1961a) notes that because the Ashkenazim were prevented from placing their resources in land and because their capital was always precarious, since it was liable to expropriation by the authorities, there was an unusual degree of fluidity in the society, in terms of both upward and downward mobility. In this type of society, scholarship was a better criterion of resource-obtaining potential even than present wealth, since it was independent of time and place, and obtaining a scholarly reputation was certainly not a matter of good fortune as wealth sometimes was. However, in some ways, scholarship and wealth were interchangeable, since property qualifications for voting were waived for scholars—another indication of the many benefits that scholarship conferred within the Jewish community.

As throughout Jewish history (Baron 1952b, 279), there was no hereditary elite of scholars. Scholars "were in a position to provide their sons with favorable facilities to continue their tradition by giving them an outstanding education and an atmosphere of learning. But they could not bequeath their learning nor block the rise of the sons of the uneducated" (Katz 1961a, 204). Nevertheless, there was a strong overlap among wealth, scholarship, family connections, and political power within the community to the point that at times scholarly position was virtually inherited. Kanarfogel (1992, 68) notes that virtually all of the prominent French Tosafists in the 12th and 13th centuries were in a direct line from Rashi or were sons-in-law in this direct line. The presence of sons-in-law in this genealogy shows the possibility of upward mobility. It was a society with "tremendous distances between its peaks and valleys. . . . He who aimed to reach the peak had a long, steep road to climb, but if he had the strength, the ability, and the will, nothing would prevent him from achieving his desire" (Katz 1961a, 209).

Another aspect of some eugenic importance is that poor Jews were relatively likely to become apostates (see Chapter 2). Such defections would also contribute to the skewing of the Jewish gene pool toward high intelligence and resource acquisition ability. This phenomenon may quite possibly be related not only to the relatively degraded political and economic position of poor Jews in the Jewish community, but also to the extreme psychological emphasis on elitism within the Jewish community apparent in this material. One would expect that individuals who failed to live up to the cultural ideal of scholarly ability and wealth would develop a negative self-image and eventually be more prone to desert the group.

This elitism persists into contemporary times: Meyer (1988) notes that early in the 20th century many American Reform congregations still set minimum dues for members, which effectively excluded poor families, and the poor could not vote in synagogue elections. These practices continued for many years thereafter, and indeed, Meyer (1988, 289) notes that "to working people the established synagogue in the first decades of the century often looked more like a 'rich man's institution,' allied with oppressive capital, than one where they felt at home." Meyer (1988, 306) describes membership in Reform congregations in the 1930s as a status symbol and as a marker of economic success.

Extreme concern with worldly success has also remained a characteristic of Judaism in the contemporary world. Herz and Rosen (1982, 368) note that "[s]uccess is so vitally important to the Jewish family ethos that we can hardly overemphasize it. . . . We cannot hope to understand the Jewish family without understanding the place that success for men (and recently women) plays in the system." Success is measured in terms of intellectual achievement, social status, and money, while failure, e.g., to graduate from college, is viewed as a problem requiring clinical counseling. Not surprisingly, a recent survey indicated that the group least likely to defect from Judaism was the highly educated (Ellman 1987).

# DIFFERENCES BETWEEN JEWS AND GENTILES IN PSYCHOMETRIC INTELLIGENCE

Given these phenomena, it is expected that Jews will tend to exceed gentiles in intellectual ability, and particularly in what psychologists term verbal intelligence. As Levinson (1958, 284) notes, traditional Jewish education emphasizes verbal knowledge, verbal concept formation, and ability to understand abstract ideas—exactly the abilities tapped by modern measures of verbal intelligence.

The belief in the superiority of Jewish intelligence has been common among Jews and gentiles alike. Patai and Patai (1989, 146ff) review data indicating that Jewish intellectual superiority was a common belief among many 19th-century and early 20th-century scholars, including some for whom the belief in Jewish intellectual superiority had anti-Semitic overtones: Galton and Pearson believed that Jews had developed into a parasitic race which used its superior intelligence to prey on gentiles. Castro (1954, 473) shows that both scholars and the populace agreed that the Jews of Spain had superior intelligence, and, indeed,

Patai (1977) summarizes data suggesting that, during the medieval period in Spain, Jews were overrepresented among outstanding scientists by a factor of 18. Data reviewed in Chapter 5 indicate a general Jewish overrepresentation in a wide range of fields in the modern world, including business, science, social science, literature, and the arts. At the pinnacle of achievement, Jewish overrepresentation is particularly striking. Patai and Patai (1989, 159) show that Jews received a highly disproportionate number of Nobel prizes in all categories from 1901 to 1985, including 11 percent for literature, 12.7 percent for chemistry, 20.2 percent for physics, 35.2 percent for physiology and medicine, and 26.1 percent for economics. Moreover, the extent of overrepresentation has increased since World War II, since Jews were awarded twice the number of prizes in the years 1943-1972 compared to 1901-1930. In Germany, Jews received 10 of 32 Nobel prizes awarded to German citizens between 1905 and 1931 despite constituting less than 1 percent of the population during this period (Gordon 1984, 14).

Studies of gifted children are of particular interest because IQs in the gifted range are unlikely to result from environmental influences acting on individuals whose genetic potential is near the population mean. Terman's (1926) classic study found twice as many Jewish gifted children as expected on the basis of their representation in the population, although the true representation of Jews in this group may have been higher because some may have concealed their Jewish identity. These subjects had IQs ranging from 135 to 200 with a mean of 151. One of Terman's Jewish subjects had an IQ of 184 when tested at age seven. His close relatives included a chief rabbi from Moscow, a prominent lawyer, a self-made millionaire, a concert pianist, a writer, and a prominent Polish scientist. His maternal great-grandfather was a rabbi famous for his compilation of a Jewish calendar spanning over 400 years, and the rabbi's descendants (the boy's cousins) had IQs of 156, 150, 130, and 122.

Research suggests an average IQ of Ashkenazi Jewish children in the range of 117.[10] In two studies of representative samples of Jewish children, Bachman (1970) and Vincent (1966) found an average IQ of 117 and 117.8, respectively, although Vincent's results are said to be an underestimate because they excluded a large percentage of an elite group of Jewish children attending fee-paying schools.[11]

There is good evidence that Jewish children's Verbal IQ is considerably higher than their Performance IQ. Brown (1944) found several sub-test differences compatible with the hypothesis that Jewish children are higher on verbal abilities, while Scandanavian children are higher on visuo-spatial abilities. Lesser, Fifer, and Clark (1965) found large differences favoring Jewish children over Chinese-American children on verbal ability, but insignificant differences in favor of Chinese-American children on visuo-spatial abilities. And Backman (1972) found that Jewish subjects were significantly higher than non-Jewish Caucasians on a measure of verbal knowledge but were significantly lower on visuo-spatial reasoning.

Large verbal/performance IQ differences have been found within Jewish populations. Levinson (1958) studied a representative sample of *yeshiva* students and found an average Verbal IQ of 125.6, an average Performance IQ of 105.3, and an average Full Scale IQ of 117.86, although he suggests that there may have been a ceiling effect for some students on the verbal portion. Whereas in the general population there was a correlation of 0.77 between Verbal and Performance IQs, among Jewish children it was only 0.31. Finally, Levinson (1960b) found that a sample of Jewish boys (age 10-13) with an average Verbal IQ of 117 had a Performance IQ of 98, while Irish and Italian samples matched for Full Scale IQ had Verbal/Performance differences of only approximately 5 points (approximately 110-105). Levinson (1959) provides evidence that the Verbal/Performance difference for Jewish children increases from pre-school to young adulthood. When children were matched on the basis of full-scale Wechsler IQ, pre-school children showed a small (3-point) difference between Performance and Verbal IQ, while elementary school-age and college student subjects showed a difference of approximately 20 points.

Taken together, the data suggest a mean IQ in the 117 range for Ashkenazi Jewish children, with a Verbal IQ in the range of 125 and a Performance IQ in the average range. These results, if correct, would indicate a difference of almost two standard deviations from the Caucasian mean in Verbal IQ—exactly the type of intellectual ability that has been the focus of Jewish education and eugenic practices. While precise numerical estimates remain somewhat doubtful, there can be no doubt about the general superiority of the Ashkenazi Jewish children on measures of verbal intelligence (see also Patai & Patai 1989, 149).

There are important implications of the finding of higher verbal intelligence among Jews. Lynn (1992) notes that higher socio-economic status groups tend to have high verbal intelligence, but these groups are not particularly high on visuo-spatial abilities. This indicates that verbal intelligence is more important for upward mobility and success in contemporary societies, and this was undoubtedly the case in traditional stratified societies as well: Wilken (1983) notes that education in rhetoric was the key to upward mobility in the Greco-Roman world of antiquity.

In this regard, it is worth mentioning that economic historians have noticed that Jewish economic activity has tended not to be characterized by technological innovation related to mechanical abilities tapped by tests of visuo-spatial abilities (i.e., Performance IQ). Thus, Mosse (1987, 166) suggests that the distinguishing features of Jewish economic activity in 19th-century Germany are to be found "less in outright innovation or invention than in a special aptitude for economic 'mediation' in the forms of the export of German goods, of 'secondary innovation', technology transfer through the introduction into Germany of processes and methods observed abroad, and new techniques for the stimulation of demand."

This is a difficult area because a theme of anti-Semitic writing in Germany was that Jews were not innovators, but only appropriated the inventions of others (Mosse 1987, 166, 404).[12] Anti-Semites emphasized that inventors of new technology such as Rudolf Diesel and Werner von Siemens were predominantly gentile, while several Jewish fortunes in technical areas, such as those of Ludwig Loewe and Emil Rathenau, were made by importing technology that originated elsewhere and were dependent on capitalization provided by Jewish private banks.[13] While among Jews ownership was divorced from technical competence, the prototypical gentile entrepreneur was the "inventor-artisan" whose technical competence was crucial to the success of the company. Whereas technical competence and inventiveness were crucial to the success of the prototypical gentile firms, among Jews success was related to having access to capital or to having "commercial flair and the ability to inspire confidence" (p. 312).[14]

The origins of Jewish and gentile entrepreneurs were also different: Mosse (1987, 244) notes that gentile manufacturers tended to come from the families of artisans, whose work is also more likely to involve visuo-spatial abilities related to Performance IQ, whereas Jewish manufacturers tended to come from old trading or banking families.

These findings suggest the hypothesis that the Jewish/gentile difference in economic activity is mediated by differences in intellectual proclivities related to Verbal versus Performance IQ. Lynn (1987) notes that visuo-spatial abilities and verbal abilities are actually negatively correlated in populations that are homogeneous for Spearman's $g$, and he provides evidence that there are neurological trade-offs such that the more the cortex is devoted to one set of abilities, the less it can be devoted to the other. Lynn finds that Mongoloids and Caucasian males are relatively high on visuospatial abilities related to mechanical science and metal work. Lynn's findings build on much older work by Wechsler (1958, 160, 228-229) indicating that individuals with high Performance IQs are more likely to have mechanical and manipulative ability (e.g., carpenters, mechanics), but that individuals with higher-level occupations in these areas (e.g., engineers) also have high Verbal IQs. These tendencies would make it more likely that gentile German males would be the type of "inventors-artisans" whose mechanical ability was a crucial ingredient in the success of their firms. And since Verbal IQ is generally related to upward social mobility in modern societies, the data are also consistent with the general finding that Jews were much better able to take advantage of the general opportunities opened up by the industrializing economy of Germany.

## Non-eugenic Explanations for Jewish Intellectual and Achievement Differences in Western Societies

The attractiveness of the eugenic explanation derives from the following argument: (1) There is heritable genetic variation for intelligence (e.g., Lynn 1992). Hundreds of behavioral genetic studies of intelligence confirm this finding, and it is only by rejecting an entire scientific discipline that one can maintain the contrary. Note that the exact level of heritability is not important for the eugenic argument. Responsible estimates of the heritability of intelligence range from approximately 0.4 to 0.8, but even if heritability is actually lower, the implication is that there is in fact some genetic variation for intelligence within human populations. (2) Given the virtual certainty that there is heritable variation for intelligence, then it is certain that the eugenic practices described above would result in natural selection within the Jewish population for the genes associated with intelligence.

Nevertheless, the eugenic argument need not deny that there have been other forces that would result in Jewish/gentile differences. Patai (1977; see also Motulsky 1977b) attributes some of the difference to natural selection imposed by gentiles—what I will term the *gentile selection hypothesis*.[15] This hypothesis states that because of the hostile gentile environment, there were strong pressures that favored the resourceful, intelligent, and wealthy members of the Jewish community.

One need not deny such a possibility in order to affirm the importance of eugenics. There is indeed evidence that at times anti-Semitic actions fell most heavily on the less wealthy individuals who were less able to flee or provide ransom for their families. For example, poor Jews who lacked the means to flee or could not be ransomed by relatives died disproportionately in the violence resulting from the Cossack uprising of 1648 (Weinryb 1972). It is difficult to determine how much weight to give to this hypothesis, however, because wars have affected all populations, and it is reasonable to suppose that intelligence may have been beneficial in escaping the ravages of war wherever it has occurred. For example, Jews have tended not to serve as combatants in military ventures, which undoubtedly resulted in high levels of mortality for common soldiers. Thus, war may well have acted as a similar eugenic selective force among gentiles.

We shall see below that Jewish intelligence appears to be lower in groups deriving from Muslim societies. The hypothesis elaborated below is that the extreme anti-Semitism of the Muslim societies actually prevented the flourishing of a highly literate Jewish culture in which intellectual ability was a key to social and reproductive success, with the result that the average IQ of Jews from these areas is lower than among the Ashkenazim. As a result, when the Ashkenazi Jews began to re-establish ties with their co-religionists in the Muslim world during the 19th century, the overwhelming picture was that Jews in these countries were much more likely to be uneducated and illiterate.

Thus, the proposal that anti-Semitism has been the most important cause of high Jewish intelligence must show that anti-Semitic actions resulting in natural selection for intelligence were stronger in Eastern Europe than in Yemen—a doubtful proposition at best (see below). Rather, high levels of Jewish intelligence and achievement have been associated with European societies where Jews have been given opportunities for developing a highly literate culture in which the educated elite were able to obtain high levels of resources and reproductive success.

Moreover, it would appear that some of the severe persecutions, such as the Spanish Inquisition, were directed much more at the successful members of the Jewish community than at the less able and therefore may not have had disproportionate effects on lower-status Jews.[16] After all, it was the wealthy Jews who were often the targets of popular hatred. Also, Jews who continued to practice Judaism in Spain during the 15th century and were subsequently expelled in 1492 were less educated and less economically successful than their Converso brethren who remained to endure the wrath of the Inquisition. In this case, the less wealthy Jews certainly suffered fewer casualties and eventually were able to emigrate to North Africa or the Levant. Eventually, the Levantine Sephardim underwent a distinct atrophy of their culture (see below), while the descendants of the Conversos continued their highly elite and exclusivist profile on the international economic scene. When these Levantine Sephardim immigrated to the United States in the 20th century, they exhibited much higher rates of illiteracy, alcoholism, prostitution, and wife abandonment than did the Ashkenazim (Sachar 1992, 338). While the Ashkenazim were quickly upwardly mobile in American society, the Sephardim achieved only "a modest economic foothold" and were more likely to engage in lower-status occupations (Sachar 1992, 340).

Finally, the gentile selection hypothesis does not provide a satisfactory explanation of the Jewish/gentile differences in the patterning of the Verbal and Performance subscales. These differences are very robust, and the gentile selection hypothesis must propose that individuals with high Verbal rather than Performance IQ were better able to escape the effects of persecutions. Now it might be the case that high verbal intelligence would be more adaptive in escaping persecutions, but it is not obvious why this would be the case. One possibility is that verbal intelligence was associated with wealth and success among Jews, and it was these attributes that were favored during persecutions. However, given the evidence that wealth and verbal intelligence were strongly associated because of Jewish religious practices and the occupational profile of Jewish elites in traditional societies, the gentile selection hypothesis really comes down to a slightly altered version of the eugenic hypothesis.

There have also been environmental hypotheses for the Jewish/gentile difference in intellectual ability. As Levinson (1958, 284) notes, the *yeshiva* curriculum may well be an environmental influence on verbal intelligence. Very strong environmental pressures for academic success in Ashkenazi Jewish families may also contribute. Although they state that there are no scientific studies measuring the phenomenon, Patai and Patai (1989, 153-154) sum up a situation that is virtually common knowledge by noting the strong emotional commitment of Jewish parents to stimulating the intellectual development of their children, sending them to the best schools, reinforcing self-perceptions of children as brilliant, and so on.

Zborowski and Herzog (1952) show that this extreme emphasis on encouraging children's academic pursuits and closely monitoring children's academic performance was characteristic of traditional Eastern European shtetl communities as well. The following quotation from a medieval Ashkenazic source shows the expectation that parents will be highly involved with their children's intellectual and moral socialization:

> They will teach him Torah and guide him in the ways of Heaven and the precepts and good deeds. They strive and work for his benefit, in order that he be able to study Torah in purity and with ease. They are partners with God, and He gave the child the intellect to grasp the teachings. (Quoted in Kanarfogel 1992, 39)

Herz and Rosen (1982) also note that Jewish families highly value the ability to articulate one's thoughts and feelings verbally. Children are encouraged to express opinions and contribute to solving family problems, and they comment on "[t]he Jewish mother's role to devote her entire emotional energy to nurturing the intelligence and achievement of her children" (p. 378).

The environment in traditional Jewish families in the Eastern European shtetl communities was intensely verbal. Zborowski and Herzog (1952, 413)) describe a preoccupation with elaborate verbalization, much of it directed at children. Communication is described as "incessant." People were even conceptualized as having a total lifetime quota of words, with women having more than men. Silence and lack of verbal expressiveness were regarded with suspicion.

From a modern behavioral genetic perspective, these pressures need not be seen as pure environmental influences. Plomin and Bergeman (1991) have shown genetic influence on commonly used instruments measuring home environment. In other words, the number of books in one's home, the amount of verbal interaction between mother and child, social class status,[17] and the commitment of parents to monitoring children's academic progress are not simply aspects of environmental influence on intelligence or other functioning, but also reflect genetic variation among the parents: Intelligent parents have large numbers of books around, talk to their children a great deal, and tend to be in the middle or upper-middle class. But their intelligence is influenced by their genetic makeup, and their genetic makeup predisposes them to enjoy reading books and entering occupations calling for high intelligence. Nevertheless, the extreme emphasis on academic accomplishment among Jews may be reasonably viewed as an important environmental pressure for high intelligence.

An evolutionary perspective is highly compatible with supposing that manipulating environments may be an important component of an evolutionary strategy (MacDonald 1988a, 1991; see Chapter 1). Given the fact that humans retain a high level of plasticity, it is quite reasonable to suppose that cultures would develop the intensive methods of socialization necessary to attain evolutionary goals within the particular context in which the group finds itself.

In the case of Jews, we have seen that the cultural commitment to education and literacy, as well as the attempt to develop a highly competent elite, can be dated to very early in the diaspora. From the present perspective, the development of Jewish education and fostering of parenting practices that result in a high level of intellectual achievement are an important aspect of Judaism as an evolutionary strategy.

These environmental pushes toward intelligence can even be seen as complementing a eugenic strategy. From a genetic point of view, these environmental practices would tend to maximize the actually achieved intelligence among Jews by creating a uniform highly favorable environment. Within this high pressure, relatively homogeneous Jewish environment, individual differences are most likely due to genetic variation. (This is a general principle of behavioral genetics: As one diminishes the environmental variation, the only remaining source of variation must be genetic.) As a result, eugenic marriage practices are assured of being based overwhelmingly on genetic variation, rather than environmental variation. As a result, one can be assured that by marrying a relatively intelligent Jew, one is marrying someone with a relatively high genetic potential for intelligence, rather than simply one who came from a relatively favorable environment.

## Between-group Variation for Intelligence among Jews: Comparisons between Ashkenazi and Oriental Jews

In addition to studies on Jews in Western societies, several studies are now available that compare Jewish groups within Israel. These studies are important because they call into question the idea that eugenic practices related to intelligence have everywhere been a component of Judaism as an evolutionary strategy. The data will be reviewed, followed by an attempt to place the data within the framework of the present theoretical approach.

Israelis originating from Middle Eastern countries where Muslim was the dominant religion are overrepresented among the lower classes in Israel, with high rates of illiteracy among the parents, low levels of formal education, little verbal interaction with their children, fewer toys and other objects that facilitate play, and authoritarian patterns of child rearing (Patai 1977, 309ff). Oriental Jews have also been found to have poorer performance on measures of intelligence and academic achievement (e.g., Burg & Belmont 1990; Preale, Amir, & Sharan [Singer]; Sharan [Singer] & Weller 1971). They also differ on personality traits related to academic success, such as being lower on attention span and delay of gratification, but higher on impulsivity. The data on fertility reviewed below indicate that Oriental Jews have higher levels of fertility than do Ashkenazi Jews, although there has been a gradual tendency for convergence within Israel (Goldscheider 1986; Shokeid 1986).[18]

Although Patai (1977) attributes the differences between Oriental- and European-derived children to cultural differences based on the differences in socio-economic status between the groups, Burg and Belmont (1990) found differences in verbal, reasoning, and numerical abilities between these groups within social class. Taken together, the data indicate that in comparison to Western Jews or, indeed, Caucasians generally, the Oriental group can be viewed as exhibiting a relatively low-investment parenting style (i.e., high fertility combined with low parental involvement; see below). The personality traits of impulsivity, short attention span, and low ability to delay gratification are also compatible with this perspective, since these traits tend to be correlated and are associated with low academic achievement (e.g., Shaywitz & Shaywitz 1988; see below). At a theoretical level, such individuals can be viewed as biased toward systems underlying attraction to reward, rather than the ability to inhibit behavior and persevere in unpleasurable tasks (MacDonald 1988a; 1992b; see below).

These results indicate that Judaism has not everywhere been characterized by a similar level of eugenic practices, high-investment parenting, and the development of a highly educated, entrepreneurial elite. However, eugenic practices appear to have been very common in the areas where Judaism underwent its largest demographic expansions and are thus central to understanding mainstream Judaism. The data imply that Oriental Jews failed to continue a policy that was well articulated in the Greco-Roman world and that not only was practiced then, but which has continued among the Ashkenazim and in at least some Sephardic groups into contemporary times.

Patai (1977) attributes these results to acculturation within a Muslim milieu. Certainly, these patterns do reflect the Muslim surroundings, but it should be noted that Jews have often pursued their cultural practices quite independently from the surrounding environment, and, in fact, "being different" is in some sense what Judaism is all about (see Chapter 4). Thus, we have noted that the Jewish emphasis on universal education was unique in the ancient world, so that these developments occurred despite the fact that all around them there was relative illiteracy. One also wonders why the fact that the great majority of peasants in pre-expulsion Spain or Eastern Europe were relatively unlettered and that education was fairly uncommon among all classes did not result in Jews rejecting their emphasis on universal education and the development of a scholarly elite. Moreover, we have seen that the emphases on education, lifelong learning, and the prerogatives of the scholarly elite can be seen quite clearly in the religious texts of Judaism, so that developing and maintaining these institutions was really something of a religious obligation. Their relative absence in the Muslim world is therefore of considerable theoretical interest.

There is in fact evidence that Jewish populations in Muslim lands responded rather quickly to opportunities for education and upward mobility. Stillman (1991) shows that the Oriental Jews at the turn of the 20th century benefited greatly from education provided by the Alliance Israélite Universelle funded by

Ashkenazi Jews. This network of schools resulted in the Oriental Jews having "a distinct advantage of opportunity over the largely uneducated Muslim masses . . . they came to have a new and unparalleled mobility and achieved a place in the economic life of the Muslim world that was far out of proportion to their numbers or their social status in the general population" (p. 25). These data indicate that an emphasis on education was highly effective during this period, but they also suggest that there must have been external reasons why this emphasis on education died out in the Muslim world. A hint is provided when Stillman (p. 45) notes that this upward mobility made possible by educational opportunity and sympathetic colonial governments was intensely resisted by the native Muslims. The Jews' new status brought about by their European co-religionists often resulted in an exacerbation of anti-Semitism by the native Muslims (see also Lewis 1984, 184-185).

As described by Lewis (1984), there was a general decline in Jewish fortunes in Muslim lands from the late Middle Ages to the 20th century. While at the beginning of the 16th century there is evidence for a highly literate Jewish culture in the Ottoman Empire, this culture gradually disappeared after the 16th century, so that from the mid-18th century until the intervention of the European powers in the 20th century, there was "an unmistakable picture of grinding poverty, ignorance, and insecurity" (Lewis 1984, 164) among Jews in the Muslim world. In the earlier period, Jews were prominent as physicians and in trade, commerce, and manufacturing. As in Western Europe, Jews were also deeply involved in finance and tax farming. Interestingly, this flourishing Jewish culture came at a time when Jews formed the ideal intermediary between the alien Ottoman elite and the subject populations (a theme of Chapter 5): Jews were favored as intermediaries over Christians because there was no possibility of collusion with the Christian enemies of the Ottoman state (Lewis 1984, 139).

After this period, there was degeneration of Jewish culture, accompanied by early marriage and a high birth rate (Lewis 1984, 141)—clearly indicative of a shift to a low-investment style of parenting. Jews became increasingly degraded in the Ottoman Empire, and their decline was far more extreme than can be explained solely by the economic fortunes of the Ottoman Empire, since it affected them far more than their Muslim and Christian co-residents.

There is some evidence that other minorities simply out-competed Jews in this area, but this was ultimately the result not of deficits in the capabilities of Jews, but of exclusionary practices analogous to Jewish kinship preferences in business ventures that effectively excluded other groups (see Chapter 6). Thus, the Ottoman Christians were able to take advantage of European education and the preference of European Christians for Ottoman Christian business contacts, thereby overturning the Jewish economic domination over Christians that had been imposed by the sultan (Shaw 1991, 77). The increased political influence of Christians resulted in a decline in Jewish influence in the government, and, indeed, discriminatory measures were enacted, and there was an increase in official and unofficial violence directed at Jews.

The decline of the Jews was also influenced by increasing Turkish anti-Semitism. As the Turkish regime became more integrated into the society, Jews were less able to play the role of intermediary between the alien rulers and the Muslim and Christian natives, and the result was an increasing strictness of the regulations enforcing degradation and humiliation of Jews.[19]

As is generally the case in times of economic and political misfortune for Jews, mysticism and *Kabbala*, rather than the intricacies of the Talmud, came to dominate religious education:

> The *Zohar* of the Kabbalists replaced the Talmud and dominated life automatically and autocratically, without discussion, commentary, or understanding. . . . Kabbalistic symbolism determined all acts of daily life, morality, sexual and hygienic behavior, housing, clothing, food, education, the shape and length of hair and beards, the furniture used in houses, all that had once been influenced by the Talmud. (Shaw 1991, 132)

In the long run, the community became too poor to provide for the education of most children, with the result that the great majority were illiterate, and they pursued occupations requiring only limited intelligence and training. However, with the resurgence of Ottoman Jews in the 19th century as a result of patronage and protection from European Jews, once again there was a flowering of a highly literate culture, including secular schools based on Western models (Shaw 1991, 143ff, 175-176).

In the case of Yemen, the degeneration of Jewish culture was more probably due to anti-Semitic actions by the host society combined with the fragility of the local economy, which did not allow for the flourishing of the typical Jewish economic specialization related to activities calling for verbal intelligence. Nini (1991) shows that in 18th- and 19th-century Yemen there was no large urban economy in which a highly educated elite could prosper. The population of Yemen was predominantly rural, and Jews resided in small groups working as artisans forced to adopt "secondary or marginal occupations" (p. 94). Communities were so small that it was often impossible to obtain a quorum for prayer. The persecution of Jews was often intense, and, indeed, the persecution of Jews in Yemen is generally considered to have been the most extreme in the Muslim world.

Because the vast majority of Jews were artisans, there was no class of wealthy property owners or middle-class entrepreneurs or traders who could support a thriving scholarly community. There was also little need for rabbis because the communities were very small and because Jewish communities were often essentially extended families. The common pattern in other diaspora communities of a wealthy, entrepreneurial elite helping the rest of the community occurred only rarely in Yemenese Jewish history, but when it did, it had the familiar features noted in Chapter 5: Thus, 18th-century Rabbi Shalom ben Aharon ha-Kohen Iraqi helped the Jewish community and generally raised the prestige of the Jews. However, his influence was short-lived, and he fell due to the envy and hostility of the local Muslim officials (Ahroni 1986, 138).

Correspondingly, there were no *yeshivot* in Yemen of the type described above as typical of Eastern Europe where scholars competed by debating questions of the law. As is typical in areas with intense anti-Semitism, intellectual activity tended toward mysticism, and there were frequent outbreaks of messianism (see Chapter 3). Moreover, because of the subsistence level of the economy, the rabbis did not live off public funds and often performed manual labor, so that religious study did not really pay off in terms of being a route to economic and reproductive success.

I conclude that the pattern of lower verbal intelligence, relatively high fertility, and low-investment parenting among Jews living in the Muslim world is linked ultimately to anti-Semitism and, in the case of Yemen, to the lack of economic development. These findings are consistent with the ecological/evolutionary model of parental investment proposed by Belsky, Steinberg, and Draper (1991). Within this model, adverse, unstable economic situations trigger a low-investment reproductive strategy, while economic prosperity and stability trigger a high investment strategy. Although traits related to parental investment also appear to be heritable (see below), the model of Belsky and colleagues is highly compatible with the shifts in parental investment patterns seen among Jewish populations over historical time.

# HIGH INVESTMENT PARENTING AS AN ASPECT OF JUDAISM AS AN EVOLUTIONARY STRATEGY

> You will see but seldom among them [i.e., Jews] guilty husbands leaving their virtuous partners for abandoned prostitutes, or shameless wives abandoning the care of their families and the sacred duties of matrimony and maternity, to plunge heedlessly into debauchery . . . .
>
> It is there that lovely chastity follows the graces and enhances their charms; there an amiable blush still overspreads the face of the modest virgin . . . . (Tama [1807] 1971, 73-75)

Evolutionary accounts of parenting emphasize investment in offspring as a critical variable (e.g., Trivers 1985; Wilson 1975). Parental investment is the cost of reproduction in terms of time, food, defense of offspring, teaching of offspring, *et cetera*. In the natural world, there are a variety of conditions which pull for high- investment parenting, including stressful physical environments, high levels of predation, and (most important for our purposes) a highly competitive environment. Competition for resources tends to result in animals having fewer and more widely spaced offspring, prolonged parental care, longer life span, and lower mortality rates at all stages of the life span. In humans, the prototypical high-investment pattern is also associated with high intelligence, delay of sexual maturation, stable pair bonding, and high levels of parental involvement with children (Belsky, Steinberg, & Draper 1991; MacDonald 1992a; MacDonald 1993; Rushton 1988).

The material summarized by Zborowski and Herzog (1952) clearly indicates a high-investment style of parenting in traditional Ashkenazi shtetl communities. Jewish mothers in these communities are said to have an "unremitting solicitude" (p. 193) regarding their children. They engage in "boundless suffering and sacrifice. Parents 'kill themselves' for the sake of their children" (p. 294).

The general pattern in traditional Poland was for early marriage (especially for the wealthy) and continued dependence on the wife's family while continuing the boy's education (Hundert 1989; see also Katz, 1961a). During this period, the son-in-law was expected to distinguish himself in study and attend to nothing else (Biale 1986; Etkes 1989). The practice of early marriage declined, but the importance of education during the adolescent years continued (Biale 1986). Kraemer (1989) emphasizes that even older teenagers were still dependent on their parents and not free from parental control and influence. He cites evidence that adulthood began only at age 20.

Hyman (1989) notes that arranged marriages were the rule among Jews until after World War I, since the economic basis of marriage was too important to leave to the vagaries of romantic love. For example, Neuman (1969, II:22) notes that it was common to arrange marriages of daughters around the time of puberty or earlier among both Sephardic and Ashkenazi Jews in all European countries in the Middle Ages. Romantic attraction was "not countenanced in good Jewish society" (Neuman 1969, II:19). Despite the lack of romance as the basis of marriage, the high level of family life and commitment to children became a rallying point for those attempting to defend Judaism from the criticisms of Enlightenment intellectuals: "In an age that held up so many aspects of Jewish experience to criticism or ridicule, they could point to traditional Jewish family life as a model of noble domestic behavior and thereby rehabilitate both Judaism and the Jews. Often they trumpeted the superiority of the Jewish family to that of the surrounding population" (Hyman 1989, 186).[20]

Guttentag and Secord (1983) note the following points relevant to the hypothesis that Jews engage in high-investment parenting:

> 1. Mortality rate is a theoretically important marker for a high investment reproductive style (Wilson 1975, 101). Peritz and Tamir (1977, 415) summarize data indicating that "almost everywhere and in all the periods for which statistical data are available, the mortality of the Jews was considerably lower than that of the surrounding populations." This is especially the case for infant mortality. In a survey of 21 countries, Schmelz (1971) found that the median infant mortality rate for Jews was a little

over one-half the rate for the general population (see also Goldstein 1981, 138). This general pattern even holds for Jewish/gentile comparisons within social class, and there is less of a social class difference in infant morality among Jews than among other groups.[21]

2. Guttentag and Secord (1983) show that Talmudic writings emphasize good child-care practices and personal hygiene, temperance, and sexual probity. Hundert (1992) suggests that lowered rates of infant mortality brought on by Jewish practices of hygiene, child rearing, and diet were responsible for the demographic explosion of Jews in pre-industrial Poland.

3. Illegitimacy, premarital conception, and divorce rates tend to be lower among Jews than the surrounding populations (Cohen 1986; Hyman 1986b; Goldstein 1981). Guttentag and Secord (1983) find that mortality rates for illegitimate children were actually higher for Jews than for non-Jews, an indication of the normative importance of male parental investment among Jews.

Guttentag and Secord (1983) also summarize several intriguing sources of data showing that Jewish populations have been characterized by high sex ratios (i.e., the number of males per 100 females). Evolutionary perspectives on variation in sex ratios (Trivers & Willard 1973; Mealey & Mackey 1990) have emphasized the idea that individuals with high social status should prefer to raise males rather than females because high-status males are better able to mate than are low-status males. Individuals with low social status are more likely to invest in females, since mating is relatively easy for females. The general finding that sex ratio is associated with social class is consistent with this perspective: The sex ratio in higher socio-economic status families tends to be skewed toward males (Boone 1988; Dickemann 1981; Guttentag & Secord 1983; Voland 1988).[22] The expectation, then, is that Jewish populations would be characterized by a high sex ratio.

The hypothesis that Judaism is a high-investment strategy implies that Jewish communities will have high sex ratios, and Guttentag and Secord summarize evidence that this is indeed the case. First, they summarize data indicating very high sex ratios among Orthodox Jews (who are presumably most likely to rigidly adhere to Talmudic injunctions regarding the timing of intercourse; see below). Although the data in many cases are admittedly less than ideal, a wide range of independent studies on Eastern European populations indicates high ratios, with the best data set, coming from six uncorrected Odessa censuses between 1892 and 1903, indicating sex ratios ranging from 109 to 118, although Guttentag and Secord (1983) themselves interpret the data as indicating ratios in the range of 135. Moreover, sex ratios ranging from 111 to 115 were found for three independent North American samples studied between 1950 and 1964, and Harlap (1979) reports an overall sex ratio of 112 for a large group of Orthodox Jewish women in Israel.[23]

Guttentag and Secord (1983) note that the Talmud requires that couples refrain from intercourse while the woman is menstruating and for a seven-day period thereafter. Following this period, they are advised to engage in frequent intercourse, with the result that intercourse is maximized at approximately the time of ovulation. Although timing intercourse exactly at ovulation would tend to result in a low sex ratio (Harlap 1979; James 1987a; James 1987b; Zarutskie, Muller, Magone, & Soules 1990), Harlap (1979) found that Orthodox Jews actually tended to resume intercourse one or two days prior to or after ovulation, resulting in an overall sex ratio of 112. The same pattern was found among wives of rabbis and students of the Talmud who are likely to be the most scrupulous followers of religious law.

It should be noted that high sex ratios would tend to result in increased sexual competition among males within the Jewish community, since some males would be unable to find a Jewish mate. These males would have to forego marriage or else marry non-Jews (the latter an unlikely prospect without defection from the Jewish community). This process would therefore have eugenic consequences, since males unable to mate would tend to be from the lower rungs of the Jewish community.

# JEWISH/GENTILE DIFFERENCES IN FERTILITY PATTERNS IN RESPONSE TO THE INDUSTRIAL REVOLUTION

Evolutionary perspectives on the demographic transition have emphasized the importance of fertility control and high-investment parenting in achieving upward mobility in response to the altered conditions following industrialization (e. g., Borgerhoff Mulder 1991). There is wide agreement that the Jews entered into the demographic transition earlier than gentiles and that Jewish fertility changed from being higher than gentile fertility to being lower than gentile fertility in the aggregate (e.g., A. Goldstein 1981; Knode 1974; Ritterband 1981).

In general, the sharp drop in Jewish fertility coincided with emancipation and a consequent awareness "of the opportunities becoming available to them for education, economic advancement, and generally better integration into the larger society" (A. Goldstein 1981, 141). For example, Hyman (1981, 1989) summarizes evidence that 19th-century Jews in France and Germany were practicing birth control and that American and European Jews had lower birthrates than the surrounding population even when controlling for education, urbanization, and social status. Alice Goldstein (1981, 124) attributes the later age of marriage and the lowered fertility of German and Hungarian Jews to the prolonged education required for the typical Jewish occupations of white-collar worker and skilled craftsman. Moreover, the Jewish/gentile difference was decreased, but not eliminated, when controlling for occupation.[24]

There is evidence that the low-fertility/high-investment pattern of most Jews after the Industrial Revolution is more characteristic of Jews who are less traditionally religious. Hyman (1981) finds that a sample of French rabbis and cantors (who would tend to be the most observant Jews) had higher fertility than the mean for French Jews. Moreover, Goldscheider and Ritterband (1981, 252) make the generalization that the highly traditional Orthodox and Hasidic Jews have higher fertility than other Jewish sects and that, within Israel, fertility is higher among those who are religiously observant than among secular Jews. Similarly, Cohen and Ritterband (1981) find that religious service attendance was associated with fertility among American Jews in the 1960s. These data are compatible with the hypothesis that, by accepting secular education and maximizing investment in their children, non-traditional forms of Judaism functioned to enable Jews to compete economically in the wider society.

There is evidence that Jewish populations adjust rapidly to the family patterns of the surrounding populations. For example, North African Jews migrating to France developed a pattern of having fewer children, marrying later, having a higher percentage of university graduates, and more frequently entering white-collar, professional occupations than those immigrating to Israel (DellaPergola 1986). Moreover, while Ashkenazi groups within Israel have a higher fertility rate than those in European or American communities (Goldscheider 1986), immigration to Israel by Asian and African Jews tends to result in lower fertility and relatively delayed marriage compared to the country of origin (Goldscheider 1986; Shokeid 1986). Within Israel, the result is a tendency toward convergence, creating a pattern intermediate between Jewish patterns in Europe and America versus the patterns in Africa and Asia and in which ethnic differences among Jews are lessening (DellaPergola 1986; Goldscheider 1986; Schmelz, DellaPergola, & Avner 1990).

The suggestion is that the general response of Jews to emancipation and the development of contexts in which upward mobility is possible has been to "keep one step ahead" of the populations they are living among by investing more in education, lowering fertility, and delaying marriage. Within Israel, Jews tend to marry later, have fewer children, and achieve higher levels of education than the co-resident Arab population (Goldscheider & Ritterband 1981, 238).

This suggests a pattern in which Jews are in direct competition with the host society and are able to manipulate their fertility in an adaptive manner relative to the social context by being able to track the investment patterns of the host society. This suggestion is an interesting parallel to the findings presented by Irons (1992), who found a general tendency for groups to adjust fertility to local (within-group) reference standards. Jews, however, appear to be tracking the investment patterns of an external group (the host society) and adjusting them accordingly in a manner that allows them to compete successfully with the host society. Such a finding is highly compatible with the present conceptualization of Judaism as an evolutionary strategy in competition with the host society: High-investment parenting is a critical aspect of this competitive strategy, but the amount of investment can be adjusted to local conditions.

Congruent with this general interpretation of Jewish/gentile competition, Patai (1971, 161ff) notes a pattern in which Jews tend to excel in just those fields that are were most highly regarded by the host country. For example, Jewish achievement in mathematics has been far more common in Continental countries, where mathematics is revered, than in England where Jews have excelled in the typically English pursuits of business. Similarly, Jewish excellence in music and art has not been characteristic of Britain, while it has been characteristic of Germany and Russia. Moreover, Jews tend to win Nobel prizes in precisely those areas where gentiles of their country excel. As Johnson (1987, 383) notes regarding the success of Jewish student prize-winning prodigies in the late 19th century and early 20th century in France, "They beat the French at their own academic-cultural game every time."

# JUDAISM AND PERSONALITY PSYCHOLOGY

> When we offer sacrifices to [God] we do it not in order to surfeit ourselves, or to be drunken...; for such excesses are against the will of God, and would be an occasion of injuries and of luxury; but by keeping ourselves sober, orderly, and ready for our other occupations, and being more temperate than others. (Flavius Josephus, *Against Apion*, 2:195)

> Judaism asks—this is the mistake of the clever people—not intelligence but, in the first instance, obedience. (Magnus 1907, 78)

Apart from providing strong environmental pressure and genetic selection for intelligence, there is some reason to suppose that Jewish eugenics and cultural practices would also influence several personality systems, although the data are far from ideal.

The personality system of conscientiousness is a biological system that underlies attention to detail, neatness, orderliness, striving for achievement, persistence toward goals in the face of difficulty, and the ability to focus attention and delay gratification (Digman 1990). At the extreme, such a person is obsessive/compulsive and guilt-ridden (e.g., Widiger & Trull 1992).[25] There is a strong positive association between conscientiousness and academic success ($r = 0.50$) (Digman & Takemoto-Chock 1981). The scales of *neat*, *careful* (of own work), *persevering*, and *planful* load positively on this dimension, while *irresponsible* and *careless* (of property) load negatively (Digman & Takemoto-Chock 1981; Digman & Inouye 1986). Correlations between high school grades and assessments of this factor performed six years previously were in the 0.50 range. Similar correlations occurred for occupational status assessed when subjects were in their mid-20s. Eugenic practices related to ability in Jewish religious studies would clearly influence this trait.

Studies of conscientiousness also indicate that this dimension includes items such as "trustworthy," "reliable," "dependable," and "responsible" which comprise what one might call "social conscientiousness" (e.g., Costa & McCrae 1992).[26] Social conscientiousness appears to be a sort of "don't let down the group" trait, originally proposed by Darwin (1871) as the basis of group allegiance. As Goldberg (1981, 161) states, "[m]y knowledge of the status of a person X on the trait of Conscientiousness answers the question 'Can I count on X?'" Because of the importance of a sense of obligation to the group for Judaism throughout its history, there is reason to suppose social conscientiousness may be of particular importance to Judaism as a group evolutionary strategy.

Individuals high on this trait would be expected to feel intense guilt for having failed to fulfill their obligations to the group. Moreover, given the importance of conformity to group norms for Judaism, it would be expected that individuals who were low on this trait would be disproportionately inclined to abandon Judaism, while successful Jews who were the pillars of the community and thus epitomized the group ethic of Judaism would be disproportionately likely to be high on group conformity and also likely to be reproductively successful. The result is that there would be strong selection pressures toward high levels of social conscientiousness within the Jewish community. And since social conscientiousness is psychometrically (and presumably biologically) linked to the other aspects of conscientiousness, these pressures would also result in a general trend toward higher levels of all aspects of conscientiousness within the Jewish community.[27]

For example, Jordan (1989, 138) notes that Jews who defected during the Middle Ages (and sometimes persecuted their former co-religionists) tended to be people who were "unable to sustain the demands of [the] elders for conformity."[28] This trend may well have accelerated since the Enlightenment because the costs of defection became lower. Israel (1985, 254) notes that after the Enlightenment defections from Judaism due ultimately to negative attitudes regarding the restrictive Jewish community life were common enough to have a negative demographic effect on the Jewish community. Moreover, in Chapter 4, it was noted that there was discrimination within the Jewish community such that the families of individuals who had apostatized or engaged in other major breaches of approved behavior had lessened prospects for marriage. To the extent that there is heritable variation for such non-conformity (and all personality traits are heritable [e.g., Rowe 1993]), such practices imply that there will be strong selection pressures concentrating genes for group loyalty and social conformity within the Jewish gene pool.

There has probably always been cultural selection such that people who have difficulty submerging their interests to those of the group have been disproportionately likely to defect from Judaism. Such individuals would have chaffed at the myriad regulations that governed every aspect of life in traditional Jewish society. In Triandis' (1990, 55; see Chapter 8) terms, these individuals are "idiocentric" people living in a collectivist culture; i.e., they are people who are less group oriented and less willing to put group interests above their own.

As in the case of intelligence, it is also highly likely that there were powerful environmental influences that facilitated the conscientiousness system. I propose that traditional Judaism, with its 613 commandments, positively facilitated the conscientiousness system. Baron (1952b, 216), writing of Jews in the ancient world, states that "[f]rom the moment he awakened in the morning until he came to rest at night his behavior was . . . governed by the multiplicity of ritualistic requirements concerning ablutions, prayers, the type of food he was allowed to eat and the time he should set aside for study. . . . It was in this vast interlocking system of observances and institutions, more and more fully elaborated by his rabbinic teachers, that he found his most integrated way of living as an individual and as a member of society."

Thus, a child reared in a traditional Jewish home would have been strongly socialized to continually monitor his/her behavior to ensure compliance with a vast number of restrictions—exactly the sorts of influences expected to strengthen the conscientiousness system. Indeed, the popular conception of the *talmid khokhem* (scholar) among the wider community of Eastern European shtetl Jews and especially among the Hasidim was that he was pre-occupied with endless rituals and consumed with anxiety that he had neglected some regulation (Zborowski & Herzog 1952, 140). Zborowski and Herzog (1952, 202) also describe individuals who are consumed with anxiety lest they omit opportunities to help others, since failure to take advantage of such an opportunity was a violation of a commandment. One function of the Hasidic rabbi was to reassure people who were anxiety-ridden because of fear that they had violated one of the myriad regulations of rabbinical Judaism (p. 179).

Among modern Hasidim too, anxiety disorders ("superego problems") are a common source of complaint (Mintz 1992, 225).[29] And one type of recognized deviance within the Orthodox community involves obsessive religious overconformity (Mayer 1979, 140-141). Such individuals become completely preoccupied with religious rituals.

Anxiety, the emotion of the conscientiousness system, is therefore a very salient psychological trait among those who represent ideal Jewish behavior in traditional societies, and thus among those who can be expected to have high social status and high reproductive success. Individuals, such as impulsive, disinhibited people, who find such requirements unduly burdensome would be prone to defect or to be excluded by the group, thereby concentrating genetic tendencies toward conscientiousness and social conformity among those who continued as Jews.

Moreover, the nature of Jewish religious writings and their role in the Jewish community would constitute effective cultural selection for individuals with high levels of conscientiousness. We have seen that these writings are extremely difficult to comprehend, so that learning them undoubtedly involves a great deal of persistence, frustration, and delay of gratification.

Also, there was little effort to make learning fun by having attractive subject matter. In the traditional Eastern European shtetl societies, studies began at age five or six with the Book of Leviticus and its very dull concern with laws and rituals, rather than with the colorful stories of other parts of the Tanakh (Zborowski & Herzog 1952, 96). Boys of all ages were expected to put in long hours of study, and even children of age three had a nine hour study routine (Zborowski & Herzog 1952, 163). In the *yeshiva*, it was customary to sleep only four or five hours a night and devote the rest of one's time to study.[30]

There were powerful social pressures encouraging children to adopt this regimen of study and thus facilitating the conscientiousness system. Zborowski and Herzog (1952) show that in traditional Eastern European shtetl societies children were exposed at an early age to the cultural ideal of scholarship. The child's introduction to study was accompanied by an elaborate ceremony, which indicated to the child the importance of this area of his life—a custom also noted by Rabinowitz (1938, 214) among the Jews of northern France during the medieval period. Books were revered, and the father's period of study was not to be interrupted with any noise. Children were shown the extreme respect accorded scholars when they came to the house. They themselves were usually named after an ancestor who was an illustrious scholar, and they were constantly encouraged to emulate the achievements of their illustrious relative. Family and community-wide ceremonies marked each advancement along the road of scholarship.

The relevance of conscientiousness as a system underlying delay of gratification and perseverance in the face of hardship and difficulty is obvious. Conscientiousness is the system that impels people to continue their efforts in pursuit of a goal even when the activity is not intrinsically rewarding and is filled with frustration and difficulty (MacDonald n.d.). High frustration tolerance would appear to be a virtual necessity for coming to grips with these works, and we have seen that individuals who were relatively successful in mastering these works were also relatively likely to be reproductively successful.

There is also considerable evidence that traditional Jewish writing strongly advocated a generally responsible, sober, hard-working attitude toward life. Boys, and especially the children of the elite, were expected to refrain from rowdy and undisciplined activities. They were expected to never get their hands dirty or soil their clothes. Fighting was labeled as extremely "un-Jewish," and even outdoor games were discouraged. Descriptions of children tended to note that their "eyes were solemn and that they 'grin but do not smile'" (Zborowski & Herzog 1952, 163). The physical ideal for an older child and an adult was to be thin and pale, what Zborowski and Herzog (1952, 358) describe as "a progressive etherealization, until he becomes the 'beautiful old man'—pale, emaciated, aflame with inner light, the epitome of the complete and 'real' Jew." Children were even scolded if they developed a physically strong, ruddy appearance. There was a very strong emphasis on the ability to delay sensual gratification.

The Books of Proverbs and Ecclesiasticus not only advocate education, but also praise psychological traits such as self-discipline and opposition to sensual gratification. There is a complete lack of any glorification of military virtues, such as physical strength, courage, and aggression, which would be necessary virtues in independently existing societies. Indeed, traditional Jewish religious rituals included practices that symbolized a rejection of military weapons. For example, during the Sabbath service, the pointer that was used by the reader of the Torah could not be made of metal because metal is used in making weapons (Zborowski & Herzog 1952, 55).

This contrasts sharply with the Biblical accounts in which the military exploits of men such as Samson, Jephthah, and King David were glorified. Swift (1919) notes that during the First Commonwealth there were two ideals of manhood, represented by craft and shrewdness ("the thrifty herdsman and farmer, the shrewd merchant, the discerning and just judge, the crafty warrior" [p. 20]) on the one hand and by strength and courage ("the stalwart and daring hunter and soldier" [p. 20]) on the other. However, in the wisdom literature, physical aggression is abjured, and Jews are advised to be obsequious to kings.[31] Self-control is valued more than military might: "He that is slow to anger is better than the mighty, and he who ruleth his spirit than he that taketh a city" (Prov. 16:32). Business, not military skill, is the route to influence: "Seest thou a man diligent in his business? he shall stand before kings; He shall not stand before mean men" (Prov. 22:29). Neusner (1987, 162-163) finds that the affective program of the rabbis during the classical period of Judaism (640-1789) was to encourage humility, patience, and self-abnegation.

Some of these virtues may well be influenced by the conscientiousness system described above. There is a clear concern with being able to delay gratification in these writings. Patai (1977) considers delay of gratification to be a central Jewish value and cites data indicating that contemporary Jews are higher on this dimension. As noted above, the ability to delay gratification is psychometrically associated with conscientiousness. Since all personality systems show significant heritability (e.g., Rowe 1993), the eugenic practices emphasized here would tend to pull the Jewish community toward a higher level in these systems. As in the case of intelligence, traditional Jewish family influences would also be expected to pull in this direction.

Interestingly, the Zionist movement emphasized a return to military virtues. "Instead of rabbis and sages, Zionism chose figures such as David or Judah Maccabee or Samson" (Neusner 1987, 204; see also Ragins 1980, 154). This development strongly suggests that the omission of these virtues from the wisdom literature was intentional and filled a need to emphasize scholarship, diligence in the pursuit of tasks, a de-emphasis on sensory pleasure, and self-control as aspects of an instrumental strategy in the diaspora. However, when confronted with the desire to establish a Jewish political entity, there was a renewed emphasis on the military virtues.

There is evidence for extremely intense relationships within the Jewish family. Alter (1989) notes the image of the overpowering father in Kafka and the "possessive, overbearing, guilt-inducing mother" (p. 227) as a fictional type, as illustrated, for example, in the work of Philip Roth. Herz and Rosen (1982) describe emotionally intense relationships within the extended family, with frequent "cut-offs" of relatives who fail to conform to very high standards for participation in family events. The mother-child relationship is particularly intense and characterized by an extreme sense of self-sacrifice and the inculcation of guilt in the child. The child can never do enough to repay the mother's sacrifice. Parental love is intimately intertwined with parental sacrifice, rather than with physical or verbal expressions of affection.

The result is an intense motivation to please parents. Jewish children are expected to provide their parents with *naches* (i.e., desired rewards) in the form of achievement, financial success, and grandchildren, and the failure to provide them causes guilt. "Of course, there can never be enough *naches*, and their failure to provide 'enough' inevitably results in guilt" (Herz & Rosen 1982, 380).

This style of parenting is also apparent in the traditional Ashkenazi shtetl communities of Eastern Europe. We have already noted that the parents were extremely solicitous and self-sacrificing for their children, but Zborowski and Herzog (1952, 294) also note that, while direct expressions of affection were never made after infancy, the children were "reminded constantly of all their parents have done and suffered in their behalf." "All the sacrifice, all the suffering, all the solicitude pile up into a monument to parental love, the dimensions of which define the vastness of filial indebtedness" (p. 297).

Besides the inculcation of guilt, there is also some indication that Jewish family life is characterized by high levels of affection and solicitude combined with hostility. Zborowski and Herzog (1952, 332) show that infants are showered with physical affection, including a great deal of kissing and caressing and that afterwards, although physical expressions of affection are rare, parents continue to be extremely solicitous about the intellectual accomplishments and physical well-being of their children.

However, there is also the suggestion that this self-sacrificing solicitude and affection are combined with high levels of anger and hostility directed toward the child. Alter (1989) notes the image of the mother as characterized by overpowering affection (and even seduction) combined with domination and hostility in Jewish fiction. And Zborowski and Herzog (1952, 301, 334-337), in their description of family life in traditional Eastern European shtetl societies, note that, in addition to extremely high levels of solicitude toward children, Jewish shtetl families typically engaged in heated arguments, a sort of "domestic pilpul"[32] in which issues were intensely discussed and there were high levels of disagreement and anger. Mothers are likely to lash out in anger and impatience toward the child and oscillate quickly between intensely positive and intensely negative emotions directed at their children. Physical punishment performed in anger was not uncommon, and fathers appear to have been rather distant figures of respect, but not affection.

Modern psychological research is highly compatible with the idea that parent-child relationships may indeed be characterized by intense affection combined with hostility (i.e., ambivalence, as in ambivalent attachment), since these emotions are associated with two independent biological systems (MacDonald 1992a). The ability to form close family relationships and engage in high-investment parenting is clearly an extremely important aspect of Judaism as an evolutionary strategy, but it is reasonable to suppose that being able to compartmentalize one's relationships is also a highly important skill (MacDonald 1992a). Being able to engage in close family relationships would thus be highly compatible with engaging in purely instrumental behavior toward other individuals outside one's group, including behavior of a hostile, exploitative nature.[33] This type of flexibility would appear to be a general feature of human evolved psychology and thus common among all human groups (MacDonald 1992a), but the literary and ethnographic evidence suggests that Jewish family relationships very strongly facilitate both the affectional system and the ability to engage in aggressive and hostile interactions with others.[34]

These data on intense, compartmentalized family relationships are also compatible with facilitating high levels of guilt. As indicated above, the emotion of guilt is associated with the conscientiousness system, but there is excellent reason to suppose that this emotion could be exacerbated by combining intense affection with hostility within the family. The affectional system is fundamentally a motivational system, and intense affection and solicitude would motivate the individual to please the other person and would induce guilt feelings upon lack of compliance (MacDonald 1992a). The combination of intense affection and unreasonable, unfulfillable demands would be expected to produce intense guilt. Indeed, these unreasonable, unfulfillable demands may be seen as an aspect of hostility. The result would be a highly conflicted child, strongly motivated to comply with parental demands and also highly motivated to reject these demands.

These findings are corroborated by Schiffrin's (1984) study of group conversational style among American Jews derived from Eastern Europe. She describes very high levels of disagreement and verbal challenging among the speakers. Speakers continually competed to be heard and used exaggerated intonation and a very rapid tempo of speech. Unlike the case with non-Jewish groups, arguments developed even when the questions asked were non-controversial. Arguments did not end with consensus, but often simply shifted to a context of sociability and intimacy—just as Zborowski and Herzog portray the rapidly oscillating emotions of traditional Jewish shtetl mothers. Although these findings are restricted to Jews derived from Eastern Europe, Schiffrin (1984) also notes the parallelism of this type of verbal argumentation to the style of the Talmuds—continual disagreement within an overall context of solidarity. This suggests a wider applicability of these findings to other Jewish groups.[35]

These findings also suggest that Jews tend to be high on the personality trait of affect intensity; i.e., they are prone to intense emotional experience of both positive and negative emotions (see Larsen & Diener 1987). Individuals high on affect intensity have more complex social networks and more complex lives, including multiple and even conflicting goals. They are prone to fast and frequent mood changes and lead varied and variable emotional lives. Clinically, affect intensity is related to cyclothymia (i. e., alternate periods of elation and depression), bipolar affective disorder (i.e., manic-depressive psychosis), neurotic symptoms, and somatic complaints (nervousness, feeling uneasy, shortness of breath). Affect intensity is also linked to creativity and the manic phase of bipolar affective disorder (see Tucker, Vannatta, & Rothlind 1990).

Consistent with the hypothesis that Jews are high on affect intensity, Zborowski and Herzog (1952, 414ff) show that emotional extremes were typical of the inhabitants of traditional Eastern European shtetl communities. The Jewish holidays were intensely emotional affairs, and the emotions that were expressed were quite opposite ones, a sort of rhythmic alternation of extremes. Rapid emotional oscillation was also characteristic of Yiddish drama.[36] However, there is also a strong emphasis on control—being able to exhibit intense, contradictory emotions at the appropriate time.

The common perception of Jewish and gentile psychiatric workers from the late 19th century until at least the end of the 1920s was that compared to gentiles, Jews (and especially male Jews), had relatively sensitive, highly reactive nervous systems, thus making them more prone to the diagnoses of hysteria, manic-depression, and neurasthenia (Gershon & Liebowitz 1977; Gilman 1993 92ff).[37] Consistent with these early findings, Gershon and Liebowitz (1977) find that Jews had a higher rate of hospitalization for affective disorder than did non-Jews in New York.[38] Strongly suggestive of a genetic basis for the greater prevalence of affective disorder among Jews is their finding that among Jews bipolar affective disorder constituted a higher percentage of all affective disorder than was the case in gentile populations in the United States or Sweden. Individuals with bipolar affective disorder have periods of intense euphoria or paranoid-anger as well as periods of despondency, worry, and hopelessness—exactly the traits expected to characterize individuals who are extreme on affect intensity.

There is some indication that Jews tend to be extreme on all personality systems. Patai (1977, 391) provides a long list of personality traits which appear to be more pronounced among American Jews. Although this type of data must be evaluated with caution, the traits involved appear to include items from all of the Five-Factor Personality Dimensions (see Digman 1990), including items suggesting a strong tendency toward neuroticism (e.g., "is more neurotic"; "anxious") and extraversion (e.g., "greater extraversion").[39] Indeed, this pattern would be expected given the supposition that Jews are higher on affect intensity. Affect intensity is related to all personality systems with a strong emotional component (Larsen & Diener 1987) and may be viewed as a behavioral energizing system that can be directed toward behavioral approach (related to extraversion) as well as behavioral avoidance and attention to danger (related to neuroticism and conscientiousness) (MacDonald n.d.). Individuals high on affect intensity are thus highly motivated to intensive interaction with the environment and often have conflicting goals because both behavioral approach and behavioral avoidance systems are prone to activation. Thus, the proposal is that a critical component in Jewish adaptation has been the elaboration of affect intensity as a personality system.

The suggestion is that via processes of cultural and natural selection Jews have developed an extremely powerful set of psychological systems that are intensely reactive to environmental contingencies. Personality systems underlie a set of adaptive interactions with the environment (see MacDonald 1988a, 1991, 1992a, 1992b, n.d.). Behavioral approach systems direct us toward active, highly motivated involvement in the world, risk-taking, and the acquisition of resources and stimulation. On the other hand, behavioral avoidance, including the conscientiousness system, underlies the ability to react intensely to anticipated danger, defer gratification, persevere in unpleasant tasks, and be dependable and orderly.

Another personality system influenced by affect intensity is the affectional system (often termed agreeableness, warmth, or love in personality research). This system underlies the ability not only to form close, intimate relationships related to high investment-parenting (MacDonald 1992a; see above), but also other types of long-term relationships of reciprocity, trust, and sympathy (Buss 1991; Wiggins & Broughton 1985). Such a trait would appear to be critical to membership in a cohesive, cooperative group such as Judaism. In this regard, it is of interest that Jews exhibit low levels of anti-social personality disorder (Levav et al. 1993), a disorder linked to being low on the agreeableness system (MacDonald 1992a; Widiger & Trull 1992).

Evolution, like a good engineer, designed people with a good engine (the behavioral approach systems) and a good set of brakes (behavioral avoidance and conscientiousness). Individuals who are very high in all of these systems are likely to have a great deal of inner conflict (also noted by Patai [1977, 391] as a trait of American Jews), since they are pulled in different directions by these biologically and psychometrically independent systems (MacDonald n.d.). Exemplars would be the sort of fictional characters who populate Woody Allen movies: individuals who have very powerful drives toward resource acquisition, social dominance, and sensual gratification, but who also have a high level of anxiety, guilt, and inhibitory tendencies.

All personality systems are adaptively important, and being high on all of them provides the ability to be flexibly (and, indeed, intensely) responsive to environmental contingencies. An individual who was high on both the behavioral approach systems and the conscientiousness systems would be strongly motivated to engage in highly rewarding approach behaviors, including extraverted behavior related to resource acquisition, social dominance, and sensual gratification (aspects of behavioral approach), but would also show an ability to react intensely to threatened danger, delay gratification, persevere in the face of difficulty, and be dependable and orderly (aspects of behavioral avoidance and conscientiousness).

This perspective is compatible with the findings of Watson and Clark (1992) indicating that high scores on the Achievement facet of the NEO Personality Inventory (Costa & McCrae 1985) are associated not only with Extraversion, but also with the Conscientiousness facets of Orderliness and Dependability. Since Jews have generally been very high achievers, it would be expected that they would be high on both of these traits. Moreover, the data cited above indicating that Jewish families have intense family relationships characterized by contradictory emotions are quite compatible with this perspective, since the suggestion is that there are intense socialization processes within the Jewish family directed at different biological systems underlying qualitatively different interpersonal relationships.

Although the hypothesis that Jews are high in all personality systems requires further study, Patai's suggestion is compatible with the general point of this section: There have been powerful eugenic and cultural selective forces that have acted on personality systems within the Jewish community over historical time.

# SOCIALIZATION FOR GROUP IDENTIFICATION

As with all collectivist cultures (Triandis 1990, 1991; see Chapter 8), Judaism depends on inculcating a very powerful sense of group identification. Socialization in collectivist cultures stresses group harmony, obedient submission to hierarchical authority, the honoring of parents and elders, ingroup loyalty, and trust and cooperation within the ingroup. Triandis (1990, 96) proposes that identification with an ingroup is increased under the following circumstances: Membership is rewarding to the individual; ingroups are separated by signs of distinctiveness; there is a sense of common fate; socialization emphasizes ingroup membership; ingroup membership is small; the ingroup has distinctive norms and values.

In addition, evolutionists such as Johnson (1986) have emphasized that socialization for group membership often includes an emphasis on the triggering of kin recognition mechanisms (such as references to the kinship nature of the group; e. g., "fatherland," "the Jewish people") and phenotypic similarity (such as similar dress and mannerisms). Operant and classical conditioning are often used, as when individuals are publicly rewarded for group allegiance and altruism.

All of these mechanisms are undoubtedly present within the Jewish community. Phenotypic similarity has been important throughout Jewish history (as indicated by community dress codes). Among contemporary Haredim, one ingredient affecting one's resource value on the marriage market is physical appearance that does not depart from the group norm on color of skin or hair. Thus, Heilman (1992, 280) reports that a haredi with red hair had great difficulty finding a wife. "They thought I looked too much like a goy." Moreover, the adulation of those who best exemplify the group ethic of Judaism is reflected in the contemporary world when major contributors to Jewish charity are honored within the Jewish community.

In the following, the emphasis will be on the reward value of group membership, as well as on ingroup membership and group distinctiveness as aspects of socialization.

There has been a very conscious attempt on the part of the Jewish community to inculcate a sense of group belongingness among all Jews. One aspect of these socialization influences is to continually place group members in situations where group activities involve very positive experiences, but there is also socialization for developing feelings of separateness from gentile culture.

In the traditional shtetl communities of Eastern Europe, beginning at birth children were socialized not simply as individuals or as family members, but also as a member of the entire community. A child's birth was celebrated by the entire community, and there were special roles for children in a variety of religious events. Thus, at the Passover celebration, the youngest child asks the Passover questions, "quivering with excitement" (Zborowski & Herzog 1952, 387). The very elaborate ceremony functions to make the child very aware of the intimate connection of the child to the family and the family to the wider group of Jews extending backward in historical time. Another holiday, *Lag ba Omer*, is given over entirely to the pleasures of children, and a very prominent part of *Hanukkah* is when children go around to relatives to receive money. The boy's *Bar Mitzvah* is fundamentally a ceremony marking his new relationship to the group (Zborowski & Herzog 1952, 351).

Positive group experiences continue into adulthood. Mayer (1979, 62; see also Heilman 1992; Kamen 1985), writing on Orthodox Jews in 20th-century America notes the "atmosphere of festivity and the sense of at-oneness that recurs so frequently in the community." The result is "a sort of collective identification. The individual is merged but never submerged; rather, he is so strongly identified with the group that it partakes of his own individuality—he *is* the group and the group is he" (Zborowski & Herzog 1952, 422; italics in text).

Besides these very positive group experiences, the goal of education was to promote the consciousness of separateness: Writing of traditional Ashkenazi society, Katz (1961a, 190) notes that "[t]he peculiar position of the Jews as a chosen people, the inherently mythic distinction between them and the nations, an understanding of the fate of the Jewish people in the Diaspora and their faith in the coming redemption—all of these penetrated the child's consciousness."

Kamen (1985) notes that the Hasidim are very concerned about contamination from the secular culture and work very hard to minimize the child's contact with or even awareness of the wider culture. Similar to all Jewish societies prior to the Enlightenment, central to this very self-conscious separatism is the use of a Jewish language (in this case, Yiddish), distinctive modes of dress,[40] and distinctive Jewish names (Kamen 1985, 43). Yiddish is the only language spoken in the home in the presence of children, and children are scolded for conversing in English outside of their English classes in school.

As throughout Jewish history, dietary practices are a potent mechanism for psychological separation. A writer on the psychology of the kosher dietary laws in a contemporary Orthodox community observes that permissible foods become "identified as Jewish food and their consumption becomes an event through which one reaffirms to himself and to others that he is, indeed, a Jew . . . (quoted in Mayer 1979, 65).

Education is of course extremely important, but a major goal in the Hasidic community is ensuring group enculturation, rather than imparting subject matter (Mayer 1979). Television and other means of integrating with the wider culture are forbidden so that the child is simply not exposed to these influences. In addition, there are numerous holidays that are utilized in the school curriculum as a means of discussing particular events important in Jewish history or religious practice.

In the synagogue, there is an emphasis on communal chanting, a communal experience "whereby the participants relive the inner time of their ancestors" (Mayer 1979, 108). There is a tendency for compartmentalization such that individual synagogues consist of endogamous subunits of relative ethnic homogeneity. The main purpose of these smaller synagogues seems to be to satisfy the need for very close feelings of group identification—what Mayer (1979, 110) refers to as a "we-feeling" of shared intimacy in a group. Mayer describes a trend in which those trained in Orthodox *yeshivas* seek out Hasidic synagogues as adults because of their greater feelings of group intimacy.

After *Bar Mitzvah* and for approximately seven years until marriage, the boys spend 16 hours per day with their peer group, including communal breakfast, communal ritual baths, communal studying, and communal prayer. At this age, studying itself is done with a great deal of emotion. The boys/men of this age are expected to relate primarily to the peer group, and if a child spends too much time at home, his behavior reflects poorly on himself and his family.

Conformity to group attitudes and behavior is an extremely important aspect of social control in traditional Jewish communities. "A sense of correct behavior, Hasidishe behavior, takes precedence over individual deviations. Indulgence in contrary behavior is not tolerated by the group; the majority acts quickly to reprimand any member whose demeanor reflects negatively on his comrades"

(Kamen 1985, 82-83). It is only with marriage that they have any independence from the peer group at all.

Mayer (1979, 136ff, 141-142) also describes elaborate mechanisms of social control within the Orthodox community, which spring into action to oppose any sign of non-conformity, such as a yarmulke that is too small or too brightly colored or a hem line that is too high.[41] Zborowski and Herzog (1952, 226-227), writing of traditional European shtetl societies, also document elaborate mechanisms that ensure conformity within the community. People are extremely concerned about the good opinions of others. Everyone knows everything there is to know about everyone else, and withdrawal and secrecy are seen as intolerable. Strangers are helped because they are fellow Jews, but their foreign ways inspire mistrust. As the Talmud states, "a man should never depart from established practice" (quoted in Zborowski & Herzog 1952, 221).

Among the Hasidim studied by Kamen (1985), group meetings and social events are common. There are weekly meetings of the males (the *tish*) at which the children participate in group singing. After the singing, there is a discourse on the Torah, followed by singing and dancing. Group dancing by males is particularly striking and also occurs at weddings and other social events. The men join arms and dance together in an atmosphere of great joy and excitement—a clear indication of the powerful positive affective forces joining together members of the group. At the social events, children are introduced in a very positive manner to group membership.

Prayer is also done in groups. Beginning in the second grade, children have group prayers in school three times a day, and the same group continues to pray together daily throughout their school years. Kamen (1985, 64) quotes a rabbi who said that the practice "makes the boys feel like comrades, more than just students together . . . if they *davn* [pray] together they get closer to God and closer to each other." Because of the importance of this social function, prayers are held an hour after the beginning of classes to make sure that all boys are present. The congregation also prays together three times daily. The prayers are performed with great emotional intensity, with "men swaying and rocking in every conceivable direction, hands motioning expressively" (p. 63; see also Mayer 1979, 111).

Another practice with affective overtones is *chazer* (cooperative learning in which a stronger student helps a weaker student). Kamen observed one boy with his arm around another during *chazer*, and a rabbi commented, "[i]n this Yeshiva there's real friendships built up, not competitions. The Rov's teachings stress good feelings and love between people. In hard times it holds people together and in good times it's that much nicer" (quoted in Kamen 1985, 74).

These trends are also apparent in the social world of the shtetl of traditional Eastern European society. Zborowski and Herzog (1952, 54) note the swaying and communal chanting as a prominent aspect of synagogue services in the traditional European shtetl communities:

> The whole room is a swaying mass of black and white, filled with a tangle of murmur and low chantings, above which the vibrant voice of the cantor rises and falls, implores and exults, elaborating the traditional melodies with repetitions and modulations that are his own. The congregation prays as one, while within that unity each man as an individual speaks directly to God.

Zborowski and Herzog (1952, 177) note that there is even more swaying and general intensity of prayer among the Hasidim. They also note (p. 86) that children are expected to go to synagogue because the group atmosphere is viewed as essential to one's education. Group chanting is also an important aspect of education (p. 93). Schoolrooms are not places of silence punctuated by individual student recitations, but very noisy places of group activities like chanting and humming.

These findings indicate major attempts within traditional Jewish communities as well as contemporary Orthodox and Hasidic communities to socialize children to the group. However, these efforts are also apparent in much less traditional Jewish groups. In Chapter 4, it was noted that Judaism in contemporary American society may be viewed as a civil religion. Perhaps because of the lessening prevalence of many of the traditional segregating mechanisms that have facilitated group cohesion over the centuries, the civil religion goes to great lengths to prevent group defection, especially by attempts to strengthen Jewish education. Those who do defect are simply written off, and group continuity and integrity are maintained by a central core of highly committed individuals. Because of the assimilatory pressures from the surrounding society, great importance is placed on "the recognition of Jewish education as the most vital element in the preservation of the Jewish people" (Woocher 1986, 34). Similarly, Elazar (1980) notes that the drive for more intensive Jewish education, including an increasing emphasis on Jewish day schools, was motivated by "the clearly pressing problems of assimilation" (p. 211).

Jewish identification is also actively facilitated by encouraging trips to Israel by high school and college students, and, indeed, Elazar refers to Israel as "the central focus of American Jewish educational effort" (p. 291). Woocher (1986, 150) notes that the trips to Israel are often overlaid with "mythic" overtones from Jewish history (p. 150) (e.g., visits to holocaust memorials) and have as their goal increased commitment to a Jewish identification on the part of the visitors. The retreats function as a sort of religious experience, which attempts to effect attitude change by removing participants from their normal lives; by emphasizing group-oriented activities and a sense of community, nostalgia, and "specialness"; and by renewing commitment to group identification and group goals (pp. 151-52). Woocher (1986) also stresses the importance of the General Assembly of the Council of Jewish Federations as a major civil religious event that functions to foster Jewish identification and a strong sense of community.

Finally, mention should be made of the role of external threat in facilitating group identification among Jews. As emphasized by evolutionists such as

Alexander (1979), external threat tends to reduce internal divisions and maximize perceptions of common interest among group members. The awareness of anti-Semitism may thus be expected to foster a sense of group identity and social cohesion in the face of threat—the "common fate" or "shared enemy" syndrome studied by psychologists (Berkowitz 1982; Hogg & Abrams 1987).

Wilson and Sober (1994) have proposed the existence of group-selected psychological mechanisms that facilitate group goals on a facultative basis, that is, in response to specific contingencies. Here it is proposed that external threat is a situation that elicits an evolved facultative tendency to more strongly identify with the group. Research on individualism/collectivism indicates that collectivist tendencies become more pronounced during periods of group conflict (Triandis 1990, 96). Thus, in Chapter 8, the extreme level of conformity and thought control that occurred among Jews in the Ottoman Empire is mentioned, based on Shaw (1991, 137ff). Although these practices occurred during a period of economic prosperity, these hyper-conformist tendencies became even more extreme during a subsequent period of persecution and economic decline. These findings are consistent with supposing that increased group competition resulted in a facultative enhancement of mechanisms related to group cohesion.[42]

External threat has commonly increased the level of group commitment among Jews. Woocher (1986, 46) notes that the European crisis of the 1930s, "as had happened so often in the past, called forth a deep sense of universal Jewish solidarity." Ragins (1980, 85-86), relying on personal testimonies, shows that anti-Semitism in Germany during the early 20th century had a strong tendency to provoke greater identification with Judaism among Jewish activists. As Freud noted in 1926, "My language . . . is German, my culture, my attainments are German. I considered myself German intellectually, until I noticed the growth of anti-Semitic prejudices in Germany and German Austria. Since that time, I prefer to call myself a Jew" (quoted in Gilman 1993, 16).[43] Feldman (1993, 43) finds very robust tendencies toward heightened Jewish identification and rejection of gentile culture consequent to anti-Semitism at the very beginnings of Judaism in the ancient world and throughout Jewish history.

A permanent sense of imminent threat appears to be common among Jews. Writing on the clinical profile of Jewish families, Herz and Rosen (1982) note that for Jewish families a "sense of persecution (or its imminence) is part of a cultural heritage and is usually assumed with pride. Suffering is even a form of sharing with one's fellow-Jews. It binds Jews with their heritage—with the suffering of Jews throughout history." Zborowski and Herzog (1952, 153) note that the homes of wealthy Jews in traditional Eastern European shtetl communities sometimes had secret passages for use in times of anti-Semitic pogroms, and that their existence was "part of the imagery of the children who played around them, just as the half-effaced memory was part of every Jew's mental equipment."

This evolved response to external threat is often manipulated by Jewish authorities attempting to inculcate a stronger sense of group identification. Hartung (1992) provides anecdotal data on the emphasis on Jewish suffering and its exaggeration as aspects of modern synagogue service. Such practices have a long history. Roth (1978, 62) notes that Jewish "martyrologists" maintained lists of Jewish martyrs for commemoration during synagogue services during the Middle Ages, and Jordan (1989, 20) refers to the "forbidding martyrocentric self-image" during this period.

Woocher (1986) shows that Jewish survival in a threatening world is a theme of Judaism as a civil religion in contemporary America. Within this world view, the gentile world is viewed as fundamentally hostile, with Jewish life always on the verge of ceasing to exist entirely. "Like many other generations of Jews who have felt similarly, the leaders of the polity who fear that the end may be near have transformed this concern into a survivalist weapon" (Woocher 1986, 73). Woocher (1986) notes that there has been a major effort since the 1960s to have American Jews visit Israel in an effort to strengthen Jewish identification, with a prominent aspect of the visit being a trip to a border outpost "where the ongoing threat to Israel's security is palpable" (p. 150).

To conclude: Judaism as a group strategy has developed a wide range of practices that serve to cement allegiance to the group and the submergence of individual goals to the overall aims of the group. Eugenic practices and the development of intensive cultural supports for group identification have resulted in a very powerful group orientation among Jews. Some of these cultural practices appear to trigger evolved psychological mechanisms related to group identification. As indicated above, this appears to be the case with the emphasis on external threat and its exaggeration. However, a similar situation may also occur with regard to socialization mechanisms in which the cultural distinctiveness of the ingroup is stressed: Social identity processes underlying group identification appear to be a biological adaptation in which a powerful sense of group identification is triggered by emphasizing the distinctive features of the ingroup (viewed as positive) and the contrary characteristics of the outgroup (viewed as negative) (see *SAID*, ch. 1). The suggestion is that mechanisms of socialization for group identification rely ultimately on a very rich set of evolved psychological systems.

# NOTES

1. It is interesting to note that the Jewish rejection of agricultural labor (i.e., primary production) is extremely deep-rooted. Nini (1991) notes that, in Yemen, Jews did not engage in agriculture, and he makes the interesting suggestion that this custom may have derived from the negative attitudes toward the *'am ha-ares* beginning in ancient times (see below) or it may be the result of continued messianic attitudes which viewed the land of Israel as the only place where one should have close links to the soil. The result, as

typical throughout Jewish history, was that Jews were not engaged in primary economic production, but lived at a higher level of the human energy pyramid. The interesting thing here is that Yemenite Jews typically performed very difficult manual labor and were extremely impoverished and uneducated. As a result, it was not an abhorrence of hard, manual labor that was involved. There is the suggestion that the avoidance of engaging in primary production has very deep cultural roots among Jews living in the diaspora.

2. These issues include the following: whether the inedible parts are to be included in the bulk necessary for imparting uncleanness; how the intention of the person eating the animal is to be considered in relation to the uncleanness of the animal; how contact between food of different degrees of uncleanness affects the cleanness of the animal; the levels of sanctification of food as related to their susceptibility to uncleanness as affected by how far they are removed from the original source of uncleanness (i.e., from the first remove, the "Father of uncleanness" [Neusner (1988a, 212], to the fourth remove); how the state of the food (i.e., whether solid, congealed, or liquid) affects all of this, especially in relation to the size of the food (e.g., if a congealed piece of the minimum size for uncleanness were to liquefy and lose one drop of liquid, it would no longer be unclean, nor would the drop of liquid exuded); how the status of the person (i. e., whether an observant Jew (*haber*) or an uneducated/non-observant Jew ('*am ha-ares*) affects the cleanness or uncleanness of the objects he/she comes in contact with; how the specific qualities of the food (e.g., the stage of ripeness for olives) affect its cleanness; the cleanness of doubts about whether an object is clean; how connections between clean and unclean things affect the whole during and after contact. Principles are enunciated, such as "All unclean things [are adjudged] in accord with [their condition] at the moment that they are found" (M. Toh. 3.5A), and then a long list of examples, which stretch the limits of the principle, is provided.

3. As discussed in *SAID* (chs. 6-8), certain predominantly Jewish intellectual movements of the 20th century, particularly psychoanalysis, have also been highly authoritarian and irrational.

4. An evolutionary perspective differs from a eugenic perspective because there is no emphasis in the eugenic perspective on resource competition between segregated gene pools or on the importance of within-group altruism. Weyl (1969, 1989) notes correctly that eugenic practices also occurred in China, but in this case there was no large, unbridgeable genetic gulf between an ethnically separate scholarly class and the rest of the population, and, indeed, successful scholars undoubtedly had large numbers of concubines from the lower levels of Chinese society. As a result, while anti-Semitism has been an extremely robust tendency, scholars were revered throughout Chinese society. (However, as indicated in Chapter 5, anti-Chinese activity has been directed against overseas Chinese when they lived as a segregated ethnic group viewed as being in competition with indigenous peoples.) In China, competition was not between a genetically isolated group of scholars and the rest of the population, but rather there was individual/family competition within the entire population, the basis of which was scholarly ability. Mainstream Judaism must be seen primarily not as an example of successful eugenic practices, but rather as a national/ethnic strategy that has a eugenic component: All the genes and gene frequencies typical of the Jewish ethnic group are involved (e.g., genes for fingerprint patterns), not simply genes for intelligence.

5. The question of whether the Pharisees (in addition to the *haberim*) discriminated against the '*am ha-ares* is controversial. (Schürer [[1885] 1979, 399] states that the *haberim* are to be identified with the Pharisees.) Many scholars, including Jeremias (1969, 246ff), Neusner (1971 III:286ff) and Schürer ([1885] 1979, 394ff), take the view that the Pharisees participated in closed communities separated from other Jews and from

the *'am ha-ares* in particular. Sanders (1992, 442) describes this tradition as one in which the Pharisees are "the only true Israel, communal meals, meals eaten in purity, sacred food, closed societies, unwillingness to mingle with others because of fear of impurity, exclusion of everyone else from the realm of the sacred, hatred of other Jews, expulsion of people who transgress food and purity laws from the commonwealth of Israel." Even though Sanders disagrees with this view, he suggests that the Pharisees only viewed the other Jews as lower on a scale of purity than themselves, but did not view the common people as entirely removed from the sacred (Sanders 1992, 434). Such a designation of relative impurity is of course compatible with considerable social and genetic discrimination against such people. The point here is that there is indeed a mainstream scholarly tradition that holds that there was a conscious attempt by organized sections of the Jewish community to exclude the *'am ha-ares* from the community of Judaism.

Because of the many negative statements about the Pharisees in the New Testament, this issue has become an issue in Christian-Jewish scholarly polemics. (Jeremias [1969, 267] states that Jesus "openly and fearlessly called these men to repentance, and this act brought him to the cross.") However, the only important issue here is whether it is reasonable to suppose that the well-documented negative attitudes toward the relatively poor and illiterate *'am ha-ares* on the part of the Jewish political and intellectual leadership had a negative effect on their genetic representation in the Jewish gene pool.

6. In the following passage, the house where the wife of an *'am ha-ares* is grinding grain for a wife of a *haber* becomes especially unclean when the wife of the *'am ha-ares* stops working, and if there are two such women there, one must always assume the worst:

A. The wife of a *haber* who left the wife of an *'am ha-ares* grinding [grain] in her house—

B. [if the sound of] the millstones ceased

C. the house is unclean.

D. The millstones did not cease—

E. unclean is only [the space] up to the place to which she can reach out her hand and touch.

F. [If] they were two, one way or the other [whether or not the grinding ceased],

G. "the house is unclean,"

H. "for one grinds, and one snoops about," the words of R. Meir.

I. And sages say, "Unclean is only [the space] up to the place to which they can reach out their hands and touch." (M. Toh. 7:4)

7. Epstein (1942, 311) emphasizes that this ceremony was intended to sever ties with anyone who had contracted a marriage of a woman of foreign blood. Clearly, both foreign blood and a marriage not made according to eugenic principles may well have both been viewed as unworthy marriages for the purposes of this ceremony.

8. Mintz (1992, 219) finds greater acceptance of professional treatment of mental disorder among the Hasidim dating from 1982, although great pains are still taken to prevent public knowledge of psychiatric disorder in the family.

9. Since marriage occurred long before the possibility of having children in many cases, it is reasonable to suppose that the practice had some other function than simply high fertility. Since the boy would be under the scrutiny of another family, marrying in early adolescence and living with in-laws would presumably result in a great deal of pressure to succeed at scholarship and to avoid the impulsivity and immediate gratification typical of adolescents (see MacDonald 1988a). There also is some indication

that Jews believed that such a practice would make adolescent sexual desire less of a disruptive force. However, there is also evidence that in some cases the children became permanently repelled by sexual relationships as a result of the practice.

10. In reviews of the early literature, Brill (1936) and Nardi (1948) found that, despite severe methodological difficulties, Jewish children were superior or at least equal to non-Jewish children in Britain and the United States, and a similar conclusion is reached by Maller (1948). Among the best of the early studies was that of Davies and Hughes (1927), which found that Jewish children aged 8-14 were superior to British children in three schools situated in a good district, a moderately poor district, and a very poor district, respectively. Lynn (1992) interprets these data to indicate a mean IQ of Jewish children of 110.5, 110.6 for arithmetic, and 113.0 for English. Although this was not a representative Jewish sample, the differences were present in all three schools and thus within the three socio-economic categories.

11. In addition, Levinson (1957) found that applicants to Jewish day schools had an average IQ of 118, and Nardi (1948) found that children in Jewish day schools had an average IQ of 115.2. Although Nardi cautions that his sample may not be entirely representative of the Jewish population, data are provided indicating that Jewish children in a public school actually had higher average IQs than Jewish children enrolled in religious schools in the same neighborhood.

12. One can detect a sensitivity to issues of anti-Semitism in Lenz's (1931, 647ff) account of "Nordic" and Jewish abilities (see especially p. 674n). His data, apart from IQ differences, are impressionistic, but I believe that he was attempting to give an unbiased account based on his experience, and his conclusions are broadly consistent with the verbal/performance distinction emphasized here. As do several modern theorists (Lynn 1992; Rushton 1988; see also my comments in Chapter 8), Lenz gives major weight to the selective pressures of the Ice Age on northern peoples. The intellectual abilities of these peoples are proposed to be due to a great need to master the natural environment, resulting in selection for traits related to mechanical ability, structural design, and inventiveness. Lenz's description of Jewish intellectual abilities conforms essentially to what is termed here *verbal intelligence*, and he notes that such abilities are important for social influence and would be expected in a people who evolved in large groups. See also Chapter 8, note 16.

13. Even more commonly, Jews tended to enter businesses that required only a simple technology, again depending on capital provided by the Jewish community (Mosse 1987, 169).

14. This does not imply that Jews were not innovators or did not contribute greatly to the development of the German economy. Quite the contrary. Mosse (1987, 404) persuasively argues that Jews were pioneers in a wide range of economic activity; they were "innovators without for that being inventors." The suggestion here is that differences in intellectual proclivities (verbal versus performance IQs) contributed to the observed patterns.

15. Although Patai (1977) accepts the idea that eugenic processes may have had some effect, he emphasizes other causes. His work is a good example of a strong apologetic tendency in social science research by Jews and is considered in detail in *SAID* (ch. 5).

16. See, e.g., Beinart's (1981) discussion of the Inquisition in Cuidad Real. Jordan (1989, 64) notes that poorer Jews were able to escape persecution from King John of England in the early 13th century.

17. Several studies have found Jewish/gentile differences in intelligence at all socio-economic levels (e.g., Davies & Hughes 1927). Socio-economic status is thus not likely to be the only factor explaining the high level of Jewish intelligence.

18. Recently, Kaniel and Fisherman (1991) found that children in a "non-culturally deprived" sample of Israelis taking the Progressive Matrices Test were either exactly at the 50th percentile (ages 9-10, 10-11, 13-14, 14-15) or somewhat below (ages 11-12 at the 45th percentile; ages 12-13 at the 40th percentile). Thus unlike Jewish children in the United States, there is no overall tendency for the Israeli population to be superior to American norms for intelligence tests—presumably reflecting the influence of the large Oriental group in Israel.

19. Similarly, in Morocco, Lewis attributes the decline of Jews to Muslim repression, which left Jews "in a state of material degradation and intellectual impoverishment" (1984, 148). Stillman (1979) attributes the economic and demographic decline of Jews in Arab lands to the development of an Islamic state bureaucracy and bourgeoisie, which gradually resulted in the economic marginalization and social isolation of Jews and other minorities. This type of exclusion by native Muslim populations also occurred much earlier in other areas: For example, Stillman (1979) notes the exclusion of Jews from a wide range of economic activities by Muslim guilds in medieval Morocco and from government service in 14th-century Egypt (p. 273).

20. This emphasis on the moral worth of Judaism as deriving from its exemplary family life occurred also in the Jewish apologetic literature in the ancient world (e.g., Philo and Josephus) during the period when Judaism first encountered Western (Greek) culture (J. J. Collins 1985, 167; see Chapter 4).

21. While all studies find lower Jewish mortality up to age 55, there are conflicting data regarding the adult mortality rate after this age (see Peritz & Tamir 1977).

22. A remarkable corroboration of this general finding comes from a recent study by Bereczkei (1993), who found a very low sex ratio among Hungarian gypsies associated with a variety of other traits characteristic of a low-investment style of reproduction compared to Hungarians: higher fertility, longer reproductive period, earlier onset of sexual behavior and reproduction, more unstable pair bonds, higher rate of single parenting, shorter interval of birth spacing, higher infant mortality rate, and higher rate of survival of low-birth-weight infants. The gypsies would appear to be a low-investment group evolutionary strategy.

23. Kaplan's (1983, 275) findings that there was a surplus of Jewish women in Germany in the late 19th and early 20th centuries may be explainable in these terms. Another intriguing set of data is presented by Mosse (1987, 216) who finds an extremely *low* sex ratio of 15/33 (0.45) among the children of a group of elite German Jews (i.e., individuals with a fortune of greater than 15 million marks) in the early 20th century. However, in a larger "sub-elite" group (individuals with a fortune of 5-15 million marks), the sex ratio of children was a very *high* 51/28 (1.8). Mosse comments that self-made men tended not to have male offspring, whereas the dynastic banking families whose wealth dated from the 18th century tended to regularly produce male heirs. These patterns were quite different for gentiles with similar incomes, the latter having both a higher fertility rate and an approximately equal sex ratio for both income categories.

24. For similar data on the Soviet Union, see Gitelman (1981) and S. Goldstein (1981). For data on the United States, see S. Goldstein (1981) and Bachman 1970, 35).

25. An early follower of Freud described a Jewish predisposition to obsessive neurosis. Freud agreed with this association and proposed that obsessive neurosis was more common among "highly developed people" (see Gay 1987, 135-136). Freud viewed Jews as genetically superior to gentiles. See *SAID* (chs. 3 and 7).

26. Factor analytic studies (Lusk, MacDonald & Newman 1993; Watson & Clark 1992) have found conscientiousness items yield separate factors for social conscientiousness and several types of asocial conscientiousness. Thus, Costa and

McCrae (1992) describe a "Dutifulness" facet of Conscientiousness, consisting of items related to performing assigned tasks conscientiously, fulfilling commitments, fulfilling social obligations, and being dependable and reliable. At least some facets of Costa and McCrae's Conscientiousness appear to be asocial, including orderliness and lack of impulsivity.

27. Johnson (1987, 138), discussing individuals such as Heinrich Heine, notes "[a] Jewish phenomenon which became very common over the centuries: a clever young man who, in his youth, accepted the modernity and sophistication of the day and then, late in middle age, returned to his Jewish roots." This suggests age changes in the tendency for group identification among Jews. Triandis (1991, 82) finds that a common phenomenon in collectivist cultures such as Judaism (see Chapter 8) is for commitment to the group (collectivism) to increase as the individual ages. Triandis speculates that older people have been socialized in the collectivist environment for a longer period of time, but the effect pointed to by Johnson suggests in addition that individuals who have fled these socializing influences tend to return to a stronger sense of group identity as they get older. I speculate that there are developmental genetic differences in attachment to group interests, perhaps resulting from the relative decline of the individualistic drives associated with the extraversion system (see MacDonald 1988a, MacDonald 1992a, MacDonald 1992b; Zuckerman 1979).

28. The Sephardic philosopher Baruch Spinoza is a famous example of a non-conformist who was expelled from the Jewish community.

29. One source of psychological stress among the Hasidim is that individuals must develop a community-oriented facade, which hides the private self. Such findings are expected in collectivist, authoritarian cultures (Triandis 1990, 77ff). Other sources of family stress are the intrusive nature of family interaction and the authoritarian style of child rearing (Mintz 1992, 176ff).

30. These tendencies are also apparent in contemporary Hasidism. The school day is very long, and after *Bar Mitzvah*, it becomes even longer. Students are strictly supervised. and it is expected that they will adopt very strict study habits. "Many nights they will fall asleep over their books . . . , awake abruptly and begin reading again with enforced vigor and concentration" (Kamen 1985, 84). "The rabbis are aware of the weariness brought on by such vigorous mental activity, but feel it builds character and resolution in a child if he 'fights physical urges to learn Torah'" (Kamen 1985, 69). As was also the case in other traditional Jewish communities, scholarly ability resulted in increased social status within the Hasidic community (p. 87).

31. For example: "My son, if sinners entice thee, consent thou not. If they say, 'Come with us, let us lie in wait for blood, let us lurk for the innocent without cause; Let us swallow them up alive as the grave, and whole, as those that go down into the pit . . .'" (Prov. 1:11-12); "The wrath of a king is as messengers of death; But a wise man will pacify it. In the light of the king's countenance is life; and his favour is as a cloud of the latter rain" (Prov. 16:14-15). The dependence of Jewish welfare on the favor of ruling elites was a major theme of Chapter 5.

32. The allusion is to the intense argumentation characteristic of *yeshiva* academic discussions; see above.

33. I speculate that one aspect of Judaism as a group evolutionary strategy is that Jews must be able to accept high levels of hostility as a normal aspect of interpersonal relationships, so that having intense hostility directed toward one does not result in self-condemnation and self-hatred. In *SAID* (ch. 2), I discuss data indicating that anti-Semitism has been virtually universal in human societies and that anti-Semitism is anticipated in canonical Jewish religious writings dating from the priestly redaction of the

Pentateuch. Indeed, Peli (1991, 110), in discussing Midrashic perceptions of anti-Semitism throughout the ages, notes that "they treat Judeophobia as an inevitable reality that Jews have to learn to live with without giving up in despair on the one hand, or trying in vain to 'correct' its causes on the other." The proposal here is that Jewish socialization emphasizes being able to "learn to live with" hostility in a context of overall self-acceptance. Consistent with this proposal, Gilman (1986) suggests that Jewish self-hatred results from internalizing gentiles' negative images of Jews. To remain a non-self-hating Jew therefore, one cannot allow the desire for acceptance by gentiles to lead to a denial of difference. One must continue to accept oneself as a Jew in the context of being hated even by a large majority of the society one lives in. A direct corollary of this is that Jewish theories of anti-Semitism have typically stressed the irrationality and projective nature of gentile beliefs about Jews. See the discussion in *SAID* (especially ch. 8).

34. As a prominent example of compartmentalized emotions, Freud ([1931] 1985, 333) observed in *The Interpretation of Dreams*, "My emotional life has always insisted that I should have an intimate friend and a hated enemy. I have always been able to provide myself afresh with both, and it has not infrequently happened that the ideal situation of childhood has been so completely reproduced that friend and enemy have come together in a single individual—though not, of course, both at once or with constant oscillations, as may have been the case in my early childhood."

Regarding this statement, McGrath (1974, 38) states that "[t]he close professional relationships with men like Josef Breuer and Willhelm Fliess are but two of the subsequent examples in which Freud sought and found fellow rebels to share his defiance of authority in the exploration of sexuality, and in both cases the relationships eventually moved from the most intimate friendship to bitter antagonism." Gay (1988, 241) notes a similar pattern: "As in earlier friendships, Freud rapidly, almost rashly, invested his affections, moved toward almost unreserved cordiality, and ended in irreparable, furious estrangement."

35. Heilman (1976) shows that the role of argumentation in creating social cohesion is well established among Orthodox Jews not only in public debates over religious law, but at more informal levels as well, including, I would suggest, the family.

36. A remarkable recent example is a scene in Paul Mazursky's film, "The Pickle," which portrays a reminiscence of a Jewish childhood in which the parents are screaming insults at each other while seated on a Ferris wheel with their son between them. The son interjects a joke and the parents immediately dissolve into laughter and the entire family then proceeds to engage in a very convivial, intimate conversation.

37. Gilman's (1993, 92ff) account indicates that Jewish psychiatrists emphasized environmental causes of the phenomenon, while gentiles were more prone to suppose it was influenced by genetic selection in the diaspora. The general attraction of Jewish social scientists to environmentalism is discussed in *SAID* (ch. 5). It is interesting in this regard that the typical sex difference found in affective disorder does not occur in Jewish populations (Levav et al. 1993). This suggests selection away from a more sex differentiated pattern typical of gentile populations. These findings are compatible with the hypothesis that gentile males have been under greater selection pressure for physical risk taking and sensation seeking in which intense emotional reactivity (which tends to trigger behavioral avoidance mechanisms energized by fear and anxiety) would be a liability (MacDonald 1988a; n.d.). Zuckerman (1984) notes that sensation seekers, a group that includes individuals who engage in physically dangerous activities, tend to be stimulus augmenters; i.e., they have strong nervous systems and do not inhibit responding even at very high levels of stimulus intensity. In other words, they tend to have low

emotional reactivity. Because of the ecological position of the Jews, however, physical risk taking and sensation seeking are expected to be of relatively little importance, while intense emotional reactivity would be an asset in motivating conscientiousness and other systems driven by negative emotions important for group living (especially anxiety) as well as positive emotions important for some aspects of behavioral approach, self-confidence, and creativity (see MacDonald n.d.).

38. In an epidemiological study based on interviews of a stratified sample of the 1949-1958 birth cohort in Israel, Levav and his colleagues (1993) found that bipolar affective disorder I (a form of manic-depression) was more common among those deriving from Europe. The most common diagnosis was generalized anxiety disorder and labile personality disorder, the latter characterized by periods of depression and hypomania. Again, the suggestion is that Ashkenazi Jews are high on affect intensity. They have highly reactive nervous systems and are prone to alternating between intensely positive and intensely negative emotions. Anxiety disorder was found less frequently in Israel than in several other areas, but the authors caution that the studies estimating prevalences used different diagnostic criteria, different interview schedules, *et cetera*.

39. One of the correlates of extraversion is risk-taking behavior. A proneness to risk-taking is a common observation of Jewish economic behavior throughout the ages (Johnson 1987; Mosse 1987, 314ff).

40. A young Hasidic man commented, "I call my clothing a personal weapon because if I am tempted to do something which by law is not right, one look at myself, my hat, my coat, my tstitsis reminds me who I am. Nobody is there to see except me, and believe me that's enough" (quoted in Kamen 1985, 88-89). In the wider Orthodox community men must wear skullcaps or hats, and women must be modestly dressed (Mayer 1979, 73).

41. See also the discussion of Turkish Jews (Shaw 1991, 65) in Chapter 8.

42. In addition, there was a shift toward mysticism (often seen in times of persecution; see Chapter 3) and asceticism and an increase in what can only be termed hypervigilance of female behavior related to sexuality. This last is particularly interesting because it suggests a concern that females might defect from the group strategy in times of crisis. Females were not allowed out of the house unless they were too poor to have servants do the shopping. Women out of the house were to remain visible from the street at all times.

43. Freud's comment is probably disingenuous. As indicated in *SAID* (ch. 7), Freud had an intense Jewish identification dating from his early childhood. He was also greatly concerned anti-Semitism dating from an incident involving his father when Freud was an adolescent.

# 8

# THE ORIGINS OF JUDAISM AS A GROUP
# EVOLUTIONARY STRATEGY

An adequate theory of Judaism must ultimately attempt to develop a perspective on the origins of Judaism as a group evolutionary strategy. Clearly, one source of the fascination that Judaism has presented over the centuries to intellectuals has been the uniqueness of Judaism and its persistence in its uniqueness over very long periods of historical time. In attempting to develop a theoretical perspective on this question, it is important to remember the general theoretical perspective developed in Chapter 1.

The theoretical perspective developed there specifically allows for "cultural" influences on evolutionary strategies. Humans are viewed as "flexible strategizers" (Alexander 1987) who are able to develop ideologies and social systems that are intended to further evolutionary ends. These evolutionary goals are assumed to have a powerful genetic component, but the means by which one attains these evolutionary goals can utilize higher-level ("domain-general") cognitive processes and be influenced by experience. In the same way that their cognitive capabilities enable humans to make inventions or learn new methods of warfare, the present perspective is highly compatible with the idea that an evolutionary strategy could be contrived on the basis of specific experiences or on the basis of a general understanding or theory of human nature.

However, in Chapter 1, it was mentioned that genetic and environmental variation in psychological mechanisms may also be important to the development of group evolutionary strategies. If indeed the type of group evolutionary strategy represented by Judaism "pulls" for certain psychological predispositions, then it is reasonable to suppose that there may be biological predispositions for engaging in the type of group evolutionary strategy represented by Judaism.

The theory eventually developed here considers three components, all of which involve cultural/environmental factors: (1) Jews are biologically predisposed to be high on psychological traits predisposing them toward collectivist social structure and ethnocentrism; (2) Jews originated as a people during the Egyptian sojourn and utilized this experience as a basis for interpreting their history and constructing their group evolutionary strategy; (3) Judaism was profoundly influenced by the invention of a hereditary (tribal) priestly class with a powerful motivation to maintain the integrity of the group.

# INDIVIDUALISM/COLLECTIVISM: THE PSYCHOLOGICAL BASIS OF ETHNOCENTRISM

> [Ethnocentrism is] a schismatic in-group/out-group differentiation, in which internal cohesion, relative peace, solidarity, loyalty and devotion to the in-group, and the glorification of the "sociocentric-sacred" (one's own cosmology, ideology, social myth, or *Weltanschauung*; one's own "god-given" social order) are correlated with a state of hostility or permanent quasi-war (*status hostilis*) towards out-groups, which are often perceived as inferior, sub-human, and/or the incorporation of evil. Ethnocentrism results in a dualistic, Manichaean morality which evaluates violence within the in-group as negative, and violence against the out-group as positive, even desirable and heroic. (van der Dennen 1987, 1)

I believe that the area of psychological research most relevant to conceptualizing Judaism as a group evolutionary strategy is that of research on individualism/collectivism (see Triandis 1990, 1991 for reviews). Collectivist cultures (and Triandis [1990, 57] explicitly includes Judaism in this category) place a great emphasis on the goals and needs of the ingroup, rather than on individual rights and interests. Ingroup norms and the duty to cooperate and submerge individual goals to the needs of the group are paramount. Collectivist cultures develop an "unquestioned attachment" to the ingroup, including "the perception that ingroup norms are universally valid (a form of ethnocentrism), automatic obedience to ingroup authorities, and willingness to fight and die for the ingroup. These characteristics are usually associated with distrust of and unwillingness to cooperate with outgroups" (p. 55).

As indicated in Chapter 7, socialization in collectivist cultures stresses group harmony, conformity, obedient submission to hierarchical authority, the honoring of parents and elders. There is also a major stress on ingroup loyalty, as well as trust and cooperation within the ingroup. Each of the ingroup members is viewed as responsible for every other member. However, relations with outgroup members are "distant, distrustful, and even hostile" (Triandis 1991, 80). In collectivist cultures, morality is conceptualized as that which benefits the group, and aggression and exploitation of outgroups are acceptable (Triandis 1990, 90).

People in individualist cultures, on the other hand, show little emotional attachment to ingroups. Personal goals are paramount, and socialization emphasizes the importance of self-reliance, independence, individual responsibility, and "finding yourself" (Triandis 1991, 82). Individualists have more positive attitudes toward strangers and outgroup members and are more likely to behave in a pro-social, altruistic manner to strangers. People in individualist cultures are less aware of ingroup/outgroup boundaries and thus do not have highly negative attitudes toward outgroup members (1991, 80). They often disagree with ingroup policy, show little emotional commitment or loyalty to ingroups, and do not have a sense of common fate with other ingroup members. Opposition to outgroups occurs in individualist societies, but the opposition is more "rational" in the sense that there is less of a tendency to suppose that all of the outgroup members are culpable. Individualists form mild attachments to many groups, while collectivists have an intense attachment and identification to a few ingroups (1990, 61).

The expectation is that individualists living in the presence of collectivist subcultures will tend to be less predisposed to outgroup hostility and more likely to view any offensive behavior by outgroup members as resulting from transgressions by individuals, rather than being stereotypically true of all outgroup members. On the other hand, collectivists living in an individualist society would be more likely to view ingroup/outgroup distinctions as extremely salient and to develop stereotypically negative views about outgroups.

## "Hyper-collectivism" as a Characteristic of Jewish Groups

As indicated above, Triandis regards Jews as a collectivist culture, and I would agree. This is indicated by the material in this volume on within-group altruism and cooperation (Chapter 6) and the data on socialization discussed in Chapter 7. However, the principle indicator of the Jewish tendency toward collectivism is the extensive material on Jewish cultural separatism among mainstream Ashkenazi and Sephardic Jewish groups discussed in Chapters 3 and 4. This cultural separatism implies a powerful sense of ingroup/outgroup barriers. Jews have retained an intense commitment to their ingroup over a very long period of historical time and despite very high levels of hostility directed at them by surrounding peoples.

In some ways, however, the data gathered in Chapters 3 and 4 represent only the tip of an immense iceberg. It is instructive to review data on just how very robust the tendency to ethnic separatism among the Jews really is. Johnson (1987, 3) calls the Jews "the most tenacious people in history," but even this judgment seems inadequate. While the general trend over historical time has been the amalgamation and assimilation of ethnic groups into larger societies (see Chapter 4), Jewish diaspora groups are known from the eighth century B.C. (Baron 1952a), long before the Babylonian exile and the development of the Jewish canon. A particularly well-described example is the non-syncretistic, endogamous community of Jews who lived in Egypt for over a century beginning before 525 B.C.—quite possibly long before this date (see Porten 1984).

From the perspective of this volume, at least some of these groups are not considered to have adopted an evolutionary strategy in quite the same sense as mainstream diaspora Jewry, since there is no evidence that they developed the eugenic practices and high-investment reproductive strategy emphasized here as essential to understanding mainstream diaspora Judaism as an evolutionary strategy. They are of interest, however, because they suggest that ethnic separatism among Jews is an extremely robust tendency, which was retained independently by several Jewish groups and which was not dependent on a large amount of the Jewish canon or on the activities of a hereditary priestly aristocracy.

The Samaritans are closely related to the Jews and are reputed to be the remnants of the tribes of northern Israel at the time of the Syrian conquest who intermarried with Syrian settlers. The schism from mainstream Judaism occurred when they were excluded from Israelite society during the Restoration era (fifth century B.C.). Despite accepting only the Pentateuch and part of the Book of Joshua, they have retained their brand of Judaism until the present time. Although the Samaritans began several diaspora communities, these never succeeded. Nevertheless, their desire to remain separate has been very strong: Avi-Yonah (1984, 241ff) describes their hopeless revolts against the Byzantine authorities in the fifth and sixth centuries. As an indication of the intense separatism of the Samaritans, Parkes (1934, 259) describes merchants in Samaria in the early Byzantine period as requiring gentiles to throw their money into water before being touched by the merchant in order to prevent pollution.

There are also several groups of Oriental Jews who claim descent from the Israelites deported to Syria in 722 B.C., including those of the Kurdistan, Persia, Bukhara, Afghanistan, Armenia, India, and China (see Mourant, Kopec, & Domaniewska-Sobczak 1978).[1] The Kurdish Jews lived for centuries without contact with mainstream Judaism and despite living as serfs under the Kurds. Although aware of the Tanakh and despite geographical propinquity to Babylon, they had little acquaintance with the Mishnah or the Talmuds. In all of these groups, separatism was retained despite persecutions (e.g., by the Zoroastrians in Persia) and through changes in the religion of the surrounding people (e.g., the shift to Islam).

The Jews of Yemen persisted in Judaism despite being completely cut off from the rest of the diaspora beginning in the early 17th century and despite being subjected to an extremely intense and persistent anti-Semitism and lacking a highly literate culture centered around traditional Jewish education (Ahroni 1986, 82). The Jews of India also existed for many centuries with no contacts with the outside world and little knowledge of Jewish practices (Patai 1971, 416).

Other groups that remained separated from the mainstream of Judaism, but nevertheless kept intact their own sect of Judaism include the Karaites (established in the eighth century; they reject the Mishnah and the Talmuds)[2] and the Falasha Jews of Africa. The Falasha Jews managed to remain separate for centuries without any contact with the rest of Judaism (Mourant et al., 211; see also Patai 1971, 423ff), and were not familiar with most of the Talmud and Midrash.

Finally, Mourant and colleagues (1978) provide evidence that, although North African Jews are predominantly of Sephardic descent, some of them may be descendants of Israelites who emigrated far earlier, even perhaps before the period of Nebuchadnezzar (seventh-sixth century B.C.). These groups tend to be geographically isolated, as in mountain regions or on the island of Djerba, but the point is that they have retained their ethnic separatism for many centuries despite being surrounded by other groups and despite isolation from mainstream Judaism. Johnson (1987, 360) also notes a group of "Mountain Jews" in the Caucausus who claim to be descendents of people expelled by Nebuchadnezzar in 597 B.C.[3]

The Israelites also showed a marked tendency toward re-establishing national identity after foreign conquest. After being conquered by the Babylonians, the Israelites rebelled against them (unsuccessfully; the result was a further exile) and then succeeded in restoring their community under the Persians. After control passed to the Greeks, they succeeded in re-establishing their national independence as a result of the Hasmonean uprising. The Jewish religion was unique in forcibly resisting Hellenizing influences during this period (Schürer [1885] 1973, 146).[4]

Later, during the Roman period, Jews alone of all the subject peoples in the Roman Empire engaged in prolonged, even suicidal wars against the government in order to attain national sovereignty. Baron (1952b) notes that Titus's victory was the result of a very difficult campaign. Even after this, the Jews remained defiant and unassimilable, and there were two other rebellions: in Alexandria and other areas in Egypt, Cyprus, Cyrenaica, Libya, and possibly Mesopotamia and Judaea during the reign of Trajan (115-117 A.D.) and in Judaea during the reign of Hadrian (131-135 A.D.) under Simon Bar Kocheba. The latter held out for over three years against the best of Hadrian's generals, with many dying as martyrs. There were also rebellions during Constantine's reign in 326 and under Patricius in 351. There were also several very bloody revolts against Byzantine authority in Palestine during the fifth and sixth centuries (Avi-Yonah 1984, 251, 254; Bachrach 1984).

The Jews were by far the most vehement in their objection to Roman rule, compared to any of the many peoples of the Empire. Alon ([1980, 1984] 1989, 698) notes "the long, drawn-out stubborn refusal of the Jews to come to any kind of terms with Roman rule" and the fact that even after the thaw Jews never completely submitted to "the wicked kingdom" (p. 698). Many authors have noted the religious fanaticism of the Jews in the ancient world and their willingness to die rather than tolerate offenses to Israel or live under foreign domination. For example, Josephus, the first-century Jewish historian and apologist, stated that

[We face] death on behalf of our laws with a courage which no other nation can equal. (*Against Apion,* 2:234)

And from these laws of ours nothing has had power to deflect us, neither fear of our masters, nor envy of the institutions esteemed by other nations. (*Against Apion,* 2:271)

Although not all Jews were willing to die rather than betray the law, "story after story reveals that this generalization is true" (Sanders 1992, 42). "No other nation can be shown to have fought so often in defence of its own way of life, and the readiness of Jews to die for their cause is proved by example after example" (Sanders 1992, 239). Crossan (1991, 103ff) shows that Jewish political activity against the Romans often included threats of martyrdom if external signs of Roman domination were not removed from Jerusalem and the Temple. Only the Jews, of all of Rome's subject peoples, were exempted from having to sacrifice to the Empire's gods, and they were the only group that was allowed to have their own courts and an *ex officio* government under the Patriarchate/Sanhedrin.

Moreover, although a later section will emphasize the unique role of the priests in maintaining ethnic and national integrity, non-elite groups, such as the Hasideans ("pious ones"), the Pharisees, and many ordinary peasants and townspeople were fanatical supporters of these goals. While this type of altruistic fanaticism is highly compatible with a group evolutionary strategy perspective as developed here, such fanaticism seems excessive even within this context. These data indicate an extremely ingrained sense of national identity and ethnic separatism.

Another widespread phenomenon indicating the extreme tendency toward cultural separatism of Jewish groups is that of crypsis during times of persecution (as, e.g., during the Iberian Inquisitions). In some cases, crypto-Jews continued to covertly separate themselves from the rest of society, practice a truncated version of Jewish ritual, and marry among themselves for centuries.[5]

One should also note the extreme sense of exclusivity that has often characterized Jewish interactions with other Jews. This is a highly robust phenomenon. Indeed, from a genetic perspective, the Jewish gene pool, and especially the Sephardic and Oriental Jewish gene pools, may be viewed as a set of genetically unique and isolated subgroups, each with its own set of recessive genetic disorders (Goodman 1979, 468). Zimmels (1958, 43-44) notes a general pattern in which immigrant Jews made their own communities when their numbers were substantial. Thus, in the early Middle Ages, Babylonian Jews immigrating to Palestine founded their own communities, as did Palestinian Jews immigrating into Cairo. Both the Ashkenazim and the Sephardim immigrating into Turkey in the 16th century formed their own communities separate from the previously existing communities of Romaniote Jews.

There was also a tendency for separatism based on community of origin. Thus, the 16th-century Sephardic community in Salonica consisted of seven Spanish communities deriving from different areas of Spain, as well as at least five communities deriving from different parts of Portugal.[6] Not surprisingly, the most turbulent synagogue was one whose members derived from different parts of Spain (Shaw 1991, 52). In other areas of the Ottoman Empire during this period, there were also Romaniote Jews (deriving from the Roman/Byzantine era) and two types of Arabized Jews, as well as Karaite Jews (who maintained complete isolation from all other Jewish groups) (Shaw 1991, 45). Each of these communities remained separate, with its own rabbis, synagogues, cemeteries, schools, hospitals, and slaughterhouses (for the preparation of *kashrut* meat). Even after Jewish ritual and law were unified with the writings of Rabbi Joseph Caro (1488-1575), "differences relating to ancestral origins still remained" (Shaw 1991, 56).

Zimmels (1958, 60ff) describes the very difficult relationships between Ashkenazic and Sephardic Jews, including especially the Sephardic sense of superiority and the tendency to develop their own communities and institutions and to reject intermarriage. In England in 1766, the Sephardic group prohibited marriage with Ashkenazim, and such marriages were regarded "with intense and unconcealed disapproval" (Zimmels 1958, 75). Baron (1973, 36) describes the Sephardic Jews of Amsterdam in the 17th and 18th centuries as rejecting marriage with Ashkenazi Jews. In 1762, Isaac de Pinto wrote that "[t]he Portuguese and the Spanish, who have the honor of being descendants of the tribe of Judah or believe to be such, have never mixed, through marriage, association, or in any other way, with the children of Jacob known under the name of German [*Tudesques*], Italian, or Avignonese Jews" (quoted in Baron 1973, 36).

Although low levels of intermarriage did occur during the 19th century, there remained a great deal of exclusivity during the 19th and 20th centuries. Benardete (1953, 145-146; see also Sachar 1992, 63) cites observations indicating that the Sephardim in the United States considered themselves "a people apart" with "hermetic groupings" and superior to Ashkenazi Jews even though they were of lower social class than the latter.

In Morocco, the Sephardim remained separate for the most part from the native Jews for whom they used the disdainful term *forasteros* (aliens) (Patai 1986). We have also noted in Chapter 6 that the Jewish communities of Palestine were closed to Jews of different origins, with the result that the Yemenese Jews, who did not have the wealthy international connections of the Ashkenazim and Sephardim, were effectively excluded from benefiting from Jewish charity derived from the Ashkenazim and Sephardim. Among immigrants to the United States, Ladino-speaking groups from different towns in Greece maintained their own institutions, and it proved impossible to develop a federation of these groups or even agree on a common prayer book (Sachar 1992, 339). This very powerful sense of separatism from other Jews was also characteristic of other Oriental Jewish immigrant groups in the United States, with the result that there were some 36 different burial and mutual-aid societies in New York in 1912 (Sachar 1992, 339). This fragmentation along intraethnic lines continues in contemporary times: Elazar (1980, 232) notes that ethnic fragmentation among Jewish groups in New York inhibits overall communal organization. Each Orthodox community, especially the Hasidim, remains "as separate and self-contained as it can possibly be . . ." (p. 233).

It is also remarkable that the Jews during the first centuries A.D. very readily developed exclusivist divisions within the society. Thus, in Chapters 3 and 4 the hierarchy of racial purity was discussed, including the segregation and eventual exclusion of the *Nethinim*, the Samaritans, the offspring of Solomon's wives, and others of mixed and foreign blood. In Chapter 7, the prolonged exclusion and denigration of the Jewish *'am ha-ares* were discussed, and Jeremias (1969, 303ff) emphasizes the fact that many ordinary trades were despised, again suggesting a strong tendency to form ingroups and outgroups within the Jewish community.

> The men who followed [these] trades were not only despised, nay hated, by the people. They were *de jure* and officially deprived of rights and ostracized. Anyone engaging in such trades could never be a judge, and his inadmissibility as a witness put him on the same footing as a gentile slave. . . . In other words he was deprived of civil and political rights to which every Israelite had claim, even those such as bastards who were of seriously blemished descent. (Jeremias 1969, 311)

It is also of some interest to note that some historical variants of Judaism have been far more exclusive even than mainstream Judaism, suggesting a very deep seated tendency in this direction. For example, the Essenes were a Jewish religious sect in Palestine dating from approximately 140 B.C. to 70 A.D. (see Sanders 1992, 341ff). The group was a sort of apotheosis of collectivism in the sense of Triandis (1990, 1991), including a surrendering of personal freedoms and economic goods to the community; extreme self-sacrifice (including willingness to be a martyr); a strict hierarchical and authoritarian group structure; a strong emphasis on exclusivism and the purity laws, which were a consistent aspect of traditional Jewish exclusivism; and a high degree of affection for other ingroup members combined with an attitude of "everlasting hatred" (Sanders 1992, 361) toward the rest of humanity, and especially other Israelites. They envisioned destroying other Jews, or perhaps converting them, before destroying the gentiles.

Interestingly, Jeremias (1969, 298) notes that the Essenes were extremely concerned with the genealogical purity of their members—a concern even greater than the very great concern of Jewish society as a whole during the period (see Chapter 4). Jeremias also points to regional variation within ancient Jewish society in Palestine at the beginning of the common era regarding the extent of exclusivity and concern with racial purity. In certain areas, such as Sepphoris and Jerusalem, extreme care was taken to ensure the rights of racially pure Israelites.

Indeed, mainstream Judaism developed out of the Pharisaic tradition whose name means "separated" (Schürer [1885] 1979, 396) and denotes the fact that the Pharisees separated themselves from the rest of the Israelites, many of whom they considered ritually unclean. Schürer ([1885] 1979, 400ff) traces the origins of the Pharisees to the Hasideans ("pious ones") who spontaneously supported the Maccabean revolt against the Greek Seleucids (second century B.C) and who had a wide following among the masses of Israelites in their emphasis on religious law. It was the Pharisees who elaborated the rituals and customs of Judaism (many of which segregated Jews from gentiles) and emphasized their strict observance as a central feature of traditional Judaism.

It should also be noted that Hasidic and other ultra-Orthodox groups (haredim) are a prominent and increasingly powerful force within contemporary Judaism, amounting to at least 650,000 Jews worldwide (see Landau 1993, xxi).[7] Historically, the type of social organization represented by these groups has been far more the norm than the exception, so that even in late-19th-century Poland the great majority of Jews were organized in ultra-Orthodox Hasidic congregations dominated by their rebbes (e.g. Litman 1984, 6).[8] These groups are extremely collectivist in Triandis's (1990, 1991) sense. They rigidly adhere to traditional exclusivist practices such as dietary and purity laws and have very negative views of outsiders, including more liberally inclined Jews. The authoritarian nature of these groups is particularly striking: "A haredi . . . will consult his rabbi or hasidic rebbe on every aspect of his life, and will obey the advice he receives as though it were an halachic ruling" (Landau 1993, 47).[9]

Like the Essenes and other Jewish extremist groups, contemporary haredim are also deeply concerned about issues of racial purity. Indeed, the resurgence of Orthodox Judaism and ultra-Orthodox Jewish fundamentalism may well result in a schism of the Jewish people along the lines of racial purity. As indicated in Chapter 4, genealogy is an extremely important aspect of status in the Hasidic community. Moreover, Landau (1993, 291ff) describes the opposition of the Orthodox and ultra-Orthodox communities to intermarriage and to procedures that facilitate conversion to Judaism.[10] Orthodox Jews and certainly the haredim do not recognize conversions performed by Reform or Conservative rabbis. Nor do they recognize the recent change in traditional Jewish law by the Reform movement that allows individuals to trace their genealogical Jewishness through the father, rather than the mother. Rabbi Aharon Soloveitchik of Yeshiva University stated that the result of the proposed policy would be that "mamzerut [bastardy] will be escalated to a maximum" (quoted in Landau 1993, 320).[11] From the perspective of the Orthodox and the fundamentalists, the rest of Jewry is highly contaminated with non-marriageable individuals whose taint derives from their genetic ancestry.

Moreover, it is not just the extremist Jewish sects that are by any measure extremely authoritarian and collectivist. The precedence of community control over individual behavior, a fundamental feature of a collectivist type of society, is a highly salient feature of mainstream Judaism, apparent throughout this volume (see especially Chapter 7). Shaw (1991, 65) provides a particularly well described example from Jews in the Ottoman Empire. The community very precisely regulated every aspect of life, including the shape and length of beards, all aspects of dress in public and private, the amount of charity required of members, numbers of people at social gatherings, the appearance of graves and gravestones, precise behavior on the Sabbath, the precise form of conversations,[12] the order of precedence at all social gatherings, *et cetera*. The rules were enforced "with a kind of police surveillance," and failure to abide by the rules could result in imprisonment in community prisons or, at the extreme, in excommunication.[13]

The tendency to set up ingroup/outgroup barriers so central to collectivist societies can also be seen by the finding that certain 20th-century intellectual movements dominated by Jews have developed a distinct flavor of cultural separatism and authoritarianism. For example, psychoanalysis from its origins has been a "science apart" from the rest of psychology and psychiatry, resulting in two separate and incompatible discourses about human behavior (see *SAID*, ch. 7). Psychoanalysis was and remains a highly authoritarian movement in which group boundaries are rigidly maintained and in which heretics are expelled.

Similarly with Jewish dominated radical political movements,[14] Liebman (1973) notes that

> [gentile intellectuals] really are not totally accepted into even the secularist humanist liberal company of their quondam Jewish friends. Jews continue to insist in indirect and often inexplicable ways on their own uniqueness. Jewish universalism in relations between Jews and non-Jews has an empty ring. . . . Still, we have the anomaly of Jewish secularists and atheists writing their own prayer books. We find Jewish political reformers breaking with their local parties which stress an ethnic style of politics, and ostensibly pressing for universal political goals—while organizing their own political clubs which are so Jewish in style and manner that non-Jews often feel unwelcome. (p. 158)

# A Genetic Perspective on Individualism/Collectivism

In summary, the data indicate that Judaism can be characterized as a collectivist (or even "hyper-collectivist") culture in Triandis's (1990, 1991) terms. In accounting for this tendency, I suggest that the ancient Israelites were genetically predisposed to be high on a cluster of traits centered around group allegiance, separatism, ethnocentrism, and collectivism. Moreover, with the adoption of a group strategy in which allegiance to the group must be a constant concern, there would also be cultural selection for individuals who were high on these traits. Highly collectivist individuals (referred to by Triandis as "allocentrics") would be more likely to maintain group membership and submerge their individual interests in favor of group goals. They would thus represent the epitome of the group ethic and would presumably be more likely to be successful within the group. On the other hand, individuals who were low on collectivism (referred to by Triandis as "idiocentrics") would be expected to be less committed to group goals, less able to submerge individual interests in favor of group goals, and therefore more likely to defect from the group.

This genetic perspective essentially states that collectivism, like many other phenotypes of interest to evolutionists (MacDonald 1991), shows genetic variation (see discussion in Rushton 1989, 553ff). This genetic variation may well have resulted because of differential selection pressures in ancestral environments. LeVine and Campbell (1972) describe variation in the extent to which human groups have been forced to adopt powerful boundary mechanisms that distinguish themselves from other groups. Groups that are geographically isolated from direct competition with other human groups for an evolutionarily significant period may not have developed the propensity toward extreme collectivism and ethnocentrism.

I speculate that such isolated groups with low population density would have been common in northern areas characterized by extremely harsh ecological conditions, as occurred during the Ice Age. Under ecologically adverse circumstances, adaptations are directed more at coping with the adverse physical environment than at competing with other groups (Southwood (1977, 1981), and in such an environment, there would be less pressure for selection of highly collectivist groups. Evolutionary conceptualizations of ethnocentrism emphasize the utility of ethnocentrism in group competition. Ethnocentrism would thus be of no importance at all in combating the physical environment, and such an environment would not support large groups.[15]

The idea would be, then, that the ancient Israelites were simply higher than average on traits predisposing them to collectivism. As a result, when they were conquered and exiled among other groups, they developed such cultural practices as endogamous and consanguineous marriage, the hierarchy of racial purity, and the segregation and eventual exclusion of racially impure groups such as the *Nethinim*, the Samaritans, the offspring of Solomon's wives, and others of mixed and foreign blood. Further, they were relatively highly predisposed to engage in self-sacrificing, altruistic behavior (including martyrdom) in the interests of the group.

Reflecting the idea that the Israelites had a strong predisposition to develop diaspora communities, Baron (1952a, 96) notes that the ideology of an ethnic group retaining its integrity in diaspora conditions followed, rather than preceded, the reality of the diaspora. The diaspora was already a reality in the eighth century B.C., long before the Babylonian exile. As a result,

Theory had to follow reality. No longer was settlement on the soil of
Palestine or life under a Jewish government essential to Jewishness. Even in
the dispersion, far from their own country and under a foreign monarch, Jews
remained Jews ethnically . . . (Baron 1952a, 96)

There is reason to believe that there is a genetic basis for this powerful
tendency toward collectivism. In Chapter 7, it was noted that one facet of
conscientiousness may be labeled "social conscientiousness" and includes items
related to performing assigned tasks conscientiously, fulfilling commitments,
fulfilling social obligations, and being dependable and reliable. This trait may
well be an important component of group allegiance. Conscientiousness, like all
other personality traits (and therefore presumably all of the traits related to
collectivism), is moderately heritable (e.g. Digman 1990; Rowe 1993).
Moreover, the data summarized in Chapter 7 indicate cultural (and ultimately
genetic) selection for conformity to group norms among Jews in the sense that
Jews who defected from Judaism tended to be non-conformists who rebelled at
the stifling life of a collectivist group.

It is of interest that there is some agreement that the Near Eastern peoples
have a more ingrained sense of ethnocentrism than has been characteristic of the
vast majority of Western societies.[16] The contrast between Eastern and Western
cultures is central to Triandis' (1990, 43-44) work on cross cultural variation on
individualism and collectivism. Triandis includes both Arabs and Jews as
exemplars of collectivist cultures in contrast to Western individualist cultures.
Western individualism originated in the Greco-Roman world of antiquity and,
although the precise dating is controversial, re-emerged after the decline of the
hegemony of medieval corporate religiosity.

Bickerman (1988) notes the relatively greater sense of ethnic exclusiveness
among the Near Eastern peoples than was apparent in the Greek world of
antiquity.[17] The Greek view of cities in the ancient world was that they were
open to any person and that any person who adopted the language and customs
of these cities could feel at home. Indeed, there is considerable scholarly
agreement that Greek anti-Semitism in the ancient world derived from the fact
that Jews wanted political rights, but were unwilling to adopt a common
language and set of customs with the Greeks (see *SAID*, ch. 2). On the other
hand, "[o]riental civilizations had no concept of naturalization and were averse
to acculturation" (Bickerman 1987, 80). This general contrast is also compatible
with Johnson's (1987, 134) point that the Greek conceptualization of a
multi-racial, multi-national society strongly conflicted with Jewish separatism
and unwillingness to respect the deities and practices of other peoples.

The Romans are generally viewed as being derived from an ethnically mixed
group of Italians and other groups (McDonald 1966). Moreover, the long-term
trend in the Roman Empire was for gradually increasing conferral of citizenship,
culminating in the granting of virtually universal citizenship in 212 A.D. by
Caracalla. There was also a gradual representation of provincials in the senate

and equestrian order, and provincials replaced Italians as emperors by the third century (Garnsey & Saller 1987, 9). Jordan (1989, 111) notes the general tolerance of "alien" groups in Roman society and the idealization of this tolerance in Roman jurisprudence.[18]

Indeed, as Schürer ([1885] 1986, 132) notes, the Roman imperial government tended to protect the Jews from repeated outbreaks of hostility in cities throughout the Empire. And the Roman government repeatedly confirmed the right of Jews (unique among the subject peoples) to their own religious communities and their exemption from sacrificing to the imperial cults and from service in the military. As a result, a major source of popular anti-Semitism in the ancient world derived from the Jewish unwillingness to participate in a homogeneous, assimilative culture: "Precisely at the time when through Roman world-rule and the levelling effect of Hellenism there was a general tendency for local cultures either to be submerged or to be absorbed in the overall Graeco-Roman culture, it must have been felt as doubly frustrating that only the Jews were unwilling to be thought of as taking part in the process of amalgamation" (Schürer [1885] 1986, 152-153; see also *SAID*, ch. 2).

The Greek and Roman pattern of conquest and empire-building, unlike that of the Israelites described in the Tanakh, did not involve genocide followed by the creation of an ethnically exclusivist state that dominated the remnants of the conquered peoples (the *Nethinim*) and never assimilated them even after many centuries. Rather, the tendency was for conquest to be followed in the long run by genetic and cultural assimilation.

The paradigm for such assimilative behavior is Alexander the Great's intention of building a universalist state in which there would be complete genetic and cultural assimilation with the conquered peoples—the dream of a universal world-state based on universal brotherhood and partnership and on cooperation between conquerors and conquered (see Hegermann 1989). Alexander adopted many Persian cultural practices (e.g., type of dress and court ceremonies), and he married an Iranian princess and forced his men to do the same.[19] In contrast, the whole point of historical Judaism has been to resist alien cultures. Moreover, Israelites who married foreign women in the period of conquest after the Exodus and in the resettlement after the Babylonian exile were condemned and excluded, and Joshua "destroyed all that breathed, as the LORD, the God of Israel, commanded" (Josh. 10:40).[20]

Similarly, the Germanic conquerors of the Roman Empire in the fifth century took their places among their new subjects largely without displacing the former citizens of the Empire, so that in some areas people were quite unaware that they were no longer members of the Empire (see Geary 1988). Eventually, there was complete cultural and genetic assimilation among the conquerors and their new subjects.

The Spanish conquest of the New World also resulted in a great deal of genetic intermingling, with the result that in the long run Hispano-American societies were not characterized by an ethnically pure elite and a genetically segregated subject population: "As the conquistadors brought the lands of America under Spanish dominion, they effectively converted the mass of the Indians into people of partially Hispanic blood, Hispanic language and manner, and Hispanic religion" (Castro 1971, 303). Genetic assimilation occurred.

The relatively greater Eastern sense of ethnocentrism is also indicated by the much greater tendency toward consanguineous marriage that is characteristic of the entire region, and thus not confined to the Jews.[21] As indicated in Chapters 3 and 6, consanguineous marriage (marriage with biological relatives) and endogamous marriage (marriage within the group) are important components of a group strategy because they result in the correlation of individual fitness with the fitness of the group. Group-oriented, collectivist societies emphasize consanguinity and endogamy based on known patterns of biological descent (e.g., tracing genealogies to prove group membership or establishing degrees of biological relationship such as first cousin or niece).

Goody (1983) shows that first cousin marriage was the norm among all Near Eastern peoples, and this practice continued into the Muslim era. Jews have also shown a very pronounced tendency toward consanguinity, including not only first cousin marriage, but also uncle-niece marriage (see Chapters 3, 4, and 6). Indeed, while uncle-niece marriage is prohibited by Muslim law, such marriages are considered ideal in Jewish law and have been practiced throughout Jewish history (see Goitein 1978, 26; Goodman 1979, 463-467), suggesting that the Jews are even   more   inclined   toward   consanguinity   than   other   Near Eastern groups. Modern groups of Samaritans also practice very high levels of consanguineous marriage, including 43 percent with first cousins and over 80 percent with some relative (Bonné 1966).

In marked contrast, there was a long tradition favoring exogamy at Rome. The ancient law prohibited marriage with second cousins (e.g., Gardner 1986; von Ungern-Sternberg 1986; Thomas 1980; Watson 1975), or, indeed all relatives, since the Romans did not count beyond second cousins (Watson 1975). Practices regarding incest became more relaxed later in the Republic and during the Empire, and, indeed, Thomas (1980) shows that first-cousin marriage was sometimes used by the aristocracy as a marriage strategy aimed at consolidating resources and power beginning near the end of the third century B.C. However, as Mitterauer (1991) notes, this does not indicate any basic change in the fundamentally exogamic marriage pattern characteristic of the West. Similarly, Saller (1991, 342) concludes that "[s]ome Romans of the pre-Christian era did marry cousins, but not with enough regularity that the late-fourth century law of Theodosius can be said to have taken away a significant inheritance strategy."

Indeed, within the Roman Empire, there was a conflict between the practices of East and West when all free inhabitants became Roman citizens in the third century. Mitterauer (1991) notes that the Christian practices regarding consanguinity had merged with the Roman perspective, and the direction of influence clearly came from Rome, so that essentially the Roman tradition came to be regarded as Christian (p. 316).

In order to rationalize these much more stringent regulations, the Christian theologians resorted to the language of Leviticus 18:6: "None of you shall approach to any that is near of kin to him, to uncover their nakedness." However, the Christians essentially adopted the Roman perspective on what constituted kin and changed the regulations entirely. Indeed, even within the Christian Church, there was a split between the Eastern branch, where consanguinity was more common, and the Western branch, which adopted the stringent Roman norms. Thus, in the fifth century, extensive Christian prohibitions on incest originating in the Western Church met with a great deal of resistance in the Byzantine Empire and were modified to accommodate local customs.

The Christian Church then went beyond both the system of Leviticus and the Roman system by inventing prohibitions on spiritual relatives. Thus, unlike the Jewish preoccupation with purity of blood and genealogy, the Christian attitude eventually granted no priority at all to actual blood relationships. Mitterauer (1991, 320) notes that a basic principle of Christianity is "the Christian rejection of endogamous tendencies among Jews: physical descent is without any religious importance."

The Christian Church, despite its obvious Jewish origins, is from an evolutionary perspective fundamentally opposed to Judaism in matters of interest to an evolutionist. Boyarin (1993, 6) contrasts the basic Jewish concern with sexuality, reproduction, genealogy, and a concept of historical peoplehood based on genetic relatedness with the denial of the importance of these qualities in Christianity. Early Christian thinkers criticized the Jewish tendency to take these Biblical themes literally, while they themselves tended to allegorize these Biblical themes and created new cultural symbols such as the virgin birth and the cultural ideal of celibacy, which were diametrically opposed to these Jewish themes.

From an evolutionary perspective, what really matters is reproductive relationships, and in this regard the Christian Church became the religious embodiment of basic Roman cultural institutions. During the medieval period, the Church's emphasis on exogamy weakened the extended kinship group, since the expanded range of incestuous marriages prevented the solidarity of extended kinship groups by excluding "the reinforcing of blood with marriage" (Goody 1983, 145; see also Bourchard 1981).

Moreover, while collectivist societies emphasize genealogy and degree of genetic relatedness in marriage, individualist societies tend to emphasize personal attraction (e.g., romantic love, common interests) (Triandis 1990). Reflecting these issues, Money (1980) has noted the relatively greater tendency of Northern European groups toward romantic love as the basis of marriage.[22] There has been a trend, beginning in the Middle Ages, toward the companionate marriage based on affection and consent between the partners, eventually affecting even the marriage decisions of the high aristocracy (e.g., Brundage 1987; Hanawalt 1986; MacFarlane 1986; Stone 1977; Stone 1990). MacFarlane (1986) notes that "[W]hereas in industrial Western societies the emotional relationship between man and wife is primary, it is not the pivot of social structure in the majority of societies" (p. 174; see also Westermarck's [1922] contrast between Eastern and Western stratified societies). The idealization of romantic love as the basis of monogamous marriage has also periodically characterized Western secular intellectual movements (Brundage 1987), such as the Stoics of late antiquity (e.g. Brown 1987; Veyne 1987) and 19th-century Romanticism (e.g., Corbin 1990; Porter 1982).

Another important contrast is that non-Western societies (including Judaism) have emphasized fertility to a much greater extent than have Western societies (MacFarlane 1986). While Jews had a religious obligation to marry and have children, Christianity legitimated celibacy and did not bestow spiritual rewards on highly fertile individuals. Whereas the role of unmarried adult was well established in Western society, unmarried individuals were extremely exceptional among the Jews (e.g., Goitein 1978, 61-63). Lack of fertility was not a grounds for Christian divorce, while for Jews infertility was a psychological and social disaster that fully justified a divorce. By contrast, although there was a strong desire to leave an heir in early modern England, failure to do so was not a psychological disaster.

Finally, while the East has a pronounced tendency toward polygyny, Western societies have tended toward monogamy. From the perspective of evolutionary theory, monogamy constitutes an egalitarian mating system, since each male is allowed only one marriage partner no matter how much wealth or power he has.[23] The Christian Church became an ardent crusader in fostering monogamy in Western Europe in opposition to the reproductive interests of the aristocracy (see MacDonald 1990). There is every indication that this concern for monogamy derives from the traditional Roman pattern of marriage (MacDonald 1990).

This contrasts strongly with the clear evidence of resource polygyny among the Jews. As indicated in Chapter 3, resource polygyny was the norm in the Tanakh. Polygyny was never prohibited among the Jews until the famous *herem* of Rabbenu Gershom dating from the 11th century in the West (Zimmels 1958, 166ff), but this only applied to Ashkenazi Jews, and polygyny continued among Sephardic and Oriental Jews into the contemporary era.[24,25]

I suggest that ultimately it was the ethnic exclusivity and powerful sense of group cohesion and collectivism of the East that resulted in the long-term degradation of Jews in Muslim societies described in Chapter 7 (see also *SAID*, ch 2). The Greco-Roman culture in the Eastern Roman Empire was essentially a civic culture that had very little influence on the indigenous cultures of the area (Bowerstock 1990; Garnsey & Saller 1987, 203). After the decline of Western influence in the area, the Jews were again confronted by societies with a powerful sense of ethnic exclusiveness and communal (group) identity. In the absence of powerful alien ruling elites who used the services of Jews as the ideal middlemen between themselves and the native populations, the Jews were rather quickly and decisively degraded in status and excluded from any possibility of economic domination. Any society with a powerful sense of ethnic identity and racial exclusiveness is expected to quickly and easily adopt a group identity in confronting a cohesive group such as the Jews.

Prominent examples of Western collectivist societies have also tended to be characterized by relatively intense anti-Semitism. For example, the development of hegemonic, corporate Catholicism during the Western Middle Ages in France was associated with high levels of anti-Semitism and exclusion of Jews.[26] Jordan (1989, 27) describes the efforts of the Church to remove Jews from the economic life of France in the 12th-14th centuries. As part of the effort to develop a corporate Christian economic community, Jews were gradually pushed out of occupations and professions they formerly engaged in. In this regard, these efforts are entirely analogous to the exclusionary effects of the cooperative, corporate thrust of Jewish economic activity throughout its history (see Chapter 6).[27]

Moreover, there was a concerted effort by the Church to prevent resources from being drained from the Christian community via Jewish moneylending to Christians.[28] Beginning in 1206 under the often reluctant King Philip II, there was increasing regulation of Jewish moneylending as a result of "a continuous chorus of criticism" (Jordan 1989, 44) emanating from the Church and ultimately from governmental authority.[29] The Fourth Lateran Council complained that "[t]he more Christians are restrained from the practice of usury, the more are they oppressed in this matter by the treachery of the Jews, so that in a short time they exhaust the resources of the Christians" (see Gilchrist 1969, 182). The council compelled secular powers to end Jewish usury, and Christians were to be excommunicated if they continued to engage in commercial dealings with Jews until this occurred. "Radical" Christian thinkers rejected the idea that Jewish religious law allowed lending at interest to Christians (Jordan 1989, 28), and Jews in turn defended the practice as conforming to their religious law. A major concern was the indebtedness of the Christian lower classes and the potential for exploitation of Christians hired as servants by wealthy Jews, but there was also concern to prevent the property of wealthy individuals from falling into Jewish hands.

The following period, under Louis IX, saw the complete triumph of the Church's hegemonic, exclusionary economic policy, the emergence of a Christian middle class,[30] and, not coincidentally, the deterioration of the Jews. Louis was extremely religious and attempted to make his state into a corporate, hegemonic Christian entity in which social divisions within the Christian population were minimized in the interests of group harmony. Consistent with this group-oriented perspective, Louis appears to have been genuinely concerned about the effect of Jewish moneylending on society as a whole, rather than its possible benefit to the crown—a major departure from the many ruling elites throughout history who have utilized Jews as a means of extracting resources from their subjects. A contemporary biographer of Louis, William of Chartres, quotes him as concerned "that they [the Jews] may not oppress Christians through usury and that they not be permitted, under the shelter of my protection, to engage in such pursuits and to infect my land with their poison" (quoted in Chazan 1973, 103). Louis therefore viewed the prevention of Jewish economic relations with Christians not as a political or economic problem, but as a moral and religious obligation. And since the Jews were present in France at his discretion, it was the responsibility of the crown to prevent the Jews from exploiting his Christian subjects.

In the end, although popular hostility and royal desire for Jewish resources (via confiscation) were important causes of the eventual expulsion of Jews from France in 1306,[31] Chazan (1973, 204) emphasizes the critical importance of the fact that France had become "a society so thoroughly organized around Christian life as to make Jewish presence inevitably peripheral and marginal."[32] In other words, France had become a collectivist society in Triandis's terms, and the Jews were excluded despite their economic benefits to the high aristocracy.[33] This "purified Christian state" persisted until the end of the Middle Ages in France (Jordan 1989, 256).[34]

On the other hand, while Eastern societies and medieval Western Christianity had very negative effects on Judaism, the main population explosions of Jews have occurred in Western societies where there has been a relative lack of concern regarding ethnicity and a strong sense of individualism rather than group interests. There have really been three major periods of Jewish population growth and development in traditional societies: during the Greco-Roman world of antiquity, during pre-expulsion Spain, and in early modern Eastern Europe. The individualistic nature of ancient Greco-Roman society, at least until the advent of Christianity as a hegemonic state religion, is well established (e.g., Triandis 1990). In the other two cases, the evidence provided in Chapter 5 indicates that the Spanish and the Polish nobility protected the Jews and allowed them to compete economically with the lower orders of their own people. Such behavior is individualist in the sense that the nobility is utilizing the Jews in a self-serving manner that compromises the interests of the lower orders.[35,36]

In the Islamic world, Judaism essentially muddled along in an extremely downtrodden and oppressed manner except during brief periods in which Jews were utilized as middlemen by alien ruling elites.[37] Following the Enlightenment and the development of individualistic societies in Western Europe, it was Jews in Western societies who reached out and attempted to obtain political and economic rights for their relatively backward and oppressed co-religionists in Muslim societies in the 19th and 20th centuries, rather than the other way around.

Indeed, Judaism has been far more successful demographically in individualistic European societies than in Arab lands characterized by collectivist social structures: Goitein (1974) notes that Jews in Arab countries constituted only 10 percent of the total Jewish population in the early 20th century, and Zimmels (1958, 75) has compiled data indicating that, while the Ashkenazi population increased by approximately 100-fold in the period from

1170 to 1900, the population of Sephardic and Oriental Jews actually declined by 36 percent after reaching its peak prior to the expulsion from Spain and Portugal.

To conclude: Whereas prototypical Western societies have shown strong tendencies toward assimilation and individualism, Judaism is at its essence exclusivist and collectivist. And there is evidence (reviewed in *SAID*, ch. 2) that individualist, assimilative Western societies, including the Greco-Roman world of antiquity and modern Western democracies (and excluding collectivist Western societies such as Naziism, communism, and medieval Christendom), have had relatively low levels of anti-Semitism. This general tendency is highly compatible with Triandis's (1991, 80) findings that people in individualist societies are much less aware of ingroup and outgroup boundaries and combat outgroups in a "rational" manner (i.e., without adopting inaccurate negative stereotypes or blaming the group for the behavior of some group members). Jewish particularism is thus expected and found to thrive precisely in Western societies that (apart from Jews themselves) are highly assimilative and individualistic.

The foregoing provides evidence that the Near Eastern peoples, and especially the Jews, tend in general toward racial exclusivity and collectivism compared to most Western societies. In the following, it will be argued that certain unique aspects of Jewish history are contributing factors to the Jews' relatively greater tendency toward these traits. I will consider two plausible candidates for such contextual influences on Judaism as a group evolutionary strategy: the experience of originating as a people during the Egyptian sojourn and the invention of a hereditary (tribal) priestly class with a powerful motivation to maintain the integrity of the group.

# SOJOURNING AND ITS ROLE IN THE DEVELOPMENT OF JUDAISM

> This way of seeing things [i.e., the belief in the cycle of exile and restoration] was not necessary, since the Jews who did not go into exile and those who did not come home had no reason to take the view of matters that characterized the Scripture. . . . Everything was invented and interpreted. (Neusner 1987, 5)

In Chapter 3, it was noted that the Tanakh assumes the reality of a diaspora and that there are many statements reflecting a positive attitude toward sojourning. This positive attitude toward sojourning can also be seen by examining several stories in which the patriarchs and/or the Israelites live as a minority among foreigners. These stories may well have a historical basis. Anthropological data indicate that a common life style in the Near East during early Biblical times would be for small clans to temporarily attach themselves to larger groups, especially in times of scarcity, and then move on after a period of sojourning (Johnson 1987, 13ff). Moreover, as Patai (1971, 6-7) points out, even if many of these sojourning events are not historical, they indicate that "in the earliest national-traditional Hebrew consciousness (i.e., in the days of the monarchy) the Diaspora had primacy over the land of Israel." Patai suggests that the point of these early stories is to show that the Hebrews had a divine right to a certain piece of land and that they desired to return there even when they had been forced to leave it.

The Biblical stories of sojourning by the patriarchs among foreigners are very prominently featured in Genesis. Typically there is an emphasis on deception and exploitation of the host population, after which the Jews leave a despoiled host population, having increased their own wealth and reproductive success. Indeed, immediately after the creation story and the genealogy of Abraham, Genesis presents an account of Abraham's sojourn in Egypt. Abraham goes to Egypt to escape a famine with his barren wife Sarah, and they agree to deceive the pharaoh into thinking that Sarah is his sister, so that the pharaoh takes her as a concubine. As a result of this transaction, Abraham receives great wealth (while his wife does not actually conceive a child by the pharaoh). But disasters afflict Egypt as a result of the immorality of the arrangement, and the pharaoh confronts Abraham with his deception. Abraham is allowed to leave with his wife and the possessions obtained as a result of the deception. A similar sequence occurs during the sojourn of Abraham and Sarah with King Abimelech and on the part of Isaac during his sojourn in Gerar. Both eventually leave with great riches.[38]

The greatest sojourn story in the Pentateuch, however, is clearly the sojourn of Jacob's family in Egypt—an event whose historicity is unquestioned (Patai 1971, 5; Sevenster 1975, 182). The details are instructive. Indeed, Baron (1952a, 41) asks

> whether this pre-Mosaic Egyptian ghetto [i.e., Goshen] did not already cast its shadows over all the future history of the people. Nevertheless, it is remarkable that there and during their migrations through the desert the Israelite tribes retained a vivid memory of their previous dwelling in Palestine and of their blood relation with the Palestinian Hebrews they were soon to join. . . . Neither the territory of Palestine, nor the desert, nor Egypt is regarded as significant, but the memory of unity, a consciousness of common history apart from that of other peoples. "They went about from one kingdom to another people," sang a later poet (Ps. 105:13).[39]

Similarly Patai (1971) states that "even in this period [i.e., during the monarchy until the collapse of the northern kingdom in 722 B.C.], the only era in Jewish history without a dispersion, the memory of the Diaspora was not allowed to fade from the consciousness of the people. On the contrary, the Egyptian bondage . . . was made by tradition into a veritable cornerstone of Biblical Hebrew religion" (p. 9). Patai notes that the sojourn in Egypt and the

Exodus had a very prominent part in Hebrew religious ritual and were related to the three annual pilgrimage festivals. The consciousness of the importance of sojourning is also said to account for the many references in the Pentateuch to being kind to strangers who live among you "for ye were strangers in the land of Egypt" (Exod. 22:20, 23:9).

Like the others, the Egyptian sojourn begins with deception and ends with the Israelites obtaining great treasure and increasing their numbers. In this case, the way is prepared by a relative who obtains great influence in the host city. Joseph obtains his power and influence in Egypt because of his great talents, and he uses them to gain admission for his family. Joseph tells them to bring only cattle and to deny ever having been shepherds, "both we, and our fathers; that ye may dwell in the land of Goshen; for every shepherd is an abomination unto the Egyptians" (Gen. 46:34).

In a pattern that we have seen was recurrent during the diaspora (see Chapter 5), Joseph acts in collaboration with the aristocratic and royal authorities against the interests of the lower classes. After collecting large amounts of grain (inevitably from the common people), he sells it back to them during the famine so that the pharaoh ends up with all of the land and the people become serfs owing one fifth of their produce to the pharaoh. The collaboration with the authorities against the interests of the lower classes pays off for the Israelites: "And Israel dwelt in the land of Egypt . . . and they got them possessions therein, and were fruitful, and multiplied exceedingly" (Gen. 47:27). Deuteronomy notes that "Thy fathers went down into Egypt with threescore and ten persons; and now the LORD thy God hath made thee as the stars of heaven for multitude" (Deut. 10:22).[40]

Moreover, the account of Exodus makes clear that the Israelites had accumulated considerable wealth during their sojourn in Egypt and that when they left, not only did they take their own flocks and herds, but also when they asked the Egyptians for jewelry and clothing, "they let them have what they asked. And they despoiled the Egyptians" (Exod. 12:36). Johnson (1987) notes that "there are hints in the Bible that the hardships were endurable; Moses' horde often hankered for 'the flesh-pots of Egypt'" (p. 30).

Sojourning and deception are also linked in the Books of Esther and Daniel, both of which are of post-exilic origin. Esther's cousin Mordecai tells Esther to reveal neither "her people nor her kindred" (Esther 2:10) to the Persians. Later, Esther uses her position to foil a plan to destroy the Jews and plunder their property because of their refusal to give obeisance to the king.[41]

The final sojourn depicted in the Bible is of course the Babylonian captivity—usually viewed as the beginning of diaspora Judaism. Here the Israelites do not come voluntarily, but there is every indication that they prospered, so that even when allowed to return, many remained in Babylon (e.g., Schmidt 1984). Johnson (1987) notes that as a result Israel itself ceased to be viewed as a necessary condition for Jewish existence. From this point on, the majority of Jews lived outside the homeland of Israel.

Indeed, Ackroyd (1968) notes that there is a very explicit "Exodus ideology" in the writings of the prophets during the Babylonian exile. For example, in the Book of Jeremiah, the Babylonian exile is explicitly compared to the Egyptian sojourn, with the point being that, as in the former case, there will be a happy ending: "Therefore, behold, the days come, saith the LORD, that they shall no more say: 'As the LORD liveth, that brought up the children of Israel out of the land of Egypt'; but: 'As the LORD liveth, that brought up and that led the seed of the house of Israel out of the north country, and from all the countries whither I had driven them'; and they shall dwell in their own land" (Jer. 23:7-8).

The Deuteronomistic writers during the Babylonian exile are able to take inspiration from the original Exodus: "The exile is no longer an historic event to be dated in one period; it is much nearer to being a condition from which only the final age will bring release. Though bound to the historical reality of an exile which took place in the sixth century, the experience of exile *as such* has become the symbol of a period, viewed in terms of punishment but also in terms of promise" (Ackroyd 1968, 242; italics in text).

These ideas are also highly compatible with the treatment of Neusner (1987). Whereas the purpose of the Yahwist writer of the Pentateuch was to rationalize the Davidic monarchy as being the result of a divine plan, the purpose of the Priestly redactors of the exilic period was to rationalize the Babylonian exile as the result of God's wrath at Israel's non-compliance. The Davidic monarchy was "politics as usual," simply another attempt at empire with the harems and political oppression typical of Oriental monarchies. In the exile context, the new hero is now Moses, who had led the Israelites out of Egypt and had established the original covenant. Within the new ideology, a cycle of exile and restoration is posited as the fate of the Jewish people, and within the exile, there must be strict segregation of Jews from their neighbors. The Priestly redaction of the Pentateuch is essentially an Exodus ideology in which the Jews during the Babylonian exile are seen as being like the Israelites wandering in the desert in the Exodus from Egypt.

These accounts make clear that it is not only the negative experiences during sojourning, such as slavery in Egypt, that are emphasized in the Biblical accounts, but also the positive. Indeed, the prototype of this view of the Egyptian sojourn is at Genesis 15:13: "Know of a surety that thy seed shall be a stranger in a land that is not theirs, and shall serve them; and they shall afflict them four hundred years; and also that nation, whom they shall serve, will I judge; and afterward shall they come out with great substance." Sojourning, while certainly dangerous and far from an ideal situation, can and does result in the acquisition of wealth and increased reproductive success. From this perspective, it is their own experience of sojourning as a *highly successful* strategy by which an ethnic group is able to retain its identity and increase its wealth and reproductive success even in a diaspora environment that is a cornerstone of Judaism as a group evolutionary strategy.

An evolutionist can only add that such a perspective makes sense within the context of viewing humans as flexible strategizers (Alexander 1987; MacDonald 1991). Within this perspective, the tendencies to value wealth and reproductive success may be viewed as biological universals, which may be analyzed as evolved motivational systems. However, the historical accounts are highly compatible with supposing that the success of the sojourning life style of the patriarchs, the successful sojourn in Egypt, and the successful sojourn in Babylon would result in the Jews learning that this was a viable strategy and could thus become a permanent feature of their outlook on life.

Such a flexible response to environmental events must be viewed as underdetermined by evolutionary/ecological theory, but nevertheless it certainly violates no principles of the theory of evolution. The priestly redactors living in exile in Babylon need not have developed a means to retain ethnic identity within a diaspora context. Nevertheless, the theory developed here proposes that they were biologically predisposed to resist assimilation, and their successful diaspora experiences then provided a framework with which to interpret their past and construct a strategy for the future.

The ultimate goals programmed by evolution had not changed, but there was a novel realization that this strategy could be made to work in the future. As Baron points out, there was undoubtedly an awareness that all empires are only temporary. By adopting the sojourning strategy, the Jews could, as Baron 1952a, 96) states, retain their ethnic identity and "increase and multiply" without facing the inevitable consequences that all the empires of the ancient world faced: destruction of political and military power and consequent ethnic fragmentation, reproductive oppression, and enforced assimilation.

Nevertheless, in evaluating the importance of the perception of sojourning success as a causal factor in the development of Judaism, one must consider the possibility that the sojourning ideology of the Tanakh is simply a rationalization of a previously existing powerful tendency toward endogamy, consanguinity, and ethnocentrism. We have noted that the ideology of sojourning followed, rather than preceded, the existence of a diaspora. And an ideology of retaining ethnic solidarity in a diaspora is scarcely required unless one is already committed to the importance of retaining ethnic integrity. Explaining fear of exogamy and ethnocentrism—central aspects of Judaism—as resulting from particular experiences thus seems misconceived. I would suggest, however, that the realization that the sojourn in Egypt had been successful would have given the exiles confidence that their strategy could succeed. And it certainly provided the basis of a very compelling diaspora ideology.

# THE UNIQUE POSITION OF THE PRIESTS AND LEVITES AS A CULTURAL FACTOR IN THE DEVELOPMENT OF JEWISH ETHNOCENTRISM

One very striking aspect of the Pentateuch from an evolutionary perspective is the designation of the tribe of Levi as a hereditary group living among all of the other tribes and supported by offerings of various kinds. Within this tribe, the sons of Aaron and their descendants assumed an exalted status as priests. From an evolutionary perspective, the designation of these groups by an archaic lawgiver (reputed to be Moses) was a masterstroke because it resulted in the creation of hereditary groups whose interests were bound up with the fate of the entire group.

Consider the difference if each tribe had had its own religious functionaries—as would certainly have happened in the absence of such a rule. There would be no group in the society whose fate was bound up with the fate of the society as a whole. Conflicts between tribes would be bound to develop as some tribes expanded more rapidly than others. The effect of the Mosaic system was to enable the formation of a very large kinship group, one whose size was many times that of the small clans of Abraham, Isaac, and Jacob, but which still had a significant force representing the common interest. The benefit clearly was that it enabled a very unified, cohesive social structure that maximized within-group cooperation and significant egalitarianism combined with outgroup hostility—presumably a very adaptive combination during the period when the Israelites were seizing their land.

There are many examples indicating that the Israelites were quite wary about the eventual results of establishing a monarchy. Any person who was raised to be king was expected not to become overly rich—"he must not multiply horses for himself . . . and he shall not multiply wives for himself, lest his heart turn away; nor shall he greatly multiply for himself silver and gold" (Deut. 17:16-17). This theme is repeated in Samuel's admonitions about a future king: "He will take your daughters to be perfumers and cooks and bakers" (1 Sam. 8:13).

There are other examples indicating that Israelite society was intended to be a relatively egalitarian kinship group. Johnson (1987) notes that the legal code of Moses prescribes less physical punishment for many crimes than several codes of the same period. This fits well with the idea that lawgivers considered the Israelites fundamentally as a large kinship group and that within-group violence should be minimized. Thus, flogging had to be performed within sight of the judge, "lest, if one should go on to beat him with more stripes than these, your brother be degraded in your sight" (Deut. 25:3).

This attempt to maximize within-group egalitarianism and minimize the fissioning of the tribes was fairly unsuccessful. As recounted in the Books of Judges and Samuel, after the founding of Israel the groups tended to fission into tribal factions that could be united only in the face of external threat. Johnson

(1987) characterizes this early phase as a democracy and meritocracy. Decision making within the tribes was egalitarian, but the result was that any large cooperative effort was very difficult to achieve: "In those days there was no king in Israel; Every man did that which was right in his own eyes" (Judg. 21:25). Johnson argues that this structure remained functional until the need to confront large local powers produced a unified state under King David. However, the problem with the Israelite monarchy was that it created so many divisions based on differences in social class as well as political power differences between the tribes that there was little unity. Tribal conflict became endemic, civil war erupted, and the northern kingdom split off from the southern kingdom. Clearly the Mosaic system was not able to prevent fissioning of the tribal system.

When Israel became a monarchy, there was a pronounced tendency to establish the typical large court characteristic of the Near Eastern civilizations, including harem polygyny. Unlike the classical Roman civilization (MacDonald 1990; see above), there were no social controls on reproductive competition, with the result that centralized power quickly resulted in enormous variation in reproductive success as well as enormous cleavages between the kinship groups.

However, the despotism was not complete: Even during this period, the kings appear to have realized that Israel was "a theocracy and not a normal state" (Johnson 1987, 57). Thus, King David was sensitive to the complaints of the religious authorities when he overstepped his authority by siring a child by Uriah's wife Bathsheba, attempting to pay him off, and finally having him killed. The punishment is appropriate: The child born to Bathsheba will die, and his wives will have intercourse with another man (in the event, his rebellious son Absalom) with the full knowledge of all Israel. Later, Elijah curses King Ahab for obtaining Naboth's vineyard through treachery. The king repents and is spared, but the king's son is cursed.

Nevertheless, the oppression, especially under Solomon, was real. Solomon employed forced labor, but exempted his own tribe, the Judans. This forced labor, along with high taxes, appears to have been a major cause of the splitting of the kingship on Solomon's death. When Solomon's son Reheboam states that he will make even more labor and financial demands of the Israelites than his father did, the result is rebellion and the split into two kingdoms. Indicating the continued importance of kinship ties in this period, the cleavage was along kinship lines, with the Judans and Benjaminites carrying on the old monarchy and a new kingdom forming from the rest of the tribes, under Jeroboam, an Ephraimite.[42]

The tendency toward centralization and oppression was also seen in the splintered kingdoms, and Johnson (1987) comments that "virtually all the kings of Israel broke with the religious purists sooner or later" (p. 68). Nevertheless, Johnson (1987) suggests that in Judah there was a revival of theocratic democracy before Jerusalem fell to the Babylonians in 586 B.C. Indeed, the forced labor of King Solomon appears to have been replaced by a taxation system when King Joash restored the Temple (2 Chron. 24:8).

Baron (1952a) notes that the prophets "castigated the oppression of the poor, the exploitation of free labor, the expropriation of small landholders, and the political, administrative and judicial system which sanctioned these crimes (p. 88). For example, Isaiah was well aware that social class differences and oppression among the Israelites prevented solidarity: "Woe to those who decree iniquitous decrees, and the writers who keep writing oppression, to turn aside the needy from justice and to rob the poor of my people of their right, that widows may be their spoil, and that they may make the fatherless their prey" (Isa. 10:1-2). Social justice is the aim, but the message is directed at the poor of "my people," that is, the kinship group, and reflects a concern over the destruction of common interests among the Israelites.[43]

Besides the tendency for class oppression, the prophets were also well aware of the tendency of Israelite society to disintegrate along kinship lines. The prolonged struggles between the house of Saul and the house of David can be seen as the struggle between two kinship groups (Benjaminites versus Judans), and when Baasha from the tribe of Issachar seizes the throne of Israel, he destroys the kinship group of Jeroboam (tribe of Joseph). Moreover, when the split in the kingship occurs after Solomon, the lines of fissure occur along tribal lines. When David becomes king, the tribes gather around him and assert their kinship links: "Behold, we are your bone and flesh" (2 Sam. 5:1). Later, the Judans take pains to deny that they have benefited in any way from their kinsman David being king (2 Sam. 19:42). In the competition among the tribes, clearly Judah becomes by far the largest: At 2 Sam. 24:9, it is stated that the men of Judah number over half of the total for the other tribes.

Isaiah is quite aware of the poisonous nature of internecine fighting between the kinship groups as well as the destructive effects of social class differences. Regarding strife among kinship groups, he says, "They eat every man the flesh of his own arm: Manasseh, Ephraim; and Ephraim, Manasseh; And they together are against Judah" (Isa. 9:19-20). In the glorious future, these rifts between kinship groups will be eradicated: "The envy also of Ephraim shall depart, and they who harass Judah shall be cut off; Ephraim shall not envy Judah, and Judah shall not vex Ephraim" (Isa. 11:13).[44]

The prophets, deriving mainly from the priests and Levites, thus appear to have been quite conscious of their role as a unifying force within Israel. Moreover, during the Babylonian exile the strategy was recast into a sojourning strategy by the only real force remaining for Israelite unity—the Priests and Levites. Although this institution was not particularly successful during the monarchy in minimizing sources of intrasocietal conflict, it was spectacularly successful during and after the exile. In the resulting diaspora strategy, the conflicts of interest were fundamentally between Jews and non-Jews and not within the Jewish community. As Baron (1952a 134) observes, in the diaspora "[g]one were the deep inner dissensions which had characterized the public life of both Samaria and Jerusalem before their downfall."[45] Rather than fissioning politically and exploiting each other, Judaism came to be conceptualized as a group strategy in which the group would exist as a diaspora living among foreigners. If one accepts the truth of the sojourning accounts of the Pentateuch, the new strategy was a return to the original strategy of competing for resources with the people they were sojourning among.

Since they lived among the other tribes and were dependent on them for support, the priests and Levites are expected to have a sort of group-selectionist outlook in which the needs of the entire group are emphasized, rather than selfish sectarian interests. It is expected that this group would be the first to criticize the oppression of the other tribes by the monarchy because such oppression would lead to social division and the eventual breakup of the state, and especially if members of this tribe continued (as they did) to live among the other tribes. In the Book of Judges 19-21, the rape and murder of a Levite's concubine by Benjaminites is depicted as resulting in a bloody civil war among the tribes—perhaps an object lesson on the importance of intertribal unity and on the need to protect the defenseless Levites from oppression by the other tribes. Such a group would therefore be expected to emphasize national solidarity even during exile (e.g., Ezekiel).

In Chapter 3, it was suggested that monotheism for the Israelites was nothing more or less than an expression of the common interests of the Jewish people viewed as a unified kinship group. In a sense, therefore, one can equate the monotheistic God, the interests of a unified Israel, and the interests of the Levites and particularly the priestly descendents of Aaron. This equation receives explicit support in the language of the Tanakh: "And the LORD said unto Aaron, 'Thou shalt have no inheritance in their land, neither shalt thou have any portion among them; I am thy portion and thine inheritance among the people of Israel'" (Num. 18:20). Indeed, the Levites are enjoined to give a tithe of their tithe, including the best meat and produce (the "Lord's offering"), to Aaron the priest (Num. 18:25-29). Thus, the priests and Levites have no right to any land, but must be supported by the rest of the tribes,[46] and there is an equation among God, group interests, and the interests of the priests and Levites.

Such a tribe also would be expected to be greatly concerned with genealogy, since membership in the tribe was entirely hereditary. Epstein (1942, 154) notes that the priests and prophets were much more opposed to exogamy than were either the political aristocracy (e.g., Solomon and his many foreign wives)[47] or the common people. And, in Chapter 4, it was noted that there was an extreme concern with genealogy on the part of the priestly aristocracy through the Second Commonwealth period, and indeed throughout Jewish history. This concern with genealogy would be expected especially in the case of the high priesthood, which was supposed to be directly descended from the sons of Aaron.

In this regard, the situation was quite unlike the situation for religious personnel in Greece and Rome, where being a priest was sometimes a mark of high social status, but never hereditary (Beard & North 1990, 7). Thus in fifth century Athens, religious decisions were made by the same democratically elected body of men as made secular decisions, while in Republican Rome, political power and religious office went together, but great precautions were taken to prevent any one lineage from monopolizing these positions. Certainly, there was no priestly tribe at the center of the state that was supported by the rest of society.[48]

The Babylonian exile appears to be a critical event for the development of the priesthood. Schürer ([1885] 1979, 257-274) notes that the prestige and power of priests increased dramatically after the exile essentially because the priests had rewritten the laws during the exile so that the divine law now coincided with priestly interests. One important result was that the contributions to priests became more like a tax, rather than being solely a part of sacrifices as set out in Deuteronomy. According to the Deuteronomic prescriptions, the priest would get a small part of the sacrificed animal, and the worshiper would get the rest. However, the Priestly Code of the Book of Numbers, written during the exile, required that the priests receive a tithe of agricultural produce and the first born of animals as well as numerous other offerings.

Later, this income was augmented from a variety of sources, including voluntary contributions and a Temple tax for diaspora Jews, which amounted to "a great deal of money" (Sanders 1992, 84), estimated to be over a million dollars in today's money. The result was that the priesthood as a class controlled vast amounts of wealth. Sanders (1992, 78, 147) estimates that the tithing system was supporting approximately 20,000 priests and Levites in the first century A.D., including a wealthy, landowning priestly aristocracy.[49]

From this perspective, it is no accident that it was the members of the Israelite priestly class, and in particular the *kohen gadol* (high priest), who led the affairs of the nation from the period of the Babylonian exile until they were replaced by a non-hereditary scholarly aristocracy of rabbis in the period following the destruction of the Second Temple, a period of over 500 years.

The Zadokite family monopolized the high priesthood for several centuries from the time of Solomon until removed from this monopoly by the Hasmoneans (who were also a priestly family) in the second century B.C. In the post-exilic period prior to the Hasmonean power, the high priests were the effective military and civil rulers of Jerusalem and had wide influence throughout Judea, even though ultimate power lay elsewhere. During the Hasmonean period, the deposed Zadokites founded at least one Temple and were intimately involved in the Essene sect (characterized by supra-normal levels of separatism, purity, and observance of the law). Loyalist Zadokites became a major component of the Sadducean party and may well have contributed two high priests under Herod the Great (Sanders 1992, 23-26).[50]

It was the priestly class who performed the final writing and redaction of the Pentateuch, which emphasized national/ethnic unity in the face of a diaspora. Chronicles 1 and 2 appear to have been written by priests, and an important theme is the status of the Zadokite priests in the affairs of Israel. The pivotal figure of Ezra, who performed a critical role in establishing the racially exclusive post-exilic community, was a Zadokite priest.

The priests also played the central role in the political events of the post-exilic period. When the Seleucid (Greek) Antiochus IV defiled the Temple with pagan sacrifice in 167 B.C., the priest Mattathias, although not a Zadokite, was the instigator of the ensuing disorders. This priestly revolt was successful, inaugurating the Hasmonean period under the leadership of Mattathias and his successors. The tribe of Levi benefited greatly during this period, and, indeed, it was during the Hasmonean period that the high priesthood was formally merged with political and military leadership, thus achieving its highest level of power and influence. An important early accomplishment of this merging of religious and political interests was the destruction of the budding assimilationist movement referred to in 1 Maccabees 1:11.[51]

Moreover, the Sanhedrin continued to be dominated by priests up until the destruction of the Temple (Alon 1989, 45; Schürer [1885] 1979, 369). Priests were also important leaders in the diaspora (Sanders 1992, 52), and retained family connections via marriage with other priestly families even though scattered over a wide area (see Epstein 1942). Even after the destruction of the Temple, there was an unsuccessful struggle with Pharisaic elements in which the priests attempted to retain their exclusive status. For this group, the integrity of the nation strongly coincided with their own interests as a hereditary elite.

The end of the Commonwealth also marked a tendency for a decline in the hereditary rights of priests and Levites (Alon [1980, 1984] 1989, 26). Leadership among Jews came to be associated with personal abilities, rather than birth, with the result that the society as a whole became more democratic or at least meritocratic. The hereditary, tribal aristocracy of the descendants of Aaron could hardly be expected to survive the complete loss of political power for very long, but while it lasted, this aristocracy was undoubtedly a potent force for retaining national and ethnic identity under even the most implausible of circumstances. From a political and a genetic point of view, the fall from centralized political power then resulted, within mainstream Judaism at least, in a coalescence between the priestly aristocracy and the scholarly, religiously observant class.

As noted in Chapter 4, being of priestly or Levitical descent continued to command respect in the Jewish community into modern times. The writings of Maimonides in the 12th century show that the requirements for ethnic purity in the marriages of priests continued to be more stringent than for the rest of the Jewish population, and establishing an unblemished genealogy continued to be of great importance. Again, one recalls Maimonides' description of a child who, recounting his immersion and eating of the heave offering, states that his companions "kept their distance from me and called me 'Johanan, the eater of dough offering'" (p. 130). And as noted in Chapter 4, individuals from the tribe of the Levites and especially the Kohanim continued to be singled out during synagogue service into modern times. Particularly striking is the role of the Kohanim in leading the synagogue service on the Day of Atonement, the most solemn Jewish holiday (Zborowski & Herzog 1952, 396). The Kohanim were also provided obligatory contributions on the birth of one's first son (Zborowski & Herzog 1952, 56, 320).[52]

It is this unique feature of ancient Judaism that I believe was critical in resisting the natural tendencies for fission among tribal societies during the early centuries after the Exodus and that was responsible for retaining national/ethnic identity even after being conquered by other groups bent on destroying ethnic ties among their subjects and enforcing assimilation. The presence of the priesthood among the Babylonian exiles and its absence among the Syrian exiles from the Northern kingdom may also explain why the latter eventually became assimilated while the former did not. Without the presence of a group that was intensely and self-interestedly committed to the integrity of the group, the eventual result was assimilation.

In Chapter 1, there was a brief discussion of the Spartan system as a group evolutionary strategy. Interestingly, there are legendary lawgivers for both the Spartans and the Israelites, Lycurgus and Moses, respectively. (Josephus relates the story that the Spartans developed the idea that they were descended from the same stock as the Jews and were brothers.) Both lawgivers stressed the importance of internal solidarity and egalitarian relationships within the society, and both emphasized ethnic and cultural separatism. Both developed means of unifying large kinship groups. Both groups dominated other ethnic groups who acted as servants among them, while retaining their genetic separatism (although the Helots appear to have had a much more prominent role in this regard than did the *Nethinim*).[53]

From a broader perspective, one can view Lycurgus and Moses as originators of group strategies. Although these individuals are perhaps mythical, the systems that developed in Sparta and among the Israelites have all the appearance of being human contrivances. This is essentially what Baron (1952a) means when he says that Judaism is not a natural political system. In a similar way, the "unnaturalness" of the Spartan system fascinated the ancients and continues to fascinate political theorists in the modern world. Both systems are quite unique when compared to the political structures that developed in surrounding areas, and both have elements of enforced intrasocietal egalitarianism, as well as attempts to deal with the divisive effects of tribalism within the society, while maintaining sufficient strength to confront external foes. Just as with political philosophers such as Plato, Hobbes, and Marx, these ancient social engineers, by using their intellectual abilities and their understanding of human nature, developed blueprints for social systems. In the case of Moses and Lycurgus, these systems were designed to have a good chance of retaining a powerful group orientation, which would be capable of withstanding external forces and preventing internal fission. As in the case of the framers of the U.S. Constitution, a political philosophy was actually constructed for a real society. However, unlike the societies envisioned by these political philosophers or the founding fathers, both Judaism and the Spartan system appear to qualify as altruistic group strategies from an evolutionary perspective.

It would appear that the system devised by the Israelite lawgiver was in some sense a better strategy for maintaining long-term ethnic coherence than that designed by the Spartan lawgiver, since the Israelite strategy, arguably, continues today (see *SAID*, ch. 10). The Spartan system was an excellent defensive system, but was ill equipped to administer an empire, and there were no provisions, such as the hereditary Israelite priestly class, that would have allowed it to survive being militarily conquered—a contingency that was all but inevitable in the ancient world and that certainly continues to some extent today.

However, I suspect that the Israelite system has been so successful in its persistence precisely because crucial aspects of the strategy were continually changed by the Jews to meet current contingencies. Thus, it is extremely unlikely that a putative Israelite lawgiver such as Moses, contemplating the design of the post-Exodus Israelite society, envisioned Judaism as a movement for national/ethnic identity in a diaspora. Nor is there any reason to suppose that the subsequent policy of favoring universal education, a highly educated elite, eugenic practices, and high-investment parenting was part of the original Israelite strategy. From the evidence presented in Chapter 7, it would appear that these latter aspects of mainstream Judaism were the invention of diaspora times and essentially involved a realization that these aspects were important if the Jews were to compete successfully in the Greco-Roman world.

However, by creating a hereditary class whose interests were to maintain the integrity of the group, the original lawgiver created a very powerful force for national/ethnic cohesion; and in the end, the only commonality for the Israelite/Jewish strategy was the need to maintain national/ethnic identity no matter what the external situation. The point here is that the invention of a hereditary tribe of priests and Levites with a centralizing function within a group of other tribes was probably a necessary condition for the development of Judaism as it developed into its peculiar form as a group evolutionary strategy.

# CONCLUSION: RETROSPECT AND PROSPECT

The material reviewed in this chapter is further confirmation of the extremely powerful centripetal forces that have resulted in an intense commitment to the group throughout Jewish history. It is this intense commitment, more than anything else, which is the *sine qua non* of Judaism as a group evolutionary strategy. However, the material reviewed in Chapter 5 also indicates that historical Judaism has often been a powerful competitor for resources within human societies. Group strategies are very powerful in competition with individual strategies within a society, and especially so in the case of Judaism with its very high degree of with-group cooperation and altruism as well as its historical commitment to eugenic practices related to intelligence and high-investment parenting.

Both the intense level of group commitment characteristic of Judaism and the power of Judaism in resource competition with gentiles are important features of the theory of anti-Semitism developed in *SAID*. Data reviewed there indicate that anti-Semitism has been a virtually universal feature of societies where Jews have resided, and, in the present volume, we have already had occasion to refer to several instances where anti-Semitism has resulted in extreme levels of intrasocietal violence (e.g., the Iberian Inquisitions, the Nazi holocaust). Given the ubiquity of anti-Semitism and the very powerful forces that it has unleashed, there is every reason to suppose that Judaism and anti-Semitic movements have had important effects on human societies. Here I will simply close by reiterating my belief that there is an urgent need to develop a scientific theory of Judaism and anti-Semitism, for it is only by developing such a theory that it will be possible to ensure that the future will not be like the past.

# NOTES

1. The derivation of these groups from those exiled by the Syrians is doubtful (Porten 1984, 343). It is interesting that the community in China eventually disappeared by becoming assimilated into the surrounding population. Mourant, Kopec, and Domaniewska-Sobczak (1978) note that records of the group indicate that there was considerable genetic admixia as a result of Chinese women marrying into the community, while women from the community were not allowed to marry outside it. The Chinese practice therefore differed substantially from that of the other Jewish communities, with the predictable result that the community was eventually assimilated culturally as well.

2. Reflecting this intense separatism, Shaw (1991, 129) mentions the fact that Turkish Karaites moved in order "to avoid contact with other Jews," and marriage with non-Karaite Jews was viewed as an abomination on both sides (pp. 47-48). The Karaites are interesting in that some groups appear not to be ethnically Semitic, and, indeed, the Nazis accepted a claim by some Eastern European Karaite groups that they were Jewish only by religion and spared them. Mourant and colleagues (1978) state that the Nazis may well have used blood group data available at the time in order to make this determination. Nevertheless, other Karaite groups in the Near East appear to be of Semitic origin.

3. It is interesting to note that, although the tendency for ethnic separatism has been maintained by all of these Jewish groups, only mainstream Judaism appears to have developed the eugenic/high-investment strategy as a component of their national/ethnic separatist strategy (although at times this policy was not pursued for external reasons; see Chapter 7). Within these other groups there does not appear to have been the extreme idealization of scholarship and the scholar that produced the enormous corpus of Jewish religious writings. Coinciding with this non-acceptance of the Jewish tradition of learning, these groups have not enjoyed anywhere near the success of mainstream Judaism. The effective breeding population of the Samaritans was estimated to be only 39 in the 19th century (see Mourant et al. 1978), while the Kurdish Jews suffered doubly, laboring as serfs of the Kurds who themselves were oppressed by the Muslims. The other

Oriental Jewish groups remained at low population levels and low social status. This suggests that the tendency for ethnic separatism is more common among the Jews and thus more likely to be of genetic origin than is the eugenic/high-investment strategy developed out of Judaism based on the complete oral and written Torah. As suggested in Chapter 7, the eugenic/high-investment strategy appears to be a purely cultural shift that has proved to be virtually indispensable for the success of a diaspora movement based on ethnic separatism. (Of course, once the eugenic/high-investment strategy was adopted, there were genetic consequences: The Jews created Judaism, and Judaism created the Jews.)

4. Even though subject to Rome, any symbol of Roman sovereignty, such as pictures of the emperor or other symbols of Roman authority, were vigorously rejected, so that, e.g., the Roman general Vitellius took a detour rather than cause an uproar among the people by bringing his military standards into Judaea. In Judaea, the image of the emperor was even removed from coins struck in Palestine out of deference to Jewish scruples (see Schürer [1885] 1979, 81ff).

5. This phenomenon is discussed extensively in *SAID* (chs. 3 and 4).

6. Only the severe decline of Ottoman Jewry (by over 50%) due to increased anti-Semitism and other factors resulted in a measure of unification in the following two centuries (Shaw 1991, 127ff). As emphasized by Alexander (1979), external threats tend to result in increased unification and common interests. Later, with prosperity, there was again more fractionation, and increasing numbers of Ashkenazim began to manage their affairs separately from the Grand Rabbinate. Moreover, the Ashkenazi group itself was highly divided on the basis of national origin (Shaw 1991, 171).

7. The haredim represent about 5 percent of the total worldwide Jewish population, while the total Orthodox population (including the haredim) represents about 12 percent of the total worldwide Jewish population (Landau 1993, xxi-xxii, 22ff). (Heilman [1992, 12] estimates the number of haredim at 550,000.) However, Orthodox Jewish leaders claim that their population is consistently undercounted by liberal Jewish demographers intent on minimizing the importance of Orthodoxy (Landau 1993, 22ff), presumably in the interests of combating anti-Semitism. Artificially low estimates of the numbers of Orthodox Jews might be expected to deceive gentiles into supposing that the extreme exclusivity of Orthodox Judaism represents only a very small minority of Jews and thus deflect potential anti-Semitism resulting from their practices.

8. Ben-Sasson (1971, 215) describes the ideals of the medieval "Hassidim of Ashkenaz" in Germany as attempting to marry completely among themselves and exclude other Jews completely from their communities. They wished to "create and maintain a community of Pious, alike in lineage and morals; it is for the sake of this ideal that the closure of the community is to be applied."

9. "The haredim's blind obeisance to rabbis is one of the most striking characteristics of haredism in the eyes of the outside world, both Jewish and Gentile" (Landau 1993, 45). Famous rebbes are revered in an almost god-like manner (*tzaddikism*, or cult of personality), and, indeed, there was a recent controversy over whether the Lubavitcher Rebbe Schneerson claimed to be the Messiah. Many of his followers believed that he was the Messiah, and Mintz (1992, 348ff) points out that it is common for Hasidic Jews to view their rebbe as the Messiah.

10. In England, the process of conversion into Modern-Orthodox Judaism takes three to four years (Landau 1993, 305). Waxman (1989, 498) reports that the Syrian Jewish community absolutely rejects intermarriage and conversion no matter how sincere the prospective convert appears.

11. The importance of genetic background among the haredim can also be seen by the fact that one ingredient affecting one's resource value on the marriage market is a physical appearance that does not depart from the group norm on color of skin or hair. Recall the comment mentioned in Chapter 7 indicating that a haredi with red hair had great difficulty finding a wife. In looking at photographs of groups of haredim one is struck by their almost clone-like degree of phenotypic resemblance.

12. It is interesting that among the psychological traits found in collectivist societies is a bifurcation of the real and the social selves (Triandis 1991). Here the ritualized form of conversation among Jews in a traditional society suggests that the social self was completely conventionalized and socially prescribed.

13. As discussed in Chapter 7, these practices intensified in a period of group conflict and economic decline.

14. Jewish radical organizations such as the Russian Bund essentially replicated traditional Jewish separatism in a secular, socialist milieu. Issues related to Jewish identity and radical intellectual/political movements are discussed extensively in *SAID* (ch. 6).

15. Lenz (1931, 657) proposed that, because of the harsh environment, "Nordic" peoples evolved in small groups and have a tendency toward social isolation. Lenz proposed that Jews evolved in larger groups (p. 667) and as a result have highly developed social skills related to social influence, such as empathy, which enable them to anticipate others' actions and desires. Such a perspective would not imply that Northern Europeans lack collectivist mechanisms for group competition, but only that these mechanisms are relatively less elaborated and/or require a higher level of group conflict to trigger their expression. See also Chapter 7, note 12.

16. I must report that Count Gobineau ([1854] 1915, 29-30) singles out the Arabs and other Middle Eastern groups, including the Jews, as having a very pronounced tendency to retain their purity of blood and resist genetic assimilation. However, he saw the tendency to resist genetic assimilation as a general human characteristic, occurring even in some areas of France, which he believed to represent a society with a high degree of genetic admixture: "The human race in all its branches has a secret repulsion from the crossing of blood, a repulsion which in many of the branches is invincible, and in others is only conquered to a slight extent. Even those who most completely shake off the yoke of this idea cannot get rid of the few last traces of it; yet such peoples are the only members of our species who can be civilized at all." For Gobineau, then, Western Europe in general was characterized less by concern with purity of blood than was typical of Eastern groups. However, Gobineau also believed that some European groups, including the Croats, Magyars, Saxons, and Wallachians had a very powerful tendency to resist genetic admixture.

17. I would suggest that Sparta is a possible exception, since the Spartans certainly did not allow others to become Spartan citizens and they appear to have had a very highly developed sense of ethnic exclusivity (Hammond 1986). Interestingly, there is good reason to suppose that the Spartan system, like Judaism, was a contrived evolutionary strategy. See below and Chapter 1.

18. In the words of Aristides, a Roman provincial in the second century addressing Rome:

> You have caused the word "Roman" to belong not to a city, but to be the name of a sort of common race, and this not one out of all the races, but a balance to all the remaining ones. You do not now divide the races into Greeks and barbarians . . . you have divided people into Romans and

non-Romans. Yet no envy walks your empire. For you yourselves were the first not to begrudge anything, since you made everything available to all in common and granted to those who are capable not to be subjects rather than rulers in turn. (Quoted in Garnsey & Saller 1987, 15)

19. Boyarin (1993, 231) argues that Western universalism beginning in the ancient world resulted in a "severe devaluation" of ethnicity. Boyarin acknowledges the exclusivist, ethnocentric nature of Judaism, but, in the manner of many recent multi-cultural ideologues, views the rabbinical writings as a "necessary critique" (p. 234) of assimilative tendencies of the ancient world. "The very emphasis on a universalism, expressed as concern for all of the families of the world, turns rapidly (if not necessarily) into a doctrine that they must all become part of our family of the spirit, with all of the horrifying practices against Jews and other Others that Christian Europe produced" (p. 235).

It is difficult to see how an assimilationist culture that de-emphasizes ethnicity would necessarily commit horrifying practices against Jews. (Anti-Semitism was relatively uncommon in the ancient world and much of what there was derived from the Jewish lack of participation in the common culture. See above and *SAID*, ch. 2.) Nor is it clear how Jews would benefit if Western culture imitated Judaism and became more ethnocentric and concerned about retaining racial purity. One would suppose that such a development would lead to intense, racially based anti-Semitism, as in the case of Naziism. Boyarin conflates the Western tendency toward individualism with medieval corporate religiosity, which did indeed have a strong tendency to exclude Jews. The latter must be seen as a departure from the tradition of Western individualism, and, indeed, in *SAID* (ch. 3) it is argued that the Church developed in the fourth century as a collectivist, authoritarian group strategy defined by its opposition to Judaism. Even at its most collectivist, however, and in radical opposition to Jewish practices, the medieval Church retained the Western tendency toward the de-emphasis on genetic relatedness as a basis for group membership or as a criterion of status within the Christian community. Boyarin's argument also ignores the exclusionary tendency of Muslim religious orthodoxy—hardly a Western phenomenon—which resulted in the long-term degradation of Jewish culture. Clearly, the best strategy for Jews has always been to retain their highly collectivist, exclusivist, and ethnocentric culture while living in a highly individualist society. Indeed, as discussed in *SAID* (ch. 8), an important strand of 20th-century Jewish intellectual activity has been to develop theories of anti-Semitism in which collectivist, authoritarian gentile groups are proposed to be indications of gentile psychopathology.

20. This is not to say that the Greeks and Romans did not exploit the conquered peoples or that they were not interested in reproductive success, as Hegermann's (1989; see also Hengel 1989, 176) account makes clear. Regarding the Hellenistic period, Hegermann (1989, 129) notes that, "as in the Roman period, powerful political ambition and ruthlessness went hand in hand with a determined search for peace and a sense of dedication to a humanizing cultural mission." I am only saying that there was much less concern with endogamy and racial purity among the Greeks than among the Jews. However, the difference is relative, not absolute: Hengel (1989, 174), while agreeing that the Jews intermarried far less than other groups, notes that Alexander's army rejected the intermarriages and provides other evidence that the Greeks did not engage in panmixia with the conquered peoples. Nevertheless, status as a Hellene definitely did not depend on genetic descent, and many intellectuals of the period emphasized the concept of a universal humanity including even the barbarians (Hengel 1989, 178, 179).

21. Mitterauer (1991) suggests that the Jews were less concerned with endogamy than were other Near Eastern groups. Thus, the Jews early on rejected a variety of common forms of Near Eastern marriage that functioned to keep a purchased wife in the family when the husband died: a daughter-in-law after death of the son, a stepmother after the death of the father, an aunt by marriage after the death of the uncle, and a sister-in-law after the death of the brother. Note that none of these prohibited marriages actually involves a blood relative. However, the Jews practiced the levirate (marriage of the brother's wife if the brother had no sons) as a religious obligation, as well as *Entochterehe* (marriage of sonless men's daughters to close male relatives; see Numbers 36:6-8).

22. Recently Salter (1994) has suggested that Northern European groups have a number of individualistic adaptations related to sexual behavior, including a greater tendency toward romantic love and genetic (rather than social) mechanisms (such as the purdah of Near Eastern civilization) to prevent cuckoldry. In general, I suppose that at the psychological level the evolutionary basis of individualism involves mechanisms in which adaptive behavior is intrinsically rewarding (e.g., romantic love) rather than socially imposed or coerced, as in collectivist cultures. See MacDonald (1991, 1992a) for discussions of the evolutionary basis of motivation.

23. An important feature of individualist societies is a tendency toward egalitarianism (Triandis 1990). Roman monogamy can thus be seen as reflecting the tendency toward individualistic social structure typical of the West.

24. Even prior to Rabbi Gershom's decree, there is evidence for a Christian influence on Jewish marriage patterns. During the (Christian) Byzantine period Jews were required to abide by Christian laws on monogamy, divorce, and consanguinity (Ruether 1974, 190; Shaw 1991, 19), but during the (Muslim) Ottoman period, Zimmels (1958, 63) notes that Ashkenazi immigrants to Turkey adopted the Sephardic pattern of polygyny. Similarly, Jews in the Roman Empire obeyed the Roman law, but in Persia during the same period, Jews were polygynous (Baron 1952b, 226). In Spain, polygamy among Jews was relatively common in Moorish areas compared to Christian areas up until the expulsion (Neuman 1969, II:37). Levirate marriages (implying polygyny) were also the common practice in Spain throughout the Middle Ages (See also Baron 1952b, 223ff).

25. Interestingly, while monogamy in Western Europe was essentially imposed by the Christian Church in opposition to the marriage strategies of the elite, among the Jews controls on concubinage were an aspect of individual reproductive strategies by the family of the woman. A common component of the *ketubah* marriage contract among the Sephardic Jews was a provision that the husband would not take a concubine, thus ensuring that the investment of the wife's family would not be diluted among the offspring of several women.

26. In *SAID* (ch. 3) I argue that the development of Christian corporate hegemony in the fourth and fifth centuries was a gentile group strategy in opposition to Judaism. This strategy represented a fundamental shift from the individualism of Greco-Roman culture to a collectivist, authoritarian movement, which has historically been more typical of Judaism.

27. Similarly, in England, the Christianization of national life excluded Jews from public administration, trade, and agriculture (Rabinowitz 1938, 37). On the other hand, Jordan (1989, 111) notes that in the south of France there was much greater tolerance of Jewish economic activity because there was no emergence of an "institutionally coherent state" that would exclude "aliens." The result was that Jews often had authority over Christians and competed with Christians in a wide range of economic activities in this area.

28. The intense popular resentment of moneylending (whether by Jews or by Christians) during this period is discussed in *SAID* (ch. 2). This resentment was rational in the sense that few individuals could hope to profit by taking a loan at the interest rates common in the medieval period. Interest rates in northern France were 65 percent and compounded until 1206, when the rate was capped at 43 percent and compounding was made illegal (Chazan 1973, 84; Rabinowitz 1938, 44). Moreover, Jordan's (1989) treatment indicates that both compounding and rates higher than the legal limit continued even after attempts to abolish these practices. The great majority of the loans were not for investment in businesses, but rather for living expenses in a society that hovered near the subsistence level (e.g., Gilchrist 1969, 62; Jordan 1989, 159). Jewish communities tended to prosper at these rates of interest (and even at much lower rates, as in 15th-century Florence [Gilchrist 1969, 73]), but the rates must be understood as including taxes by authorities who used Jewish moneylending as a source of revenue. Rabinowitz (1938, 113) provides statements of contemporaries indicating that moneylenders themselves viewed their occupation as extremely lucrative compared to artisanry or agriculture.

Interest rates of this magnitude therefore resulted in a net flow of resources out of the gentile community into the Jewish community with no compensating increase in economic activity within the gentile community. The opposition of the Church during this period to usurious moneylending (which was not without effect [see Gilchrist, 1969, 106ff]) was thus rational in the sense that the eradication of moneylending at rates typical in the Medieval period would benefit the gentile community as a whole. The medieval Church, like traditional Judaism, must be understood as a collectivist, exclusionary entity with a strong sense of Christian group interests. (Thus, the common medieval metaphor for society is a body in which the Church is the head and eyes, the nobility the hands and arms, and the peasantry the legs and feet [Rabinowitz 1938, 117]). Like traditional Judaism, this group conceptualization was one in which there was harmony of all social classes, including a responsibility of charity for the poor (Gilchrist 1969, 118ff; see also Hill 1967).

29. The following is based on Chazan (1973, 78ff) and Jordan (1989, *passim*).

30. In both Poland and Spain, on the other hand, the evidence reviewed in Chapter 5 indicates that Jewish competition substantially hindered the emergence of a Christian middle class. Jordan (1989, 182) indicates that Christian merchants were also instrumental in the expulsion of the Jews as a means of removing a source of competition, again suggesting that the removal of the Jews was an important factor in the development of a gentile middle class.

31. During the reign of Philip IV, the Church and the monarch clashed over treatment of Jews and there was a marked increase in popular hatred of Jews, leading, beginning in the 1290s, to expulsions from particular areas and in 1306, from the entire kingdom. Popular hatred also led to a later expulsion in 1322 after Jews were readmitted in 1315 (Jordan 1989, 244ff). The expulsion order of Charles II of Sicily (Count of Anjou and Maine) of 1289 reflects popular animosity winning out over royal revenues: "[F]or the honor of God and the tranquillity of [the area] . . . although we enjoy extensive temporal benefit from the . . . Jews—, preferring to provide for the peace of our subjects rather than to fill our coffers with the mammon of iniquity . . ." (quoted in Chazan 1973, 185). (To an evolutionist, it is interesting that besides the complaint that Jews obtained riches via usury, the order also complained that Jews seduced Christian maidens.) Charles's subjects were forced to pay for the privilege of living without Jews with a special tax, a practice then followed by Philip IV of France. Immediately prior to the expulsion of 1306 in France there was an increase in the number of communities that were willing to pay the

crown to rid themselves of Jews, as also occurred in England prior to the expulsion of 1290 (Roth 1978).

32. Similarly, in northern Italy in the late 15th century, Franciscans led a campaign against Jewish moneylending because of perceived negative effects of this activity on the Christian community (Shulvass 1973, 118). The campaign included the development of charitable *Monti di Pieta* lending institutions, which gave loans on a non-profit basis. The following period was characterized by much greater community control over the interest rates Jews could charge on loans.

33. Castro (1954, 496-497) suggests that the situation in which an unassimilated ethnic group (Jews) was placed over the masses of Spaniards by the nobility resulted in the impossibility of a modern (i.e., individualist) European state developing in Spain because it prevented the development of the homogeneous, corporate, feudal state that was the historical forerunner of the modern state.

> It is a serious affair when the services that we lend or are lent to us do not mesh with a system of mutual loyalties and common values, as they did where the feudal organization was an authentic reality. In important areas of Spanish life, loyalty and esteem were replaced by the tyranny of the lord and the flattering servility of the Jews, forced to pay this price to subsist. This false situation was fatal, and equally so was the situation in which the common people had to accept a group whom they hated and despised as their superiors, legally entitled to prey regularly upon their meager resources. And the more evident that the superiority of the Jews turned out to be, the worse it became. From such premises it was impossible that there should be derived any kind of modern state, the sequel, after all, of the Middle Ages' hierarchic harmony. . . . The main paths that were open to the Christian feudal state were obstructed in Spain by the Jew, as necessary as he was foreign.

34. During the modern era, Naziism is another example of a highly cohesive, collectivist group that strongly opposed Judaism. The collectivist, exclusionary aspects of Naziism are discussed further in *SAID* (ch. 3). Given the propensity for gentile collectivist societies to exclude Jews, it is not surprising that a powerful strand of Jewish intellectual activity in the 20th century has been to pathologize highly cohesive, collectivist gentile social structures, gentile nationalism, gentile authoritarian political groups, and gentile ethnocentrism (e.g., the Frankfurt School of Social Research; see *SAID* (ch. 8). It is clearly in the interests of Jews to advocate the continuation of the quintessential Western cultural commitment to individualism as the best environment for the continuation of Jewish collectivism.

35. On the basis of his cross-cultural data Triandis (1990, 1991) finds that upper-status individuals are more likely to be individualist in their outlook and therefore not identify with group aims. In Chapter 5, it was noted that there were often very close relationships between Jews and upper-class gentile elites combined with widespread anti-Semitism among the lower classes. Upper-class gentiles are thus more likely to ally themselves with Jewish interests and fail to develop a sense of collective gentile interests in opposition to Judaism as a group evolutionary strategy.

36. As indicated in Castro (1954; see note 33 above), the role of Jews in Spain may have been essential, at least during the period of the Reconquest.

37. Data on anti-Semitism in Muslim societies are discussed in *SAID* (ch. 2).

38. In the Isaac story, Isaac is apparently draining too many resources from the Philistines, for he later says to their leaders when they come to him, "Wherefore are ye

come unto me, seeing ye hate me, and have sent me away from you?" (Gen. 26:27). He is forced to leave and finally finds a spot in the valley of Gerar where he could dig a well without conflict with the neighboring groups. Speiser (1970, 12-13) notes that there has been a polemical literature regarding the morality implicit in these stories of deception. He also notes that a wife designated as a wife-sister had a higher status than an ordinary wife in cultures of the area.

39. Note the emphasis in Baron's (1952a) comment on the consciousness of ties of biological relatedness as crucial to the diaspora mentality. The 19th-century proto-Zionist Moses Hess (1943, 235) also points out that both the Talmud and the Midrash emphasize that the Israelites in Egypt did not assimilate by taking Egyptian names and that their women remained faithful to their "Jewish nationality."

40. Exodus 12:37 states that the leaving group consisted of about 600,000 men plus women and children. From an ecological perspective, it was the very large economy of Egypt that made this large increase in population possible, while still retaining a strong sense of group identity. Had they remained in the desert, the groups would have undoubtedly fissioned long before they had achieved this population. (Even Abraham and Lot must go their separate ways after the first Egyptian sojourn because they have accumulated so much wealth [Gen. 13:6].)

41. The Book of Esther was an inspiration for crypto-Jews attempting to deceive the gentile society regarding their true affiliations during the period of the Iberian Inquisitions (Beinart 1971b, 472).

42. This new kingdom was apparently far less orthodox than the Judan kingdom (Johnson 1987), and it is stated in both Kings and Chronicles that the Levites were expelled. A major theme of these works, and especially the Book of Hosea, is the impending doom for the northern kingdom as a result of straying from proper religious observances. Quite possibly the oppression at the hands of Solomon resulted in a much more general distrust of orthodox religion in the north.

43. Amos 8:4; Jeremiah 5:28, 6:6, 7:5, and 22:3; Micah 6:11; Zechariah 7:8; and Malachi 3:5 also decry the oppression of the Israelite state.

44. The choice of Manasseh and Ephraim is significant because these are two half-tribes in the tribe of Joseph and therefore represent the idea that even closely related kinship groups had developed large conflicts of interest, although together they continued to harass the more distantly related tribe of Judah. After the death of Solomon, the fracture resulted in two states, one under the leadership of Judah and the other under the leadership of an Ephraimite.

45. See also Chapter 6.

46. Interestingly, in the numerical count of the tribes at Numbers 26, the tribe of Levi has the fewest members. Since the tribe was (from an ecological perspective) parasitic on the rest of the Israelites, it is quite possible that there were subtle controls on their population, while at the same time they were protected from oppression from other tribes (the story of the rape of the Levite's concubine by Benjaminites [Judg. 19-21] comes to mind).

47. Besides Solomon, Epstein (1942, 183n) notes two other instances in which members of the royal family married foreign wives.

48. Moreover, the tribal nature of the priesthood is not apparent in other ancient societies. Kuhrt (1990) finds that religious personnel in Babylon were appointed by the king. Temple personnel were highly diverse, "drawn from a specified group of the urban community, in an apparently independent and spontaneous fashion, sometimes dictated by economic exigencies" (p. 154). These individuals may well have had commercial or

industrial power, but in any case there is no evidence that the priesthood had a tribal organization as in Israel.

The situation in Egypt was more similar to that in Israel, but there were important differences. Thompson (1990) finds that the priestly offices were hereditary and the priesthood itself was possessed of considerable wealth and power. (A high priest of Ptah writes, "I was a great man, rich in all riches, whereby I possessed a goodly harem . . ." [quoted in Thompson 1990, 115].) For example, there was a small elite group of intermarrying families of high priests of the cult of Ptah in which the high priesthood was passed from father to son over several generations. However, unlike the case of Israel, there was a variety of cults, and priests participated in an official capacity in several of them. There would thus appear to be a variety of cults maintained by an interlocking set of families, with the cult of Ptah at the pinnacle of power and wealth. However, priesthoods could be purchased and ceded by the government, and there was a wide variety of cults supported by the people and the government. As a result, although the Egyptian priesthood was clearly far more the focus of a family strategy than was the case in the Greco-Roman world, there is no indication that the priesthood as a whole in any sense constituted an endogamous tribe in which a subset was priests and in which an even more exclusive subset was the high priests. Lacking this strong sense of belonging to a kinship group, the priesthood itself disappeared quickly when the Romans reduced the power and wealth of the Egyptian temples.

49. There is also a scholarly tradition emanating mainly from Christian sources that emphasizes the business aspect of the Temple. There was a great deal of buying and selling of sacrificial animals at the Temple and some suggestion that the priests and Levites were directly involved in this commerce (Sanders 1992, 85ff, 185ff) as well as in their normal role as consumers of the sacrificial products. Nevertheless, while Sanders (1992) himself demurs from this judgment (if only because the Jewish system may have been less exploitative than other Oriental religions), he notes that "[m]odern scholars, both Jews and Christians, are inclined to see the temple system as corrupt, or as detrimental to the people's welfare" (p. 91). The only point here is that the system produced a hereditary class with a vital stake in a continuing national/ethnic identity and non-assimilation with surrounding peoples.

50. In a comment consistent with the heightened role of genealogy in Eastern cultures emphasized in this chapter, Jeremias (1969, 193) notes that: "[i]t is very enlightening to see that the Zadokite family, though politically obscure, stood in the popular view high above the influential but illegitimate high-priestly families. In the east, ancestry has always counted more than power, in fact it is regarded as divinely ordained. . . . ."

51. The Hasmonean period also produced its share of despots. For example, according to Josephus, Alexander Jannaeus (r. 103-76 B.C.) executed 800 of his Jewish opponents by crucifying them. Before they died, he had "the throats of their wives and children cut before their eyes; and these executions he saw as he was drinking and lying down with his concubines" (Flavius Josephus, *The Wars of the Jews*; 1:97). I suppose that an evolutionist should not be surprised at such a deed, but I also suppose that only an evolutionist can comprehend the exquisite symbolism represented by one man calmly flaunting his reproductive assets while his opponents are forced to observe their reproductive assets being slaughtered prior to themselves being subjected to an extremely painful death.

52. Recently the marriage of a convert female to a man named Cohen produced a national crisis in Israel and in diaspora circles. The issues centered around the age-old prohibition against priestly marriage to converts (see Landau 1987, 304ff).

53. There were some differences as well. The Spartans were far more egalitarian and centralized than were the early Israelites. Moreover, it would appear that tribal lines within the Spartan society were de-emphasized to a greater extent than among the early Israelites, and there was no provision for a hereditary class (tribe) of religious personnel supported by the rest of the society.

# BIBLIOGRAPHY

## PRIMARY

Tanakh quotations are from *The Holy Scriptures According to the Masoretic Text.* Philadelphia: Jewish Publication Society of America, 1955.

Babylonian Talmud quotations are from *The Talmud of Babylonia: An American Translation*, trans. J. Neusner. Atlanta: Scholars Press, 1992.

Apocrypha quotations are from *The New English Bible: The Apocrypha*. Oxford University Press and Cambridge University Press, 1970.

Book of Jubilees quotations are from *Apocrypha and Pseudepigrapha of the Old Testament in English II*, ed. R. H. Charles. 1-82. Reprint. Oxford, England: Clarendon Press, [1913] 1966.

Mishnah quotations are from *The Mishnah: A New Translation*, trans. J. Neusner. New Haven and London: Yale University Press, 1988.

Quotations from Josephus are from *The Works of Josephus* (complete and unabridged), trans. W. Whiston. Peabody, Mass.: Hendrickson Publishers, 1989.

Code of Maimonides quotations are from *The Code of Maimonides*, ed. L. Nemoy. Yale Judaica Series, New Haven, Conn.: Yale University Press, 1965.

## SECONDARY

Abramsky, C., M., Jachimczyk, & A. Polonsky, (1986). Introduction to *The Jews in Poland*, ed. C. Abramsky, M. Jachimczyk, & A. Polonsky. London: Basil Blackwell.

Ackroyd, P. R. (1968). *Exile and Restoration*. Philadelphia: Westminster Press.

———. (1984). The Jewish community in Palestine in the Persian period. In *The Cambridge History of Judaism*. Vol. 1, ed. W. D. Davies & L. Finkelstein. Cambridge: Cambridge University Press.

Adler, M. N. (1907). *The Itinerary of Benjamin of Tudela: Critical Text, Translation and Commentary*. New York: Philip Feldheim.

Ahroni, R. (1986). *Yemenite Jewry: Origins, Culture, and Literature*. Bloomington: Indiana University Press.

Alexander, R. (1979). *Darwinism and Human Affairs*. Seattle: University of Washington Press.

———. (1987). *The Biology of Moral Systems*. New York: Aldine.

Allegro, J. M. (1972). *The Chosen People*. Garden City, N.Y.: Doubleday & Co.

Alon, G. (1977). *Jews, Judaism, and the Classical World*, trans. I. Abrahams. Jerusalem: Magnes Press, Hebrew University.

———. ([1980, 1984] 1989). *The Jews on Their Land in the Talmudic Age (70-640 C.E.)*, trans. G. Levi. Jerusalem: Magnes Press, Hebrew University; Cambridge: Harvard University Press.

Alter, R. (1989). Literary refractions of the Jewish family. In *The Jewish Family*, ed. D. Kraemer. New York: Oxford University Press.

Altshuler, M. (1987). *Soviet Jewry Since the Second World War: Population and Social Structure*. New York: Greenwood Press.

Amussen, S. D. (1988). *An Ordered Society: Gender and Class in Early Modern England*. London: Basil Blackwell.

Anderson, K. E., H. Lytton, & D. M. Romney (1986). Mothers' interactions with normal and conduct-disordered boys: Who affects whom? *Developmental Psychology* 22:604-609.

Applebaum, S. (1974a). The legal status of the Jewish communities in the Diaspora. In *The Jewish People in the First Century*. Vol. 1, ed. S. Safrai & M. Stern. Philadelphia: Fortress Press.

———. (1974b). The organization of the Jewish communities in the Diaspora. In *The Jewish People in the First Century*. Vol. 1, ed. S. Safrai & M. Stern. Philadelphia: Fortress Press.

Aschheim, S. E. (1982). *Brothers and Strangers: The East European Jew in Germany and German Jewish Consciousness, 1800-1923*. Madison: University of Wisconsin Press.

———. (1985). "The Jew within": The myth of "Judaization" in Germany. In *The Jewish Response to German Culture: From the Enlightenment to the Second World War*, ed. J. Reinharz & W. Schatzberg. Hanover and London: University Press of New England for Clark University.

———. (1976). *The Jews Under Roman and Byzantine Rule: A Political History of Palestine from the Bar Kokhba War to the Arab Conquest*. Jerusalem: Magnes Press.

———. (1984). *The Jews under Roman and Byzantine rule: A Political History from the Bar Kochba War to the Arab Conquest*. Reprint. Jerusalem: Magnes Press, Hebrew University.

Bachman, J. G. (1970). *Youth in Transition, Vol. II: The Impact of Family Background and Intelligence on Tenth-Grade Boys*. Ann Arbor: University of Michigan Institute for Social Research.

Bachrach, B. S. (1984). The Jewish community in the Later Roman Empire as seen in the *Codex Theodosianus*. In *"To See Ourselves as Others See Us": Christians, Jews, "Others" in Late Antiquity*, ed. J. Neusner & E. S. Frerichs. Chico, Calif.: Scholars Press.

Backman, M. E. (1972). Patterns of mental abilities: Ethnic, socio-economic, and sex differences. *American Educational Research Journal* 9:1-12.

Baer, Y. (1961). *A History of the Jews in Christian Spain.* Vols. I & II, trans. L. Schoffman. Philadelphia: Jewish Publication Society of America.

Balch, S. N. (1986). "The neutered civil servant": Eunuchs, abductees, and the maintenance of organizational loyalty. In *Biology and Bureaucracy: Public Administration and Public Policy from the Perspective of Evolutionary, Genetic and Neurobiological Theory,* ed. E. White & J. Losco. Lanham, Md: University Press of America.

Bamberger, B. J. ([1939] 1968). *Proselytism in the Talmudic Period.* Reprint. New York: KTAV Publishing House.

Barkow, J. (1991). *Darwin, Sex, and Status: Biological Approaches to Mind and Culture.* Toronto: University of Toronto Press.

Baroja, J. C. (1961). *Los Judios en la España Moderna y Comtemporanea.* Vol. 3. Madrid: Ediciónes Arion.

Baron, S. W. (1952a). *A Social and Religious History of the Jews. Vol. I: To the Beginning of the Christian Era.* 2nd ed. Philadelphia: The Jewish Publication Society of America.

——. (1952b). *A Social and Religious History of the Jews. Vol. II: Christian era: The First Five Centuries.* 2nd ed. Philadelphia: The Jewish Publication Society of America.

——. (1969). *A Social and Religious History of the Jews: Vol. XIII: Late Middle Ages and Era of European Expansion.* 2nd ed. Philadelphia: The Jewish Publication Society of America.

——. (1973). *A Social and Religious History of the Jews: Vol. XV: Late Middle Ages and Era of European Expansion.* 2nd ed. Philadelphia: The Jewish Publication Society of America.

Beard, M., & J. North (1990). Introduction to *Pagan Priests: Religion and Power in the Ancient World,* ed. M. Beard & J. North. Ithaca, N.Y.: Cornell University Press.

Beauvois, D. (1986). Polish-Jewish relations in the territories annexed by the Russian Empire in the first half of the nineteenth century. In *The Jews in Poland,* ed. C. Abramsky, M. Jachimczyk, & A. Polonsky. London: Basil Blackwell.

Beinart, H. (1971a). The Converso community in 15th century Spain. In *The Sephardi Heritage.* Vol. I, ed. R. D. Barnett. New York: KTAV Publishing House.

——. (1971b). The Converso community in 16th and 17th century Spain. In *The Sephardi Heritage.* Vol. I, ed. R. D. Barnett. New York: KTAV Publishing House.

——. (1981). *Conversos on Trial: The Inquisition in Cuidad Real.* Jerusalem: Magnes Press, Hebrew University.

Belsky, J., L., Steinberg, & P. Draper (1991) Childhood experience, interpersonal development, and reproductive strategy: An evolutionary theory of socialization. *Child Development* 62:647-670.

Benardete, M. J. (1953). *Hispanic Culture and Character of the Sephardic Jews.* New York: Hispanic Institute in the United States.

Bender, R. (1986). Jews in the Lublin region prior to the January uprising, 1861-1862. In *The Jews in Poland,* ed. C. Abramsky, M. Jachimczyk, & A. Polonsky. London: Basil Blackwell.

Ben-Sasson, H. H. (1971). The "Northern" European Jewish community and its ideals. In *Jewish Society Through the Ages,* ed. H. H. Ben-Sasson & S. Ettinger. New York: Schocken Books.

Bereczkei, T. (1993). r-selected reproductive strategies among Hungarian Gipsies: A Preliminary Analysis. *Ethology and Sociobiology* 14:71-88.

Berkowitz, L. (1982). Aversive conditions as stimuli to aggression. In *Advances in Experimental Social Psychology.* Vol. 15, ed. L. Berkowitz. New York: Academic Press.

Bermant, C. (1971). *The Cousinhood: The Anglo-Jewish Gentry.* London: Eyre & Spottiswoode.

Bernáldez, A. ([1898] 1962). *Historia de los Reyes Catolicos.* Reprint. Madrid: Real Academia de la Historia.

Betzig, L. (1986). *Despotism and Differential Reproduction.* New York: Aldine.

——, & P. Turke (1986). Parental investment by sex on Ifaluk. *Ethology and Sociobiology* 7:29-37.

Biale, D. (1986). Childhood marriage and the family in the Eastern European Jewish enlightenment. In *The Jewish Family: Myths and Reality*, ed. S. M. Cohen & P. E. Hyman. New York: Holmes & Meier.

Bickerman, E. J. (1984). The Diaspora: B. The Babylonian captivity. In *The Cambridge History of Judaism.* Vol. 1, ed. W. D. Davies & L. Finkelstein. Cambridge, UK: Cambridge University Press.

——. (1988). *The Jews in the Greek Age.* Cambridge: Harvard University Press.

Birnbaum, N. (1956). *The Bridge*, ed. S. Birnbaum. London: Post Publications.

Blain, J. & J. Barkow (1988). Father involvement, reproductive strategies and the sensitive period. In *Sociobiological Perspectives on Human Development*, ed. K. MacDonald. New York: Springer-Verlag.

Blalock, H. M. (1967). *Toward a Theory of Minority-Group Relations.* New York: John Wiley & Sons.

Bonné, B. (1966). The Samaritans: A demographic study. *American Journal of Human Genetics* 18:61-89.

Bonné-Tamir, B., Ashbel, S., & Kenett, R. (1977). Genetic markers: Benign and normal traits of Ashkenazi Jews. In *Genetic Diseases Among Ashkenazi Jews*, ed. R. M. Goodman & A. G. Motulsky. New York: Raven Press.

Boone, J. L. (1988). Parental investment, social subordination and population processes among the 15th and 16th century Portuguese nobility. In *Human Reproductive Behavior*, ed. L. Betzig, M. Borgerhoff Mulder, & P. Turke. New York: Cambridge University Press.

Borgerhoff Mulder, M. (1991). Human Behavioural Ecology. In *Behavioural Ecology: An Evolutionary Approach.* 3rd ed., ed. J. R. Krebs & N. B. Davies. London: Blackwell Scientific Publications.

Bourchard, C. B. (1981) Consanguinity and noble marriages in the tenth and eleventh century. *Speculum* 56:268-287.

Bowerstock, G. W. (1990). *Hellenism in Late Antiquity.* Ann Arbor: University of Michigan Press.

Boyajian, J. C. (1983). *Portuguese Bankers at the Court of Spain 1626-1650.* New Brunswick, N.J.: Rutgers University Press.

Boyarin, D. (1993). *Carnal Israel: Reading Sex in Talmudic Culture.* Berkeley: University of California Press.

Boyd, R. & P. J. Richerson (1985). *Culture and the Evolutionary Process.* Chicago: University of Chicago Press.

——, & P. J. Richerson (1992). Punishment allows the evolution of cooperation (or anything else) in sizable groups. *Ethology and Sociobiology* 13:171-195.

Bracher, K. D. (1970). *The German Dictatorship: The Origins, Structure, and Effects of National Socialism*, trans. by J. Steinberg. New York: Praeger.

Braude, W. G. (1940). *Jewish Proselytizing in the First Five Centuries of the Common Era, the Age of the Tannaim and Amoraim.* Brown University Studies, Vol VI. Providence, R.I.: Brown University Press.

Brigham, C. C. (1930). Intelligence tests in immigrant groups. *Psychological Review* 37:158-165.

Brill, M. (1936). Studies of Jewish and non-Jewish intelligence. *Journal of Educational Psychology* 27:331-352.

Bristow, E. J. (1983). *Prostitution and Prejudice: The Jewish Fight Against White Slavery, 1870-1939.* London: Oxford University Press.

Brown, F. (1944). A comparative study of the intelligence of Jewish and Scandinavian kindergarten children. *Journal of Genetic Psychology* 64:67-92.

Brown, P. (1987) Late antiquity. In *A History of Private Life*, ed. P. Veyne. Cambridge: Harvard University Press.

Brundage, J. A. (1975). Concubinage and marriage in medieval Canon law. *Journal of Medieval History* 1:1-17.

———. (1987). *Law, Sex, and Christian Society in Medieval Europe.* Chicago: University of Chicago Press.

Burg, B, & I. Belmont (1990). Mental abilities of children from different cultural backgrounds in Israel. *Journal of Cross-Cultural Psychology* 21:90-108.

Buss, D. M. (1991). Evolutionary personality psychology. *Annual Review of Psychology* 42:459-491.

Calleo, D. (1978). *The German Problem Reconsidered: Germany and the World Order, 1870 to the Present.* Cambridge: Cambridge University Press.

Carlebach, J. (1978). *Karl Marx and the Radical Critique of Judaism.* London: Routledge & Kegan Paul.

Carmelli, D., & L. L. Cavalli-Sforza (1979). The genetic origin of the Jews: A multivariate approach. *Human Biology* 51:41-61.

Castro, A. (1954). *The Structure of Spanish History*, trans. E. L. King. Princeton, N.J.: Princeton University Press.

———. (1971). *The Spaniards: An Introduction to Their History*, trans. W. F. King & S. Margaretten. Berkeley: University of California Press.

Castro, F. P. (1971). España y Judios Españoles (English summary, pp. 314-322). In *The Sephardi heritage.* Vol. I, ed. R. D. Barnett. New York: KTAV Publishing House.

Cavalli-Sforza, L. L., & D. Carmelli (1977). The Ashkenazi gene pool: Interpretations. In *Genetic Diseases Among Ashkenazi Jews*, ed. R. M. Goodman & A. G. Motulsky. New York: Raven Press.

Chagnon, N. (1983). *Yanomamo: The Fierce People.* 3rd ed. New York: Holt, Rinehart and Winston.

Chase, G. A., & V. A. McKusick (1972). Founder effect in Tay-Sachs disease. *American Journal of Human Genetics* 25:339-352.

Chazan, R. (1973). *Medieval Jewry in Northern France: A Political and Social History.* Baltimore: Johns Hopkins University Press.

Ciechanowiecki, A. (1986). A footnote to the history of the integration of converts into the ranks of the *szachta* in the Polish-Lithuanian Commonwealth. In *The Jews in Poland*, ed. C. Abramsky, M. Jachimczyk, & A. Polonsky. London: Basil Blackwell.

Cohen, Shaye (1987). *From the Maccabees to the Mishnah.* Philadelphia: Westminster Press.

Cohen, Stephen M. (1980). *Interethnic Marriage and Friendship.* New York: Arno Press.

——. (1986). Vitality and resilience in the American Jewish family. In *The Jewish Family: Myths and Reality*, ed. S. M. Cohen & P. E. Hyman. New York: Holmes & Meier.

——, & P. Ritterband (1981). Why contemporary American Jews want small families. In *Modern Jewish Fertility*, ed. P. Ritterband. Leiden: E. J. Brill.

——, & C. S. Liebman (1987). *The Quality of American Jewish Life-Two Views*. New York: The American Jewish Committee.

Collins, A. Y. (1985). Insiders and outsiders in the Book of Revelation and its social context. In *"To See Ourselves as Others See Us": Christians, Jews, "Others" in Late Antiquity*, ed. J. Neusner & E. S. Frerichs. Chico, Calif.: Scholars Press.

Collins, J. J. (1985). A symbol of otherness: Circumcision and salvation in the first century. In *"To See Ourselves as Others See Us": Christians, Jews, "Others" in Late Antiquity*, ed. J. Neusner & E. S. Frerichs. Chico, Calif.: Scholars Press.

Corbin, A. (1990) Intimate relations. In *A History of Private Life, Vol. IV. From the Fires of the Revolution to the Great War*, ed. M. Perrot. Cambridge: Harvard University Press.

Costa, P., & R. McCrae (1980). Influence of extraversion and neuroticism on subjective well-being. *Journal of Personality and Social Psychology* 38:668-678.

——, & R. McCrae (1985). *The NEO Personality Inventory Manual*. Odessa, Fla.: Psychological Assessment Resources, Inc.

——, & R. McCrae (1992). *The Revised NEO Personality Inventory*. Odessa, Fla: Psychological Assessment Resources, Inc.

Crespo, V. P. (1987). Thought control in Spain. In *Inquisition and Society in Early Modern Europe*, ed. S. Haliczer. Totowa, N.J.: Barnes & Noble.

Crossan, J. D. (1991). *The Historical Jesus: The Life of a Mediterranean Jewish Peasant*. San Francisco: HarperSanFrancisco.

Dandamayev, M. (1984). The Diaspora: A. Babylonians in the Persian Age. In *The Cambridge History of Judaism*. Vol. 1, ed. W. D. Davies & L. Finkelstein. Cambridge: Cambridge University Press.

Danzger, H. M. (1989). *Returning to Tradition: The Contemporary Revival of Orthodox Judaism*. New Haven, Conn.: Yale University Press.

Darwin, C. (1871). *The Descent of Man and Selection in Relation to Sex*. New York: Freeman.

Davidson, N. (1987). The inquisition and the Italian Jews. In *Inquisition and Society in Early Modern Europe*, trans. and ed. S. Haliczer. Totowa, NJ: Barnes & Noble.

Davies, M. & A. G. Hughes (1927). An investigation into the comparative intelligence and attainments of Jewish and non-Jewish school children. *British Journal of Psychology* 18:134-146.

DellaPergola, S. (1986). Contemporary Jewish family patterns in France: A comparative perspective. In *The Jewish Family: Myths and Reality*, ed. S. M. Cohen & P. E. Hyman. New York: Holmes & Meier.

Deshen, S. (1986). The Jewish family in traditional Morocco. In *The Jewish Family: Myths and Reality*, ed. S. M. Cohen & P. E. Hyman. New York: Holmes & Meier.

Dickemann, M. (1979). Female infanticide, reproductive strategies, and social stratification: A preliminary model. In *Evolutionary Biology and Human Social Behavior*, ed. N. A. Chagnon & W. Irons. North Scituate, Mass.: Duxbury Press.

Dickemann, M. (1981). Paternal confidence and dowry competition: A biocultural analysis of purdah. In *Natural Selection and Social Behavior: Recent Research and New Theory*, ed. R. D. Alexander & D. W. Tinkle. New York: Chiron Press.

Digman, J. M. (1990). Personality structure: Emergence of the five-factor model. *Annual Review of Psychology* 41:417-440.

——, & J. Inouye (1986). Further specification of the five robust factors of personality. *Journal of Personality and Social Psychology* 50:116-123.

——, & N. K. Takemoto-Chock (1981). Factors in the natural language of personality: Re-analysis, comparison, and interpretation of six major studies. *Multivariate Behavioral Research* 16:149-170.

Dinnerstein, L. (1991). Anti-Semitism in crisis times in the United States: The 1920's and 1930's. In *Anti-Semitism in Times of Crisis*, ed. S. L. Gilman & S. T. Katz. New York: New York University Press.

Dobrosyzcki, L. (1981). The fertility of modern Polish Jewry. In *Modern Jewish Fertility*, ed. P. Ritterband. Leiden: E. J. Brill.

Duby, G. (1978). *Medieval Marriage*. Baltimore: Johns Hopkins University Press.

——. (1983). *The Knight, the Lady, and the Priest*, trans. B. Bray. New York: Penguin Books.

Eichorn, D. M. (1965a). Introduction to *Conversion to Judaism: A History and Analysis*, ed. D. M. Eichorn. New York: KTAV Publishing House.

——. (1965b). From expulsion to liberation. In *Conversion to Judaism: A History and Analysis*, ed. D. M. Eichorn. New York: KTAV Publishing House.

Eksteins, M. (1975). *The Limits of Reason: The German Democratic Press and the Collapse of Weimar Democracy*. New York: Oxford University Press.

Elazar, D. J. ([1976] 1980). *Community and Polity: Organizational Dynamics of American Jewry*. Reprint. Philadelphia: Jewish Publication Society of America.

Eldridge, R. (1970). The torsion dystonias: Literature review and genetic and clinical studies. *Neurology* 20:1-78.

——, & T. Koerber (1977). Torsion dystonia: Autosomal recessive form. In *Genetic Diseases among Ashkenazi Jews*, ed. R. M. Goodman & A. G. Motulsky. New York: Raven Press.

Ellman, Y. (1987). Intermarriage in the United States: A comparative study of Jews and other ethnic and religious groups. *Jewish Social Studies* 49:1-26.

Endelman, T. M. (1991). The legitimization of the diaspora experience in recent Jewish historiography. *Modern Judaism* 11:195-209.

Engel, D. (1986). Patriotism as a shield: The liberal Jewish defence against anti-Semitism in Germany during the First World War. *Leo Baeck Institute Yearbook* XXXI:147-171.

Epstein, L. M. (1942). *Marriage Laws in the Bible and the Talmud*. Cambridge: Harvard University Press.

Etkes, I. (1989). Marriage and Torah study among the *Lomdim* in Lithuania in the nineteenth century. In *The Jewish Family*, ed. D. Kraemer. New York: Oxford University Press.

Feldman, L. H. (1993). *Jew and Gentile in the Ancient World: Attitudes and Interactions from Alexander to Justinian*. Princeton, N.J.: Princeton University Press.

Feldman, W. M. (1939). Ancient Jewish eugenics. *Medical Leaves* II: 28-37.

Finkelstein, L. (1924). *Jewish Self-Government in the Middle Ages*. Westport, CT: Greenwood Press.

——. (1962). *The Pharisees: The Sociological Background of Their Faith*. 3d ed., 2 vols. Philadelphia: Jewish Publication Society of America.

Fischel, W. J. ([1937] 1968). *Jews in the Economic and Political Life of Medieval Islam*. Reprint. London: Royal Asiatic Society for Great Britain and Ireland.

Fishberg, M. (1911). *The Jews: A Study of Race and Environment*. New York: W. Scott.

Flaceliére, R. (1962). *Love in Ancient Greece.* New York: Crown Publishers.

Fohrer, G. (1968). *Introduction to the Old Testament,* trans. D. E. Green. Nashville: Abingdon Press.

Fraikor, A. L. (1977). Tay-Sachs disease: Genetic drift among the Ashkenazi Jews. *Social Biology* 24:117-134.

Frank, R. (1973). Marriage in 12th and 13th century Iceland. *Viator 4:*473-484.

Freud, S. ([1931] 1985). *The Interpretation of Dreams,* trans. D. Brill. Cutchogue, N.Y.: Buccaneer Books.

Friedman, M. A. (1989). Marriage as an institution: Jewry under Islam. In *The Jewish Family,* ed. D. Kraemer. New York: Oxford University Press.

Gabba, E. (1989). The growth of anti-Judaism or the Greek attitude toward the Jews. In *The Cambridge History of Judaism.* Vol. 2, ed. W. D. Davies & L. Finkelstein. Cambridge: Cambridge University Press.

Gafni, I. M. (1989). The institution of marriage in rabbinic times. In *The Jewish Family,* ed. D. Kraemer. New York: Oxford University Press.

Gager, J. G. (1983). *The Origins of Anti-Semitism: Attitudes Toward Judaism in Pagan and Christian Antiquity.* New York: Oxford University Press.

Gampel. B. R. (1989). *The Last Jews on Iberian Soil: Navarrese Jewry 1479-1498.* Berkeley: University of California Press.

Gardner, J. F. (1986). *Women in Roman Law and Society.* Bloomington: Indiana University Press.

Garnsey, P., & R. Saller (1987). *The Roman Empire.* Berkeley: The University of California Press.

Gay, P. (1988). *Freud: A Life For Our Time.* New York: W. W. Norton.

Geary, P. J. (1988). *Before France and Germany: The Creation and Transformation of the Merovingian World.* New York: Oxford University Press.

Gershon, E. S., & J. H. Liebowitz (1977). Affective illness. In *Genetic Diseases Among Ashkenazi Jews,* ed. R. M. Goodman & A. G. Motulsky. New York: Raven Press.

Gilchrist, J. (1969). *The Church and Economic Policy in the Middle Ages.* New York: St. Martin's Press.

Gilman, S. L. (1986). *Jewish Self-Hatred: Anti-Semitism and the Hidden Language of Jews.* Baltimore: Johns Hopkins University Press.

————. (1993). *Freud, Race, and Gender.* Princeton, N.J.: Princeton University Press.

Gilson, E. (1962). *The Philosopher and Theology.* New York: Random House.

Ginsberg, B. (1993). *The Fatal Embrace: Jews and the State.* Chicago: University of Chicago Press.

Gitelman, Z. (1981). Correlates, causes, and consequences of Jewish fertility in the USSR. In *Modern Jewish Fertility,* ed. P. Ritterband. Leiden: E. J. Brill.

————. (1991). The evolution of Jewish culture and identity in the Soviet Union. In *Jewish Culture and Identity in the Soviet Union,* ed. Y. Ro'i & A. Beker. New York: New York University Press.

Gobineau, Count Arthur de ([1854] 1915). *The Inequality of Human Races,* trans. A. Collins. Reprint. London: William Heinemann.

Goitein, S. D. (1971). *A Mediterranean Society. Vol. II: The Community.* Berkeley: University of California Press.

————. (1974). *Jews and Arabs: Their Contacts through the Ages.* 3rd ed.. New York: Schocken Books.

————. (1978). *A Mediterranean Society. Vol. III: The Family.* Berkeley: University of California Press.

Golczewski, F. (1986). Rural anti-semitism in Galicia before World War I. In *The Jews in Poland*, ed. C. Abramsky, M. Jachimczyk, & A. Polonsky. London: Basil Blackwell.

Goldberg, J. (1986). The privileges granted to Jewish communities of the Polish Commonwealth as a stabilizing factor in Jewish support. In *The Jews in Poland*, ed. C. Abramsky, M. Jachimczyk, & A. Polonsky. London: Basil Blackwell.

Goldberg, L. R. (1981). Language and individual differences: The search for universals in personal lexicons. *Review of Personality and Social Psychology* 2:141-166. Beverly Hills, Calif.: Sage Publications.

Goldman, I. M. (1975). *Lifelong Learning Among Jews*. New York: KTAV Publishing House, Inc.

Goldscheider, C. (1986). Family change and variation among Israeli ethnic groups. In *The Jewish Family: Myths and Reality*, ed. S. M. Cohen & P. E. Hyman. New York: Holmes & Meier.

———, & Ritterband, D. (1981). Patterns of Jewish fertility in Israel: A review and some hypotheses. In *Modern Jewish Fertility*, ed. P. Ritterband. Leiden: E. J. Brill.

Goldschmidt, E., A. Ronen, & I. Ronen (1960). Changing marriage systems in the Jewish communities of Israel. *Annals of Human Genetics* 24:191-197.

Goldstein, Alice (1981). Some demographic characteristics of village Jews in Germany: Nonnenweier, 1800-1931. In *Modern Jewish Fertility*, ed. P. Ritterband. Leiden: E. J. Brill.

Goldstein, A. S. (1965). Conversion to Judaism in Bible times. In *Conversion to Judaism: A History and Analysis*, ed. D. M. Eichorn. New York: KTAV Publishing House.

Goldstein, S. (1969). Socioeconomic differentials among religious groups in the United States. *American Journal of Sociology* 74:612-631.

———. (1974). American Jewry: A demographic analysis. In *The Future of the Jewish Community in America*, ed. D. Sidorsky. Philadelphia: Jewish Publication Society of America.

———. (1981). Jewish fertility in contemporary America. In *Modern Jewish fertility*, ed. P. Ritterband. Leiden: E. J. Brill.

Goodman, M. (1989). Proselytizing in rabbinic Judaism. *Journal of Jewish Studies* 40:175-185.

Goodman, R. M. (1979). *Genetic Disorders Among the Jewish People*. Baltimore: Johns Hopkins University Press.

Goody, J. (1983). *The Development of the Family and Marriage in Europe*. Cambridge: Cambridge University Press.

Gordon, S. (1984). *Hitler, Germans, and the "Jewish Question."* Princeton, N.J.: Princeton University Press.

Graetz, H. ([1898] 1967). *History of the Jews*, 6 vol., abridged, trans. P. Bloch. Reprint. Philadelphia: Jewish Publication Society of America.

Grant, M. (1973). *The Jews in the Roman World*. New York: Charles Scribner's Sons.

Grossman, A. (1989). From father to son: The inheritance of spiritual leadership in Jewish communities of the Middle Ages. In *The Jewish Family*, ed. D. Kraemer. New York: Oxford University Press.

Gunneweg, A. H. J. (1978). *Understanding the Old Testament*, trans. J. Bowden. Philadelphia: Westminster Press.

Gutman, Y. (1986). Polish and Jewish historiography on the question of Polish-Jewish relations during World War II. In *The Jews in Poland*, ed. C. Abramsky, M. Jachimczyk, & A. Polonsky. London: Basil Blackwell.

Guttentag, M., & P. F. Secord (1983). *Too Many Women: The Sex Ratio Question.* Beverly Hills, Calif.: Sage Publications.

Haliczer, S. (1987). The first holocaust. In *Inquisition and Society in Early Modern Europe*, trans. and ed. S. Haliczer. Totowa, NJ: Barnes & Noble.

———. (1990). *Inquisition and Society in the Kingdom of Valencia 1478-1834.* Berkeley: University of California Press.

Halverson, C. F. Jr., & M. F. Waldrop (1970). Maternal behavior toward own and other preschool children. *Developmental Psychology* 12:107-112.

Hamilton, W. D. (1964). The genetical theory of social behaviour, I, II. *Journal of Theoretical Biology* 7:1-52.

Hammond, N. J. L. (1986). *A History of Greece to 322 B.C.* Oxford, England: Clarendon Press.

Hanawalt, B. (1986). *The Ties That Bound: Peasant Families in Medieval England.* New York: Oxford University Press.

Harlap, S. (1979). Gender of infants conceived on different days of the menstrual cycle. *New England Journal of Medicine* 30:1445-1448.

Harter, S. (1983). Developmental perspectives on the self-system. In *Handbook of Child Psychology: Socialization, Personality and Social Development.* Vol. 4, ed. E. M. Hetherington. New York: Wiley.

Hartung, J. (1992). The Torah, Talmud, and Maimonides on rape. Paper presented at the meeting of the Human Behavior and Evolution Society, Abuquerque, N. M., July 25.

———. (n.d.). *Thou Shalt Not Kill Who?—An Inquiry into the Moral Code of Judeo-Christianity.* Forthcoming.

Hegermann, H. (1989). The Diaspora in the Hellenistic age. In *The Cambridge History of Judaism.* Vol. 2, ed. W. D. Davies & L. Finkelstein. Cambridge: Cambridge University Press.

Heilman, S. (1976). *Synagogue Life.* Chicago: University of Chicago Press.

———. (1992). *Defenders of the Faith: Inside Ultra-Orthodox Judaism.* New York: Schocken Books.

Hengel, M. (1989). The interpenetration of Judaism and Hellenism in the pre-Maccabean period. In *The Cambridge History of Judaism.* Vol. 2, ed. W. D. Davies & L. Finkelstein. Cambridge: Cambridge University Press.

Herlihy, D. (1985). *Medieval Households.* Cambridge: Harvard University Press.

———. (1991). Biology and History: Some suggestions for a dialogue. Brown University. Unpublished manuscript.

———, & C. Klapische-Zuber (1985). *Tuscans and Their Families.* New Haven, Conn.: Yale University Press.

Hertzberg, A. (1969). *The Zionist Idea: A Historical Analysis and Reader.* New York: Atheneum.

———. (1979). *Being Jewish in America.* New York: Schocken Books.

———. (1993a). Is anti-Semitism dying out? *New York Review of Books* XL(12):51-57.

———. (1993b). Letter. *New York Review of Books* XL(15):68-69.

Herz, F. M., & E. J. Rosen (1982). Jewish families. In *Ethnicity and Family Therapy*, ed. M. McGoldrick, J. K. Pearce, & J. Giordano. New York: The Guilford Press.

Herzl. T. ([1896] 1988). *The Jewish State*, trans. J. M. Alkow. Reprint. New York: Dover Publications.

Hess, M. ([1918] 1943). *Rome and Jerusalem: A Study in Jewish Nationalism*, trans. M. Waxman. Reprint. New York: Bloch Publishing Company.

Hilberg, R. (1979). *The Destruction of the European Jews.* New York: Harper Colophon.

Hill, J. E. C. (1967). *Society and Puritanism in Pre-Revolutionary England.* 2nd ed. New York: Schocken Books.

Hill, K. & H. Kaplan (1988). Tradeoffs in male and female reproductive strategies among the Ache: Parts 1 & 2. In *Human Reproductive Behavior: A Darwinian Perspective,* ed. L. Betzig, M. Borgerhoff Mulder, & P. Turke. New York: Cambridge University Press.

Hillgarth, J. N. (1976). *The Spanish Kingdoms, 1250-1516, Vol. I, 1250-1410.* Oxford, England: Clarendon Press.

———. (1978). *The Spanish Kingdoms, 1250-1516, Vol. II, 1410-1516.* Oxford, England: Clarendon Press.

Hodges, W. F., R. C. Wechsler, & C. Ballantine (1979). Divorce and the preschool child: Cumulative stress. *Journal of Divorce* 3:55-67.

Hogg, M. A., & D. Abrams (1987). *Social Identifications.* New York: Routledge.

Hooker, J. T. (1980). *The Ancient Spartans.* London: Dent.

Hostetler, J. A. (1992). An Amish beginning. *American Scholar* 61:552-562.

Howe, I. (1976). *The World of Our Fathers.* New York: Harcourt Brace Jovanovich.

Hughes, A. G. (1928). Jews and gentiles: Their intellectual and temperamental differences. *Eugenics Review* (July):89-94.

Hundert, G. D. (1986a). The implications of Jewish economic activities for Christian-Jewish relations in the Polish Commonwealth. In *The Jews in Poland,* ed. C. Abramsky, M. Jachimczyk, & A. Polonsky. London: Basil Blackwell.

———. (1986b). Approaches to the history of the Jewish family in early modern Poland-Lithuania. In *The Jewish Family: Myths and Reality,* ed. S. M. Cohen & P. E. Hyman. New York: Holmes & Meier.

———. (1989). Jewish childhood and adolescence in Talmudic literature. In *The Jewish Family,* ed. D. Kraemer. New York: Oxford University Press.

———. (1992). *The Jews in a Polish Private Town: The Case of Opatow in the Eighteenth Century.* Baltimore, Md.: Johns Hopkins University Press.

Hyman, P. E. (1981). Jewish fertility in nineteenth century France. In *Modern Jewish Fertility,* ed. P. Ritterband. Leiden: E. J. Brill.

———. (1986a). Introduction: Perspectives on the evolving Jewish family. In *The Jewish Family: Myths and Reality,* ed. S. M. Cohen & P. E. Hyman. New York: Holmes & Meier.

———. (1986b). Afterword to *The Jewish Family: Myths and Reality,* ed. S. M. Cohen & P. E. Hyman. New York: Holmes & Meier.

———. (1989). The modern Jewish family: Image and reality. In *The Jewish Family,* ed. D. Kraemer. New York: Oxford University Press.

Irons, W. (1979). Cultural and biological success. In *Evolutionary Biology and Human Social Behavior,* ed. N. A. Chagnon & W. Irons. North Scituate, Mass: Duxbury Press.

———. (1983). Human female reproductive strategies. In *Social Behavior of Female Vertebrates,* ed. S. K. Wasser. New York: Academic Press.

———. (1992). Niche homogeneity and reproductive competition. Paper presented at the meeting of the Human Behavior and Evolution Society, Albuquerque, N.M., July 26.

Israel, J. I. (1985). *European Jewry in the Age of Mercantilism.* Oxford, England: Clarendon Press.

Itzkoff, S. W. (1993). Orthoselection and the corticalization of behavior. *Mankind Quarterly* 33:283-293.

James, W. H. (1987a). The human sex ratio. Part I: A review of the literature. *Human Biology* 59:721-752.

———. (1987b). The human sex ratio. Part II: A hypothesis and a program of research. *Human Biology* 59:873-900.

Jeremias, J. (1969). *Jerusalem in the Time of Jesus: An Investigation into Economic and Social Conditions During the New Testament Period*, trans. F. H. Cave & C. H. Cave (based on an earlier draft of a translation by M. E. Dahl). Philadelphia: Fortress Press.

Johnson, G. (1986). Kin selection, socialization, and patriotism: An integrating theory. *Politics and the Life Sciences* 4:127-154.

Johnson, P. (1987). *A History of the Jews*. New York: Harper & Row.

Jones, A. H. M. (1964). *The Later Roman Empire 284-602: A Social, Economic and Administrative Survey*. 2 vols. Norman: University of Oklahoma Press.

———. (1967). *Sparta*. Oxford: Basil Blackwell.

Jordan, W. C. (1989). *The French Monarchy and the Jews: From Philip Augustus to the Last Capetians*. Philadelphia: University of Pennsylvania Press.

Kallen, H. M. (1915). Democracy versus the melting pot. *Nation* 100 (18 and 25 February):190-194; 217-220.

———. (1924). *Culture and Democracy in the United States*. New York: Arno Press

Kamen, H. (1965). *The Spanish Inquisition*. New York: New American Library.

———. (1985). *Inquisition and Society in Spain in the Sixteenth and Seventeenth Centuries*. Bloomington: Indiana University Press.

Kamen, R. M. (1985). *Growing Up Hasidic: Education and Socialization in the Hasidic Community*. New York: AMS Press.

Kanarfogel, E. (1992). *Jewish Education and Society in the High Middle Ages*. Detroit: Wayne State University Press.

Kaniel, S., & S. Fisherman (1991). Level of performance and distribution of errors in the Progressive Matrices Test: A comparison of Ethiopian immigrant and native Israeli adolescents. *International Journal of Psychology* 26:25-33.

Kaplan, Marion A. (1983). For love or money: The marriage strategies of Jews in Imperial Germany. *Leo Baeck Institute Yearbook* XXVIII:263-300.

———. (1986). Women and tradition in the German-Jewish family. In *The Jewish Family: Myths and Reality*, ed. S. M. Cohen & P. E. Hyman. New York: Holmes & Meier.

Kaplan, Mordecai ([1934] 1967). *Judaism as a Civilization*. Reprint. New York: Schocken Books.

Karlin, S., R. Kenett, & B. Bonné-Tamir (1979). Analysis of biochemical genetic data on Jewish populations II. Results and interpretations of heterogeneity indices and distance measures with respect to standards. *American Journal of Human Genetics* 31:341-365.

Katz, J. (1961a). *Tradition and Crisis: Jewish Society at the End of the Middle Ages*. New York: The Free Press of Glencoe.

———. (1961b). *Exclusiveness and Tolerance*. Oxford: Oxford University Press.

———. (1973). *Out of the Ghetto: The Social Background of Jewish Emancipation, 1770-1870*. Cambridge: Harvard University Press.

———. (1985). German culture and the Jews. In *The Jewish Response to German Culture: From the Enlightenment to the Second World War*, ed. J. Reinharz & W. Schatzberg. Hanover, N.H.: University Press of New England for Clark University.

———. (1986). *Jewish Emancipation and Self-Emancipation*. Philadelphia: Jewish Publication Society of America.

Kieniewicz, S. (1986). Polish society and the Jewish problem in the nineteenth century. In *The Jews in Poland*, ed. C. Abramsky, M. Jachimczyk, & A. Polonsky. London: Basil Blackwell.

Klier, J. D. (1986). *Russia Gathers Her Jews: The Origins of the "Jewish Question" in Russia.* DeKalb: Northern Illinois University Press.

Knode, J. (1974). *The Decline in Fertility in Germany, 1871-1979.* Princeton, N.J.: Princeton University Press.

Kobyliansky, E., & G. A. Livshits (1985). morphological approach to the problem of the biological similarity of Jewish and non-Jewish populations. *Annals of Human Biology* 12:203-212.

———, E., S. Micle, M. Goldschmidt-Nathan, B. Arensburg, & H. Nathan (1982). Jewish populations of the world: Genetic likeness and differences. *Annals of Human Biology* 9:1-34.

Kosmin, B. A., S. Goldstein, J. Waksberg, N. Lerer, A. Keysar, & J. Scheckner (1991). *Highlights of the CJF 1990 National Jewish Population Survey.* New York: Council of Jewish Federations.

Kohler, K. ([1918] 1968). *Jewish Theology.* Reprint. New York: KTAV Publishing House.

Kotkin, J. (1993). *Tribes: How Race, Religion and Identity Determine Success in the New Global Economy.* New York: Random House.

Kraabel, A. T. (1982). The Roman diaspora: Six questionable assumptions. *Journal of Jewish Studies* 33:445-464.

Kraemer, D. (1989). Images of childhood and adolescence in Talmudic literature. In *The Jewish Family*, ed. D. Kraemer. New York: Oxford University Press.

Krebs, D. L. (1970). Altruism: An examination of the concept and a review of the literature. *Psychological Bulletin* 73:258-302.

———, K. Denton, & N. C. Higgins (1988). On the evolution of self-knowledge and self-deception. In *Sociobiological Perspectives on Human Development*, ed. K. B. MacDonald. New York: Springer-Verlag.

Kroll, J., & B. S. Bachrach (1990). Medieval dynastic decisions: Evolutionary biology and historical explanation. *Journal of Interdisciplinary History* 23:1-28.

Kuhrt, A. (1990). Nabonidus and the Babylonian priesthood. In *Pagan Priests: Religion and Power in the Ancient World*, ed. M. Beard & J. North. Ithaca, N.Y.: Cornell University Press.

Lacey, W. K. (1968). *The Family in Classical Greece.* Ithaca, N.Y.: Cornell University Press.

Ladurie, E. L. ([1977] 1986). *The French Peasantry 1450-1660*, trans. A. Sheridan. Berkeley: University of California Press.

Landau, D. (1993). *Piety and Power: The World of Jewish Fundamentalism.* New York: Hill and Wang.

Laqueur, W. (1974). *Weimar: A Cultural History 1918-1933.* London: Weidenfeld and Nicolson.

Larsen, R. J., & E. Diener (1987). Affect intensity as an individual difference characteristic: A review. *Journal of Research in Personality* 21:1-39.

Laslett, P. (1983). Family and household as work group and kin group: areas of traditional Europe compared. In *Family Forms in Historic Europe*, ed. R. Wall, J. Robin, & P. Laslett. New York: Cambridge University Press.

Lea, C. H. ([1906-07] 1966). *History of the Inquisition of Spain.* 4 Vols. Reprint. New York: American Scholar Publications.

Lenz, F. (1931). The inheritance of intellectual gifts. In *Human Heredity*, trans. E. Paul & C. Paul, ed. E. Baur, E. Fischer, & F. Lenz. New York: Macmillan.

Leon, H. J. (1960). *The Jews of Ancient Rome*. Philadelphia: Jewish Publication Society.

Leroy, B. (1985). *The Jews of Navarre*. Jerusalem: Magnes Press, Hebrew University.

Lesser, G. S., G. Fifer, & D. H. Clark (1965). Mental abilities of children from different social-class and cultural groups. *Monographs of the Society for Research in Child Development.* Ser. no. 102, vol. 30, no. 4.

Levav, L., R. Kohn, B. P. Dohrenwend, P. E. Shrout, A. E. Skodel, S. Schwartz, B. G. Link, & G. Naveh (1993). An epidemiological study of mental disorders in a 10-year cohort of young adults in Israel. *Psychological Medicine* 23:691-707.

Levenson, A. (1989). Reform attitudes, in the past, toward intermarriage. *Judaism* 38:320-332.

Levin, N. (1977). *While Messiah Tarried: Jewish Socialist Movements, 1871-1917*. New York: Schocken Books.

LeVine, R. A., & D. T. Campbell (1972). *Ethnocentrism: Theories of Conflict Resolution*. New York: Wiley.

Levinson, B. M. (1957). The intelligence of applicants for admission to Jewish day schools. *Jewish Social Studies* 19:129-140.

———. (1958). Cultural pressure and *WAIS* scatter in a traditional Jewish setting. *Journal of Genetic Psychology* 93:277-286.

———. (1959). Traditional Jewish cultural values and performance on the Wechsler tests. *Journal of Educational Psychology* 50:177-181.

———. (1960). A comparative study of the verbal and performance ability of monolingual and bilingual native born Jewish preschool children of traditional parentage. *Journal of Genetic Psychology* 97:93-112.

———. (1962). Jewish subculture and WAIS performance among Jewish aged. *Journal of Genetic Psychology* 100:55-68.

Lewis, B. (1984). *The Jews of Islam*. Princeton, N.J.: Princeton University Press.

Lichten, J. (1986). Notes on the assimilation and acculturation of Jews in Poland, 1863-1943. In *The Jews in Poland*, ed. C. Abramsky, M. Jachimczyk, & A. Polonsky. London: Basil Blackwell.

Liebman, A. (1979). *Jews and the Left*. New York: John Wiley & Sons.

Liebman, C. (1973). *The Ambivalent American Jew: Politics, Religion, and Family in American Jewish Life*. Philadelphia: Jewish Publication Society of America.

Lindemann, A. S. (1991). *The Jew Accused: Three Anti-Semitic Affairs (Dreyfus, Beilis, Frank) 1894-1915*. New York: Cambridge University Press.

Litman, J. (1984). *The Economic Role of Jews in Medieval Poland: The Contribution of Yitzhak Schipper*. Lanham, Md.: University Press of America.

Longhurst, J. E. (1964). *The Age of Torquemada*. 2nd ed. Lawrence, Kan.: Coronado Press.

Lowenstein, S. M. (1981). Involuntary limitation of fertility in nineteenth century Bavarian Jewry. In *Modern Jewish Fertility*, ed. P. Ritterband. Leiden: E. J. Brill.

———. (1983). Jewish residential concentration in post-emancipation Germany. *Leo Baeck Institute Yearbook* XXVIII:471-495.

———. (1989). *Frankfurt on the Hudson: The German-Jewish Community of Washington Heights, 1933-1983, Its Structure and Culture*. Detroit: Wayne State University Press.

Lusk, J., K. B. MacDonald, & J. R. Newman (1993). Resource appraisals among self, friend and leader: Toward an evolutionary perspective on personality and individual differences. Paper presented at the meeting of the Human Behavior and Evolution Society, Binghamton, N.Y., August 7.

Lynn, R. (1987). The intelligence of the Mongoloids: A psychometric, evolutionary and neurological theory. *Personality and Individual Differences* 8:813-844.

——. (1991). Race differences in intelligence: A global perspective. *Mankind Quarterly* 31:255-296.

——. (1992). Intelligence: Ethnicity and culture. In *Cultural Diversity and the Schools*, ed. J. Lynch, C. Modgil, & S. Modgil. London and Washington, D.C.: Falmer Press.

Maccoby, H. (1982). *Judaism on Trial: Jewish-Christian Disputations in the Middle Ages.* Rutherford, N.J.: Fairleigh Dickinson University.

MacDonald, K. B. (1983). Production, social controls and ideology: Toward a sociobiology of the phenotype. *Journal of Social and Biological Structures* 6:297-317.

——. (1984). An ethological-social learning theory of the development of altruism: Implications for human sociobiology. *Ethology and Sociobiology* 5:97-109.

——. (1985). Early experience, relative plasticity and social development. *Developmental Review* 5:99-121.

——. (1986a). *Civilization and Its Discontents* revisited: Freud as an evolutionary biologist. *Journal of Social and Biological Structures* 9:213-220.

——. (1986b). Biological and cultural interactions in early adolescence: A sociobiological perspective. In *Biological-Psychosocial Interactions in Early Adolescence: A Life-Span Perspective*, ed. R. Lerner & T. Foch. Hillsdale, N.J.: Erlbaum.

——. (1986c). Early experience, relative plasticity and cognitive development. *Journal of Applied Developmental Psychology* 7:101-124.

——. (1986d). Developmental models and early experience. *International Journal of Behavioral Development* 9:175-190.

——. (1988a). *Social and Personality Development: An Evolutionary Synthesis.* New York: Plenum.

——. (1988b). The interfaces between sociobiology and developmental psychology. In *Sociobiological Perspectives on Human Development*, ed. K. B. MacDonald. New York: Springer-Verlag.

——. (1989). The plasticity of human social organization and behavior: Contextual variables and proximal mechanisms. *Ethology and Sociobiology* 10:171-194.

——. (1990). Mechanisms of sexual egalitarianism in Western Europe. *Ethology and Sociobiology* 11:195-238.

——. (1991). A perspective on Darwinian psychology: Domain-general mechanisms, plasticity, and individual differences. *Ethology and Sociobiology* 12:449-480.

——. (1992a). Warmth as a developmental construct: An evolutionary analysis. *Child Development* 63:753-773.

——. (1992b). A time and a place for everything: A discrete systems perspective on the role of children's rough and tumble play in educational settings. *Early Education and Development* 3:334-355.

——. (1993). Parent-child play: An evolutionary analysis. In *Parent-child Play: Descriptions and Implications*, ed. K. B. MacDonald. Albany, N.Y.: State University of New York Press.

——. (1994). Group evolutionary strategies: Dimensions and mechanisms. *Behavioral and Brain Sciences, 17*(4). Forthcoming.

———. (1995). *Separation and Its Discontents: Toward an Evolutionary Theory of Anti-Semitism*. Westport, Conn.: Praeger. Forthcoming. (Cited in the text as *SAID*.)

———. (n.d.). Evolution, the Five Factor Model, and Levels of Personality. *Journal of Personality*. Forthcoming.

———. (n.d.). The Establishment and Maintenance of Socially Imposed Monogamy in Western Europe. Under submission.

MacFarlane, A. (1986). *Marriage and Love in England: Modes of Reproduction 1300-1840*. London: Basil Blackwell.

MacMullen, R. (1969). *Constantine*. New York: The Dial Press.

Magnus, L. (1907). *Religio Laici Judaici*. New York: Bloch Publishing Co.

Maller, N. (1948). Studies in the intelligence of young Jews. *Jewish Education* 2:29-39.

Marcus. J. (1983). *Social and Political History of the Jews in Poland, 1919-1939*. Berlin: Moulton Publishers.

Margalit, A. (1993). Prophets with honor. *New York Review of Books* XL(18):66-71.

Massing, P. W. (1949). *Rehearsal for Destruction: A Study of Political Anti-Semitism in Imperial Germany*. Publication no. II of The American Jewish Committee Social Studies Series. New York: Harper & Brothers.

Mayer, E. (1979). *From Suburb to Shtetl: The Jews of Boro Park*. Philadelphia: Temple University Press.

McCullough, W. S. (1975). *The History and Literature of the Palestinian Jews from Cyrus to Herod*. Toronto: University of Toronto Press.

McDonald, A. H. (1966). *Republican Rome*. New York: Praeger.

McGrath, W. J. (1974). Freud as Hannibal: The politics of the brother band. *Central European History* 7:31-57.

McKnight, S. (1991). *A Light Among the Gentiles: Jewish Missionary Activity in the Second Temple Period*. Minneapolis: Fortress Press.

Mealey, L., & W. Mackey (1990). Variation in offspring sex ratio in women of differing social status. *Ethology and Sociobiology* 11:83-96.

Memmi, A. (1966). *The Liberation of the Jew*. New York: Orion Press.

Meyer, M. A. (1988). *Response to Modernity: A History of the Reform Movement in Judaism*. New York: Oxford University Press.

Mille, S., & Kobyliansky, E. (1985). Dermatoglyphic distances between Israeli Jewish population groups of different geographic extraction. *Human Biology* 57: 97-111.

Mintz, J. R. (1992). *Hasidic People: A Place in the New World*. Cambridge: Harvard University Press.

Mishkinsky, M. (1968). The Jewish labor movement and European socialism. *Cahiers d'Histoire Mondiale* 11:284-296.

Mitterauer, M. (1991). Christianity and endogamy. *Continuity and Change* 6:295-333.

Money, J. (1980). *Love, and Love Sickness: The Science of Sex, Gender Differences, and Pair Bonding*. Baltimore: Johns Hopkins University Press.

Moore, G. F. (1927-30). *Judaism in the First Centuries of the Christian Era: The Age of the Tannaim*. 2 vols. Cambridge: Harvard University Press.

Morton, F. (1961). *The Rothschilds*. New York: Atheneum.

Mosse, G. (1985). Jewish emancipation: Between *Bildung* and respectability. In *The Jewish Response to German Culture: From the Enlightenment to the Second World War*, ed. J. Reinharz & W. Schatzberg. Hanover, N.H.: University Press of New England for Clark University.

Mosse, W. E. (1985). Wilhelm II and the *Kaiserjuden*: A problematical encounter. In *The Jewish Response to German Culture: From the Enlightenment to the Second*

*World War*, ed. J. Reinharz & W. Schatzberg. Hanover, N.H.: University Press of New England for Clark University.

——. (1987). *Jews in the German Economy: The German-Jewish Economic Élite 1820-1935.* Oxford, England: Clarendon Press.

Motulsky, A. G. (1977a). Possible selective effects of urbanization on Ashkenazi Jews. In *Genetic Diseases Among Ashkenazi Jews*, ed. R. M. Goodman & A. G. Motulsky. New York: Raven Press.

——. (1977b). Epilogue to *Genetic Diseases Among Ashkenazi Jews*, ed. R. M. Goodman & A. G. Motulsky. New York: Raven Press.

Mourant, A. E., A. C. Kopec, & K. Domaniewska-Sobczak (1978). *The Genetics of the Jews.* Oxford, England: Clarendon Press.

Muhlstein, A. (1981). *Baron James.* New York: Vendome Press

Nardi, N. (1948). Studies in the intelligence of Jewish children. *Jewish Education* 19:41-51.

Neuman, A. A. ([1942] 1969). *The Jews in Spain: Their Political and Cultural Life During the Middle Ages.* Vols. I & II. Reprint. New York: Octagon Books.

Neusner, J. (1965). *History and Torah: Essays on Jewish Learning.* New York: Schocken Books.

——. (1986a). *Judaism: The Classical Statement: The Evidence of the Bavli.* Chicago: The University of Chicago Press.

——. (1986b). From Moore to Urbach and Sanders: Fifty years of "Judaism": The end of the line for a depleted category. *Religious Studies and Theology* 6(3):7-26.

——. (1986c). *Judaism, Christianity, and Zoroastrianism in Talmudic Babylonia.* Lanham, Md: University Press of America, Inc.

——. (1987). *Self-Fulfilling Prophecy: Exile and Return in the History of Judaism.* Boston: Beacon Press.

——. (1988a). *The Philosophical Mishnah.* 4 vols. Brown Judaic Studies, nos. 158, 163, 164, and 172. Atlanta: Scholars Press.

——. (1988b). Introduction to *The Mishnah: A New Translation*, trans. and ed. J. Neusner. New Haven, Conn.: Yale University Press.

——. (1992). Introduction to Qiddushin. In *The Talmud of Babylonia: An American Translation.* Vol. XIX.B: Qiddushin Chapters 2-4. Atlanta: Scholars Press.

Nini, Y. (1991). *The Jews of the Yemen 1800-1914*, trans. H. Galai. Chur, Switzerland: Harwood Academic Publishers.

Noonan, J. T. (1973). Power to choose. *Viator* 4:419-34.

Ortiz, A. D. (1965). Historical research on the Spanish Conversos in the last 15 years. In *Collected Studies in Honour of Américo Castro's Eightieth Year*, ed. M. Hornik. Oxford, England: Lincombe Lodge Research Library.

Parkes, J. (1934). *The Conflict of the Church and the Synagogue: A Study of the Origins of Antisemitism.* London: The Soncino Press.

Patai, R. (1971). *Tents of Jacob: The Diaspora Yesterday and Today.* Englewood Cliffs, N.J.: Prentice-Hall.

——. (1977). *The Jewish Mind.* New York: Charles Scribner's Sons.

——. (1986). *The Seed of Abraham: Jews and Arabs in Contact and Conflict.* Salt Lake City: University of Utah Press.

——, & J. Patai (1989). *The Myth of the Jewish Race.* Rev. ed. Detroit: Wayne State University Press.

Peli, P. H. (1991). Responses to anti-Semitism in Midrashic literature. In *Anti-Semitism in Times of Crisis*, ed. S. L. Gilman & S. T. Katz. New York: New York University Press.

Peritz, E., & A. Tamir (1977). Remarks on the mortality of Ashkenazim, with data on European-born Jews in Israel. In *Genetic Diseases Among Ashkenazi Jews*, ed. R. M. Goodman & A. G. Motulsky. New York: Raven Press.

Pettigrew, T. F. (1958). Personality and sociocultural factors in intergroup attitudes: a cross-national comparison. *Journal of Conflict Resolution* 2:29-42.

Phillips, R. (1988). *Putting Asunder: A History of Divorce in Western Society*. Cambridge: Cambridge University Press.

Pinkus, B. (1988). *The Jews of the Soviet Union: A History of a National Minority*. Cambridge: Cambridge University Press.

Plakans, A., & J. M. Halpern (1981). 18th-century Jewish families in Eastern Europe. In *Modern Jewish Fertility*, ed. P. Ritterband. Leiden: E. J. Brill.

Plomin, R., & C. S. Bergeman (1991). The nature of nurture: Genetic influence on "environmental" measures. *Behavioral and Brain Sciences* 14:373-427.

——, & Daniels, D. (1987). Why are children in the same family so different from one another? *Behavioral and Brain Sciences* 10:1-16.

Pogrebin, L. C. (1991). *Deborah, Golda, and Me*. New York: Crown Books.

Porten, B. (1984). The Diaspora: D. The Jews in Egypt. In *The Cambridge History of Judaism*. Vol. 1, ed. W. D. Davies & L. Finkelstein. Cambridge: Cambridge University Press.

Porter, R. (1982). Mixed feelings: The Enlightenment and sexuality in eighteenth-century Britain. In *Sexuality in Eighteenth-Century Britain*, ed. P. Bouce. Manchester, England: Manchester University Press.

Porton, G. G. (1988). *GOYIM: Gentiles and Israelites in Mishnah-Tosefta*. Brown Judaic Studies, no. 155. Atlanta: Scholars Press.

Praele, I., Y. Amir, Y., & S. Sharan (Singer) (1970). Perceptual articulation and task effectiveness in several Israeli subcultures. *Journal of Personality and Social Psychology* 15, 190-195.

Prinz, J. (1973). *The Secret Jews*. New York: Random House.

Pullan, B. (1983). *The Jews of Europe and the Inquisition of Venice, 1550-1670*. London: Basil Blackwell.

Purvis, J. D. (1989). The Samaritans. In *The Cambridge History of Judaism*. Vol. 2, ed. W. D. Davies & L. Finkelstein. Cambridge: Cambridge University Press.

Quaife, G. R. (1979). *Wanton Wenches and Wayward Wives: Peasants and Illicit Sex in Early Seventeenth-Century England*. London: Croom Helm.

Rabbie, J. M. (1991). Determinants of instrumental intra-group cooperation. In *Cooperation and Prosocial Behaviour*, ed. R. A. Hinde & J. Groebel. Cambridge: Cambridge University Press.

Rabinowitz, L. (1938). *The Social Life of the Jews of Northern France in the XII-XIV Centuries as Reflected in the Rabbinical Literature of the Period*. London: Edward Goldston.

Ragins, S. (1980). *Jewish Responses to Anti-Semitism in Germany, 1870-1914*. Cincinnati: Hebrew Union College Press.

Raisin, J. S. (1953). *Gentile Reactions to Jewish Ideals*. New York: Philosophical Library.

Ravid, B. (1992). An introduction to the economic history of the Iberian diaspora in the Mediterranean. *Judaism* 41:268-285.

Reynolds, V. (1991). Socioecology of religion. In *The Sociobiological Imagination*, ed. M. Maxwell. Albany, N.Y.: State University of New York Press.

Ringer, F. K. (1983). Inflation, antisemitism and the German academic community of the Weimar period. *Leo Baeck Institute Yearbook* XXVIII:3-9.

Ritterband, P. (1981). Introduction to *Modern Jewish Fertility*, ed. P. Ritterband. Leiden: E. J. Brill.

Rodríguez-Puértolas, J. (1976). A comprehensive view of Medieval Spain. In *Américo Castro and the Meaning of Spanish Civilization*, ed. J. Rubia Barcia. Berkeley: University of California Press.

Rogoff, H. (1930). *An East Side Epic: The Life and Work of Meyer London*. New York: Vanguard Press.

Rose, P. L. (1990). *Revolutionary Antisemitism in Germany from Kant to Wagner*. Princeton, N.J.: Princeton University Press.

Rosenbloom, J. R. (1978). *Conversion to Judaism: From the Biblical Period to the Present*. Cincinnati: Hebrew Union College Press.

Rosenthal, J. (1956). The Talmud on trial: A disputation at Paris in the year 1240. *Jewish Quarterly Review* XLVII:58-76; 145-169.

Roth, C. (1937). *The Spanish Inquisition*. New York: W. W. Norton.

———. (1974). *A History of the Marranos*. 4th ed. New York: Schocken Books.

———. (1978). *A History of the Jews in England*. 3rd ed. Oxford, England: Clarendon Press.

Rothman, S., & S. R. Lichter (1982). *Roots of Radicalism: Jews, Christians, and the New Left*. New York: Oxford University Press.

Rowe, D. C. (1993). *The Limits of Family Influence: Genes, Experience, and Behavior*. New York: Guilford Press.

Rouche, M. (1987) The early Middle Ages in the West. In *A History of Private Life*. Vol. I, ed. P. Veyne. Cambridge: Harvard University Press.

Round, N. G. (1969). Politics, style and group attitudes in the *Instrucción del Relator*. *Bulletin of Hispanic Studies* XLVI:289-319.

Roychoudhury, A. K. (1974). Genetic distance between Jews and Non-Jews of four regions. *Human Heredity* 32:259-263.

Rubin, I. (1982). *Salmar: An Island in the City*. Chicago: Quadrangle Books.

Ruether, R. R. (1974). *Faith and Fratricide: The Theological Roots of Anti-Semitism*. New York: The Seabury Press.

Rushton, J. P. (1988). Race differences in intelligence: A review and evolutionary analysis. *Personality and Individual Differences* 9:1009-1024.

———. (1989). Genetic similarity, human altruism, and group selection. *Behavioral and Brain Sciences* 12:503-559.

Russell, D. S. (1987). *The Old Testament Pseudepigrapha*. Philadelphia: SCM Press.

Sachar, H. M. (1992). *A History of Jews in America*. New York: Alfred A. Knopf.

Sachs, L., & M. Bat-Miriam (1957). The genetics of Jewish populations. *American Journal of Human Genetics* 9:117-126.

Safrai, S. (1968). Elementary education, its religious and social significance in the Talmudic period. *Cahiers d'Histoire Mondiale* 11:148-169.

———. (1974). Jewish self-government. In *The Jewish People in the First Century*. Vol. 1, ed. S. Safrai & M. Stern. Philadelphia: Fortress Press.

———. Education and the study of the Torah. In *The Jewish People in the First Century*. Vol. 1, ed. S. Safrai & M. Stern. Philadelphia: Fortress Press.

Salbstein, M. C. M. (1982). *The Emancipation of the Jews in Britain: The Question of the Admission of the Jews to Parliament, 1828-1860*. Rutherford, N.J.: Fairleigh Dickinson University Press.

Saller, R. (1991). European family history and Roman law. *Continuity and Change* 6:335-346.

Salomon, H. P. (1974). Introduction to *A History of the Marranos*, by C. Roth. 3rd ed. New York: Schocken Press.

Salter, F. (1994). Does female beauty increase male confidence of paternity? A blank slate hypothesis. Forschuungsstelle Für Humanethologie in der Max-Planck-Gesellschaft, Andechs, Germany. Unpublished manuscript.

Sanders, E. P. (1977). *Paul and Palestinian Judaism*. Philadelphia: Fortress Press.

———. (1992). *Judaism: Practice & Belief 63 BCE—66 CE*. London: SCM Press.

Scarr, S., & R. Weinberg (1978). The influence of "family background" on intellectual attainment. *American Sociological Review* 43:674-692.

———, & R. Weinberg (1983). The Minnesota adoption studies: Genetic differences and malleability. *Child Development* 54:260-267.

Schiffrin, D. (1984). Jewish argument as sociability. *Language in Society* 13:311-335.

Schmelz, U. O. (1971). *Infant and Early Childhood Mortality Among Jews of the Diaspora*. Jerusalem: Institute of Contemporary Jewry, Hebrew University of Jerusalem.

———, S. DellaPergola, & U. Avner (1990). Ethnic differences among Israeli Jews. *American Jewish Committee Yearbook 1990*:3-204.

Schmidt, W. H. (1984). *Old Testament Introduction*, trans. M. J. O'Connell. New York: Crossroad Publishing Co.

Schürer, E. ([1885] 1973). *The History of the Jewish People in the Age of Jesus Christ (175 B.C.-A.D. 135)*. Vol. I, rev. and ed. G. Vermes & F. Millar. Edinburgh: T. & T. Clark.

———. ([1885] 1979). *The History of the Jewish People in the Age of Jesus Christ (175 B. C.-A. D. 135)*. Vol. II, rev. and ed. G. Vermes, F. Millar, & M. Black. Edinburgh: T. & T. Clark.

———. ([1885] 1986). *The History of the Jewish People in the Age of Jesus Christ (175 B. C.-A. D. 135)*. Vol. III, rev. and ed. G. Vermes, F. Millar, & M. Goodman. Edinburgh: T. & T. Clark.

Schusterman, A. (1965). The last two centuries. In *Conversion to Judaism: A History and Analysis*, ed. D. M. Eichorn. New York: KTAV Publishing House.

Seeley, T. (1989). The honey bee colony as a superorganism. *American Scientist* 77:546-553.

Segal, A. F. (1988). The costs of proselytism and conversion. In *Society of Biblical Literature 1988 Seminar Papers*, ed. D. J. Lull. Atlanta: Scholars Press.

Seligson, D. J. (1965). In the post-Talmudic period. In *Conversion to Judaism: A History and Analysis*, ed. D. M. Eichorn. New York: KTAV Publishing House.

Sevenster, J. N. (1975). *The Roots of Anti-Semitism in the Ancient world*. Leiden: E. J. Brill.

Shaffir, W. (1986). Persistence and change in the Hasidic family. In *The Jewish Family: Myths and Reality*, ed. S. M. Cohen & P. E. Hyman. New York: Holmes & Meier.

Sharan (Singer), S., & L. Weller, L. (1971). Classification patterns of underprivileged children in Israel. *Child Development* 42:581-594.

Shaw, S. J. (1991). *The Jews of the Ottoman Empire and the Turkish Republic*. New York: New York University Press.

Shaywitz, S. E., & B. E. Shaywitz (1988). Attention Deficit Disorder: Current Perspectives. In *Learning Disabilities: Proceedings of the National Conference*, ed. J. F. Kavanagh & T. J. Truss, Jr. Parkton, Md: York Press.

Sherman, A. J. (1983). German-Jewish bankers in world politics: The financing of the Russo-Japanese war. *Leo Baeck Institute Yearbook* XXVIII:59-73.

Shibituni, T., & Kwan, K. M. (1965). *Ethnic Stratification: A Comparative Approach.* New York: Macmillan

Shokeid, M. (1986). The impact of migration on the Moroccan Jewish family in Israel. In *The Jewish Family: Myths and Reality*, ed. S. M. Cohen & P. E. Hyman. New York: Holmes & Meier.

Shulvass, M. E. (1973). *The Jews in the World of the Renaissance*, trans. E. I. Kose. Leiden: E. J. Brill and Spertus College of Judaica Press.

Silverman, J. H. (1976). The Spanish Jews: Early references and later effects. In *Américo Castro and the Meaning of Spanish Civilization*, ed. J. Rubia Barcia. Berkeley: University of California Press.

Simon, M. ([1948, 1964] 1986). *Verus Israel: A Study of the Relations Between Christians and Jews in the Roman Empire (135-425)*, trans. M. McKeating. Reprint. Oxford, England: Oxford University Press for the Littman Library.

Sofaer, J. A., P. Smith, & E. Kaye, (1986). Affinities between contemporary and skeletal Jewish and non-Jewish groups based on tooth morphology. *American Journal of Physical Anthropology* 70:265-275.

Soggin, J. A. (1980). *Introduction to the Old Testament from Its Origins to the Closing of the Alexandrian Canon.* 2nd ed. Philadelphia: Westminster Press.

Sorkin, D. (1987). *The Transformation of German Jewry, 1780-1840.* New York: Oxford University Press.

Southwood, T. R. E. (1977). Habitat, the temple for ecological strategies? *Journal of Animal Ecology* 46:337-66.

———. (1981). Bionomic strategies and population parameters. In *Theoretical Ecology: Principles and Applications*, ed. R. M. May. Sunderland, Mass.: Sinauer Associates.

Sowell, T. (1993). Middleman minorities. *The American Enterprise* (May-June):31-41.

Speiser, E. A. (1970). The Biblical idea of history in its common Near Eastern setting. In *The Jewish Experience*, ed. J. Goldin. New York: Bantam Books. (Originally published in *Israel Exploration Journal* VII, no. 4 (1957).

Stein, S. (1955). The development of the Jewish law on interest from the Biblical period to the expulsion of the Jews from England. *Historia Judaica* XVII:3-40.

———. (1959). A disputation on moneylending between Jews and gentiles in Me'ir b. Simeon's Milhemeth Miswah (Narbonne, 13th Cent.). *Journal of Jewish Studies* 10:45-61.

Stern, M. (1974). *Greek and Latin Authors on Jews and Judaism.* Vol. 1. Jerusalem: The Israel Academy of Sciences and Humanities.

———. (1976). Aspects of Jewish society: The priesthood and other classes. In *The Jewish People in the First Century.* Vol. 2, ed. S. Safrai & M. Stern. Philadelphia: Fortress Press.

Stern, S. (1950). *The Court Jew*, trans. R. Weiman. Philadelphia: Jewish Publication Society of America.

Stevenson, H. (1991). The development of prosocial behavior in large scale collective societies: China and Japan. In *Cooperation and Prosocial Behaviour*, ed. R. A. Hinde & J. Groebel. Cambridge: Cambridge University Press.

Stillman, N. A. (1979). *The Jews of Arab Lands: A History and Source Book.* Philadelphia: Jewish Publication Society of America.

———. (1991). *The Jews of Arab Lands in Modern Times.* Philadelphia: Jewish Publication Society of America.

Stone, L. (1977). *The Family, Sex, and Marriage in England: 1500-1800.* New York: Harper & Row.

————. (1990). *The Road to Divorce*. Oxford: Oxford University Press.

Swift, F. H. (1919). *Education in Ancient Israel*. Chicago: Open Court Publishing Co.

Szeinberg, A. (1977). Polymorphic evidence for a Mediterranean origin of the Ashkenazi community. In *Genetic Diseases Among Ashkenazi Jews*, ed. R. M. Goodman & A. G. Motulsky. New York: Raven Press.

Tajfel, H. (1981). *Human Groups and Social Categories: Studies in Social Psychology*. Cambridge: Cambridge University Press.

Tama, M. D. ([1807] 1971). *Transactions of the Parisian Sanhedrim*, trans. F. D. Kirwan. London: Charles Taylor. Westmead, Farnborough, Hants, England: Gregg International Publishers.

Teitelbaum, S. (1965). Conversion to Judaism: Sociologically speaking. In *Conversion to Judaism: A History and Analysis*, ed. D. M. Eichorn. New York: KTAV Publishing House.

Tellegen, A. (1985). Structures of mood and personality and their relevance to assessing anxiety, with an emphasis on self-report. In *Anxiety and Anxiety Disorders*, ed. A. H. Tuma & J. D, Maser. Hillsdale, N.J.: Lawrence Erlbaum.

Terman, L. M. (1926). *Genetic Studies of Genius*. 2nd ed. Stanford, Calif.: Stanford University Press.

————, & M. H. Oden (1947). *The Gifted Child Grows Up*. Stanford, Calif.: Stanford University Press.

Thomas, Y. (1980). Mariages endogamiques à Rome. Patrimoine, pouvoir et parente depuis l'époque archaïque. *Revue de l'Histoire du Droit Français et Étranger* 58:345-382.

Thompson, D. J. (1990). The high priests of Memphis under Ptolemaic rule. In *Pagan Priests: Religion and Power in the Ancient World*, ed. M. Beard & J. North. Ithaca, N.Y.: Cornell University Press.

Tigerstedt, E. N. (1974). *The Legend of Sparta in Classical Antiquity*. Vol. II. Uppsala, Sweden: Almqvist & Wiksell.

Tollet, D. (1986). Merchants and businessmen in Poznan and Cracow, 1588-1668. In *The Jews in Poland*, ed. C. Abramsky, M. Jachimczyk, & A. Polonsky. London: Basil Blackwell.

Triandis, H. C. (1990). Cross-cultural studies of individualism and collectivism. *Nebraska Symposium on Motivation 1989: Cross Cultural Perspectives*. Lincoln: University of Nebraska Press.

————. (1991). Cross-cultural differences in assertiveness/competition vs. group loyalty/cohesiveness. In *Cooperation and Prosocial Behaviour*, ed. R. A. Hinde & J. Groebel. Cambridge: Cambridge University Press.

Trivers, R. (1985). *Social Evolution*. Menlo Park, Calif.: Benjamin/Cummings.

————, & D. E. Willard (1973). Natural selection for parental ability to vary the sex ratio of offspring. *Science* 179:90-92.

Tucker, D. M., K. Vanatta, & J. Rothlind (1990). Arousal and activation systems and primitive adaptive controls on cognitive priming. In *Psychological and Biological Approaches to Emotion*, ed. S. L. Stein, B. Leventhal, & T. Trabasso. Hillsdale, NJ: Lawrence Erlbaum.

Turner, J. C., M. A. Hogg, P. J. Oakes, & P. M. Smith (1984). Failure and defeat as determinants of group cohesiveness. *British Journal of Social Psychology* 23:97-111.

van der Dennen, J M. G. (1987). Ethnocentrism and in-group/out-group differentiation. A review and interpretation of the literature. In *The Sociobiology of Ethnocentrism*, ed. V. Reynolds, V. Falger, & I. Vine. Athens: The University of Georgia Press.

——. (1991). Studies of conflict. In *The Sociobiological Imagination*, ed. M. Maxwell. Albany: The State University of New York Press.

Veyne, P. (1987). The Roman Empire. In *A History of Private Life*. Vol. I, ed. P. Veyne. Cambridge: Harvard University Press.

Vincent, P. (1966). The measured intelligence of Glasgow Jewish children. *Jewish Journal of Sociology* 8:92-108.

Vogel, F., & A. G. Motulsky (1986). *Human Genetics: Problems and Approaches*. 2nd ed. Berlin: Springer-Verlag.

Voland, E. (1988). Different infant and child mortality in evolutionary perspective: Data from late 17th to 19th century Ostfriesland (Germany). In *Human Reproductive Behavior*, ed. L. Betzig, M. Borgorhoff-Mulder, & P. Turke. New York: Cambridge University Press.

Volkov, S. (1985). The dynamics of dissimulation: *Ostjuden* and German Jews. In *The Jewish Response to German Culture: From the Enlightenment to the Second World War*, ed. J. Reinharz & W. Schatzberg. Hanover, N.H.: University Press of New England for Clark University.

von Ungern-Sternberg, J. (1986). The end of the conflict of the orders. In *Social struggles in archaic Rome: New perspectives on the conflict of the orders*, ed. K. A. Raaflaub. University of California Press.

Walsh, W. T. (1940). *Characters of the Inquisition*. Port Washington, N.Y.: Kennikat Press.

Watson, A. (1975). *Rome of the XII Tables*. Princeton, N.J.: Princeton University Press.

Watson, D., & Clark, L. A. (1992). On traits and temperament: General and specific factors of emotional experience and their relation to the five-factor model. *Journal of Personality* 6:441-476.

Waxman, C. (1989). The emancipation, the Enlightenment, and the demography of American Jewry. *Judaism* 38:488-501.

Wechsler, D. (1958). *The Measurement and Appraisal of Adult Intelligence*. 4th ed. Baltimore, Md.: Williams and Wilkins Co.

Weinryb, B. D. (1972). *The Jews of Poland: A Social and Economic History of the Jewish Community in Poland from 1100 to 1800*. Philadelphia: Jewish Publication Society of America.

Weisfeld, G. (1990) Sociobiological patterns of Arab culture. *Ethology and Sociobiology* 11:23-49.

Werblowsky, R. J. Z. (1968). Messianism in Jewish history. *Cahiers d'Histoire Mondiale* 11:30-45.

Wertheimer, J. (1987). *Unwelcome Strangers: East European Jews in Imperial Germany*. New York: Oxford University Press.

Westermarck, G. (1922). *The History of Human Marriage*. 5th ed. New York: Allerton.

Weyl, N. (1963). *The Geography of Intelligence*. Chicago: Henry Regnery Co.

——. (1989). *The Geography of American Achievement*. Washington, D. C.: Scott-Townsend Publishers.

Widiger, T. A., & T. J. Trull (1992). Personality and psychopathology: An application of the five factor model. *Journal of Personality* 60:363-393.

Wiggins, J. S., & R. Broughton (1985). The interpersonal circle: A structural model for the integration of personality research. *Perspectives in Personality* 1:1-47.

Wilken, R. L. (1983). *St. John Chrysostom and the Jews: Rhetoric and Reality in the Late 4th Century*. Berkeley: University of California Press.

———. (1984). The restoration of Israel in biblical prophecy. In *"To See Ourselves as Others See Us": Christians, Jews, "Others" in Late Antiquity*, ed. J. Neusner & E. S. Frerichs. Chico, Calif.: Scholars Press.

Williams, G. C. (1966). *Adaptation and Natural Selection: A Critique of Current Evolutionary Thought.* Princeton, N.J.: Princeton University Press.

Wilson, David S. (1989). Levels of selection: An alternative to individualism in biology and the human sciences. *Social Networks* 11:257-272.

———. (1991). Nepotism vs Tit-for-tat, or, why should you be nice to your rotten brother? *Evolutionary Ecology* 5: 291-299.

———, G. B. Pollock, & L. A. Dugatkin (1992). Can altruism evolve in purely viscous populations? *Evolutionary Ecology* 6:331-341.

———, & E. Sober (1994). Re-introducing group selection to the human behavioral sciences. *Behavioral and Brain Sciences* 17(4). Forthcoming.

Wilson, Derek (1988). *Rothschild: The Wealth and Power of a Dynasty.* New York: Charles Scribner's Sons.

Wilson, E. O. (1975). *Sociobiology: The New Synthesis.* Cambridge: Harvard University Press.

———. (1978). *On Human Nature.* Cambridge: Harvard University Press.

Wirth, L. (1956). *The Ghetto.* Chicago: University of Chicago Press.

Wistrich, R. S. (1990). *Between Redemption and Perdition: Modern Anti-Semitism and Jewish Identity.* London and New York: Routledge.

Woocher, J. S. (1986). *Sacred Survival: The Civil Religion of American Jews.* Bloomington: Indiana University Press.

Wrightson, K. (1980). The nadir of English illegitimacy in the seventeenth century. In *Bastardy and Its Comparative History*, ed., P. Laslett, K. Ooseterveen & R. M. Smith. London: Edward Arnold.

Wrigley, E. A. & R. Schofield (1981). *The Population History of England, 1541-1871.* Cambridge: Harvard University Press.

Yee, A. H. (1993). Sino-Judaic reflections: The Stepping Stone Syndrome. *Points East: A Publication of the Sino-Judaic Institute* 8(3):11-13.

Zarutskie, P. W., C. H. Muller, M. Magone, & M. R. Soules (1990). The clinical relevance of sex selection techniques. *Fertility and Sterility* 52:891-905.

Zborowski, M., & E. Herzog (1952). *Life Is with People: The Jewish Little-Town of Eastern Europe.* New York: International Universities Press.

Zenner, W. P. (1991). *Minorities in the Middle: A Cross-Cultural Analysis.* Albany, N.Y.: State University of New York Press.

Zimmels, H. J. (1958). *Ashkenazim and Sephardim: Their Relations and Problems as Reflected in the Rabbinical Responsa.* London: Oxford University Press.

Zuckerman, M. (1984). Sensation seeking: A comparative approach to a human trait. *Behavioral and Brain Sciences* 7:413-471.

# INDEX

**About the Author**

KEVIN MACDONALD is an Associate Professor in the Department of Psychology, California State University, Long Beach. Among his earlier books are *Social and Personality Development, Sociobiological Perspectives on Human Development,* and *Parent-Child Play.*

ISBN 0-275-94869-2

90000>

EAN

9 780275 948696

HARDCOVER BAR CODE